14.95

Moral Differences

Moral Differences

TRUTH, JUSTICE AND CONSCIENCE
IN A WORLD OF CONFLICT

Richard W. Miller

PRINCETON UNIVERSITY PRESS

PRINCETON, NEW JERSEY

Library of Congress Cataloging-in-Publication Data

Miller, Richard W.
Moral differences : truth, justice and conscience in a
world of conflict / Richard W. Miller.
p.   cm.
Includes bibliographical references and index.
1. Ethics. 2. Truth. 3. Justice. 4. Conscience. I. Title.
BJ1012.M54   1992   170—dc20   91-40205   CIP

ISBN 0-691-07409-7 (hard) — ISBN 0-691-02092-2 (pbk.)

This book has been composed in Linotron Goudy

Princeton University Press books are printed on acid-free paper,
and meet the guidelines for permanence and durability of the
Committee on Production Guidelines for Book Longevity of the
Council on Library Resources

Printed in the United States of America

1   3   5   7   9   10   8   6   4   2

1   3   5   7   9   10   8   6   4   2
(Pbk.)

For Laura

CONTENTS

Moral Differences

INTRODUCTION

THIS BOOK is about the conflicts that trouble morality—confrontations between contrary moral convictions, conflicts of interests that we seek to resolve justly and conflicts between the demands of one's conscience and what one would do, conscience to one side. These are the differences that add most pain to moral living. People look to moral philosophy for help in easing the pain, but they are disappointed in their most urgent hopes. I believe that this disappointment is not inevitable. Moral philosophy fails to help because of two kinds of self-confinement that should be ended: distorting views of rational inquiry in general and false assumptions about the resources needed to answer the particular questions that moral philosophers pose.

The distortions about rational inquiry are assumptions that certain centrally important appraisals only require the application of utterly general rules or rules that are acceptable to all rational inquirers. A prime example is the characteristic positivist assumption that a truth claim is justified in light of a given body of data just in case the proposition and the data are effectively connected by principles of scientific method that are valid for all fields, which no one could possibly reject except on pain of irrationality. This worship of generality takes other forms, as well, producing constraints on reference, rational choice and moral deliberation that constantly get in the way of insight.

The strategic mistakes about resources are assumptions that this or that traditional problem in moral philosophy can be resolved without commitment to empirically controversial hypotheses about social or psychological processes characteristic of specific historical settings. (Of course, the attempt to base rational inquiry on a canon of topic-neutral, a priori rules encourages such mistakes.) For example, the standard philosophical questions about economic justice are largely investigated through reflection confined to obvious facts about economic activity, thought-experiments about such characters as farmer Smith and farmer Jones on their otherwise uninhabited island, and price-theoretic models of economic activity employed without detailed attention to whether the models are true enough. Similarly, philosophical questions about our access to truth in moral matters are supposed to be answerable by reflecting on obvious facts about what happens when one judges and deliberates.

In recent years, discontent, along these lines, with the abstractness of standard moral philosophy has grown, but it has not yielded many answers to questions about moral conflict. Most intriguing positive proposals come from philosophers who do not profusely offend the worship of generality and who do avoid detailed empirical inquiry. Meanwhile, those discontented with the mainstream have argued that these proposals do not work and diagnosed the failures, without creating at all as much. I hope to show how freedom from confinement high and low, i.e., liberation from the constraints on rationality epitomized by positivism and abundant resort to empirical inquiry into specific processes, can make possible a variety of constructive answers to longstanding questions about moral conflict.

In the first three chapters, I will be concerned with worries about truth and justification in morality, worries which are first aroused—in many of us, at least—by encounters with disagreements in moral convictions. I will argue for truth without universality. We, i.e., most reflective, informed people in modern industrial societies, are often in a position to claim that our moral judgments are true. Our moral inquiries give us nondogmatic access to truth in the same way as our scientific inquiries. For we are justified, in scientifically normal ways, in explaining our judgments as the exercise of capacities for detection. Nonetheless, in many of these cases, other actual moral inquirers would rationally dissent from our judgments, in light of all our evidence, even all the evidence for which we could, rationally, hope. Indeed, every moral judgment we make could be rejected by a possible (though, presumably, nonactual) rational person, possessing all evidence. Such limitless, rational, informed dissent is unavailable to any possible person who ever ascribes a moral property, but it is available to a moral nihilist who rejects all moral affirmations as false.

The case for this mixture will depend on violating the limits that I protested before. For example, the justification of our claims to truth in moral matters will depend, indispensably, on topic-specific principles for rating explanations, in ways that conflict with the positivists' demand for a canon of general rules. It will also depend on empirical and contingent claims about the causes of our ways of forming moral judgments. (So the worry about whether those judgments refer to anything responds to a real possibility, though one that we can tentatively put to one side, on empirical grounds.) Similarly, the argument that evidence and reason could not overcome many actual, important moral disagreements will depend on case studies of particular ways of moral learning in different cultures. And the evaluation of such radical disagreements as a normal aspect of rational inquiry such as science pursues will depend on a postpositivist account of justification in science.

Other obstacles to my mixed metaethics will have to be overcome, for example, oversimplified accounts of the relation between desires, beliefs and reasons which would rule out the possibility of moral nihilism or make our nonnihilism a matter of desire as against belief. The most important obstacle of all is a challenge to the coherence of the mixture itself. This challenge, the subject of chapters four and five, creates the most fruitful of all the many connections between controversies concerning truth and justification in morality and issues in philosophy at large.

According to all current accounts of content, my assertions of moral truth are incompatible with my denials of universality. Above all, the alleged disagreements among rational moral inquirers which reason and evidence cannot overcome could not, in fact, be genuine disagreements. Differences in frameworks for assessing evidence which are sufficiently radical to prevent agreement on the basis of shared evidence would guarantee that the different asserters do not address themselves to the same subjectmatter. Positivism is a prime example of an approach to truth and justification in which my denial of universality would be incoherent. Suppose that all rational disputants implicitly rely on the same rules for connecting their evidence with their truth claims. Then, if common evidence does not lead to agreement, people are either irrational or not really making contrary claims as to the truth of the same hypothesis. However, positivism is by no means the only obstacle (which is why the difficulty is so fruitful). Every current alternative to positivism which is definite enough to assess the relevant distinctions between genuine and merely verbal disagreement would rule out the evaluations of genuine, radical disagreement that are central to my account of access to truth in moral matters.

In chapters four and five, I will develop an approach to the nature of content which overcomes these obstacles. According to this account, the limits of content, the boundaries that someone cannot cross without changing the subject, are determined by common projects of advancing learning through communication. In science, morality and nontechnical inquiries into ordinary properties of matter or mind, the criteria for shared content are set by communicative strategies which often depend on mere questions of convenience and given facts of common response. However, the criteria singled out by strategic advantages can, and often do, tie content to objective facts about the local environments of language-users. After showing that the strategic approach fixes the limits of content correctly in a variety of obvious or well-studied cases apart from moral discourse, I will show that our needs in moral discourse establish limits that fit my claims about morality. The strategic limits, here, are broad enough to accommodate the radical disagreements described in my case studies while excluding as necessarily irrational the judgments that I portrayed as unavailable to any rational maker of moral judgments.

Turning from conflicts in belief to conflicts among interests, I will go on to use the discussions in the first half of the book as the framework for a theory of justice. Part of this framework, my account of our access to moral truth, includes a description of a process in which premises for political deliberation adjust to equality of power, a process that is a source of insight into justice. This initial account of the detection of justice implies a vague principle that I will call "justice as social freedom." Roughly, social arrangements are just in case they are freely and rationally acceptable to anyone who desires such acceptability to all. The difficulty of developing a standard adequate to distinguish just from unjust arrangements in a modern industrial society largely reflects the vagueness of this initial principle, which has been specified in ways as different as Nozick's libertarian premises for laissez-faire capitalism and Rawls' insistence on terms for cooperation requiring liberal egalitarianism.[1]

Here, as elsewhere in moral philosophy, disputes among partisans of rival specifications have largely compared general principles in light of empirically uncontroversial hypotheses. These disputes have reached an impasse—a morally disturbing one, given the moral urgency of the search for means of persuading people of good will to accept social arrangements which are, inevitably, coercively enforced. I will try to end the impasse through a strategy that is more piecemeal and empirical. Rather than eliminating all but one specification of justice as social freedom, I will try to establish a minimal specification, rationally compelling for all partisans of social freedom despite their other differences, and then to show that the minimum is enough to determine what arrangements are just for modern industrial societies, i.e., to show this through appeal to empirical facts about the workings of such societies.

The main subject of this reconciling project will be economic justice, because this is where partisans of the vague principle are now far apart. In chapter six, I will argue for a minimal principle of equal opportunity, according to which imposed inequalities in competitive resources are unjust unless they are inevitable by-products of arrangements that are best for the most disadvantaged. This turns out to be a special instance of a general principle identifying justice with the provision of equal inducements to willing cooperators. Then, in chapter seven, I will rely on social data and economic theory to show that the competitive inequalities are inevitably imposed in capitalist societies, and imposed in ways that are just only if the worst-off are as well-off as they can be under capitalism. The case for such egalitarianism is strengthened by considering how actual, inevitable departures from certain models of perfect competition impose risks that would violate justice as social freedom unless the effects of markets are mitigated through the provision of a guaranteed minimum. After establishing these conditions for justice in a capitalist setting, I will argue that everyone in an advanced industrial society has reason to avoid noncapitalist alternatives, on account of their distinctive burdens of inefficiency. In sum, because of facts about how we get in one another's way in modern industrial economic activity (not in every kind of economy, much less every coherent thought-experiment), the freedom that constitutes justice requires economic equality. Finally, in chapter eight, I will extend the mini-

---

[1] There is one major exception to the rule that current approaches to questions of justice are specifications of justice as social freedom—namely, utilitarianism. I will argue that virtually everyone's acceptance of utilitarianism as a political philosophy rests on wishful thinking or confusion, above all, confusion about the nature of the evenhandedness that moral political choice requires.

mal specification of social freedom to questions of civil liberty, including the abortion controversy, problems in imposing constraints on rational, informed dissenters from justice as social freedom, and issues of international economic justice.

I will conclude by turning to the moral microcosm of one's self and examining conflicts between what conscience demands and what one wants, morality to one side. Recently, important writing on morality has sought to lift some of these burdens of conscience, arguing, for example, that even a decent, morally insightful person sometimes is not unreasonable to do what is morally wrong, or that what is morally wrong is not always wrong all-told, or that the sort of person one should try to become is not always the sort of person one should try to become morally speaking. Though the urge to lift these burdens is almost entirely misguided, it is extremely revealing. For an adequate response forces one to free rational choice and moral deliberation from the confines of the philosophical worship of generality.

In chapter nine, I will begin investigating the burdens of conscience by arguing for a mixed conclusion: doing what is morally wrong is sometimes a reasonable choice even for a decent, morally insightful person, but avoiding what is morally wrong is never an unreasonable choice for any morally insightful person. Just as the earlier mixed appraisal of truth and justification violated theories in which rational belief was a response to data conforming to topic-neutral rules, this mixed appraisal of morality and reason violates theories of rational choice in which rational choice responds to desires and beliefs in accordance with general rules assigning maximum expected utility. I will develop an alternative account, in which reasons with specific kinds of content, including moral reasons, have a special power to make choice rational, even though (as burden-lifters insist) the rationality of a choice depends on its being grounded in the chooser's system of desires.

In chapter ten, I will examine and ultimately reject the powerful case for saying that what is morally wrong is not always wrong all told. This way of lifting moral burdens would be right if morality required ultimate impartiality, as it does in consequentialist theories. Even the addition of a general "agent-centered prerogative" to consequentialism would produce prohibitions that do not correspond to wrongness all-told. At a farther remove from consequentialism, contractualist accounts of moral wrongness misidentify what is wrong through excessive concern with the impact of social interactions on participants' interests.

These are the main current philosophical descriptions of what makes an act morally wrong. But the gaps between wrongness all-told and moral wrongness that they would create reflect misconceptions of morality, not a real limitation of morality. Morality does not impose an impartial ultimate basis for choice. There is no valid general rule, such as standard moral theories seek, which ascribes moral wrongness on the basis of general properties that are discernible without further moral discrimination. Instead, moral wrongness is what violates the self-imposed constraints of morally responsible people, people whose status is specified in part through diverse concrete norms of character which permit ultimate partiality toward intimates and personal projects. Moral responsibility does require principled self-regulation on a basis that all other responsible people could accept. But it does not consist of choice from an impartial point of view, closer to just legislators' deliberations than to routine personal concerns. After further developing this account of moral wrongness, I will show how it removes the basis for lifting the burdens of conscience. What is morally wrong is always wrong.

Going beyond questions of obligation and responsibility, I will end by considering the role of morality in deciding how one should live. Morality, I will argue, gives us a correct and complete grasp of all objectively valid answers to questions of what one should do and what kind of person one should strive to be which are not just questions of what would fit one's goals, desires or interests. The adequacy of moral deliberations, here, depends on the norms of character that figure (less directly) in the discernment of moral wrongness. Morality directs us to consult these concrete norms, which make limited demands. It also gives scope to authenticity, as opposed to the engineer's perspective on oneself that is a typical outcome of philosophical morality.

In a way, these conclusions are tranquilizing, and so are earlier conclusions in this book. The deep attachments to particular people and projects which most of us require for our flourishing create no need for something different from ordinary modern morality, such as a partial return to more ancient ways of life; ordinary modern morality, quite as much as ancient Greek morality, is governed, quite indispensably, by diverse concrete norms to be pursued authentically. Similarly, when we are well-informed and suitably reflective, our ordinary moral deliberations put us in a position to assert moral truths, even if others, rational and possessing all relevant evidence, can deny them. And the normal modern ways of pursuing questions of justice are capable of yielding adequate common answers among those who pursue justice in these ways. So some worries are ended.

But I hope that the right worries are preserved from soothing kinds of despair. A certain complacency can arise when distortions of philosophy are misidentified as limitations of morality. Morality, as I will describe it, can be extremely demanding, especially in matters of justice. It is tranquilizing to suppose that a source of difficult demands cannot, after all, lay claim to truth, is hopelessly indeterminate, or must, in any case, be exchanged for some other, richer basis for living. Discontent with the confines of philosophical morality tends to encourage such escapes. But our morality will turn out to be, basically, in order, for reasons that imply that much is out of order in our world.

. . .

Although the later discussions of justice and of conscience take place within the framework of the earlier account of truth and justification, most of the later arguments do not assume earlier conclusions. So if need be, one can enter this book at midstream.

Occasionally a section which is addressed to the literature on a topic is not essential to my own argument about the topic. I have indicated each of these sections by putting an asterisk beside the heading that introduces it.

The approach to moral truth and moral justification which I present in the first three chapters was first sketched in "Reason and Commitment in the Social Sciences," *Philosophy & Public Affairs* 9 (1979), pp. 241–66, and developed in some more detail in "Ways of Moral Learning," *Philosophical Review* 94 (1985), pp. 507–56. Work on this book was supported by an American Council of Learned Societies/Ford Fellowship for 1988–89.

Chapter One

REASON AND RIGHTNESS

IN PHILOSOPHY these days, disputes about 'realism' are at the center of most stages. In particular, attention is fixed on disputes over topics entitled "scientific realism" and "moral realism," respectively. In the former, people discuss what justification, if any, we have for supposing that science reveals the existence of kinds of things that could not be known to exist without the aid of scientific theories. In the moral realism dispute, the direct concern of the first part of this book, people discuss what kinds of justification, if any, we have for supposing that moral inquiry reveals to us objective moral facts.

Whether moral realism is true is, in a way, a good question. Many people ought to be obsessed with it, now. In the generation now passing from the scene in English-speaking philosophy, large questions about justification, truth and meaning were often resolved in a positivist framework, by applying utterly general rules concerned with logical form, rules dictating appropriate relations between truth claims and sense-experience. In the 1950's and 1960's, the positivist project was devastated, by Goodman, Kuhn, Quine, Putnam and others, where it had been most vigorous, in the discussion of scientific inquiry and of everyday inquiry concerning material things. On this same terrain, in the course of the late 'sixties and early 'seventies, Putnam, Boyd, Kripke, Feyerabend and others began to construct a variety of new, often opposing standpoints to replace the one that had been destroyed. Though the work of construction, collaboration and debate furiously continues, the new ideas about truth and justification, first employed in the "scientific realism" controversy, have been seized upon to advance the "moral realism" controversy, as well. Similarly, Wittgenstein's new ways of thinking about justification and truth found important parallels in Foot's work on moral belief and justification, topics far removed from Wittgenstein's favored terrain in the philosophy of mind and mathematics.

In addition to these academic reasons why the question of moral realism is good to ask now, there is a frighteningly nonacademic reason. While responsible people continue to seek a secure moral basis for assessing the proposals that dominate political controversy, many now wonder whether any satisfactory means of assessment exists. In the 'fifties and early 'sixties, at least among most English-speaking intellectuals, broad political outlooks tended to be the same. Later, differences sharpened, but still it seemed to most that shared moral first principles would dictate a single just politics if only the relevant social facts were known. In the present gray haze, it is unclear to many people how the facts, as they seem to be, can sustain any adequate basis for political choice. Partisans of noninterference in market processes have never promised so little. Believable defenders of capitalism have largely given up proposing that it can provide jobs, decent housing and a reasonably crime-free environment for everyone willing to work in advanced industrial societies, much less the poorer ones. In the United States in the 1980's, a decade in which the Gross National Product increased by 29.2% in constant dollars, those who worship at the altar of capitalist growth confronted these trends: a decline, from 1979 to 1987, in average real income among the poorest fifth of families of 9.2% while the real income of the highest fifth increased by 18.7%; a decline, in the same period, of real income of the poorest fifth of families with children of 13.8% while the highest fifth with children gained the same 18.7%; a 1.8% decline in real hourly wages from 1980 to 1989 while dividend and interest income per capita increased by 44.2%.[1] Yet while the social impact of market-based production has become disheartening for people in market economies, socialism has never seemed less attainable in a form that might attract most people in an advanced industrial society. Once basic necessities are provided for all, the rigidities and inefficiencies of central planning come to the fore. And experiments in "market socialism" have, so far, been as self-destructive as the sternest defender of central planning ever supposed. To the similar dismay of politically responsible people, electoral choices often seem empty to those who live in long-established democracies, while the fate of those who do not is often settled by international economic transactions over which they would lack influence in any feasible political arrangement. Among those who are impressed by failures of central planning, but not swept up by capitalist triumphalism, our turn-of-the-century gives rise to a general moral anxiety. This is a good time to wonder what justification there could be for supposing that any basic political program is based on moral truths. Other cultures have posed broad questions about justification and truth when old political assumptions were destroyed yet not replaced. Hume's Britain comes to mind, and so does the Central Europe of Mach, Nietzsche and Freud, an intellectually gratifying, otherwise horrifying analogue to the circumstances that make it right to debate moral realism today.

At the same time, the question of whether moral realism is valid is a bad one. When people debate this issue, they raise a variety of questions. The label, "moral realism," reflects and encourages a tendency to assume that

---

[1] *United States Statistical Abstract, 1990* (Washington, D.C.: Government Printing Office, 1990); *Survey of Current Business*, 1990 (70), p. 6; *New York Times*, "News of the Week in Review," March 4, 1990, drawing on reports to the Council of Economic Advisers and the House Ways and Means Committee. In addition to adjustments for inflation, the family income figures are adjusted for family size, government benefits and taxes, which increases the decline in income of the lowest fifth.

these questions all have the same answers. Yet they need not. I will argue that they do not. Here, in particular, are three important questions about truth, justification and morality that could have very different right answers, "realist" in response to some, "anti-realist" in response to others, as those terms are usually applied.

First, there is a question about truth. In what cases, if any, is one in a position to claim that a moral judgment is a true description of a state of affairs? Since nothing is right or wrong just because one thinks it is (perhaps along with fellow-thinkers), this amounts to the question of whether one is in a position to make claims about objective moral facts.

A judgment could have the special warrant that the first question describes because of a justification provided by one's own framework of background principles, i.e., principles that one applies to evidence in the form of non-moral statements of empirical fact in order to reach moral conclusions. (Of course, the framework and its use may have to be of special kinds to justify claims to moral truth. Different answers to the first question often depend on different views of the appropriate constraints.) A second important question is concerned with confrontations between different frameworks.

It is an utterly uncontroversial fact about us humans that we often present justifications of moral judgments, justifications partly appealing to empirical findings that are not, taken individually, intrinsically moral. One might well ask in what instances, if any, one could support one's judgment with a case so strong that any actual person who has lived would have to share the judgment, if she accepted the same nonmoral findings, rationally reflected on the arguments, and was not a victim of some process or attitude (or of the absence of some process or attitude) which *she* regards as a source of misjudgment. In posing this question, one reaches far beyond oneself to consider one's capacity to resolve disagreements with every potential disputant who has actually existed. Every framework for answering moral questions that has actually been employed is a relevant basis for disagreement. But in two respects, the scope of the relevant disputes is narrow. First, one only considers what room for rational dissent there is among those who accept the same nonmoral findings. In assessing the security of most moral judgments, this restriction is a way of avoiding a waste of time on the obvious. For usually it is obvious that a rational, otherwise qualified moral judge would reach a different judgment in light of different findings. Also, one matches one's powers of justification against all frameworks that there have been, but not against all possible ones. The goal is not a justification that would end all possible rational dissent.

Special though its scope may be, this question about justification is important, in two ways. First, it is the question about the justification of morality that has the most direct bearing on what might be called the morality of justification, those moral constraints on action that require the existence of justifications of certain kinds. The most important claim in the morality of justification is that an action backed by coercion—for example, a normal exercise of state power—should be justifiable, in principle, to anyone who is hurt. It will prove extremely hard to say what is necessary to satisfy this requirement, as it is intended. However, a justification with the special scope that has been singled out would surely be sufficient. Suppose there is an imposition justified by an argument that every actual person would accept if he or she were well-informed, grasped relevant concepts and arguments and otherwise exercised all the capacities and attitudes whose positive relevance he or she accepts. Then the interference has a justification as universal as anyone requires. It is not suspect in the same way as a criminal statute producing results that most of us value on the basis of ultimate standards that some of us do not share, even though equally well-informed, rational and conscientiously seeking undistorted moral judgment. If some possible person who has never lived would not approve, despite relevant qualifications for judgment, that will hardly matter for the morality of justification, which seeks to avoid actual harm. (Admittedly, frameworks which no one applies any longer would be irrelevant as well. One might frame a more restricted version of the second question, addressed to contemporaries. But there is always a risk that a generally obsolete framework will turn out to have living partisans. In this preliminary survey of major distinctions, I will not bother to distinguish these two versions.)

The second question also singles out a kind of justification that is of special cognitive interest. Such justification would meet the demands that are satisfied when a hypothesis is confirmed in the development and testing of scientific theories. For scientific confirmation requires fairness to all actual competing frameworks, not neutrality among all possible frameworks.

The demands of fairness in confirmation are due to the need to rely on a framework of background principles to connect data with hypotheses. The findings of ordinary, unaided sense perception (for example, the perception of a curly streak in a cloud chamber as against the perception of a K-meson using a cloud chamber) only confirm hypotheses in theoretical science in light of background principles used to interpret the raw findings. More specifically, any argument from data to hypothesis can be put in the form, "These are the data and the best explanation of how they came to be would entail the approximate truth of this hypothesis and the basic falsehood of its rivals"; which explanation of the data is best will depend on further propositions, as grand as the most all-embracing principles of symmetry and conservation in physics or as humble as descriptions of circuitry in an apparatus. If a disagreement about a hypothesis depends on a difference in background principles, it is question-begging to argue that data confirm the hypothesis when this argument presupposes the falsehood of principles in the framework of some who reject the hypothesis. Confirmation is less question-begging than this. It is a

process of fair explanatory comparison, fair to rival hypotheses and their accompanying frameworks.

For example, it would have been question-begging for Galileans seeking
evidence that confirmed their heliocentric claim to assume that if telescopes
reveal terrestrial reality better than the naked eye, they had to give superior
access to celestial reality as well. For this conflicted with Aristotelian beliefs
about the radical difference between celestial and terrestrial matter and the
prima facie fitness of natural organs for observation. As it happens, Mars,
when viewed from the earth with a telescope, varies in brightness in the
course of a year, the heliocentric expectation of Galileans, while it does not
vary significantly when viewed with the naked eye, the geocentric expectation of Aristotelians. Neither side had a non-question-begging argument from
the total data about variations in the brightness of Mars to the truth of the
astronomical hypotheses at issue. So neither could claim that the data confirmed their favored hypothesis, even though a Galilean (or, an Aristotelian)
could argue from data to the favored hypothesis within the framework he
believed and employed in his research.

In the natural sciences as we now catalog them, physics, astronomy, biol-
ogy and geology, it has turned out to be possible to resolve most important
disagreements through a fair process of explanatory comparison. Of course,
the originators of a new option that will ultimately triumph sometimes lack
the means to defeat the old outlook while treating its framework fairly. But
when we look at the great consolidators of scientific revolutions, Newton in
contrast to Galileo, Charles Darwin in contrast to Erasmus Darwin and La-
marck, it is striking how well they succeed in being fair. Newton takes advantage of a shared optics, very close to commonsense lore of light and shadow,
to show that Aristotelians and, for that matter, Cartesians, lack a valid mechanics of celestial motion. Optical reasoning, even from naked eye observations, shows that comets would smash the celestial spheres, and that they
lack the swerves that Cartesian vortices would produce.[2] Yet everyone accepts
that the regularities of celestial motion stand in need of an explanation. And
Newton's larger astronomical success, as he describes it, extracting an ascription of causal influences from some data which dictates trajectories fitting
quite different data, is strong support for his celestial mechanics, on any
view.[3] Charles Darwin's tact in treating rival explanatory frameworks fairly is
even more obvious. In The Origin, he constantly demonstrates that natural
selection is a source of superior explanations, rated in light of beliefs about
variation, competition, inheritance and creative intelligence that creationists
share. Thus, the most delightful of his many arguments concludes with appro-

[2] See, for example, section 1 of The System of the World, in F. Cajori, ed., Newton's Principia
(Berkeley: University of California Press, 1962), pp. 549f., and the beginning of the General
Scholium to Book III of the Principia, ibid., p. 543.
[3] See, for example, ibid., pp. xvii f., 192, 550.

priate gloating over the fairness of his triumph, "Why, it may be asked, has the supposed creative force produced [distinctive endemic species of] bats and [of] no other mammals on remote islands? On my view this question can easily be answered; for no terrestrial mammal can be transported across a wide space of sea, but bats can fly across."[4]

In seeking to confirm hypotheses, scientists mean to be fair to rival frameworks actually applied to the actual data. But they do not seek any greater universality. Obviously, they do not seek a justification that would be acceptable no matter what the data. Science is empirical. A bit less obviously, they do not seek a justification that any possible rational investigator would accept, on the basis of the actual data, no matter what possible framework was employed to interpret it. Indeed, there is no need to be fair to all future frameworks. Newton's use of astronomical observations is a paradigm of confirmation. But given the limits of accuracy of which he was aware, his data do not discriminate between his celestial mechanics and relativistic celestial mechanics. The rational consensus that scientists seek, in testing hypotheses, is the same mix of the actual and the hypothetical as singled out by the second question about moral judgments. They seek a consensus to which all actual investigators would be led if each were to respond rationally to all the evidence actually available, rationally responding in light of principles each actually employs in interpreting evidence. (Of course, in this process of response, it might be irrational for someone acquiring certain evidence and arguments not to modify some principle which he would otherwise have employed to interpret evidence.)

Because it refers to actual bases for rational dissent, the second question, concerning the scope of moral justification, will mire us in the rich details of specific cases. Fortunately, the initial statement of the question itself can be simplified. Part of the specification of relevant dissent, though sometimes helpful, is, strictly speaking, dispensable. In defining the second question, I referred to three tools of criticism which one might mobilize to set limits on relevant dissent. The first was the appeal to evidence, i.e., to factual findings that do not by themselves entail moral judgments when each is taken in isolation. The second was the demand for understanding of one's arguments; the relevant dissenter does not reject their conclusions when this is a mark of muddle or a failure to grasp the concepts involved. The third was the discovery that dissent depends on the presence (or the absence) of some causal factor, a presence (or absence) that the dissenter would regard as a source of distortion. I singled out this last possibility since otherwise the question about disagreement might seem to presuppose an unduly intellectualist account of moral judgment. In addition to standards for the possession of moral proper-

---

[4] *The Origin of Species*, J. M. Burrow, ed. (Baltimore: Penguin Press, 1968), p. 383; for other paradigms of fair causal comparison see pp. 132f., 217, 228–30, 237, 351, 359, 378–91.

ties, people have standards for ways of reaching judgments of moral properties, standards referring to attitudes or motivations of fully qualified moral judges. For example, someone might reject a judgment as wrong because such a response to all the features of the act in question would essentially depend on an absence of appropriate sympathy or respect. Still, the third requirement, that the relevant dissenter arrive at the dissent in a way that is not defective by his standards, adds nothing, strictly speaking, to the other requirements, that dissent be rational and well-informed on the part of someone employing a framework actually used. This framework will include whatever standards for judging he has, and his ignorance of his own deviations from his standards for judging will be ignorance of relevant empirical facts.

There is a significant variant of the second question, which I will discuss, as well. In science, even when one acknowledges that one's evidence and arguments are not enough to make one's hypothesis rationally compelling for all actual inquirers, one hopes that more evidence or arguments will fill the gap. Often, this is a rational hope. In thinking about moral judgment, one can raise a corresponding question: is it rational to hope that the totality of evidence that there will ever be, together with all arguments that could make use of this totality, would preclude rational dissent from one's moral judgment in all actual frameworks?

The third question under the heading of "moral realism" arises when one considers mere possibilities, the notorious tendency of philosophers. Even if the constraints of morality and the usual goals of science do not push beyond the limits of the frameworks actually employed in justification, people can be more ambitious, and will be if they philosophize. One can ask in what cases, if any, one's moral judgments are supported by arguments that would lead to their acceptance by any possible person who is rational, possesses all relevant nonmoral findings, and has any qualification for rightly answering moral questions whose relevance must be accepted by anyone who understands the questions.

Some hypotheses about unobservable entities in theoretical science seem to have such a broadly universal warrant. In light of the data they seem to be immune from rational rejection because they are connected to data by criterial principles, principles which no one with our actual experience could possibly reject except out of confusion or a failure to understand. For example, there is a burden of proof on someone who denies that anything external has acted on a nonliving thing in erratic motion; blindness to this specific burden of proof seems as much a token of unreasonableness as blindness to the general need to modify at least one of two contradictory beliefs. There is a similar burden of proof on someone who denies that the fact that something seems to make clear and distinct what is otherwise perceived vaguely is evidence that it makes the otherwise invisible visible. The argument from Brownian motion to molecules depends, in part, on the first burden-of-proof principle, as the argument for microscopic life depends on the second.[5]

One might wonder whether there are moral judgments whose justification is similarly independent of contingent historical limits on the frameworks that have actually been employed. To what extent are reason and evidence, unaided by those limits, sufficient to compel acceptance of one's moral judgments? This is a third good question that might be raised under the heading of "moral realism."

Of course, there are more than three important and importantly different questions whose answers might be thought to separate moral realists from others. However, even in their present, vaguely developed state, these three will serve to mark off the most important distinctions that tend to be neglected in the moral realism dispute. In each case, some answers would normally be rated realist, others anti-realist. Yet for some moral judgments, for most moral judgments, and for typical and important moral judgments, the right answer could—on the face of it—be realist for one question but not for another. Perhaps when one claims that certain moral judgments are true descriptions of states of affairs one is justified, but only as a Galilean would be in arguing from telescopic observations of the brightness of Mars to the heliocentric hypothesis—justified in one's truth claim, but not justified in claiming that all actual dissenters are irrational or uninformed. In addition, on the face of it, one might be in a position to claim that evidence and argument would compel agreement with a moral judgment in every moral framework actually employed, without supposing that dissent in every possible framework would be a sign of ignorance or unreason. Moreover, there is no obvious need for either kind of universal justification to be a justification of a claim that a moral judgment is a true description of a state of affairs. The subjectmatter of a justification is often something else, an attitude, for example. Perhaps, even the more universal justification is sometimes available when it is wrong to claim that what is justified is a description of a moral fact.

THE MIXED VERDICT

I will be defending answers to the three questions of moral realism (and others) which do diverge from one another. More precisely, there will turn out to be significant cases in which some right answers to a question posed of a moral judgment are realist, while others are anti-realist. The question, "Is moral realism valid?", is bad, not just in principle, but in practice.

In the view of justification and moral truth that I will defend in the next chapter, most of our well-established moral judgments are justified true beliefs

---

[5] I set out the detailed arguments, in their original historical settings, and a further account of the underlying truisms in chapter 10 of *Fact and Method* (Princeton: Princeton University Press, 1987).

concerning objective states of affairs. By "our well-established" moral judgments I mean those that most people in advanced industrial societies would make after rational reflection on relevant arguments and well-established empirical facts. These judgments refer to objective moral properties because they result from ways of responding to evidence and argument which are ways of detecting rightness and wrongness.

This highly realist answer to the first question about morality needs to be defended against suspicions of dogmatism. The defense will partly consist of a criticism of overly simple accounts of how explanations (including explanations of the sources of moral judgment) ought to be tested and compared. It will partly consist of an argument that controversial claims about processes of detection are a normal foundation for claims about reference and content.

We are often justified in claims as to moral truth—yet, when we are, there is sometimes another framework actually employed that would lead to a contrary judgment on the basis of rational response to all of our own data and arguments. In the rest of this chapter, I will defend this anti-realist answer to the second question by investigating two sorts of frameworks for moral judgment quite different from our own, the traditional morality of the Tiv, an agrarian people in Nigeria, and the outlooks characteristic of Greco-Roman antiquity, especially in Aristotle's version. I hope to show that there are some significant moral differences beyond the reach of reason and evidence—indeed, beyond the reach of all the evidence we could rationally hope to acquire.

None of these efforts to set boundaries on the scope of reason and evidence will put beyond the boundaries such paradigmatic judgments of moral wrongness as the condemnation of the Nazis' murders of Jews or Caligula's alleged recreational killings. As moral realists sometimes note in a tone of indignation, any means of moral assessment that rational people have employed condemns these acts, and all too many others, in light of the facts of each case. Still, the third question of realism can be asked. Could some merely possible rational person, possessed of all the evidence, dissent from the judgment all actual informed and rational judges share? I will argue for an anti-realist "Yes" in all cases, including cases in which the question about actual dissenters merits a realist "No." Even though no possible rational, informed person who affirms judgments of right or of wrong could dissent in the paradigmatic cases, a possible informed, rational person could—namely, a nihilist who rejects every ascription of a moral property, as false. The possibility of such a nihilist will, in essence, consist of the possibility of a certain attitude of radical unconcern for others on the part of an informed and rational person. So, to establish the relevance of such nihilism to questions of justification and truth, I will have to argue for an intermediate position on morality and motivation: there is an intrinsic connection between moral belief and moral desires, and yet this relation is compatible with a construal of moral beliefs as beliefs in objective truths.

Taken one by one, these diverging hypotheses have (I hope) seemed worth pursuing. Yet well-established conceptions of justification, truth and meaning would insure that the proposed answers could not all be right. For example, the logical positivists all assumed that any truth claim justifiable in light of the evidence someone possessed was justifiable by reasoning from that evidence which only employed principles that no one could possibly rationally reject. In the empirical sciences those universal premises were supposed to consist of definitions together with a single canon of rules of empirical inference, holding in all fields at all times. Many still assume that a good argument from evidence will meet the demand for universality, even though few share the positivists' more specific expectations about the content of the canon. And the general assumption is enough to exclude the mixed verdict that I will defend. If anyone were justified in a claim of moral truth in light of certain evidence, any possible person (much less any actual one) would have to be led to the same conclusion by an argument from the same evidence which only depended on universally compelling principles.

One response to such objections to mixed verdicts about moral judgments would be to construct a distinctive account of truth or justification in morality, distinctive, that is, from the analysis applied in the sciences, the home territory of the most powerful positivist writings. But this response would be doubly misguided. In the first place, it would give too much credit to the constraints imposed on science by positivism and its modern heirs. Analogous cases within science itself provide equally good motivations for similarly mixed verdicts. For example, Maxwell took current data to support the hypothesis that the movement of one charge would produce movement in another, with a regular time-delay, by producing stress in an intervening massless medium. His justification relied on the principle that "the propagation of electrical action in time" must be "either the flight of a material substance in space or the propagation of a condition of motion or stress in a medium already existing in space."[6] Neumann, responding to the same data, took them to support the hypothesis that the movement of the first charge acts on the other at a distance and with a delay, with no relevant change in intervening matter. Potential was the primary causal factor in his explanatory framework; it was not ascribed to further underlying forces or attributed to matter.[7] Because of the difference in frameworks, each theorist was rational, though their evidence was the same.

At any rate, even apart from the misrepresentation of science, the response that treats rational truth-claims in morality as a special case will not cope with

[6] A Treatise on Electricity and Magnetism, II, p. 492.
[7] See Das Newton'sche Princip der Fernwirkungen (Leipzig: B. G. Teubner, 1896), pp. v, 22, 27.

the general worry that the mixed verdict violates limits that are appropriate in every realm of true-or-false belief. There is a powerful and quite general tendency to suppose that people cannot genuinely disagree in their beliefs when their difference in response is entirely due to their different bases for responding to evidence, not to a difference in the evidence that each possesses. Such a fundamental difference in means of response is supposed to constitute a difference in the subjectmatter of the judgments. All current efforts to distinguish sameness from difference in content, including the most important alternatives to positivism, will turn out to sustain this denial of sameness with enough force to rule out the mixed verdict on moral realism. So a principled argument for the verdict must include an alternative, general account of content.

I will develop that account at length in chapter five, after a critical survey (in chapter four) of current options and their barriers to the mixed verdict. In my account, the limits of content, the boundaries that someone cannot cross without changing the subject, are determined by practical considerations in a common project of advancing learning through communication. Tactical rationales, sometimes quite superficial, taking goals, practices and spontaneous inclinations as given, determine when someone is addressing herself to a given subjectmatter. These rationales often single out, as relevantly advantageous, standards for common content. Often, these standards, though pragmatically grounded, emphasize objective constraints; they dictate that asserters differing radically in beliefs address themselves to the same subjectmatter, nonetheless, on account of their similar interactions with similar environments. Applied to moral discourse, this account of content will be just permissive enough to sustain the mixed verdict.

Whether all these conclusions add up to a position that is "realist," "anti-realist" or "relativist" I do not know. I hope that their defense will lead the reader to join me in not caring.

MORAL DIVIDES

Answering the various questions of moral realism requires a clear grasp of disagreements more radical than any we normally try to resolve. So it is useful to begin with the second question, seeing whether actual people might ever reach different moral judgments of the same state of affairs, when the judgment of neither side depends on irrationality or ignorance of empirical facts.

As usual in such discussions, the base point for measuring moral distance will be the judgments on which most people brought up in a modern industrial society would agree, if they rationally responded to relevant facts. I will speak of these as "our" judgments, for short. Even if (as I very much doubt) you would not make them, you will appreciate that they would be the moral verdict of the vast majority.

I will begin with two detailed descriptions of sources of moral disagreement with us, well-documented, respectively, in the anthropological literature and the literature of Greco-Roman antiquity. The first case is the moral outlook of the Tiv, a traditional African society. The second is the moral outlook of Aristotle, especially concerning hierarchies and especially where he is representative of important themes in literate opinion in Greco-Roman civilization. I will argue that we would indeed disagree morally with these people in cases in which their different moral judgments would not depend on ignorance or confusion. If traditional Tiv, or Aristotle, possessed all our evidence and arguments, indeed, if they possessed all evidence and arguments that we could rationally hope to acquire, reason would not be enough for agreement. The disagreements would result from their employing different frameworks for moral inquiry, reasonable frameworks which are not subject to non-question-begging criticism.

I will sometimes speak of the crucial difference as a difference in ways of moral learning. This turn of phrase brings to the fore the crucial role of disagreements as to what processes contribute to moral insight. The processes that we take to contribute to moral insight are, primarily, processes of choice among acts and institutions on the basis of evenhanded concern or respect for all affected, provided that they are willing to choose on the same basis. As with any quick statement of a way of learning in a complex domain, this one is vague, incomplete and in need of qualification. Indeed, more than half of this book, i.e., chapters six through eleven, will be an effort to understand the demands of respect, concern and evenhandedness. Still, it will, I hope, become apparent that our shared reliance on evenhanded concern or respect is definite, strict and important enough to come in conflict with other people's ways of moral learning.

The Tiv

The Tiv are a farming people in Nigeria, whose practices, though adjusted to the colonial regime, were still traditional in many ways when the Bohannans studied them in the 1950's. They resemble many so-called "tribal agriculturalists" in the literature. There is an abuse of ethnography in which pathetic refugees or demoralized remnants of a defeated society, too desperate to subject themselves to moral constraints or burdened by challenges for which they were not remotely prepared, are supposed to present informative contrasts to our standards of behavior and assessment. Turnbull's Ik and Veblen's Kwakiutl are widely used instances. By contrast, the Tiv cope with challenges in the normal range of severity, with normal stability and success. (In any case, they did at the time of their classic description by Paul and Laura Bohannan, in the 1950's. I will relate these accounts in the present tense, in anxious ignorance of subsequent stresses on the Tiv.)[8]

The Tiv are organized in family compounds consisting primarily of brothers, their wives, and their children. These groups are distributed more or less uniformly over a district of patrilineally related kin, known as a *tar*. Tivland is a loose confederacy of such districts, but the Western political term "confederacy" conceals the problem that was the despair of British administrators. No one is in charge, in traditional Tiv society. There are local councils of leaders, who are even thought to have mystical powers. But their function is to mediate disputes and tensions, in a process which leads people to interact in relative tranquillity, despite the characteristic assertiveness and individualism of the Tiv and the traditional absence of any central coercive apparatus. The most important social bonds are, of course, not contract or citizenship, but bonds of kinship and common locale.

Apart from consequences of European invasion, the Tiv maintain these bonds and the obligations they generate without drainage of resources and liberties toward a central administration. Indeed, they initially regarded jails as a barbaric horror. Usually, Tiv live up to one another's expectations because of certain stable attitudes and interests: concern, respect or liking that develops among immediate family and cooperating neighbors, interest in continued cooperation from those on whom one's livelihood depends, and interest in minimal approval from those whose resentment or dislike could be a lifelong burden. However, individuals' desires sometimes conflict with obligations generated by Tiv social ties. The central moral problem of the Tiv is to protect the network of relationships from consequent rupture without unnecessary harm to individuality and self-esteem. As the Tiv sometimes put it, when conflicts threaten to "spoil the *tar*," there is an urgent need to bring disputants together and "repair the *tar*."

The main means of repairing the tar is organized discussion, consultation, social pressure and, occasionally, coercion in the *jir*, the "native court" in colonial jargon. These "courts" are led by judges who, if all goes well, sensitively and firmly evoke both angers and loyalties in a way that repairs strains on interpersonal connections. Usually this means reestablishing fluent interaction among the disputants. Sometimes it means ending their relationships while establishing their new location in the network of interpersonal ties. A decision that is acceptable to the disputants (often as a result of pressure from the assembled, kibitzing community) is right, just by that token. Working out threats to relationship through the processes epitomized in the *jir* is the distinctively Tiv way of moral learning.

[8] I will mainly rely on Paul Bohannan, *Justice and Judgment Among the Tiv* (Oxford: Oxford University Press, 1968) and Paul and Laura Bohannan, *The Tiv of Central Nigeria* (London: International African Institute, 1953).

Although it has its attractive side, this version of moral learning can lead to much that we find wrong. The troubling cases, of course, are those in which the Tiv, in our view, give too much weight to the maintenance of interpersonal ties of kinds that are important for coordination in Tivland.

Consider the Tiv ethic of testimony in local courts. Except for police, witnesses are, almost exclusively, brought to court by individual disputants and are of two categories: relatives, who are expected to testify in the interests of their disputant, and witnesses preselected by the disputant and paid for their testimony. The payment is important, since it helps the witness to avoid animosity from the other side. The testimony was "nothing personal," just a service for a fee. As a result, there is much false testimony by relatives, and the burden of finding and negotiating with witnesses keeps much truth out of court. Yet for the Tiv, the witness who freely steps forward and gives incriminating evidence does wrong if, as is likely, he or she "spoils the *tar*."

Similarly, marital ethics, the central source of moral problems for the Tiv, is, from our standpoint, too heavily biased toward the maintenance of social ties. Traditional Tiv society was held together by exchanges of wives, over long periods of time, among the brother-centered family groups. The major goal in such exchanges was the gain in children for the group. The practice, in this original form and as modified in light of colonial restrictions, puts a heavy burden on women to stay in unhappy marriages. Even when separation is allowed, the husband's right to the child is absolute. While there is social pressure on him not to demand the custody due to him when the child is young, he is expected to demand the return of a teenager, who is expected to obey.

Here are two cases in a *jir* displaying the burdensome limits on choice, especially choice by women, that are the price for relying on interpersonal relations instead of a state. In the first, Chenge, a good judge in the Tiv process of adjudication, combines his usual appreciation of the difficulties of both sides with his usual sternness in defending the network of ties that coordinates interactions.

The next *jir* concerned the custody of a child—a young girl of about ten years. Her mother had died a year or so after she was born and she was then reared by her mother's mother. Gbegba, hearing this much of the matter, observed that there seemed to be no problem: the child's father should give the old woman a gift of ten shillings for rearing her, and the matter would be finished. The child should then accompany her father home; her filiation was not in doubt. . . .

The girl began to whimper. As her father came towards her, she began to scream. When persuasion failed he tried to carry her away. She screamed more loudly. Chenge walked over to them: 'Softly, softly,' he said to the father. 'Look, my child, this man is your father. He won't do anything to you. He will give you plenty of food. And besides, in a year or so you will be getting married and will go to your husband in a new compound in any case. Go with your father and don't give us all this trouble.'

I have seen Chenge make this sort of speech on several occasions. Either the youngster becomes quiet and says she will go, or she kicks and screams more loudly than before. Today's child screamed. Chenge lost his temper and told the father to get this noisy youngster out of the compound so that the *jir* could proceed. When the father tried to pick her up to carry her away, the mother's mother's classificatory sister—an old woman who is half mad, and who was angry with Chenge in any case because all her sons were in gaol for larceny—went after Chenge with a stick and had to be forcibly restrained by a policeman. Everyone, including Chenge, thought this very funny.[9]

In his commentary, Bohannan notes that the girl's stay with her father probably will not be as burdensome as she fears. And the Tiv certainly think that fathers should be kind to daughters. Still, even if the father proves painfully unkind, he will retain a right to custody.

The second case makes even clearer the Tiv commitment to preserve the basic source of interfamilial ties. Marriage would not work as the social cement of Tivland if the preservation of marriage depended on mere liking. Though most cases in *jir* feature effusive banter and a strong preference for the use of persuasion, in this one, the appeal to liking is dismissed as abruptly and forcefully as we would dismiss a tax collector's assertion that he may tax as he pleases.

Adetsô, of Shangev Ya, married Bukwagh, an MbaDuku girl. She left him and returned home. He came after her. Because he would not stop annoying her in her kinsmen's compound, and kept trying to induce her to return to him, she called a case before the MbaDuku *mbatarev* [i.e., the judges of the MbaDuku district, those whom Bohannan studied.] She said that her husband had given her sufficient cloth (a more or less literal metaphor for caring for her material wants), he had not fought with her and he did not beat her much; she simply did not like him.

The judges gave her a lecture to the effect that she was lucky to have such a husband, and told her to go with him. She said she would not. They told the husband to take her and get her out of there. She said nothing more, but she put up a pretty good fight. In the long run, it took two of her husband's kinsmen to carry her off: one grasping her arms, the other her ankles. There was no noise, but she was still kicking and struggling as they carried her out of the compound.[10]

To cite one further example, from precolonial Tiv morality, the moral limits on aggression among the Tiv are highly sensitive to one's degree of kinship to the potential victim. "The Tiv lineage system . . . provides a . . . scale of

[9] Bohannan, *Justice and Judgment*, pp. 23f.
[10] Ibid., p. 90.

social distance by which moral values may be measured. . . . To strike a close agnate [paternal kin] is a moral offense for which one's agnates may justifiably bewitch one. To get into a fight with a non-Tiv is sometimes foolhardy, but never immoral. . . . From the morally reprehensible nature of theft within the minimal segment to the morally laudable nature of such raiding between very large segments lies an almost imperceptibly graded scale of moral judgment attaching to the same physical act and depending on the social closeness of the two lineages involved."[11]

It would be stupid of me to judge Chenge's judgments by the standards I apply to Tompkins County Family Court. In Tivland, as in my land, there is an inherited network of practices, relations and rules, which must be taken into account in any morally responsible choice. Because of the nature of the Tiv network, respect for the desires of individuals who are trapped in family or marital relations can be especially dangerous to others. Certainly, it is important to appreciate the social point of the troubling decisions. Nonetheless, the Tiv and we still disagree when the context of Tiv choices is fully characterized. Chenge does not judge the runaway daughters and unhappy wives in a spirit of moral anxiety, like Admiral Vere in Melville's "Billy Budd." In Tiv judgment, unlike our judgment, he does not wrong those women at all, so there is no question of his wronging innocents to prevent social disaster. Similarly, a reformist argument to change the Tiv system of obligations to broaden freedom of choice in marriage would be inadequate for the Tiv when it would succeed in our eyes. Such reform would inevitably disrupt Tiv social life for a while and the Tiv put much greater weight than we on the maintenance of interpersonal ties that are actually present, sustained by rules that actually command general acceptance.

Analogously, though we think it understandable that a Tiv might not volunteer important information in court, we think that volunteering would constitute heroism where it would be an outrage for the Tiv. Certainly, we think it wrong to prey on strangers in the manner of the precolonial Tiv— even if we take Queen Victoria's army to have been the greatest raiding party of all.

That people in different cultures may disagree in moral judgments of the same acts settles no philosophical issue and only surprises the most naive. The present issue is whether such disagreement could exist among people who are fully informed and rationally responding to all relevant information. These qualifications for relevant dissent can be quite demanding. Someone cannot arrive at answers to moral questions in a rational way if he does not understand the terms of those questions. One does not understand the terms of

[11] Bohannan and Bohannan, The Tiv, pp. 25–27. For a similar structuring of aggression in a totally different ecological setting, see Asen Balikci, The Netsilik Eskimo (Garden City, N.Y.: Natural History Press, 1970), pp. 179–93.

moral questions if one accepts answers to them when one knows that the answers essentially depend on certain incapacities. Some of these constraints on understanding are relevant to moral judgment and to nonmoral judgment, as well. If one doesn't take it to be a serious criticism of a judgment of wrongness that it depends on ignorance of facts about the case at hand, or confusion, or inconsistency, one doesn't understand what wrongness is. Other intrinsically relevant incapacities are more specific to moral judgment. Above all, a moral judgment must not be accepted if it depends on an incapacity for imaginative empathy with others. It is a piece of nonsense to report, "It was right to beat up that stranger, although I would not say this if I could imagine how it must have felt to him."

In all respects that are intrinsically relevant to moral judgment, the Tiv function well, on occasions in which they disagree with us. They show great intelligence and a sound grasp of relevant facts about Tiv society. The Tiv had extensive familiarity with alternative ways of life, European and African, which they rejected so long as the traditional economy was viable.[12] Wide-ranging empathic imagination is an especially impressive characteristic of the inquests conducted when Tiv die or are seriously ill. Death is the unavoidable break in the network of relations. The inquests are, at once, investigations of sorcery and witchcraft and, quite consciously, heroic sessions of family therapy, in which emotional understanding extends across barriers of gender and lineage. No one reading the account of Chenge's leadership of such inquests could suppose that he lacked the capacity to imagine the deprivation of the woman trapped in an unhappy marriage or the suffering of a child forced to live with a cruel father.[13]

In this case, as in many others, it is vital to distinguish empathy from sympathy. Otherwise, a capacity that is essential to judging well in any framework will be confused with an attitude that only has an essential connection with sound judgment in some frameworks. Chenge's distinctive responses to unhappily married women and to girls who fear their fathers do not depend on a lack of empathy, an inability to grasp what their situations are like for them. But his responses do sometimes depend on a lack of sympathy, a failure to care about them to the same extent as he would care about others who are just as troubled. If he has self-knowledge, Chenge will accept that his judgments do not reflect evenhanded sympathy for all, when such sympathy would conflict with the ongoing project of maintaining the current network of social ties. Yet despite such self-knowledge, he can rationally engage in moral judgment. In effect, he can say, "I take the claim of the husband to be right, even though I would not accept his claim if I were decisively influenced by evenhanded sympathy for all affected."[14]

---

[12] Bohannan and Bohannan, *The Tiv*, pp. 37–42.

[13] See *Justice and Judgment*, pp. 23–25, 79, 93, 94f., 126f., 131, 132–34, 140f.

[14] The cleavage between empathy and sympathy is even more dramatic among men in the

For all the appearance of difference, the Tiv way of moral learning would be the same as ours in the final analysis, if Tiv practices of judgment ultimately depend on a rationale that we would accept as well. The central Tiv interest in repairing the *tar* would certainly be valued, to some extent, from the standpoints of relatively impartial concern or respect that supply our ways of moral learning. This might suggest that their fundamental standpoint is our own. But it is not. The well-being of all, impartially assessed, is never in question among the Tiv. While what a Tiv denotes, referring to his or her *tar*, varies in extent from context to context, it rarely includes more than a small fraction of the Tiv, much less non-Tiv. Unequal weighing according to degree of kinship is always treated as preferable to impartial promotion of human welfare in Tiv discussions of morality, to a far greater extent than we would allow at a similarly fundamental level.[15] Moreover, while we can well imagine worse means of social coordination in Tiv circumstances, worse, that is, when assessed from our point of view, there is no reason to believe that other patterns found among tribal agriculturalists, some more atomized, some more reliant on official leadership, would not work out better. A variety of influences and accidents, now largely forgotten, produced Tiv agricultural techniques that were adequate but somewhat wasteful.[16] Why suppose Tiv moral techniques are better, when assessed from a European consequentialist point of view?[17] In any case, even if the general emphasis on "repairing the *tar*" were optimific, it is only in the most rigid rule-utilitarianism, which few

traditional culture of the Yanomamo, a hunter-gatherer people of the Amazon basin. In relations between villages and between the sexes, Yanomamo men cultivate and admire relentless fierceness. For example, they force their wives to do their bidding, often through such violent tactics as shooting a barbed arrow into the thigh of a wife who is late with dinner. They engage in raids on rival villages, trying to kill as many men as possible and to rape and kidnap as many women as possible. While villages cultivate alliances in response to this state of war, treachery is a common and admired device of warfare, often taking the form of a "treacherous feast": allies are invited to a banquet and ambushed when they enter the village compound. For all these resemblances to emotional cripples of sadistic kinds in our culture, Yanomamo men are capable of the full range of emotions and able to grasp the perspectives and experiences of others. The Yanomamo are portrayed in vivid detail in Napoleon Chagnon, *Yanomamo: The Fierce People* (New York: Holt, Rinehart and Winston, 1977) and *Studying the Yanomamo* (New York: Holt, Rinehart and Winston, 1974). For some examples of Yanomamo imaginativeness and insight in understanding the perspectives of others, see *Yanomamo*, pp. 48f., 68, 93, 98–100, 107, 135. Perhaps Yanomamo male approval, in the troubling cases, is not moral judgment. Still, Yanomamo men are not led by their empathy to corresponding sympathy, confirming the view that others, more clearly engaged in moral judgment, reject claims of sympathy without displaying inadequate mental access to others.

[15] See Bohannan and Bohannan, *The Tiv*, pp. 25–27, 29; Bohannan, *Justice and Judgment*, p. 136.

[16] Bohannan and Bohannan, *The Tiv*, p. 1.

[17] For example, the Bohannans believe that abiding dilemmas concerning leadership are inherent in the Tiv's combination of egalitarianism with the acceptance of leadership, judicial and otherwise, of outstanding individuals. Periodic violent uprisings were the most dramatic result. See *The Tiv*, pp. 31f., 39f., 90–92.

if any of us accept, that this morally justifies the extreme but specific losses of a daughter forced to live with a cruel father, or a harmless wanderer, beaten up and robbed.

Examples can only provide a prima facie case that there are moral disagreements which reason and evidence cannot overcome. A variety of general considerations, concerned with moral psychology, meaning or justification, could be used in an attempt to explain away the appearance of fundamental disagreement. However, even before these rebuttals are encountered, there is a need for a different example with the same appearance of fundamental division between an alien way of moral learning and our own. After all, if only the Tiv and similar societies departed from the way of learning of the rest of humanity, that would be a prima facie case that the Tiv are victimized by some intrinsically relevant defect that further analysis will reveal. Another example is needed, from a different social setting. A much more famous reasoner than Chenge provides it.

DIFFERENCES WITH ARISTOTLE

Of the several banal generalities that people bring to their reading of Aristotle, the view that his ethics is virtue-based is perhaps the truest and most useful. His assessment of acts and institutions is based on an account of the best way for a human to live. And the best way is the one that fully exercises what is best in us. These excellences, or virtues, are concerned either with intellect or with character. Aristotle claims to have a comprehensive description of them (EN 1115 a 3–5), and has much to say about their relative importance. The description and the ranking are a recipe for assessing lives that most of us would reject. Moreover, when Aristotle deploys this assessment of lives in his judgments of institutions, the vast majority of us would reject his political assessments. In disagreeing with Aristotle, we sometimes find that his distinctive judgments do not depend on his ignorance of empirical findings and arguments acquired in the intervening millennia. In these respects, his morality, unlike his chemistry, is a source of disagreement that reason and evidence would not resolve.

In the *Nichomachean Ethics*, the longest, most detailed project is the description of virtues of character. Almost half of the virtues that Aristotle describes concern competence in dealing with wealth, power or honor, greater (in several cases, much greater) than the norm. The liberal man gives for the sake of noble ends, setting no store by wealth (iv.1). The magnificent man spends large sums like an artist to create splendid, fine things (iv.2).

Greatness of soul is the crowning virtue of character. The great-souled man deserves and claims "the prize appointed for the noblest deeds; and this is honor" (1123 b 20).[18] He gives, but is ashamed of receiving benefits. When he does receive a benefit, he is apt to respond by giving something greater, so that his original benefactor will be in his debt. He has utter contempt for honors from ordinary people or on trifling grounds. Even in response to great honors from excellent people he is only "moderately pleased, thinking that he is coming by his own or even less than his own; for there can be no honor that is worthy of perfect virtue" (1124 a 7–9). He acquires fine, useless things, which expresses his self-sufficiency.

Aristotle is well aware that it would be pointless for anyone but a person of considerable wealth and leisure to cultivate these dispositions. "A poor man cannot be magnificent . . . and he who tries is a fool" (1122 b 28f.). Even when such resources are not obviously and generally required, the possibility of virtue sometimes depends on social circumstances. Thus, the truly brave are fearless not just in the face of lethal dangers, but of those calling for prowess or promising a noble death (1115 b 5f.).

Even those of us who think it poisonous mush to deny that poverty makes it hard to flourish will find much to question in Aristotle's catalog and rankings. Most of us think it good to encourage the self-esteem of people whose accomplishments are not first-rate, rather than reinforcing their sense of inferiority or dependence. We admire the artful liberality of rich philanthropists, but no more (probably, less) than the stubborn, limited dedication of a mother on welfare trying to protect the most basic prospects for her child.

In general, the virtues of wide-ranging, fine and effective discrimination do not play such an important role in our account of the best sort of life. In his discussions of virtues of character, Aristotle repeatedly notes that the virtuous person acts for the sake of to kalon (in EN alone, see 1115 b 13, 119 b 16, 1120 a 24, 1121 a 5, 1122 b 6f., 1168 a 10). The term kalos has various translations, defensible in context, usually implying prowess and refinement: "noble," "fine," "worthy," and "beautiful." "Beautiful, beauteous, fair" is the primary definition in the standard Greek-English lexicon. Our consequent worries about aestheticism in Aristotle's ethics are confirmed by his remark in the Metaphysics that "the chief forms of to kalon are order and symmetry and definiteness, which the mathematical sciences demonstrate in a special degree" (1078 b 1–3).[19]

Aristotle also discusses intellectual virtues, in addition to virtues of character. His rankings are especially emphatic, and their difference from our own assessments especially great. "If happiness is activity in accordance with virtue, it is reasonable that it should be in accordance with the highest virtue . . . That this activity is contemplative we have already said" (EN 1177 a

---

[18] I will use Ross' translation of the Nichomachean Ethics, in The Basic Works of Aristotle, R. McKeon, ed. (New York: Random House, 1941).

[19] Ross' translation in ibid. I am indebted to John Cooper, "Virtues and Values" (manuscript, 1988) for pointing out the importance of this passage.

12f., 18). In this activity, one contemplates eternal truths, concerning things that do not change, without consideration of practical human concerns (see EN VI, 3; X, 7). In advocating the supremacy of this activity, Aristotle emphasizes the self-sufficiency that comes with its successful pursuit. Unlike the just man, the wise man does not "need people towards whom and with whom he shall act justly" (1177 a 30f.). Theoretical contemplation, he adds, "alone would seem to be loved for its own sake" (1177 b 2). In part, he seems to have in mind that even an entirely and appropriately enjoyable activity of material creation depends for its enjoyment on the survival of a created thing that is vulnerable to destruction.

Aristotle is at one with us in regarding a life entirely devoted to theoretical contemplation as inhuman and (for humans) incomplete. Successful theoretical contemplation would not be the whole story of a flourishing human life. For example, something is missing if friendship is missing. Still, Aristotle takes the fact that theoretical contemplation is the best part of the story to have important consequences for human choice. A virtuous human will give priority to those goals which contribute to expressing what is best in him. For example, the best sort of life will include friendships with fellow-contemplators, which stimulate theoretical contemplation in humans, however unnecessary such relationships might be to a contemplative god. But the best sort of life will exclude attachments of other kinds when they interfere with contemplative activity, as they certainly often do among humans. A life dominated by just benefaction is worse than a life dominated by theoretical contemplation (EN 1177 a 30f.). Much worse would be a life in which one provided benefits to others who do not excel, while depriving oneself of resources for theoretical contemplation.

Even when we consider relatively self-centered human achievements, we are far from insisting on the priority of insightful contemplation over other activities, more material, transient or collective. And in fact, concern for others is central to our conception of those traits which are to be admired or developed. Here, we do not think it wrong for someone to disengage somewhat from successful intellectual activity in order to act on concern for others outside of a mutually admiring society of the intellectually elect. Indeed, apart from certain extreme and rare circumstances, we think an Aristotelian degree of absorption would be wrong.

Admittedly, the main subjectmatter of Aristotle's ethics differs from our main moral concern. Our central moral anxieties are directed at questions of how to avoid objectionable interference with others, not how to develop ourselves in the best possible way. For this reason, among others, our most intense moral disagreements with Aristotle concern the hierarchies that he defends in the Politics, hierarchies sustained by organized force and appropriately biased education, as he is acutely and explicitly aware.

Our most notorious disagreement concerns slavery. But here, it is at least open to question whether he would have maintained his position if he possessed our biological data and responded rationally to it. For he objects to the enslavement of those whose natural capacities are equal to their masters', and claims that barbarians are typically congenitally retarded, in a way that makes their enslavement by Greeks best for all. The uncharacteristic shoddiness of his arguments for the latter, biological conclusion suggests that he may rely on background principles in light of which slavery stands less in need of justification for him than for us. Elsewhere, I have defended this assessment of our disagreement.[20] However, there is much firmer ground than slavery for the pursuit of disagreements about hierarchies that reason and evidence would not resolve.

Aside from the alleged natural incapacities that preclude the significant exercise of virtue in natural slaves—and other natural incapacities he attributes to Greek women—Aristotle claims that various social circumstances prevent the exercise of virtue, at least to any high degree, among Greek men whose natural capacities are intact. Far from depending on ignorance on Aristotle's part, these claims of defect combine an acute awareness of the human consequences of social roles in classical antiquity with his catalog of individual human excellences. Yet because he rates social arrangements according to the best lives they create, his social insight leads him to judge as best arrangements that we would reject because of burdens of degradation or drudgery imposed on the majority of nonslaves. Our agreement about the relevant data is partly responsible for our rational disagreement about what is best.

Those who are slaves by nature will not be craftsmen, wage-laborers, tradesmen or independent farmers—presumably because the absence of the deliberative capacity in natural slaves makes them too stupid for these jobs. Thus, "[w]hile the slave exists by nature, this is not so of the shoemaker or other artisan" (Pol., 1260 b 1f.).[21] Tradesmen and craftsmen play a role in the political arrangement that Aristotle regards as ideal. Independent farmers do, as well, in the best feasible arrangement. Yet Aristotle is adamant about the limitations that these occupations place on virtue. In the ideal state, "the citizens [i.e., those who play a role in governing] must not lead the lives of mechanics and tradesmen, which is ignoble, and far from conducive to virtue. Nor must they be drawn from among the farming class, because leisure is necessary for the growth of virtue" (1328 b 33–1329 a 3).

The degradation of tradesmen, craftsmen and wage-laborers is especially severe—and especially important politically, since these roles are filled by nonslaves in all arrangements that Aristotle recommends. Tradesmen are so occupied with monetary gain through buying and selling that they come to

[20] At the end of "Marx and Aristotle: The Unity of Two Opposites," *Proceedings of the American Political Science Association* (1978).

[21] I will rely on John Warrington's translation of the *Politics*, *Aristotle's Politics* (London: Dent, 1959).

regard the acquisition of as much money as possible as an end in itself, neglecting the exercise of the diverse nonacquisitive faculties for which money should simply serve as a means (see 1257 b 1–1258 a 18). Speaking of craftsmen and wage-laborers, Aristotle declares, "their way of life is despicable, and there is no room for excellence in any occupation to which people of that sort put their hand" (1319 a 24–31). This radical unworthiness reflects at least three defects, from the standpoint of the catalog of virtues that Aristotle employs.

In the first place, since artisans and day-laborers obtain their whole income by selling, they are prone to the unnatural acquisitiveness that Aristotle explicitly attacks in connection with a merchant's way of life. Also, they must make the same kind of product again and again in order to live. Hence, they are frequently engaged in production which is engaged in only for the sake of the resulting product, a form of doing which Aristotle repeatedly stigmatizes as inferior to activity engaged in for its own sake. Aristotle gives us a clue to the third reason for his disdain when he characterizes artisans and laborers as "servants of the public" (1278 a 112f.). By this phrase, he presumably means to remind us that these workers depend on the vagaries of taste and prosperity in others. Being prey to unpredictable and uncontrollable market forces, they cannot subject their lives to purposive control (see EN 1112 a 26f.) in the same way as the master of the self-sufficient aristocratic household.

These ratings of lives are premises for statecraft, since "the state exists for the sake of a *good* life, and not for that of life *as such* . . . for the sake of good actions, and not merely of social life" (1280 a 31f., b 2f.). More specifically, the best social arrangements will provide resources and opportunities promoting the best lives on the part of those who live best. ("In nature, as well as in the arts, the inferior always exists for the sake of the superior . . ." 1333 a 21f.) Aristotle sees very clearly that those resources and opportunities of the best require that others live in ways that degrade or stultify them, according to his own standards. In pursuit of the highest degree of virtue, he would approve of political choices that we would judge wrong, wrong because they condemn the vast majority to inferior lives that they could otherwise avoid.

Aristotle's elitist assessment of social sacrifices is epitomized in his preference between two societies he describes in the *Politics*. One is a democracy of small farmers (see 1318 b 6–1319 a 19). Aristotle believes such a society could be highly stable. While the farmers will lack the leisure that the best sorts of life require, they could certainly have sufficient leisure to exercise significant moral virtues in their periodic political deliberations and in their personal interactions. And they are not vulnerable to the special degradation of artisans, day-laborers or merchants. The other society is an aristocracy in which leisured philosophers, politicians, and military men are provided for by the farming of their slaves and the handiwork of artisans and tradesmen who are excluded from politics (see xii.9). Aristotle makes it clear that the well-being of the leisured minority will require extremely inferior lives on the part of the vast majority. And, at least for the nonslave noncitizens, this inferiority would be the product of social circumstances. Yet Aristotle does not hesitate to rate the second arrangement as ideal, the farmers' democracy as simply the best version of a bad political form. An arrangement in which most of those capable, by nature, of leading the best sorts of lives lead utterly degraded ones instead is better than an arrangement in which all who are capable of excellence develop and exercise virtue to a significant, though mediocre degree.

Except (perhaps) in rare and extreme circumstances, the burdens that Aristotle approves are, for us, unjust. For example, we would not approve of the late-Tsarist social order, with all of its repression and its deprivations for the vast majority, on the basis of a finding that a more democratic and humane alternative would have somewhat dimmed the flames of high culture in Moscow and St. Petersburg.

Do Aristotle's distinctive judgments of lives and hierarchies depend on his ignorance of empirical facts about lives and societies? This seems very far from the source of our disagreements. In his discussions of friendship in books VIII and IX of the *Nichomachean Ethics*, he shows an acute awareness of phenomena of caring about others. Indeed, every aspect of living that we think is good receives perceptive treatment somewhere in Aristotle. Our disagreements with him concern, not what is good in general and to some degree, but the relative importance of different kinds of goods. (The same is true of our disagreements with Chenge.) These similarities lessen the extent of our disagreements with Aristotle. But, at the same time, his perceptiveness in exploring the common terrain makes it highly unlikely that he disagrees with us in crucial preferences among lives because of his ignorance of a fact about lives, or a failure to respond rationally to such facts.

Similarly, Aristotle's discussions of inequalities among nonslave males are informed by an erudite grasp of the institutions of the various Greek city-states, Egypt, Persia, and many barbarian peoples. We know more facts than he did about inequalities and their consequences. But what do we know that ought, rationally, to make a difference for Aristotle? His awareness of the human costs of social constraint is clear-sighted. The disagreements concern the moral importance of those costs.

Another realm of social facts that Aristotle grasps well enough for his purposes, even if he has fewer facts to grasp than we, connect equality with stability. He is well aware that hierarchical ideals may not be feasible because of the discontent they inspire in the worse-off. In fact, his ideal constitution is unrealizable on just these grounds, in his own view. Ideally, he thinks, the soil would be tilled by slaves in the service of leisured aristocrats, while other material goods would be provided by tradesmen and craftsmen who, though nonslaves, are strictly excluded from citizenship (1328 b 33–40, 1330 a 25–28. The exclusion is, at once, a denial of power and a denial of opportunity to develop and exercise important virtues). If it were stable, this arrangement would provide the most for the best, but it is doomed to instability because poor freemen excluded from citizenship tend to become enemies of the state (1281 b 29–31).

These considerations, among others, lead Aristotle to regard a different constitution as the best feasible arrangement. To this extent, evidence and reason move him in our direction. But the movement is limited by his moral framework. The political goal that he recommends is shaped by the distinctive elitism registered most directly in the ideal constitution. In the best feasible arrangement, the property requirement for citizenship is the highest that allows citizens to outnumber (adult male) noncitizens. Excluded from citizenship to the extent that this strategy permits, the poor are treated in such a way that they will tend to keep quiet and to serve in the lower ranks in time of war. The means to such acquiescence that Aristotle describes are relatively cheap, avoidance of violence toward the poor or confiscation of their property and the provision of subsistence allowances for military service. (See 1297 b 1–13.) Though the recommended arrangements might be inadequate means to stability in modern settings, they are feasible strategies in response to the ancient distribution of resources for coercion and disruption. (Indeed, Aristotle emphasizes at the outset that citizenship will be confined to those who possess weapons; 1297 b 1f.) Once again, his vision of the facts is clear-sighted, even though his moral response departs from ours.

How widely shared were views of virtue and hierarchy of Aristotle's kind? If moral views are only held by an intellectual and those under his or her direct influence, this limitation suggests that eloquence, intellectual pride and the architectonics of a philosophical system explain their currency. Such causes are hardly sources of moral insight, in any framework. Also, my interpretations of Aristotle are, in some respects, controversial. So it is important that distinctively elitist bases for assessing lives and society did have wide currency in the ancient world.

That political power belongs to those who excel must have been a premise of broad currency in classical Greek society, since even democrats felt obliged to address themselves to it. Thus, Thucydides has Athenagoras, a Sicilian advocate of the common people, preface arguments for broad citizenship with the remark, "It will be said, perhaps, that democracy is neither wise nor equitable, but that the holders of property are also the best fitted to rule."[22] In the *Meno*, the eponymous target of Socrates' probing is a rich young noble who would soon become an important military leader. When Socrates asks what virtue is, he answers, "There will be no difficulty, Socrates, in answering your question. Let us take first the virtue of a man—he should know how to administer the state, and in the administration of it should benefit his friends

---

[22] *The Complete Writings of Thucydides: The Peloponnesian War*, J. H. Finley, ed. (New York: Modern Library, 1951), p. 362 (vi, 39).

and harm his enemies."[23] This is rather less refined and elaborate than Aristotle's discussion of virtues of character, but the emphasis on prowess in self-assertion is common to both. The parallel is even closer when Meno responds a little later, to a request for a more general definition: "Well, then, Socrates, virtue, as I take it, is when he who desires things which are lovely [kala], is able to provide them for himself; so the poet says, and I say too that 'virtue is the desire for things that are lovely, with power to attain them.' "[24] Perhaps Aristotle's assumption that theoretical contemplation is the best part of life had a limited appeal outside of intellectual circles. But the extreme emphasis on self-sufficiency that underlies his arguments for this ideal had broad currency. In the *Rhetoric* he offers the desirability to the virtuous of extreme self-sufficiency as an obvious suppressed premise in a sample of banal fallacious reasoning. "In the *Alexander*, for instance, it is argued that Paris must have been greatsouled, since he despised society and lived on Mount Ida: because the greatsouled do this kind of thing, therefore Paris too, we are to suppose, had a great soul."[25]

In short, Aristotle seems to have been faithful to his announced procedure in discussing character traits. "We must, as in all other cases, set the observed facts before us and, after first discussing the difficulties, go on to prove, if possible, the truth of all the common opinions about these affections of the mind, or, failing this, of the greater number and the most authoritative" (EN, 1145 b 1–6). As this declaration of method allows, current opinion might have been divided, in Aristotle's time, over just these issues of virtue and hierarchy. It probably was. In opposition to the ethic of prowess, others, in the generations of Socrates, Plato and Aristotle, may well have been advancing an ethic more deeply concerned with cooperation, and more acceptable to us. Indeed, Aristotle's discussion may have seemed old-fashioned in his own time.[26] But the central question is whether a framework contrary to our own was actually employed, whose employment did not depend on ignorance or unreason. In any case, the future actually lay with the elitist trend, for about two millennia. Appeals to democratic cooperation were soon to be muted, and finally ended with Roman domination.[27]

[23] 71 e, Jowett's translation, *The Dialogues of Plato*, vol. 1 (Oxford: Oxford University Press, 1953), p. 266.

[24] 77 b, ibid., p. 273. Lamb, the translator in the Loeb edition, suggests that the poet may have been Simonides, a traditional source of solid advice.

[25] 1401 b 20–23, adapting the Roberts translation in *The Basic Works of Aristotle* to fit my literal translation of *megalopsychia*, in the previous discussion of the *Nichomachean Ethics*.

[26] See J. P. Vernant, *The Origins of Greek Thought* (Ithaca, N.Y.: Cornell University Press, 1982); L. Gernet, *The Anthropology of Ancient Greece* (Baltimore: Johns Hopkins University Press, 1981), especially chapter 11; A.W.H. Adkins, *Merit and Responsibility* (Oxford: Oxford University Press, 1960).

[27] See G.E.M. de Ste. Croix, *The Class Struggle in the Ancient Greek World* (Ithaca, N.Y.: Cornell University Press, 1981), especially chapter 5, section iii and chapter 7.

Moral Learning and Moral Development

To establish the existence of moral disagreements that do not depend on ignorance or unreason, it is not enough to trace them to basically different ways of moral learning. It is not even enough to show that the disagreements in moral judgment would not be ended by the acquisition of data concerning the objects of the contrary judgments, and similar acts, institutions or traits. For perhaps the differences in judgment could be ended by non-question-begging arguments concerning the ways of moral learning themselves. Through evidence or reasoning, one side, if rational, would come to share with the other certain propositions about ways of learning what is right and wrong. Applying those shared principles to empirical facts about processes of moral-judgment-formation, they might be forced to abandon their alien moral judgments—because of revised views about judging, not new facts about the objects of judgment. The crucial new data might be far-flung, surprising and hard for us moderns to acquire. After all, it took more than a little ingenuity for Newton to establish, in a non-question-begging way, that the telescope was giving humans superior access to celestial reality when it conflicted with the naked eye.

This indirect route to universality is especially promising because of a fact that Hume noted on several occasions. It is striking how many beliefs about the right way to evaluate are shared even when people disagree in their evaluations. Chenge, the Tiv judge, usually seeks information that would interest us as a basis for judgment. And Tiv value his counsel, in large part, on account of capacities that we appreciate, too. To this day people learn about balance in judgment by deriving lessons from Aristotle, in passages close by his most alien descriptions of virtue. A general theory of reliable moral learning might be based in part on universal principles about the gaining of increased moral insight, for example, this principle of maturity: the experience of problems of choice in coping with conflicts tends to contribute to moral insight if the experience is undergone by an emotionally open, informed and reflective person. Such truisms combined with far-flung data, the like of which was unfamiliar to either Chenge or Aristotle, might confirm a theory of reliable learning which could then be used to criticize the alien ways of Chenge, Aristotle and others as unreliable. After all, reason and evidence can, in this way, overcome the characteristic divisions of scientific revolutions, as in the fair arguments for Newtonian celestial mechanics that showed neo-Aristotelian attitudes toward telescopes to be wrong.

The only way to assess whether psychological data can resolve moral differences through a fair argument about moral learning is to assess the most successful efforts of this kind so far. Fortunately, for present purposes, this survey can be short. There are a number of current theories of how moral beliefs are acquired. Most of these theories could not be used by us to criticize moral frameworks different from our own. Most theories of moral belief acquisition—for example, Freudian or neo-behaviorist theories—describe processes which *we* do not take to constitute increasing moral insight. Even if identification with one's father as a means of escaping from castration anxieties happened to produce conscientious adherence to just the moral principles we approve, our moral principles are not so patriarchal or phallic that we would take a moral judgment to be unreliable just because it did not have this source. Similarly, we are not so traditionalist in morality that we approve of principles because they are supported by internalizations of reinforcements that grownups have used to train children. (Such traditionalism would lapse into incoherence, in any case, since incompatible moralities have been so inculcated.)

Our morality imposes strict limits on what a theory of reliable moral learning could be. Among current empirical theories, Lawrence Kohlberg's theory of moral development is the prime example of such an account. It is the only theory that has been used in a justification of our way of learning meant to be compelling for all fully informed, adequately reflective makers of moral judgments. Kohlberg describes a process of change which is, as such, a process contributing to insight, on our view. In effect, he goes on to argue that this assessment of the process would be shared by people who currently learn in radically different ways, if they responded rationally to the information he provides.

According to Kohlberg, reliable moral learning is organized, chronologically, into three general levels and five or six more specific stages. They describe a sequence of styles of reasoning about moral problems. Level I, the so-called preconventional level, begins at stage 1, where children respond to questions of what ought to be done by looking for a means of avoiding punishment by satisfying powerful people's desire that rules be obeyed. At the next preconventional stage, the child's model of a solution is a deal in which his or her interests are satisfied without conflict with others. At stage 3, the "conventional" level of moral reasoning begins. People pursue a "nice boy/nice girl" ideal, seeking to conform to a model of character which others like to see. At stage 4, the other conventional stage, people seek to live up to the obligations of their social roles, and promote the general welfare of their social group. Finally, some people reach the "postconventional" level, which Kohlberg once divided into distinct stages, 5 and 6. He describes this as the level of empathetic role-taking. One judges all alternatives, including the rules presupposed by social roles, from a standpoint of equal concern for all people affected, with no bias toward one's social group.[28]

[28] In the exposition of Kohlberg's views, I will rely primarily on his longest and most philosophical statement, "From Is to Ought: How to Commit the Naturalistic Fallacy and Get Away With It" (originally 1971) in his *Essays on Moral Development*, vol. 1 (San Francisco: Harper and Row, 1981), chapter 4 and Appendix. I will use the figures on the frequency of moral judgment stages by age and locale in "Indoctrination versus Relativity" (originally 1971), ibid., chapter 1.

In Kohlberg's view, if people learning how one ought to behave encounter the richest combination of experiences, problems and concepts, responding intelligently and sensitively to tensions and dissatisfactions produced by new kinds of encounters, they will come to reason at Level III. In effect, he argues that this conclusion is the best explanation of three kinds of data. The first is epitomized in the study of seventy-two Chicago area males that he conducted for over twenty-five years. The stages through which they passed are an ordered chronological sequence. People end up at various stages, but only after passing through lower numbered ones, in numerical order.

Because this finding might simply reflect the fact that different messages are indoctrinated at different ages, Kohlberg emphasizes a second kind of study, by Rest, Turiel, Blatt and others, suggesting that people are moved by their own pursuit of understanding, not indoctrination. In these studies of United States schoolchildren, the subjects turn out to understand stages up through their own, and to understand partially reasoning one stage above. If the understanding of the higher state is increased through classroom discussion, it tends to be adopted more rapidly.

The interpretation of the latter advances as genuine learning must still confront the possibility that they reflect the prestige of complex, abstract and cosmopolitan types of reasoning in the American classroom setting. This gives special importance to the third kind of data, derived from utterly different cultural environments. In rural preindustrial communities, in Malaysia, Taiwan, the Yucatan and elsewhere, Kohlberg and others have found the same ordering of stages, among people who would seem to attach no special and extraneous prestige to the fancier forms of moral learning. In the most isolated rural settings, in the Yucatan and Turkey, almost no one engaged in postconventional reasoning. Indeed, preconventional reasoning dominated at age sixteen, when stage 5 is the most prevalent single stage among middle-class urban boys in the United States. Still, in all the studies, people moved from stage to stage in precisely the same ordered sequence.

According to Kohlberg, the cross-cultural studies make the case for his learning theory a fair means of criticizing ways of moral learning different from the highest stage in his typology. His proposal is promising because this case for the highest stage seems just to depend on universally shared background principles, above all the principle of maturity according to which the growth of experience and understanding contributes to moral judgment. On the alternative view of maturity that I will be defending, Kohlberg's sequence of stages describes only one process of maturing as people cope with one kind of problem, made increasingly salient and difficult by the experience of one kind of social environment. To regard those who have reached other kinds of ma-

---

Kohlberg sketches changes in his views during the decade after "From Is to Ought" in his contribution to the symposium "Cognitive Development Theory," *Ethics* 92 (1982), pp. 513–28.

turity as retarded, because they are only at a low Kohlbergian state, is like regarding the Parthenon friezes as inferior to *Bleak House*, because the inscriptions are not good literature.

Among survey data of Kohlberg's kind, the most important work that supports this pluralism is Carolyn Edwards' Kenyan study.[29] Edwards' subjects were in three main groups: students at the University of Nairobi (median age: 22.2), high school students from a variety of Kenyan communities (median age: 19.6), and "community leaders" in those same communities, people who "had reputations as responsible citizens, people noted for giving useful advice and counsel" (ages 23 to 75, median age: 48).[30] Using Kohlberg's techniques in his cross-cultural studies, Edwards and her Kenyan co-workers assessed the stages of development of these subjects. The community leaders, while significantly in advance of the high school subjects, were substantially retarded in moral development compared with the university students. The median "moral judgment score" (that is, location among the stages) of the community leaders was below that of 13-year-old urban middle-class boys in the United States.

No one who has seriously studied the lives and environments of African community leaders supposes that they have encountered fewer problems of coping or dealt with them less sensitively and reflectively than 22-year-old African university students, much less 13-year-old American boys. It looks as if some achievement in maturity is not scored in Kohlberg's ratings. Edwards strengthens and specifies this interpretation when she contrasts the scores of different community leaders. The substantially retarded leaders, by Kohlberg's standards, are those whose experience was largely confined to traditional village settings, much like those studied in the Bohannans' Tiv ethnographies. For example, 72% of the community leaders with no formal education were below stage 3. On the whole, they score at the level of moral maturity of a United States urban 10-year-old. By comparison, 84% of the college-educated leaders are at stage 3 or higher. To explain this dramatic difference, Edwards proposes, in effect, that Kohlberg's ratings neglect what the Tiv would call talent in "repairing the *tar*." Indeed, Kohlberg's moral judgment scores tend to identify maturity in this endeavor as moral retardation.

In the most famous of the dilemmas with which Kohlberg evokes subjects'

---

[29] "Societal Complexity and Moral Development: A Kenyan Study," *Ethos* 3 (1975), pp. 505–27. For an argument to similar effect concerning non-Kohlbergian moral growth among women in the contemporary United States, see Carol Gilligan, *In a Different Voice* (Cambridge, Mass.: Harvard University Press, 1982). Edwards' work on the moral skills of adults in different cultures is complemented by her investigations of processes by which moral beliefs are acquired, for example, her comparison of such processes in a Kenyan village and in the Vassar College Nursery School, "Culture and the Construction of Moral Values: A Comparative Ethnography of Moral Encounters in Two Cultural Settings," in J. Kagan and S. Lamb, *The Emergence of Morality in Young Children* (Chicago: University of Chicago Press, 1987).

[30] Edwards, "Societal Complexity," p. 515.

moral reasoning, Heinz, whose wife is dying of cancer, must choose whether to steal a cancer cure monopolized by a selfish druggist, asking an impossibly high price. (Of course, the details, but not the substance, of the story are suitably adapted to the local scene when moral judgment scores are assigned in settings different from the United States.) The answer, "Heinz should steal the drug, because human life is an ultimate value, more important than property," means instant access to stage 6. When preteens in the United States and 72-year-old Kenyan community leaders show a special concern to devise a mutually acceptable arrangement between Heinz and the druggist and to find courses of conduct conforming to local views of how a good person behaves, both display "good boy/good girl" stage 3 reasoning, for Kohlberg. But to rate their emphasis in the same way is to equate maturity with shallowness. These are leading emphases of the preteens because they do not appreciate how recalcitrant disagreements can be, how excessive someone's minimal demands can be, how many people may be affected by a bargain, or how contradictory or stultifying the demands of conformity can be. They are leading emphases among the community leaders because they want to help life go on in a self-assertive way while protecting the interpersonal ties that keep the peace that a central authority cannot preserve or will only preserve at an unacceptable cost.

Moral learning, as it actually unfolds in different environments, can represent different processes of matured coping, in response to different problems. Kohlberg's problem, especially salient for middle- and upper-class males in urban industrial settings, is to find a generally acceptable rule by means of which one can peacefully pursue one's self-interest while respecting the self-interests of others. This is different from the tribal-agriculturalists' problem emphasized by Edwards and the Bohannans. In developing a justification meant to be rationally compelling to all, it would beg the question to assume that Kohlberg's problem is uniquely revealing. And it would be anthropologically naive to suppose that the experiences of those who cope with this problem are uniquely rich.

When each of two outlooks is a mature response to distinctive circumstances in which it develops, it might seem that both can be justified to all, in a roughly Kohlbergian way, as valid, complementary ways of learning applicable to different situations: each is applicable only within its special scope, the scopes do not overlap, and each outlook is justified as far as it extends, justified using shared principles of matured coping. There might be such an array of universally justifiable moralities if humans were more modest in the scope of their moral judgments, restricting them to their own or similar social circumstances. But in fact we think that a Tiv who is pressured into accepting a loss in court because witnesses have lied for their relatives' sake has been wronged. Rather than endorsing the Tiv judgment as a morally insightful response to locally salient problems, we conclude that matured coping with situations in which prospects of cooperation are largely based on substantial interpersonal ties can give rise to moral blindness. Certainly, if Chagnon, the brave ethnographer of the Yanomamo, persuades us that the fierceness of male Yanomamo is a mature response to constant threats of conflict, we still condemn the action of the Yanomamo husband who shoots a barbed arrow into his wife's thigh when she is a bit slow to bring him supper.[31] And the people whom we are prepared to judge are ready to judge us, too. People from agrarian societies such as the Tiv are shocked by our readiness to override concrete interpersonal ties. Aggressive hunter-gatherers, such as the Yanomamo, and aggressive pastoralists, such as Evans-Pritchard's Nuer, look with contempt on the weak-willed European way of life.[32]

SELF-SUSTAINING FRAMEWORKS

There is a general source of relativism of which the barriers to Kohlberg's argument are only special instances. More than one contrary framework for moral inquiry defends itself through a self-sustaining account of reliable moral learning, i.e., an account which explains away contrary judgments of rational, informed users of rival frameworks as the result of departures from reliable moral learning. Because of the connections between detection, justification and truth that I will explore in the next chapter, any framework from which justified truth-claims emerge must have this self-sustaining character. It must support the attribution of the claims that emerge to processes of detection and the attribution of contrary claims that others make to defects in detection.

"Self-sustaining" does not mean "incorrigible in principle." Every account of moral learning actually employed has diverse aspects, relies on empirical presuppositions and leads to the endorsement of a variety of independent moral beliefs as well-learned. In principle, the encounter with empirical data could put any account of reliable moral learning in conflict with itself, leading any rational, well-informed inquirer to seek an alternative. But in fact, more than one framework for moral inquiry survives encounters with all relevant data, helped by an account of moral learning that explains away facts of moral disagreement which would otherwise undermine the framework.

Our framework includes such a self-sustaining account. We think (putting it very roughly) that the morally right choice is the one to which a well-informed person would be led by equal concern or respect for everyone affected. In our complementary account of moral learning, we take attitudes toward choice to be morally insightful if they are promoted by sustained contact with and dependence on women and men of many different backgrounds, including many strangers, interacting from positions of equal power. This cos-

---

[31] See Chagnon, *Yanomamo*, p. 82.

[32] See E. E. Evans-Pritchard, *The Nuer* (New York: Oxford University Press, 1972), pp. 90, 134, 182.

mopolitan and egalitarian experience is apt to encourage the attitudes in choice which we take to be insightful. When we have traced our disagreements with Chenge or Aristotle to the limits of such experience in their cultures, we can conclude that their disagreements with us reflect defects in their moral learning.

At the same time, their frameworks are similarly equipped with a self-sustaining epistemology. For Chenge, moral insight most centrally depends on the intelligent use of communal resources to protect the actual network of interpersonal ties. He knows that a life of dependence on strangers will weaken the preference for defending interpersonal ties by local informal means. In his framework, it is a criticism of a choice that it reflects such impersonality. Aristotle thought that respect for excellence in achievement was the source of valid choices. In the *Politics*, he is acutely aware of the tendency of certain social environments to erode such respect. Certainly, he would appreciate that the cosmopolitan, egalitarian experience that promotes right choice in our view discourages his favored attitude. Like his modern heirs, he would take the need to interact with people from many different walks of life on a footing of interdependence and relatively equal power to distort choice, through excessive modesty, sentimentality and other vices of which greathearted men are free.

In this chapter, the evidence about difference has the following shape. There are frameworks for making moral judgments, dictating judgments contrary to our own, which do not depend on any irrationality in those who employ them or any ignorance of relevant data concerning the objects of the distinctive judgments. In support of this quite empirical hypothesis, it turned out that Chenge and Aristotle already possess data of all the kinds that are relevant to our contrary judgments. Any further data for which we could, rationally, hope, which we would interpret as supporting our distinctive judgments, would not be so interpreted by them, on account of their different frameworks. The remaining sort of argument that might make disagreement unreasonable concerns the processes leading to moral judgment. Here, shared principles concerning processes whose operation adds to acceptability turned out to be too vague to resolve disagreements, in light of any evidence we have or could rationally hope to have. Our best hope for rational reconciliation was the principle of maturity because it is shared and is genuinely concerned with validity. But there turned out to be too many ways in which people achieve maturity in coping for the vague principle to resolve outstanding differences. On the other hand, a specification of reliable moral learning that is specific enough to undermine the alien moral judgments will be rejected, and rationally so, by those employing the alien frameworks. The rejections depend on principles of moral learning already in place, principles that yield self-sustaining interpretations of any data about learning that we have or for which we can rationally hope. So some disagreements in moral judgment do not depend on either side's being irrational or ignorant of any evidence. Here, it is as if Galileans and Aristotelians could only resolve their disagreements in light of data about the brightness of Mars and were stuck forever in the situation in which each side rationally responded to all the data as sustaining its cosmology.

This answer to a question about the limits of rational dissent makes it urgent to face questions about truth. Having conceded that dissent is rational among the well-informed and would be rational in light of all the evidence for which one hopes, is one still in a position to assert the truth of a moral judgment? In the answer to this question, in the next chapter, the verdict on moral realism will start to be mixed.

Chapter Two

MORAL TRUTH

OFTEN, an argument that an alien, contrary moral framework does not depend on ignorance or unreason has been a first step toward denying that moral judgments are ever justified true beliefs. This is, I think, a step in just the wrong direction. In our disagreements with Chenge about treatment of wives and strangers and our disagreements with Aristotle about hierarchies, our beliefs are true and theirs are false. In making these claims as to truth, we are not dogmatic. We can point to features of the case at hand that justify our judgments, i.e., our judgments of right and wrong *and* our assessment of those judgments as truths. What would be dogmatic, indeed, downright false would be to claim that the other side is judging irrationally or on the basis of inadequate information. We are justified, but we could not justify our position to them, even if they reflected on our arguments and data in a rational way.

Before looking at charges that this mixed verdict is incoherent, charges that raise deep questions about the nature of reference and content, it is best to begin by looking at the case for moral truth. Suppose I judge an act or institution to be morally wrong, supporting the judgment in the usual ways by pointing to moral obligations that are violated, respect for persons that was not shown, or harm inflicted without a commensurate benefit elsewhere. If I am functioning well, no one could point to further facts that would override my judgment according to moral principles in my framework. If this is the measure of my success, I am certainly justified in my moral judgment. That there are facts that would dictate a contrary judgment according to principles that I do not share hardly shows that I am unjustified. But why suppose that I am justified in a truth claim, an ascription of an objective property of wrongness to an act or institution? Surely, we can be justified in what we say when we make no statement of fact. Whatever their failings may have been, emotivists were right that movie-lovers are often justified in saying, "Let's take in a movie," even though they express an attitude rather than making a statement of fact.

We are justified in the belief that moral truths exist on the same kinds of grounds as those that justify us in believing that molecules and elephants exist. (Here and on through the next two sections, I will be pursuing the lines of argument I first presented in "Reason and Commitment in the Social Sciences," *Philosophy & Public Affairs* 8 [1979], especially on pp. 248–55, 263. See also "Ways of Moral Learning," *Philosophical Review* 94 [1985], especially on pp. 526–29, 553f.) The existence of moral truths is entailed by causal explanations of the data we possess that are better than any rival explanations of those data. Of course, a moral fact causes nothing independent of the ways in which people respond to it. Similarly, an electromagnetic field causes nothing independent of the ways in which charges respond to it. However, successful explanations of belief or action often refer to moral properties or to processes entailing the existence of moral properties—properties or processes that do affect human responses.

Some explanations entailing the existence of moral facts refer to the detection of moral properties. A moral judgment is attributed to someone's ability to detect rightness, wrongness, or whatever moral property is in question combined with the presence of that property in the case at hand. Or alternatively, a false moral judgment or the absence of a moral judgment is attributed to the absence of the normal ability to detect wrongness, or whatever. In another class of explanations which are often better than any rival, an action is attributed to good character or bad character, as when someone's playing music at top volume is attributed to his insensitivity to other people's rights. In yet another category, discontent is explained as a response to injustice, or acceptance and participation are explained as a response to justice.

Explanations referring to moral detection, to seeing what is wrong, realizing what is right, telling the difference between right and wrong, are specially important for present purposes. If one's use of a term is a successful exercise of one's capacity to detect a property, in the course of learning about its presence or absence, then one uses the term to refer to the property in a true ascription of the latter. So the frequent superiority of explanatory appeals to moral detection directly supports the thesis that we are often justified in making claims as to moral truth. If a person's characterization of an act as wrong is an exercise of her capacity to detect wrongness, and if she is justified in taking herself to be exercising this capacity, then she is, precisely, making a justified claim as to the truth in moral matters. On the other hand, if moral judgments are never attributed to capacities for moral detection, it might be doubted whether the other kinds of "because"-claims involving moral judgment really are causal explanations. Someone might admit that we often rightly say that a person intrudes on others because of bad character yet deny that this moral assessment of character is a description of a state of affairs.

In short, in metaethics, as elsewhere, talk of reference is parasitic on talk of detection. I will often be specifying and defending, piecemeal, an approach to the philosophically central characterization, being justified in a belief concerning an objective state of affairs, which grounds it in diverse, specific processes of detection, often familiar and humble ones. These ways of learning include the processes of telling color and shape by looking, discerning signs of life, and seeing effects of interference which are described by the prima facie truisms that I sketched in the last chapter. They also include processes

of moral detection, which I will illustrate and describe. As a whole, the process of inquiry expands, contracts and modifies the repertoire of processes of
detection through further specification and testing, of kinds that I will also
describe. Some principles of detection are sufficiently fundamental that their
justifying force solely depends on their not failing the tests, rather than their
being derivable from further principles and data. I hope to show that certain
processes of moral detection are described in such fundamental principles,
and that no dogmatism is involved in basing justified belief in moral facts on
these principles.

To return to the preliminary argument in favor of our access to objective
moral truths: it is not controversial that what we offer in the way of explanation often seems to include an attribution of a capacity for moral detection.
Moreover, many of these explanations seem better than all rivals in light of
all relevant data. Usually these explanations are part of an effort to explain
action taken in spite of costs. Perhaps a child has broken a playmate's toy.
Her playmate asks for it back, and she is tempted to say she never had it. But
she decides to confess because she sees that it would be wrong to lie. Or consider a decision that Bela Bartok made. Purely Aryan and a national hero, he
decided to leave Hungary shortly after the Horthy regime consolidated its ties
with the Hitler regime, because he realized his presence would lend prestige
to an evil government, and was filled with disgust and anger at the prospect.
In a converse realm in which we explain responses worse than the norm, some
people are said to kill when most would suppress homicidal impulses, because
they lack the normal ability to tell the difference between right and wrong.

Someone who thinks that such explanations are always better than their
rivals is naive. Sometimes, children resist the temptation to lie just because
they are afraid of being found out and punished. Sometimes children think
that lying is wrong just because their parents have told them so. The rule has
the same status for them as parental injunctions to tuck in one's shirt and
keep a clean face. So they do not know that lying is wrong, though they
respect this principle—rather as children of a certain age quickly memorize
storybooks read to them, and say the right words while looking at the letters
on the page, but cannot read. Similarly, some eminent Aryans emigrated because they feared the outbreak of war, and some condemned Nazi actions as a
result of haughty and resentful disdain of the crass arrivistes brought to power
by the Nazi triumph. That these various nonmoralizing causal descriptions
could be true, could explain, and are rivals to the moralizing alternatives is
evidence that the latter are substantive explanatory proposals. A nonmoralizing rival is sometimes superior. But someone who always favors these or
similar nonmoralizing rivals over every explanatory appeal to moral insight
displays a pervasive cynicism that cries out for empirical justification.

In the rest of this chapter, I will defend and develop this case for the existence of moral facts and this conception of our access to them. First, I will

consider some of the leading arguments that there are no moral facts. This will be a long defense, because of the power of those arguments and the importance of crucial issues concerning explanation, justification and detection. Then, the more constructive part of this chapter will begin with a more detailed account of some fundamental processes of moral detection. Next, I will explain why justified belief that there are moral facts is tentative, compatible with certain legitimate anxieties about their existence. Finally, I will relate the pursuit of truth to the other goals of moral discourse.

SOME ATTACKS ON MORAL TRUTH

Pervasive cynicism is not, of course, the position of those who currently argue against the existence of moral facts. Rather, they make one or both of two claims: the apparent references to moral detection in the course of explanation are not literally intended; reference to moral detection never helps to explain. Thus, Gilbert Harman, in a powerful and influential argument against explanatory inference to the existence of objective moral facts, dismisses the appearance of moral explanation on both of these grounds. He contrasts our practice in moral discourse with our talk of colors where "[w]e are willing to assume that there are facts about color, despite our not knowing precisely how to reduce them, because in practice we assume that there are such facts in many of our explanations of color perception, even if in theory this assumption is dispensable."[1] And he also says, "Moral hypotheses do not help explain why people observe what they observe."[2] Of these claims, the second is essential to the first. Explanatory talk of "seeing what is wrong," "realizing what is right," or "knowing the difference between right and wrong" seems to refer to capacities for detecting facts. A grasp of obvious truths about English usage does not require the denial that such reference is intended. Rather, if the usages are explained away as no more than dead metaphors of detection, the dismissal must be based on the pointlessness of moral hypotheses in explanation: given speakers' beliefs about causes, they would have to be more muddled than they are to attribute moral judgment to moral detection. Indeed, the point about the pointlessness of moral explanation could stand on its own as a criticism of belief in moral truth, even if people are admitted to be so muddled as to offer explanations entailing the existence of moral facts. Thus, John Mackie, in arguments against moral facts that are similar to Harman's, takes most people to intend to refer to them as a result of a shared error, rather as young children intend to refer to a fat elf who slides down chimneys at Christmas.[3]

---

[1] *The Nature of Morality* (New York: Oxford University Press, 1977), p. 23.

[2] Ibid., p. 11.

[3] See his *Ethics: Inventing Right and Wrong* (Harmondsworth: Penguin, 1977), chapter 1. Harman's and Mackie's arguments have a highly influential precursor in aspects of Max Weber's

Do hypotheses entailing the existence of moral facts help in explaining why we observe actions, choices, beliefs and inclinations in others and in ourselves? Contrary to Harman's dismissal, such hypotheses do have the explanatory power that normally justifies a truth claim.

Reference to moral detection (or traits of moral character or moral features of institutions) can help in explanations in the same way as justifies belief in the existence of any causal factor to which an explanation refers. The attribution of the phenomenon directly in question to that causal factor can be part of an explanation that is better than any rival explanation. By a "rival" explanation, I mean one whose truth would be incompatible with the former explanation's correctly answering the question of why the phenomenon occurred. Often, explanatory hypotheses concerning the same phenomenon are different, but not rivals, in this sense—say, because the second describes in more precise detail the aspect of the causal factor mentioned in the first that was effective on the occasion in question. Thus, there is always a more specific alternative to an explanation appealing to the presence of dirt. Rather than attributing the premature breakdown of the watch to dirt in the wheels one can attribute it to the presence of irregular, rigid clusters of carbon in the wheels, and so forth. But even if the alternatives are always, on balance, superior to explanations in terms of dirt, we are, alas, justified in believing that dirt exists. The superior alternatives would not be rivals, incompatible with the presence and explanatory relevance of dirt, but specifications of what dirt was present and doing its dirty work.

If the confessing child had formed the belief that it would be wrong to lie *just* because her parents had told her lying is wrong, this would be a rival to the hypothesis that she forms the moral belief because she realizes that lying is wrong. Believing what one's parents say in moral matters may happen to yield valid moral beliefs if one's parents are sufficiently insightful. But it would be absurd, a form of parent-worship, to suppose that detecting the difference between right and wrong could consist in believing in whatever one's parents say about right and wrong. One might as well say that a Fahrenheit thermometer is an avoirdupois scale in a population of people with normal body temperatures and weights of 98.6 pounds. Suppose, however, that the child forms the belief that lying would be wrong as a result of the attitude that Hume, Piaget, Rawls and Kohlberg describe in their writings on the sense of justice.[4]

famous advocacy of value-freedom. I discuss Weber's position in detail in "Reason and Commitment in the Social Sciences."

[4] See, for example, Hume, *A Treatise of Human Nature*, iii.ii.2 ("Of the Origin of Justice and Property"); J. Piaget, *The Moral Judgment of the Child* (New York: Free Press, 1965—first edition, 1932); John Rawls, "The Sense of Justice," *Philosophical Review* 72 (1963); L. Kohlberg, "From Is to Ought." The list could easily be extended. For example, the account of moral development in Book IV of Rousseau's *Emile* is very similar, especially once one makes allowance for Rousseau's anxieties about interdependence.

When she has benefited from cooperation with others that depends on participants respecting certain terms of cooperation, she wants to respect those
terms when she can expect others to do the same; to decide what would be
right in responding to the playmate, she put herself under the sway of that
cooperative desire, to see what choice would emerge.[5] It would be absurd for
one of us to say, "Consulting the desire to respect terms of cooperation from
which one has benefited might happen to produce a valid judgment as to how
to respond, but that is all. It is no more a source of moral insight than believing whatever one's father or one's guru says." Consulting that cooperative
desire is a way of telling the difference between the right and the wrong response. By the same token, the attribution of the child's belief to such a process is not, remotely, incompatible with the claim that the child's belief was
an exercise of her capacity to detect moral rightness and wrongness.

Similarly, suppose that Bartok believed that evil was pervasive in Hungary
because he resolved questions of good and evil from a standpoint of equal
concern and respect for all affected. It would be absurd for one of us to say
that this hypothesis is incompatible with the claim that his moral belief was
due to moral insight. But if his belief was wholly due to disdain for parvenus,
or to protective beliefs about Jews that were isolated from larger principles,
then the explanatory appeal to moral detection really is excluded.—Perhaps
it would not be absurd for Aristotle or Chenge to deny that the cooperative
or egalitarian attitudes are sources of moral insight. That is a different issue
from the one at hand. The present question is whether one of us could be
justified in an explanation entailing the existence of moral facts.

Of course, Harman is very well aware that "the explanation of your making
the judgment you make" depends on further characterizations of your psychology. In challenging belief in moral facts, he emphasizes this dependence.
In explaining "your making the judgment you make," he says, "all we need
assume is that you have certain more or less well articulated moral principles
that are reflected in the judgments you make, based on your moral sensibil-
ity."[6] But he thinks that the premise that this is all we need assume entails
that "an assumption about moral facts would . . . be totally irrelevant to the
explanation of your making the judgment you make . . . [T]he truth or falsity

[5] This is a common feature of six-year-olds' reasoning, in Piaget's reports of discussions with
them. And six-year-olds do not regard such adjustment to others as a mere matter of conformity
to conventional standards. On the average, by the age of six, children are almost as good as
adults at distinguishing questions of moral principle from questions of custom and decorum,
reaching adult standards around the age of ten. See Deborah Pool, Richard Schweder and Nancy
Much, "Culture as a Cognitive System: Differentiated Rule Understandings in Children and
Other Savages" in E. T. Higgins et al., *Social Cognition and Social Development* (Cambridge, England: Cambridge University Press, 1983); Elliott Turiel, Melanie Killen and Charles Helwig,
"Morality: Its Structure, Functions, and Vagaries" in Kagan and Lamb, *The Emergence of Morality
in Young Children*, especially pp. 171–82.

[6] *The Nature of Morality*, p. 7.

of the moral observation seems to be completely irrelevant to any reasonable explanation of why that observation was made."[7] There are a variety of ways in which these remarks might be understood. Each is an important source of skepticism about moral facts. But each ultimately depends on a false account of the justification of truth claims.

Harman's emphasis on the absence of any "need to make assumptions about any moral facts to explain"[8] suggests a standard for explanatory inference different from the one I have proposed: one should only accept what is part of the *minimal* explanation that is needed to explain all relevant facts, i.e., the explanation that entails the fewest factual claims. Relying on this standard, someone might argue that any explanation that entails a claim as to moral facts goes beyond the minimum, and, so, is not justifiable by its power to explain. Such an opponent of justified moral truth-claims might appeal to possibilities of disagreement as revealing the explanatory excessiveness. There is always (he claims) a neutral redescription of a process of belief-acquisition that we take to be a process of moral detection, a description which only contains morally neutral terms, so that it would be acceptable to one who rejects the claim of moral detection: it would be acceptable to Chenge or Aristotle or, quite generally, to a nihilist who does not believe there is any such thing as the detection of moral facts. Such nonmoralizing descriptions would also explain relevant data (the argument against moral facts continues). They are not incompatible with the appeal to moral detection. But the appeal to moral detection asserts something more, what Chenge or Aristotle or, in any case, the nihilist would reject. And similarly for all the explanatory hypotheses which entail moral judgments, for example, ascriptions of personality traits entailing moral assessments of character. So an explanation that entails a moral judgment is not justifiable by virtue of its role in explanation. For what is not part of the minimal description of the relevant cause is not justified through its role in explaining.

In this initial version, the argument relies on an overly demanding standard for justification. If a hypothesis serves to explain, and explains *better* than any rival, surely that is justification for believing it, whether it is minimal or not. Still, the excessive demand points the way to a deeper challenge. It might be argued that the less-than-minimal explanation provides a worse explanation than the nihilist's alternative, so that the two standards of justification have the same result. The nihilist's whole proposal is that the nonmoralizing alternative is true, while every attribution of moral properties is false, since no such properties exist. This is a genuine rival, not a mere alternative. This rival hypothesis entails the existence of fewer kinds of entities than the appeal to moral detection (or whatever). And (the argument continues) ontological sparseness is a virtue that is only overridden by countervailing virtues in a

---

[7] Ibid.
[8] Ibid., p. 6.

rival hypothesis, superiorities which are absent from the moralizing alternative.

The deeper challenge depends on the following premises:

1. Corresponding to any moralizing explanation, there is at least one description of what caused the phenomenon to be explained, true if the former is, which entails the existence of no moral fact or property.

2. Ontological sparseness is a virtue which is, in itself, a basis for justifying a hypothesis as relevantly best. By itself, it is one of the virtues which, in the final analysis, can be crucial in justifying the claim that an explanatory hypothesis is true.

3. Combine a morally neutral description which is part of a moralizing explanation (in the sense of premise 1) with the denial that there are moral facts; the result of at least one such combination is not inferior to the moralizing explanation in ways that override the gain in sparseness.

I think that the first premise is true, for reasons that will emerge in the next chapter, in the course of a detailed examination of a grand, grim possibility of moral nihilism. But the second and third premises are false.

Ontological sparseness is not, by itself, relevant to the justification of an explanatory claim. It is only a basis for inferring the truth of a hypothesis when it minimizes explanatory loose ends, cases in which the framework of inquiry combined with the data locate phenomena in need of explanation but lacking one. Here, it is important to distinguish explanatory need from mere potential explanatory gain (just as it was important to distinguish a rival explanation from a mere alternative). It is always a good thing if a fact receives an otherwise acceptable explanation. But often the absence of the explanation is not a defect, i.e., a defect which could be crucial in justifying belief in the falsehood of what is not explained. It is a good and difficult thing to explain why the kicking of an empty tin can caused it to sail in the general direction in which the kicking toe pointed. But the claim that the can so moved because someone kicked it is not defective until such an explanation is established. On the other hand, that speaking well of someone reduces her prosperity does stand in need of explanation. It is unsatisfactory to be given this explanation of misfortune unless the connection is further explained in an otherwise acceptable way. Even if good reports generally brought misfortune, there would be a need to explain this. (Appeals to the Evil Eye of a jealous Providence acknowledge this burden, though the attempt to support it is lame.) In general, inquirers operate with a repertoire of principles according to which some causal connections are perfectly acceptable at rock bottom, while others are not.[9] We apply these principles in judgments of causal simplicity, the reduction of explanatory loose ends.

Causal simplicity is so different from ontological sparseness that consider-

---

[9] This is one aspect of the core conception of causality that I present in chapter 2 of *Fact and Method*. See especially pp. 73–86.

ations of causal simplicity can justify ontologically bloated hypotheses. Thus, the molecular-kinetic theory of gases has long been a prime example of a hypothesis justified by its explanatory power. Yet this theory, with its appeals to molecules and novel molecular properties, was bloated in comparison with a mere listing of the best-established empirical relations between observable properties of gases. The great scientists, such as Maxwell and Boltzmann, who justified the theory as the best explanation of those regularities were well aware of its extra content. They took it to be justified by its capacity to explain thermodynamic regularities which stood in need of explanation. Other scientists, such as Poincaré and Ostwald, had different principles of explanatory need. They took the regularities initially explained by kinetic-molecular theory to stand in no special need of explanation, and denied that the theory was anything more than a useful means of summarizing those regularities, among others. Their initial dissent from the molecular hypothesis was finally ended by the investigations of Brownian movement early in this century, in which the molecular-kinetic hypothesis was brought to bear on phenomena of motion which stood in need of explanation according to everyone's framework of inquiry.[10]

The same considerations of causal simplicity, regulated by specific principles of explanatory need, dominate our nontechnical inquiries. In those investigations, each of us routinely attributes his or her own experiences to causal happenings involving people or things. Such explanations are often better than any rivals. But the ordinary world-picture is hardly minimal. The sparser world of the subjective idealist admits only the idealist's experiences. Admittedly, the many regularities displayed in the course of experience have no explanation compatible with the idealist's sparse ontology. Still, that our bloated ontology permits more explanations cannot, by itself, be the reason for its superiority. Reckless speculations often provide the same superabundance. Neither is our ontology superior because it reduces the sum of unanswered questions. Our ordinary ways of explaining themselves raise further questions that do not arise for the subjective idealist. Questions of why certain kinds of nonmental processes have regular mental sequels are prime examples of such open questions, which scientific extensions of common sense have barely begun to close in the most elementary cases. Rather, the subjective idealist's sparse hypothesis is worse because it does not explain what stands in urgent need of explanation. Regular sequences among sensations stand in need of explanation, as standard causal connections (say, between being hit hard and feeling pain) do not. It would be mysterious that pain regularly follows visual experiences of fist trajectories' seeming to end at the surface of one's body, if the painfulness of hitting did not explain the regularity. In contrast, it is only a disappointment, not a mystery, if the means by which

---

[10] I discuss these disputes and their resolution in more detail in *Fact and Method*, pp. 470–82.

hitting produces pain are not known. Distinctions between what stands in need of explanation and what does not are presupposed in our rating of the relatively bloated, standard world-picture as the best source of explanations. Note that here, as in the technical, molecular case, the underlying principles of explanatory need are not obviously based on further, absolutely general principles of explanation, the same for all subject-matters at all times.

So far, these rational preferences for the more-than-minimal could be seen as the overriding of a virtue of sparseness by countervailing virtues of causal simplicity. But once the force of the latter is appreciated, ontological sparseness turns out to be nothing more than one frequent result of achieving other virtues, the ones that are part of inference to the best explanation. In the cases—the many important cases—in which a sparse rival is preferred, the preference is always justified on grounds other than sparseness, typically grounds of causal simplicity. Thus, the addition of witchcraft hypotheses to our repertoire of explanations of misfortunes would certainly be unreasonable. But ontological surplus would not distinguish witchlore from the molecular-kinetic hypothesis. Believers in witchlore can sometimes explain a fact that disbelievers cannot, for example, the fact that a particular roof collapsed right after a particular person sat under it. Witchlore opens questions by introducing new entities, but so did molecular-kinetic theory. For example, the question of how to explain the elasticity of molecules in collision was an open question that was not closed until decades after the molecular hypothesis was justified. If witchlore is worse because it is not simple enough, the relevant simplicity is causal simplicity. For example, according to witchlore, the resentments of witches bring disaster to their enemies, yet witchlore identifies as witches people whose ill-will is often inefficacious—most dramatically, when they are caught and punished. These are important anomalies according to witchlore itself, loose ends whose absence in a witchless framework are reasons not to posit witches. In contrast, our inability to explain why someone sat under a roof as it was about to collapse would not make it defective to explain his death as due to a roof's collapsing without encouragement by incantation. Someone's being at the wrong place at the wrong time is not, in general, in need of explanation.

In short, the second premise mistakes a typical symptom of explanatory virtue for virtue itself (typically, the virtue of causal simplicity). As it happens, the crucial distinction between a need for explanation and a mere open explanatory question sheds light on the defects in the third premise, as well.

According to the third premise (which includes the first, but goes beyond it), any moralizing explanation has an ontologically sparser rival to which the former is not superior in ways that override the ontological excess; the rival combines an alternative which is morally neutral with the outright denial that moral facts exist. This premise is needed, since otherwise the sparser rival can be rejected as inferior on balance. And perhaps this premise is sufficient by itself to block claims that moral facts exist. If premise 2 is rejected, so that the independent relevance of sparseness is denied, then acceptance of premise 3 commits one to denying that the moralizing explanation is in the least superior to the nonmoralizing rival. Perhaps, in such a case suspension of belief is the only rational position.

In fact, premise 3 is false as well. The tactic that produces a genuine rival produces one that is inferior, on balance. To see the falsehood of premise 3, one has to keep in clear view both the difference between a rival and an alternative and the difference between a need for explanation and an open explanatory question. That Bartok's disgust was due to his equal concern and respect for all affected is not a rival to the hypothesis that his disgust was due to moral insight. The rival is the more complex, incompatible hypothesis that Bartok's disgust was due to his equal concern and respect for all affected and not to a capacity to detect evil. But it is a loose end, in need of explanation, that someone's equal concern and respect for all affected should not constitute a capacity to detect evil. Perhaps this severe anomaly can sometimes be explained away, as when other aspects of someone's personality make it inevitable that evenhanded concern and respect will lead to mere squeamishness. But presumably in Bartok's case the loose end could not be tied in this way. The noninferior alternative was not a rival, and this genuine rival is inferior.

The Normality of Moral Inquiry

Of course, a moral nihilist would not accept these judgments of explanatory need or explanatory rivalry. If, as I shall argue in the next chapter, a moral nihilist could be rational and aware of all data, then inferences to the best explanation are powerless to introduce moral properties into all possible explanatory frameworks that lack them. Without irrationality or ignorance of data, someone could always deny that a process constitutes a source of moral insight, yet, despite this denial, claim to have explanations as good as ours. Perhaps the appeal to the dispensability of moral assertion in explanation is best understood, not as insistence on the virtues of economy, but as this claim that explanatory inference will not expose the irrationality or ignorance of every possible position that dispenses with appeal to a moral fact. If it is, indeed, this denial of universality, the premise about dispensability is right. But if this is the premise about explanatory inference on which the skeptical arguments rely, they fail to show that we are not justified in claims as to moral facts.

A skeptical inference from the absence of universality might appeal to some general requirement that a justified true belief have an appropriately universal warrant. In effect, I will consider such general concerns when I defend the coherence of the mixed verdict in chapters four and five. But this appeal to a distinctive general principle concerning justification would not be Harman's or Mackie's way of connecting justified true belief with universality. Rather than defending detailed general accounts of justification, Harman and Mackie take justification in science and in nontechnical investigations of material and psychological reality as their standard, and insist that moral judgments cannot be justified in those standard ways. Harman begins presenting his powerful doubts about moral facts by posing the question, "Can moral principles be tested and confirmed in the way scientific principles can?"[11] Mackie calls his main anti-realist argument "the argument from queerness." It is meant to cast doubt on our alleged capacity to describe moral facts on the grounds that such a capacity would have to be "utterly different from our ordinary ways of knowing everything else."[12] If these arguments for skepticism about moral facts really are based on the denial of universality that I have just described, then they only work if standard scientific practice in justifying hypotheses always has the universality that all justification of moral truth-claims lacks. But there is no such difference between the two realms.

Reason and evidence would not require acceptance of some of our moral judgments by those pursuing all actual ways of moral learning (or so I have argued). Reason and evidence would not require acceptance of any of our moral judgments by all possible people (including the possible, but presumably nonactual nihilist—or so I will argue). However, scientific inquirers are often justified in tentative beliefs about reality when such universality is lacking. I have already described three such episodes from the past, the dispute over what the telescope reveals, the dispute about what delayed electromagnetic responses reveal, and the dispute as to the truth as opposed to the mere usefulness of the kinetic-molecular theory. Such rational indeterminacy continues in present-day science. There is no reason to suppose that it will ever end.

For example, now as in the time of Maxwell and Neumann, the latest fundamental theories of the elementary constituents of matter continue to be asserted or denied on the basis of different weights assigned to alternative considerations, rankings permitted by reason but not required by reason. String theory is the best explanation of relevant data for those who seek to reduce fundamental laws to requirements of symmetry and who give priority to ending the situation in which relativity theory and quantum physics can only be rendered mutually compatible by ad hoc restrictions.[13] It is defective for others, such as Richard Feynman, who take such unification to be inadequate to justify the positing of additional spatiotemporal dimensions. Of

[11] *The Nature of Morality*, p. 3.

[12] *Ethics*, p. 38.

[13] For a brief sketch of the case for string theory, in which these background considerations are clear, see Steven Weinberg, "Towards the Final Laws of Physics," pp. 95–106 in R. Feynman and S. Weinberg, *Elementary Particles and the Laws of Physics: The 1986 Dirac Memorial Lectures* (Cambridge: Cambridge University Press, 1987).

course, if the past is any guide, this specific dispute will be resolved through future argument and evidence gathering. But, by the same token, if the past is any guide, all actual evidence that humans will ever acquire will leave it open for informed people to disagree, in as yet unspecified, deeply important ways, about the elementary structure of matter. In any case, outside of the physical sciences, specific disagreements have long endured and can be expected to continue, in the face of future evidence, because of framework differences. Thus, good historians continue to disagree as to whether the English Civil War was due mainly to the rising power and aspirations of a dynamic capitalist class centered on nonaristocratic, entrepreneurial landowners. Their different answers often reflect different weights that they put on various ways of learning historical causes. Some emphasize the motives revealed in individual actions and self-portrayals, while others appeal to general tendencies for actions to reflect objective interests or social circumstances.[14] Similarly, in psychopathology, different assessments of an explanation in terms of nonconscious motives are sometimes sustained by different ways of learning about psychological causes, each compatible with reason and evidence. A framework giving greater weight to the principle that people normally engage in costly actions in order to pursue a suitably urgent goal will be more receptive to depth-psychological explanations than a framework giving greater weight to the principle that people can normally discern their own motives upon reflection.[15]

It would be a remarkable fluke if, in all of these cases, all of the facts that would constitute relevant evidence would overcome all framework differences, if we were to know those facts. Of course, one might, in each case, vaguely imagine a total data base that would resolve all disputes, i.e., imagine this without believing that such data exist. In this spirit, historians must sometimes dream of ideal diaries or county-by-county comparisons. However, this imaginable resolution could not distinguish "normal" science from "queer" moral inquiry. In the same spirit of suspended disbelief, one can dream of such future data as would persuade every rational moral disputant. In this neat and quite unlikely resolution, no hierarchy objectionable to us would promote excellence as assessed by Aristotle's standards. The interpersonal ties that Chenge tries to consolidate never require neglect of legitimate individual complaints. In short, one can engage in wishful thinking about evidence in morality as well as in science.

In all of my characterizations of scientific controversies, I have supposed that empirical justification of truth claims is, as it always seems to be, inference to the best explanation, an inference which rates explanations as best

---

[14] For more analysis and examples, see *Fact and Method*, pp. 113–18 and my "Methodological Individualism and Social Explanation," *Philosophy of Science* (1978).

[15] I describe the role of the rationale-demanding principle in some detail in "A Clinical Science," *Canadian Journal of Philosophy* 18 (1988).

according to topic-specific principles, differing from field to field and (in many cases) from inquirer to inquirer. When scientific inquiry is seen in this way, it looks no different in kind from moral inquiry. However, another approach dominated the philosophy of science when the most creative work was done by those who accepted the label "logical positivist." Data and hypotheses were supposed to be connected by a single canon of topic-neutral principles, the same for all fields and all times. Later, at the start of chapter four, I will present some of the good reasons for abandoning this assumption. Though the rejection of positivism is essential to our main goal, viz., the accurate description of moral justification and moral truth, current suspicions that access to moral truth would be strangely different from standard scientific practice cannot even be defended in a positivist framework. Whatever the canon of general rules of inference is supposed to be, it cannot exclude the justification of moral truth-claims without excluding quite standard scientific claims, as well.

The positivists took hypotheses concerning regular associations among observables to be justified by the observation of instances. But, as they recognized, two important kinds of empirical hypotheses do not seem to be justified in this way. Theoretical hypotheses make assertions about unobservable things and properties. Explanations of events assert that a prior event brought about the event to be explained—which can hardly be established by observing the occurrence of each event. (A cough may have been coughed just before Lee decided to surrender, but it did not bring about Lee's decision.)

The positivists tried to admit justified theoretical hypotheses by broadening the canon of rules to include the entailment of observable regularities by a theoretical hypothesis taken together with auxiliaries connecting the unobservable with the observable. To avoid admitting absurdities by this route, they tended to impose a requirement that the total body of theoretical and auxiliary hypotheses simplify the scientific account of the empirical regularities. Of course, the goal was not causal simplification, as assessed using topic-specific principles of explanatory need. That would have meant the abandonment of the whole project of describing an effective canon of topic-neutral rules. Rather, the deduction of regularities or expected sequels had to be simplified according to some general yardstick of formal simplicity.

However, this formalist project, which probably would have excluded moralizing hypotheses, had to be abandoned by those who sought the inclusion of standard scientific hypotheses. So it is not a viable means of distinguishing morality from normal scientific inquiry. Even in the physical sciences, well-established theories often reduce simplicity, by any formal standard. When molecular-kinetic theory is supplemented with all the specifications and auxiliaries needed to entail observational expectations concerning temperature, pressure and volume in gases, it becomes much more complicated than the mere statement of the observable regularities. Not just the premises but the chains of deductive reasoning are utterly elaborate and ingenious, as physics students discover to their surprise and dismay. The theory can be further augmented to unify diverse fields, but only through further complications, adding diverse parameters and subtheories.

Worse yet, outside of the physical sciences, some well-established hypotheses do not serve at all as means of deducing observational sequences. In his paradigmatic inference to the best explanation, Darwin refrains from claiming that any biological observation could be deduced from the theory of evolution and confirmed auxiliary principles, and wisely so, since such deduction was impossible. Still, he could appeal to many cases in which what stands in need of explanation, according to all frameworks for inquiry, is, according to all frameworks, better explained by the theory of natural selection. Admittedly, as Darwin confesses, there are other cases in which the theory cannot explain, in any satisfactory way, facts which cry out for explanation. But the overall pattern of explanatory success and failure is best explained as due to the basic truth of the theory and the uneven development of auxiliary sciences.[16] These claims about power to explain data using the theory do not correspond to any claim to deduce data or regularities using the theory together with auxiliaries confirmable apart from prior knowledge of the derived phenomena. For Darwin lacked any basis for ascertaining relevant features of variation or advantage in the course of natural history.[17] To this day, the emergence of new species cannot be deduced in this way, since we cannot establish selective advantages within the needed limits.[18]

Positivist accounts of event-explanation had a similar outcome: the confirming connections with data cannot wholly consist of an appropriate pattern of deduction and instantiation. The most tempting proposal, incisively advanced by Hempel, was that confirming an explanation meant confirming the

---

[16] "I have felt these difficulties far too heavily during many years to doubt their weight. But it deserves special notice that the more important objections relate to questions on which we are confessedly ignorant; nor do we know how ignorant we are," *The Origin of Species*, p. 440.

[17] "Our ignorance of the laws of variation is profound. Not in one case out of a hundred can we pretend to assign any reason why this or that part differs, more or less, from the same part in the parents" (ibid., p. 202). "It is good thus to try in our imagination to give any form some advantage over another. Probably in no single instance should we know what to do, so as to succeed. It will convince us of our ignorance on the mutual relations of all organic beings; a conviction which is as necessary, as it seems to be difficult to acquire" (p. 129). It would not help to portray the theory as a source of derivations in some loose sense, involving the expectations to which the theory would give rise, or to emphasize the role of the theory in making certain sequences less, or more surprising. For, as Darwin forcefully acknowledges, especially at the start of his concluding chapter, those expectations are often disappointed, and important theoretical surprises do occur. The degree of disconfirmation, by such standards, would be as great as that of theories which rational inquirers reject as false.

[18] See Richard Lewontin, *The Genetic Basis of Evolutionary Change* (New York: Columbia University Press, 1979), chapter 5 for a compelling description of the obstacles. Elliott Sober presents a similar view in rich detail, philosophical and biological, in *The Nature of Selection* (Cambridge: M.I.T. Press, 1984).

claim that sequel was entailed by antecedent together with a general empirical law associating the two. But event explanations are frequently justified by the data when no such regularity is confirmed. Lee's letters make it clear that he decided to surrender because he thought his cause was lost after the fall of Richmond. But this suggests no general empirical law that has ever been confirmed connecting general properties of military leaders and their circumstances with their decisions to surrender.

In response to such difficulties, much ingenuity has been devoted to further elaborations of the canon of general methodological standards—including, most recently, enrichments from probability theory and model theory. Yet despite half a century of effort, no one has described general rules that would admit the well-established scientific hypotheses which I have described, unless the criteria are further amended to permit inclusion on grounds of pragmatic, quasi-aesthetic or psychological advantage. And these standards would, then, admit moral hypotheses as well. For example, kinetic-molecular theory has been a suggestive source of further hypotheses, some of which have been borne out. But the same can be said of our moral lore, for example, our lore concerning character traits. Thus, Robert Caro's hypothesis that Lyndon Johnson's rise to power depended on self-centered moral depravity well beyond the norm for political leaders suggests explanations of his later stubbornness in pursuing victory in Indochina. Evolutionary theory singles out causally relevant similarities among situations that are otherwise diverse. But so does the hypothesis that people who are insensitive to the rights of others are dangerous to deal with. It is often hard to call to mind chemical and thermodynamic relations among observables unless one pictures those regularities as resulting from molecular properties. It is also much easier to remember the details of Frederick Douglass' life if one pictures it as a moral struggle, a struggle for the recognition of his moral worth (a worth of which he was not himself fully aware, at first) and, toward the end, a struggle to resist the forms of moral blindness that respectability encourages (a danger which he did not fully appreciate).

Similarly, resources for explanation might be located outside the covering-law model and its nonpragmatic variants by taking explanatory questions to demand ascription from some repertoire of alternatives which is sufficiently entrenched in the thinking of the inquirers. Thus, in our routine mental explanations, we call upon a wide-ranging repertoire of explanatory factors, and we actually, easily believe that such factors exist. The same can be said of our appeals to moral insight and moral character.

I do not mean to claim that these pragmatic, quasi-aesthetic or psychological virtues really are sufficient for the justification of a truth claim. On the face of it, most have little to do with the true description of a world which was not created by a being with an interest in our mental ease. In any case, hypotheses which are obviously unjustified can claim these virtues. My point is rather that the alleged contrast between the normality of scientific truth-claims and the queerness of moral truth-claims is so farfetched that it cannot contend with the bare facts of standard scientific practice. The contrast collapses even before one takes the fateful step of abandoning the assumption that a canon of topic-neutral a priori rules must connect the data with an empirically justified hypothesis.

Detecting Moral Truth

Because I have based our claims to truth in moral matters on our capacities for moral detection, my defense of moral facts is susceptible to another charge of strangeness, the charge that any such process of detection would be bizarre. Most people are not embarrassed to speak of telling the difference between right and wrong or recognizing a bad state of affairs. But some philosophers have insisted that a genuine process of moral detection, entailing the existence of moral facts, would challenge all our normal expectations concerning the nature of detection. This is part of Mackie's warning that ". . . if we were aware of them [viz., objective values], it would have to be by some special faculty of moral perception or intuition, utterly different from our ordinary ways of knowing everything else."[19] It is important, then, to see what is asserted in ordinary, nonmoral claims that a process is a process of detection, and to find out whether processes of moral detection have these characteristics. It turns out that talk of moral detection generates commitments as to the existence and causal role of states of affairs in the usual way that talk of detection does. The resulting commitments are themselves quite unpeculiar moral and causal judgments.

Suppose I claim that my watch keeps good time, i.e., that looking at the position of the hands and reading the time in the usual manner is a way of telling what time it is. Then, I am, in part, making a statement about what causes the hands to be in their position. I am saying that there is some process determining the position of the hands which is unlikely to give rise to the observed position unless the local time is the one corresponding to that position. Of course, I may know very little about that process. However, if I did not think such a process was responsible for the position of the hands, I would concede that hands and time only correspond, if at all, by accident. Such a watch is not a time-detector.

In general, the assertion that a phenomenon D is a means of detecting a state of affairs S involves the claim that there is some process P which brings about instances of D in the circumstances in question and which is unlikely to do so in the absence of S. However, this necessary condition is not sufficient. The 'procedure', looking at a nonworking clock which has both hands

[19] *Ethics*, p. 38.

pointing to twelve at midnight or noon, is not a means of detecting whether the time is precisely twelve o'clock, even though this source of twelve-ish dial images is infallibly correlated with twelve o'clock times. Keeping a thermometer stuck at 98.6 degrees in the mouth of a healthy human for three minutes results in a final reading which is unlikely to be far from the actual Fahrenheit temperature of the human's insides. But this is not a rough means of detecting body temperature.

On what grounds should one exclude these sequences as non-detection? This question might seem a good occasion to revive demands for indispensability: D does not detect if some process P' gives rise to D and, given the existence of P', D is just as likely to occur whether or not S obtains. Thus, if a watch has stopped with both hands pointing to "12" it will lead to twelve-ish dial appearances regardless of whether it is twelve o'clock. The process of putting the blocked thermometer in a person's mouth is just as likely to give a normal reading whether or not the person's temperature is normal.

As usual, the demand for dispensability is excessive. Consider a paradigmatic case of detection, one's detecting the physical color of an object by determining its apparent color when one looks at it in moderate sunlight (provided, of course, that one has healthy eyesight). There is a true description of causes of any such color appearance that does not refer to anything outside the surface of one's retina. Given the retinal irradiation, the color appearance is just as likely regardless of whether there is a surface in front of one's eyes with the corresponding physical color. But this hardly makes it false that the apparent colors are a means of detecting the physical colors of outside surfaces. There is some process involving light bouncing off the outside surface, entering one's eye and giving rise to one's color-experience and color-judgment which is unlikely to occur if the surface doesn't have the corresponding color. But the whole process is not indispensable in describing a sufficient antecedent for the end result.

It might seem that the initial description of conditions for detection was inadequate because the requirements neglect the threat of "false negatives" in a test procedure. It is not enough (in the proposed, stricter construal) for the underlying process to be unlikely to bring about D in the absence of S. It must make the presence of S unlikely given the nonoccurrence of D. If the stuck watch seen at noon had given rise to a non-twelve-ish appearance, that would not have made it unlikely that the time was twelve, at noon. The failure would have reflected some optical quirk. Similarly, a highly non-98.6-ish reading of the stuck thermometer emerging from the healthy body reflects optical deviation, and is as likely as ever to be accompanied by a temperature of about 98.6 Fahrenheit in the body from which the thermometer emerges.

No doubt, our ideals in the way of detection have this characteristic of reliably indicating both presence and absence. But suppose a process, say a test for a disease, has "positives" that are unlikely in the absence of the disease, even though there are plenty of "negatives" accompanied by the disease. Surely, the observation of the positive, that pink spot, say, where the patch test was applied, is a means of detecting the disease, even though observance of nonoccurrence of the sign is not a means of detecting nonexistence of the disease.

The appropriate demand, in all these cases, would require that the production of D by some process P be connected with S in two ways, absolute and comparative. The production of D by P must be unlikely in the absence of S and it must be more likely in the presence than in the absence of S. This demand for probabilistic S-dependence is a general expression of the basic source of our epistemic outrage at the claim to tell time, ever, using a stopped watch: a stopped watch always gives the same time regardless of what time it is. Unlike the demand for indispensable S-dependence, this one does not require that there be no equally efficacious process screening off dependence on the presence of S. Rather, there must be some process, perhaps much more than minimal, whose operation is relevantly dependent on S. Some process involving moderate sunlight bouncing off a surface is both unlikely to give rise to the appearance of red in a person with healthy eyesight if the surface is not red, and more likely to do so if the surface is red than if it is not.

Still, the list of requirements is not complete. Moreover, the requirement of probabilistic dependence just stated is just one entailment of the pragmatic requirement which does seem to complete the list: one must be able to use the occurrence of D to justify the claim that S obtains, when justification would otherwise be missing. Thus, although characteristic patterns in stellar spectra are a means of detecting the presence of chemical elements in stars, the presence of the elements in the stars is not a means of detecting the corresponding spectral lines. The nonpragmatic conditions for detection are met. The presence of argon, say, is due to a process of condensation which is unlikely to locate argon in a star unless the star's spectrum contains the characteristic argon pattern—and more likely to do so if the pattern is present than if it is absent. (Note that the laws underlying stellar spectroscopy are among the most fundamental laws of nature. The absence of characteristic lines when argon is present would not be a small, localized irregularity.) Still, we can only justify the attribution of such a content to a star on the basis of patterns in spectral lines. So we cannot use the compositional claim to justify a spectral claim that would otherwise be unjustified. Similarly, consulting the stopped watch does not justify the claim that it is twelve o'clock, since a needed premise, that the watch is being consulted at twelve, would have to be justified independently of the watch-reading, and this would establish a justification of the time-claim to which the reading adds nothing. There is this much, then, to the demand for indispensability. Detection-claims should be capable of doing independent work in the tasks of justification.

Ordinary claims that something is a means of detecting something else have turned out to be demanding and complex. I hope it is also obvious, from the examples given and many others that readily come to mind, that the processes connecting the detecting and the detected phenomena are extremely diverse, that the connections need be no more than probabilistic, that the belief that an appropriate process exists may be justified on the part of someone with only the vaguest idea of its nature, and that there may be similar vagueness in commitments concerning the conditions under which the probabilistic relations exist. Before the middle of the twentieth century, there were only the most fragmentary warranted beliefs concerning the nature of human color-vision, and there was only vague knowledge of the general conditions for color detection, with much reliance on tautologies concerning healthy eyesight. Still, people have been able, since some time before, to tell by looking when apples are red.

These normal, jointly sufficient conditions for detection are met when people exercise their capacity to tell the difference between right and wrong, good and evil. To reverse Mackie's claim: moral detection is utterly similar to our ordinary ways of detecting everything else. Perhaps no specific process of moral insight closely resembles a specific process of nonmoral detection. Certainly, any way of telling right from wrong differs in important ways from telling by looking what is green and what is red. But the same can be said of pairwise comparisons of uncontroversial nonmoral processes of detection. Telling colors by looking, telling whether a piano is in tune using a tuning fork, determining length with a yardstick, finding out what someone thinks by asking and detecting voltage with a voltmeter differ from one another in important ways. What does unify them unites them with moral detection, as well.

Consider the cases already at hand, of the little girl and Bartok. The girl's inclination to own up to breaking her playmate's toy is due to her disposition to respect the demands of practices from which she has benefited in cooperation with others. More specifically, she is disposed to bear the burdens of such practices when her turn has come in circumstances of present cost, past gain and expected benefit which are not too demanding and which are not forced on her in inappropriate ways, circumstances of which her present situation is an instance. This disposition toward reciprocity is unlikely to lead to an inclination unless that inclination does incline her toward the right thing to do.

But is the disposition to reciprocate more likely to produce the inclination to avoid a course of conduct when such conduct is wrong than when it is not? Yes, when the disposition to reciprocate does not produce an inclination to avoid a contemplated course of action, that action does not violate terms of cooperation from which one has benefited. Such nonviolation is less apt to be characteristic of acts that are not wrong than those that are. It is the same with Bartok's responding with disgust to happenings in Hungary: the disgust was due to his evenhanded concern and respect for all affected; this attitude is unlikely to give rise to disgust when events are considered unless those happenings are evil; and the attitude is more likely to give rise to disgust when the happenings are evil than when they are not.

In both cases, there is an alternative, causally sufficient description of how the detecting phenomenon was produced which would screen off probabilistic dependence on the presence or absence of the moral property. For example, the girl's inclination not to say what is false is a response to the following characteristic of falsehood-telling: it would violate terms of cooperation from which she has benefited. Such a disinclination in her in response to the presence of this characteristic is not more likely to occur when the presence of this characteristic is accompanied by wrongness than when it is not. However, this is no more relevant to the detection-claim than the fact that appropriately irradiated retinas give rise to the appearance of red regardless of whether a physically red surface is present. What is relevant to telling colors by looking is the truth of the alternative causal description, involving light bouncing off a surface, which singles out a process more likely to give rise to the relevant experience and judgment if the surface is red than if it isn't. In both of the moral cases, there are such descriptions, involving reflection, guided by certain dispositions or attitudes, on certain alternatives or happenings.

Finally, the ascription of someone's moral response to a process with these general features can make an independent contribution to the justification of the moral claim in question, satisfying the pragmatic requirement for detection. Such uses are common when we rely on the moral judgments of others. Suppose we know that someone's moral response arose in the ways I described in the case of the child or of Bartok, i.e., we know this because we know how he or she tends to respond, in general. Then this knowledge that a response resulted from a process is grounds for supposing he or she is right in the corresponding moral judgment when we do not know enough about the object of the judgment to form an independent moral assessment of our own. In one's own case, principles concerning the origins of one's responses are most apt to play an independent role when principles unconcerned with detection come into conflict or when one worries whether an argument from such principles is a mere rationalization, not a valid moral rationale. For example, I would not be justified in relying on an egalitarian principle in assessing distributions if my reliance on it were essentially due to envy.

INSIGHTFUL ORIGINS

What kinds of processes constitute the acquisition of moral insight? Are we justified in supposing that our moral judgments are, in many instances, the outcomes of these processes? Now that the initial challenges to the very possibility of moral detection have been met, it is time to pursue these constructive questions in more detail.

There are at least three general sources of moral insight whose positing does not require strenuous moral argument yet is definite enough to be useful. First, judgments as to whether a state of affairs is morally good or bad are apt to be valid if they reflect equal concern and respect for everyone whose interests are affected (i.e., they correspond to preferences satisfying this attitude which rationally respond to all relevant evidence). Second, judgments as to what actions are right or wrong are apt to be valid if people are led to make them by an upbringing in which basic trust and love in early childhood is a basis for friendship later on, and friendship is a basis for a desire for cooperation on a footing of equal power. More precisely, attitudes formed in this way lead to preference for what is right and avoidance of what is wrong in well-informed rational responses to relevant choices. Third, the choice of social arrangements is apt to be just if the underlying standards (rationally applied in light of adequate information) are the outcome of a social history in which terms for political deliberation evolved in response to the growth of equality in power: standards came to be employed as shared premises for judging complaints against institutions because they were more effective as a generally acceptable basis for acquiescence as inequalities in coercive power diminished.

That our frameworks for moral inquiry identify these origins as sources of moral insight distinguishes us modern industrial folk from some other folk, and from the moral nihilist. Yet there are notorious differences among us as to the right specification of crucial terms in each description, for example, "equal," "cooperation" and "generally acceptable." Quite apart from the rational persuasion of others, most of us would have to rely on strenuous moral argument with ourselves before discovering adequate grounds for adopting any very determinate specification. Fundamental principles of moral detection are vague, and the moral principles that we employ in specifying them are by no means limited to principles directly concerned with detection. I hope that it is clear, by now, that these concessions, though important, do not distinguish fundamental principles of moral detection from fundamental principles of detection elsewhere.

Of these three sources of moral insight, the first concerns the assessment of goodness, the second the discernment of wrongness, and the third the attribution of justice. The three processes are distinct, as described. And I do not mean to propose that the first is basic in the final analysis since the choice of justice and the avoidance of wrongness are, as such, means of creating the most good overall. Indeed, my frequent argument in the second half of this book will be that consequentialism is an invalid moral theory.

One can see why consequentialism has frequently been associated with insistence that we are in a position to describe moral facts. Consequentialists have frequently sought a reductive account of overall goodness which identifies it with some property, usually psychological, which can be described without using the distinctive vocabulary of moral judgment. Our capacity to make factual claims about this property would not be in doubt. Admittedly, the status of the claim identifying the nature of goodness is less clear to many consequentialists. But it is sometimes thought to be justifiable as an explication or "reforming definition." In any case, the combination of consequentialism with an objectively valid, reductive account of goodness is the simplest possible way to establish our access to moral facts. One receives all the facts in one gulp, as it were.

Nonetheless, if consequentialism is bad morality, any partisan of moral truth should regard the traditional connection as a burden. Later, I will argue that it is a burden. Now, I will be providing means to avoid it. Indeed, commitment to develop reductive accounts is, in general, a burden best left behind. There is no reason why anyone concerned for moral truth should insist on an account of any moral property in a nonmoral vocabulary. Perhaps the needed specifications of such terms as "equal concern and respect," "cooperation," and "generally acceptable" unavoidably make use of the distinctive terms of moral discourse. That would not entail that the production of moral insight operates through strange causes, but only that the difference between causes giving rise to moral insight and causes that do not can only be described in moral terminology. In a similar way, our only means of singling out the neural processes in which pain consists might be via the term "pain." As Richard Boyd has trenchantly emphasized, pain can be wholly neural, for all that.[20] Since accounts of moral properties in a nonmoral vocabulary have never worked, so far, it is a relief to have a basis for moral truth-claims that is uncommitted to such projects.

Two large questions might be raised about the claim that the three sources of moral insight are responsible for broadly important judgments that we make. First, are we in a position to take these causes as sources of insight? In the next chapter, I will complete the argument that we are justified by showing that we give the corresponding principles of detection a fundamental role in inquiry, without lapsing into dogmatism. Second, do broadly important judgments of ours actually result from these processes (no doubt along with other causes which are, however, dispensable)? My present concern is to argue that they do, and also to show that worries about such causal questions are the legitimate basis for anxiety about our access to moral truth.

Among other ways, one can discern the operation of equal concern and respect by exercising one's capacity for psychological self-description, which is usually pretty good. Looking into ourselves we (i.e., you, me and other

[20] See Richard Boyd, "Materialism without Reduction" in N. Block, ed., *Readings in the Philosophy of Psychology*, vol. 1 (Cambridge: Harvard University Press, 1980).

decent modern folk) find that we are often led to rank some states of affairs as preferable to others because of our appropriately equal respect and concern for all affected; and we find ourselves inclined to assess moral desirability according to this preference. Notoriously, one sometimes thinks one's preferences are based on evenhanded concern and respect when in fact one is moved by special concern for oneself and those one loves. But often these special interests are not in question. In any case, our capacity to suppress such distortion is often confirmed when we consult others whose special interests are not affected.

The influence of the second source of insight is harder to establish, since it concerns the course of upbringing. Still, it is a reasonably well-established finding that the standards and the modes of response underlying normal judgments of wrongness in modern industrial societies are normally due to a process with the following major phases. At the start, one is cared for by a basically loving person (or, even more happily, two). Soon, that person sets limits to his or her satisfaction of one's needs. One starts to try to be the somewhat self-constraining person the other person wants because one's inner security depends on secure awareness of the caregiver's basic approval and on his or her willingness to mirror and encourage one's emotions. A bit later, the initial dependence of inner security on relations with others starts to be extended, with suitable change in its terms. One enters a world of play in which enjoyment of oneself and others depends on participation by others not at all committed to nurturing, viz., playmates. So sharing becomes a condition for activities without which one would be parentally smothered or painfully alone. Openness and trust are part of what makes such cooperation satisfying; this is especially clear in the frequent cases in which the interaction has no payoff beyond enjoyment of the process itself. So, to the obstinate accompaniment of many tantrums, one becomes a person who shares in order to enjoy interaction with equals on a basis of integrity. If one's emotionally significant relations with those not committed to nurturing are of this sharing kind, one's self-esteem in relations with nonintimates comes to depend on the uncoerced acceptability to others of what one does. Of course, one doesn't want to be a pushover. So one seeks relations in which the self-esteem of each depends on the acceptability to all of the terms for interaction. By making choices which reflect this preference for reciprocity, one begins to tell the difference between right and wrong.

This narrative is embodied in the findings of Piaget, Kohlberg and their modern heirs among researchers on upbringing.[21] Of course, these findings

---

[21] Judy Dunn, "The Beginnings of Moral Development: Development in the Second Year," Carolyn Edwards, "Culture and the Construction of Modern Values" and Carol Gilligan and Grant Wiggins, "The Origins of Morality in Moral Development" in Kagan and Lamb, *The Emergence of Morality in Young Children* are revealing examples of current research along these lines. The pursuit of a secure, valued and well-integrated self is especially central according to

are close to the accumulated lore of parents and teachers, as well. The capacity of processes of interaction such as I have described to mold moral outlooks is also confirmed by certain artificial interventions. For example, the programs that most effectively change the inclinations of teenage criminals create milieus in which cooperation and nurturance are hard to avoid.[22]

This process of moral learning would not be effective unless adults set limits, preventing the child from getting what she wants and giving reasons for the intervention (which ultimately become conditions for the child's own self-acceptance). This truth can be exaggerated into the following falsehood: elders' interventions in the way of punishment, reward and preaching are the only indispensable causes of our moral judgments, and the direction of these interventions has no cause in turn that makes them a source of insight. Perhaps this exaggeration contributes to the force of attacks on moral truth-claims like the following: "If you . . . see a group of young hoodlums pour gasoline on a cat and ignite it, . . . you can see that it [what they are doing] is wrong. But is your reaction due to the actual wrongness of what you see or is it simply a reflection of your moral 'sense', a 'sense' that you have acquired perhaps as a result of your moral upbringing?"[23] Without the exaggeration of the role of mere inculcation, such attacks would obviously require a quite tendentious view of the actual course of one's upbringing. For otherwise, there is no general opposition between insight and upbringing.

The exaggeration depends on neglecting the contributions to the direction and effectiveness of learning made by a variety of factors other than the vigor of the episodes of preaching and the pleasantness or unpleasantness of the episodes of reinforcement. These other factors include the child's needs and uncontrolled activities, the nurturers' and the playmates' noneducational desires, and the contexts of power and objective dependence. It is because of

---

the work on attachment surveyed in Inge Bretherton, "New Perspectives on Attachment Relations: Security, Communication and Internal Working Models," in J. Osofsky, ed., Handbook of Infant Development, second edition (New York: John Wiley, 1987). M. Main, K. Kaplan and J. Cassidy, "Security in Infancy, Childhood and Adulthood" in I. Bretherton and E. Waters, eds., "Growing Points of Attachment Theory and Research," Monographs of the Society for Research in Child Development 50 (1985), is an important longitudinal study emphasizing the importance of mutual emotional openness in this process of security.

[22] For a description and detailed evaluation of such "milieu therapy," at the Wiltwyck School, see W. McCord and Joan McCord, Psychopathy and Delinquency (New York: Grune and Stratton, 1956). Claude Brown, Manchild in the Promised Land (New York: Macmillan, 1965) includes a detailed account of his experience of this mileu. The founding text, with further narratives, is August Aichhorn, Wayward Youth (New York: Viking, 1935).—Of course, the resident counselors must be energetic, sensitive and utterly devoted.

[23] The Nature of Morality, p. 4. Harman does not propose that the question is especially threatening when "your moral upbringing" is identified with preaching and reinforcement. But surely one thinks of such causes, not, say "your past experience of nurturing and cooperation" when the challenge gives rise to anxieties about access to moral truth.

the role of these factors in the process of learning that I described that it constitutes movement in the direction of insight.

Thus, in crucial measure, the adult interventions result from a nurturer's need to set limits to a child's often intolerable demands, and their effectiveness depends on a child's need to trust in the basic approval of a nurturer. Self-constraint acquired on this basis has a tendency to involve valid insights into what is a violation of moral limits, even though inculcation based on differential reinforcement and preaching has no such tendency in general. In addition, inculcation is only apt to result in genuine moral belief if the child uses the inculcated rules, for her own purposes, as in the incessant three-year-old plea, "It's not fair." Such uses are governed by the child's desire to get her way, but also by her need for acceptance by others who seek to get in her way, a tension that also encourages moral insight. Finally, when use is extended beyond the family circle—as it must for moral belief to result—the child encounters others of approximately equal power whose enjoyable participation depends on their free acceptances. In this context, most rules that might have been inculcated by nurturers are not viable means of achieving stability and comfort in oneself. A six-year-old seeking enjoyable interaction at the playground finds it hard to keep faith with the rule that he is worthy of better treatment than most people.—In these and other ways, the nature and entrenchment of most people's moral beliefs depend on causes different from mere inculcation, causes that are insight-enhancing.

The third source of insight that I sketched gives rise to a heightened capacity to detect justice, through a social history appropriately responsive to growing equality of power. Just as the other processes are real forces in personal histories, this one has been a real force in social histories leading to our times.

The crucial historical shifts in terms for assessing justice have reflected the declining opportunities of some to benefit from social rules that others would not willingly accept if they had equal information and power. In the great revolutions of the seventeenth and eighteenth centuries, large-scale changes in the direction of democratic equality began when rising elites in combat with old regimes took the risk of relying on the active and violent support of people without substantial property. Even though participation in Cromwell's New Model Army did not lead to broadly defined electoral suffrage in the Commonwealth and the levée en masse did not lead to a permanent republic in France, the millions who took part in successful well-coordinated revolutionary violence were, along with their children, a recurrent threat to order until their demands for participation were met. In the course of the nineteenth century, broader political participation was instituted, as a result. (In the United States, where power was more equally dispersed among white males from the start, broad political participation among them came sooner, as a consequence.) However, the loyalty of the new political participants could only be sustained, in the long run, on the basis of further new elements in the terms of political justification, for example, special solicitude for extreme material deprivation. Nineteenth- and twentieth-century observers, right and left, used words such as "class warfare" to describe the alternative. In this way, the greater equality in political power generated further changes in the terms of political debate.

In contrast, in societies in which the social power of subordinate groups is trivial, the terms for justifying their subordination are quite undemanding. The Roman law on slavery, as presented in the first substantive section of Justinian's code, begins with the forthright specification, "Slavery . . . is an institution conforming to common practice in which someone is subjected to external domination contrary to nature."[24] Modern hypocrisy is repulsive in its own way, but the absence of such blithe acknowledgment of subordination at least pays tribute to the modern need to argue from broadly acceptable principles. The causal influence of this need makes deliberations insightful.

EXPANDING DETECTION

The means of moral detection that I have described are fundamental in the following sense: a nondogmatic person need not have a further, informative description of what it is in virtue of which each is a means of access to truth. Without further development of the process of detection (which I will now describe), such fundamental principles of moral detection are troublingly vague. If shared information is limited to the topic of a specific moral question, people can often be led to contrary answers by processes that fit one or another construal of the relevant fundamental principle.

This indeterminacy afflicts deliberations over particular choices. For example, people whose upbringings and social settings fit my vague descriptions and who share full information about the alternatives immediately in question often disagree as to which of two fiscal policies should be adopted if one improves life for most by encouraging investment and efficiency while another improves life for the worst-off. Indeed, an individual with such an upbringing and background will often be unsure in herself how to answer the particular question of which policy is just.

A similar overabundance of initially acceptable options is often a burden when one asks those who conform to the descriptions of insight-enhancing influence to choose among general principles—for example, principles of justice. No doubt, such answerers will all seek standards for justifying political measures which evenhandedly appeal to the interests of all willing cooperators in order to induce acquiescence in a noncoercive way. Aristotle's elitism and Chenge's patriarchy will be excluded. But in specifying this vague com-

[24] "Servitus . . . est contitutio iuris gentium, qua quis dominio alieno contra naturam subicitur," *Institutes of Justinian*, I.iii.

mon principle of evenhanded inducement, some will be inclined to insist that a genuine cooperator would require no inducement to forbear from interfering with others' nonfraudulent commercial self-advancement. Others will insist on equality of outcome as a condition for appropriately equal inducement, others on equal prospects of success given equal willingness to try, yet others on equal prospects given equal willingness and equal talents.

Because of these hazards of vagueness, there had better be means of expanding moral detection beyond immediate applications of fundamental principles to moral questions. Otherwise, moral detection might largely involve dead issues in modern times, such as the injustice of chattel slavery.

The scope of detection can be expanded, and often is, by taking advantage of the variety of initial vague principles or narrow moral judgments to which all would be led. Often, further specification proceeds in the following way. One considers various possible ways of specifying a vague principle whose acceptance would result from a fundamental process of moral detection, for example, the vague principle enjoining evenhanded inducement of willing cooperators. One tests the possible specifications to which some who form judgments in an insightful way are initially inclined, by looking for securely established particular moral truths which rule out specifications, in light of relevant facts and other, well-secured principles. The secured truths, here, are those to which everyone with an insightful upbringing and background would be led by reflection on facts and arguments. So the particular moral truths are narrow in significance and the auxiliary principles vague at the start of such reflection. Still, the sifting process may eliminate some construals of vague principles as false. What survives the test may be a specific enough construal to resolve particular questions that were previously open, and justify the specification of other general principles. For example, in my discussion of justice I will, in part, exclude the libertarian construal of equal inducement to cooperate by arguing that it would conflict with narrow judgments of processes involving pollution and the withholding of benefits, judgments whose pervasiveness and stability is best attributed to the influence of the ways of learning that I vaguely described. This determination might make it possible to resolve particular questions about redistribution that are otherwise open.

Note that it is part of moral detection as I have already described it that a more specific view of the truth results from such a process. It is fundamental that moral insight tends to be enhanced by rational consideration of more facts on the part of someone whose upbringing and social background are insight-enhancing. The process of specification is no more a matter of subjective harmony as against objective detection than the oiling of a mainspring is a matter of reducing wear in a watch as against enhancing its capacity to tell time.

This process of specification is apt to take one far afield from particular questions that first motivated attention to the vague principle. For these initial motivating questions could not, as yet, be said to have answers solely dependent on reliable ways of learning; the initial diversity of answers put that assessment in doubt. In addition to its tendency to range far afield, this process of specification may also produce revisions of initially rational assessments of particular, narrow judgments as secure truths. After all, it is part of the underlying account of moral detection that judgments arrived at in relevant ways are more apt to reveal truth as they rationally respond to more and more arguments as well as more and more data. As vague principles become more specific, they may become the basis for arguments undermining judgments that would otherwise have been secure.

These transitions back and forth between the general and the particular parallel the main phases in the quest for "reflective equilibrium," the ultimate stability in the whole system of judgments that Rawls takes to be the goal of moral theorizing.[25] A seeker of moral truth must certainly take seriously the warnings against one-sidedness that are part of Rawls' account: moral justification does not just consist of deductions from general principles joined to nonmoral facts, and also does not just consist of uncritical recording and summary of particular judgments. However, the pursuit of moral truth is not the same as the pursuit of reflective equilibrium.

Though moral truth is accessible, the appeal to internal harmony among moral acceptances and rejections could hardly establish access to moral truth. We are justified in taking our moral judgments to be true only if we are justified in taking them to be the successful exercise of a capacity for moral detection. But none of us does regard it as fundamental that his or her achievements of stable harmony in acceptance and rejection reveal moral truth. It would be the height of arrogance to declare, "It would be a fluke, an anomaly in need of explanation, if my acceptance of this tax policy as just harmonized, on reflection, with my other judgments, while the tax policy was nonetheless unjust." Indeed, someone who regarded it as fundamental that her reflective equilibrium revealed truths about justice, wrongness and the like would hardly understand the corresponding concepts.

Reflective equilibrium is important in moral deliberations, important, in particular, in deciding when to stop deliberating. If my acceptance of a tax policy as just harmonizes on reflection with my other judgments, this may justify me in fully embracing an attitude of acceptance, ending any suspension of commitment. Moreover, the process of specification and testing that I have described is, among other features, a way of achieving reflective equilibrium. However, for this development to justify a claim to truth it must develop fundamental principles of certain kinds, namely, principles of detection. And such principles do not consist of the endorsement of reflective equilibria. This

[25] See Rawls, A Theory of Justice (Cambridge: Harvard University Press, 1971), section 9.

helps to explain Rawls' own reluctance to categorize this method as a basis for asserting truth in moral matters.

I hope that the discussions of justice and discussions of moral responsibility in this book will establish our access to a variety of useful and interesting moral truths. No doubt, in morality, as in science, there are also questions that are urgent to us, yet lack true answers. Still, in both realms of inquiry, fundamental principles that yield only vague or narrow findings in their first applications can be used to establish more specific and far-reaching truths, through further specification and testing.

THE ANXIETY OF REFERENCE

Any believable argument for our right to lay claim to moral truth must sustain a further justification of the worry that our claim might, in fact, be illegitimate. If claims of moral insight are aspects of moral thinking, so, too, is the worry that all such claims may be invalid, that our moral judgments may be, at best, a coherent and stable system of acceptances and rejections corresponding to nothing that makes the judgments true. Those who think that claims to describe moral facts rest on confusions are in a position to argue that the anxiety about external reference is itself confused, some misconstrual of our rational goals of internal coherence and stability. But if, as I have argued, we could have access to moral truths, then there would seem to be nothing muddled about worries as to whether we do have access. And a worry that is so pervasive among rational people ought to correspond to real fallibility.

The fallible, tentative nature of the previous arguments about the actual causes of our moral practices is an advantage, at this point, because it establishes the legitimacy of this anxiety of reference. There is reason to suppose that our basic practices of moral justification have causes that are apt to give rise to true beliefs, including true beliefs about the means of discerning moral properties. But the evidence for these causal ascriptions is hardly conclusive. We are justified in worrying that our moral judgments might, instead, have causes with no tendency to give rise to true moral beliefs.

As a clear example of a debunking causal attribution that could, in principle, be true, consider the Nietzschean social hypothesis that modern ways of assessing justice are the result of envy and convenient ideology. At the outset (the hypothesis goes), Middle Eastern subject peoples in Greco-Roman antiquity envied the activities and power of their Hellenic superiors. They wished they could be as cultured, beautiful and dominant, and assuaged their jealous sense of failure by adopting the thesis that all are equally deserving regardless of personal excellence so long as they obey a god who will equally redeem all the faithful. Eventually, it was sound imperial strategy to maintain this faith as the official religion of the Roman Empire, since it had become widespread, was universalistic in its rules, and promised people that their present burdens had no significance in the long run. Over the millennia, religious faith waned, but the underlying envy of the less able did not, so Christianity became secularized in a conviction that institutions should provide equal inducement to cooperate to all willing cooperators, regardless of excellence or power.

According to this hypothesis, modern insistence on equal inducement to all willing cooperators indispensably depends on wishful thinking due to envy, the usefulness of certain forms of wishful thinking in maintaining social order, and a variety of historical accidents, such as the somewhat greater success of Christians than devotees of Mithras in spreading the faith. If our insistence on equal inducement has these causes, and is not actually due to the causes I previously ascribed, then attributing justice on the basis of equal inducement is not a way of detecting truths about institutions. After all, the Nietzschean process is as likely to set unjust limits on striving for excellence as to lead to the endorsement of just institutions. There is nothing remotely anomalous in the claim that envy, wishful thinking and cultural accident have led to a commonly accepted standard which is not a source of insight into justice.

Indeed, apart from assessments of justice, suppose that our inclination to base assessments of moral goodness on equal concern and respect for all was indispensably rooted in this same cultural history combined with our infantile jealousy of the power of the big people who first control our lives. Then our process of forming preferences would not be a way of detecting facts about goodness.

This debunking story, which I have extracted with some dramatic license from Nietzsche's *The Genealogy of Morals*, is coherent and consistent with a number of relevant historical facts. It does not fit all the historical facts. However, it contains some troubling grains of truths. Equal concern and respect, the achievement of self-esteem through honest reciprocity, and stabilization through reliance on practices rationally acceptable among well-informed equals are not the only possible mechanisms contributing to moral belief. Envy, wishful thinking, the achievement of order through tranquilizing ideology, historical accidents, inculcation, and psychological resistance to departures from one's culture's routines all have an influence on people's ways of responding to moral problems. Our evidence that modern ways of judging goodness, justice and rightness result from mechanisms such as those on the first list, and not, indispensably, on some combination of mechanisms such as those on the second list is tentative and fallible. The consequent worry that our means of making moral judgments result from pressures, habits and accidents with no tendency to give rise to true moral beliefs is our legitimate anxiety that our best-established moral judgments are not justified true beliefs.

The tentative, fallible case for external reference does depend on fundamental commitment to prima facie principles that certain causes of belief are revealing. But this is not a special feature of morality. External reference can never be established in any realm of inquiry, not even tentatively and fallibly, without reliance on such principles. One cannot recognize the coincidence of what one believes with what exists independent of one's psychology, in any other way. Admittedly, people have sometimes tried to model all such recognition on a very different process, the comparison of two items both present in perception in order to establish their similarity. But when one item is a mental representation, the other nonmental, no such process can establish access to external facts. In any case, the universality of the demand for recognition by comparison is self-defeating. For recognition by comparison to succeed the *relevant* similarities have to be consulted. So there must be some noncomparative means to recognize the objective presence of something, namely, of a relevant kind of resemblance. Otherwise, recognition would be blocked by an infinite regress.

Crudely pictorial theories of access to truth require access more direct than moral reference can provide. Similarly, positivism tended to require more security than moral reference can provide. Semantics was supposed to be the secure foundation for the rest of inquiry. The connections between terms and referents which determine the truth conditions for sentences were supposed to be facts of language, infallibly guaranteed by stipulation or convention prior to the risky work of empirical inferring and testing. This blueprint never fit theoretical inquiry, where the fate of such terms as "phlogiston" made it clear that reference, if it occurred, was insecure. For reasons that I will describe in developing an approach to content, the positivist blueprint itself is now taken to be defective. The actual structure of science is rational in the absence of secure semantic foundations. Insistence on secure semantic foundations is just as inappropriate for moral inquiry.

I have emphasized questions of what actually gives rise to this or that aspect of moral thinking, rather than questions of what thinking would arise on a certain, perhaps hypothetical basis. In most moral contexts, emphasis on the hypothetical questions would be appropriate, instead. The distinction helps to set limits to the consequences of referential anxiety.

On the whole, our basic means of moral deliberation consist of discerning what preference would result if informed choice were molded by certain processes. Belief in a principle of moral detection entails reliance on such a method of deliberation; for example, the belief that accommodation to growing equality of power enhances access to truth about justice entails resolving questions of justice by asking what people would accept if they had equal power and sought stability through willing cooperation. However, one can rely on the hypothetical questions in forming judgments without taking the answers to be truths. Their truth depends on whether the reliance has actual causes that are truth-revealing. Thus, if the Nietzschean, debunking story explains why we actually rely on the questions about hypothetical molding by cooperation and equality, then our reliance is not a means of access to truth. We might rationally accept this debunking while still relying on the same hypothetical method to form moral judgments. But we will no longer regard our conclusions as discoveries of truth.

Those who think mere confusion is the basis for claims of access to moral facts almost always add that we should maintain most, if not all of our moral judgments when we are disabused of illusions concerning their truth. Though I have argued at length that moral insight is no illusion, it does seem right that most of our moral judgments are more secure than their assessment as truths. Now one can see why. Our methods of moral-judgment-formation consult hypothetical effects. Our belief that reliance on these methods reveals truths depends on the assignment of actual causes to these reliances. The reliance would not be irrational if the causal attributions were to prove wrong. And, like all attributions of actual causes, these are tentative and fallible.

If this distinction between the rationality of reliance and the rationality of belief were special to morality, that would be grounds for suspicion that moral truth, if it exists as more than a metaphor, is truth of a very special kind. So a defender of the plain truth of moral judgments needs to consider at least one further topic, the relationship between truth and other goals, in morality and elsewhere.

The Unimportance and Importance of Moral Truth

If they continue as long as this one has, arguments that our justified moral judgments are often justified truth-claims begin to evoke a stiff and academic portrait of moral justification. The argument so far in this chapter might suggest that the goal of moral justification is the establishment of the truth of the moral judgment in question, in an argument showing that its truth follows from the best explanation of the data. This is a caricature of moral justification. But the caricature is not required by the ascription of justified moral truth.

Whenever one bases a conclusion on moral considerations or moral principles, one is engaged in moral justification. Though establishing the truth of a moral judgment, in an argument relying on a principle of moral detection, is sometimes one's goal in this activity, other goals are much more common. One's self-esteem depends on conformity to one's moral principles, and often one's goal in moral justification is preserving self-esteem by pursuing conduct that does conform. Even more commonly, one's engagement in moral justification is motivated by a search for common ground with others. In such activity, we seek sufficient common ground in shared moral principles to make agreement as to a costly choice rational, in light of relevant nonmoral findings. This goal is morally urgent, quite as much as the pursuit of conscientious self-acceptance. If an option would impose costs on some, while benefiting others, one has a duty to seek rationales for accepting such a choice that those burdened would, rationally, accept. In the absence of such a rationale, the burden is an injury that should usually (though not invariably) be avoided. The moral importance of this pursuit of common ground is especially great when the option involves the use of coercion, as virtually all government policies do.

Most people would, rationally and responsibly, prefer to spend their time on other projects in the absence of a moral reason to engage in moral reasoning. The needs for conscientiousness and for common ground are the usual reasons for engaging in moral justification, nonetheless. Usually, their successful fulfillment does not involve justifying the claim that a moral judgment is a true description of an objective state of affairs.

Thus, in my annual argument for affirmative action with about half the members of my Freshman Seminar, I seek common ground, appealing to various facts and to shared principles of fairness, freedom and equality. Success consists in establishing that their most deeply held criteria for acceptance or rejection are similar enough to mine to sustain acceptance of affirmative action including racial and sexual quotas, given certain empirical facts. In my annual effort I do not argue that the best explanation of our common inclinations entails their truth. I do not even do this quite informally and inexplicitly. I make no reference to considerations bearing on moral detection. I do not expect the freshmen to fill in gaps, so as to connect the arguments I offer with an argument that the positive judgment of affirmative action is true. After all, these are Cornell freshmen, many of whom are convinced that there is no such thing as moral truth. Their delight in denying that there are moral truths may not be typical of humankind in general, but the kind of project I pursue surely is typical of moral justification in general. It is not a project of establishing that a moral judgment is true.

It is important that the pursuit of common ground, not truth, is the most frequent goal of moral justification. Indeed, I will argue in chapter five that this assessment is essential to an understanding of the content of moral ascriptions which is required by my mixed verdict on the questions of moral realism. However, the typical irrelevance of truth-justification does not show that we are not typically justified in claims as to moral truth. Justification of a claim as true need not be the only goal of rational, principled, nonmanipulative justification in a field in which truth claims are, in fact, justified. Scientific cases show this.

Often, scientific reasoning aims at justifying tentative belief in approximate truths through fair explanatory comparison. But often, even in fields where truth is pursued, scientific reasoning aims at the choice of convenient means of summary or prediction, or the formal simplification of a system of propositions through the derivations that scientists praise as "elegant." These goals are not goals of truth as such. Indeed, people sometimes, quite rationally, pursue them in the absence of any expectation that the favored propositions will be true. For example, when someone finds the linear relation best fitting a scattergram, this often justifies its use as a means of summarizing the data, even if the investigator has no idea whether the actual relation is linear, quadratic, or of some higher degree. Because they fix the rate of change for the whole curve, linear relations are easiest to use, truth to one side. Similarly, the formal simplification of a body of theory through elegant derivations need not be the project of someone who thinks the theory describes mechanisms underlying observed events. Perhaps the simplifier seeks a less clumsy device for summarizing observed regularities . . . or just prefers elegance to mess. Still, the derivations provide a justification for using the simpler body of theory.

That certain goals can motivate non-truthseekers in developing scientific justifications for relying on propositions shows that these are not goals of establishing truth. But the same goals can also be dear to truthseekers, who also prefer convenience and elegance. Without inconsistency, the same person can at one time justify the use of a scientific hypothesis to describe reality, at another justify its use in truth-independent ways. So our frequent motivation by truth-independent goals when we engage in moral justification hardly shows that moral inquiry never consists of justifying the truth of moral judgments.

So far, I have used the analogy of science to show that there is room for justifications aiming at goals other than truth in a practice generally regarded as achieving justified true beliefs, as well. But this attention to the goals of rational practice could prove dangerous to truth. The truth-independent goals might be so effective in providing rationales for actual practices of deliberation that there is no room left for justified belief in the truth of moral judgments, or of theoretical hypotheses. For suppose that the explanation of what rational practitioners do and of why it is rational never requires the ascription to them of beliefs in these truths. If such ascription is never part of the best explanation of rational practice, this is a reason to deny that the controversial truth-claims are rationally asserted. For surely the characterization of people's beliefs should play a role in rationalizing what they do (including what they utter).

In principle, the claims to truth could, nonetheless, be distinctive claims of philosophers, supported by special philosophers' reasons. But this is far from my actual strategy of taking truth claims to be conveyed by normal moral judgments and supported by principles of detection implicit in normal practice. Indeed, there is something crazy about the idea of moral truth solely accessible by means utterly different from normal moral deliberations pursued in favorable circumstances—or truth about the subjectmatter of science achieved by means utterly different from actual scientific argument. So it is important to see whether the pursuit of truth is an artificial additive to ordinary rational practice.

In the case of science, the conduct of rational inquirers sometimes is rational because they are believers, not just accepters. Berzelius guessed (correctly) that pure substances in which the same elements were combined in the same proportions would sometimes react in different ways. This was a rational guess because he took Daltonian chemistry literally, as a description of how chemical combinations were controlled by capacities for attachment linking the surfaces of atoms. Different, sufficiently complex hookups among atoms of the same kinds and proportions should create differences in capacities to hook up with similarly complex molecules. On the other hand, someone who took Daltonian chemistry to be just a means of summing up and unifying already-established regularities would lack grounds for this rational practitioner's guess. Similarly, Maxwell appealed to the ether hypothesis to justify his guess that radiant heat is due to vibrations in molecules. (The ether conveys the energy through spaces devoid of mass.) If, like Hertz, he had only believed in Maxwell's equations, putting questions of mechanisms to one side, he would have lacked grounds for the rational guess. Elsewhere, attitudes toward anomaly and inconsistency are explained and rationalized by appealing to belief, where mere acceptance would not be sufficient.[26]

In morality, is it, similarly, the case that what a rational practitioner does is sometimes to be explained on the basis of her taking a moral judgment to be true, not just by ascribing to her a goal of seeking common ground with others, or conforming to her own convictions? Yes, and as in the case of science, the ways in which truth can have a point in practice are diverse and specific. Two ways in which truth counts concern the justification of coercion and the demands of conscience.

The imposition of a law that rational, informed people would disobey were it not for the coercive power of the state is always in need of justification. If one's best justification depends on moral premises that have no claim to truth, then, by that token, the justification may be too weak to provide an adequate moral justification of the intrusion. It will not be too weak, if the harms prevented by the imposition are great enough. But the harms must be especially grave to justify intrusions that others would conscientiously reject without

[26] Richard Boyd has, for many years, emphasized the distinctive contribution of literal belief to practices of inference that rely on considerations of intratheoretical plausibility. See "Realism, Underdetermination and a Causal Theory of Evidence," *Nous* (1973), pp. 8f. and "*Lex Orandi est Lex Credendi*" in P. Churchland and C. Hooker, eds., *Images of Science* (Chicago: University of Chicago Press, 1985), pp. 9, 18. Elsewhere, I have criticized the arguments for scientific realism that he bases on this characterization; but it is certainly an important means of revealing the role of genuine belief in much actual scientific practice. For the doubts about the argument, see *Fact and Method*, pp. 453–59. Hilary Putnam describes how insistence on intertheoretical consistency can imply commitment to theoretical truths in "Explanation and Reference" (1973) collected in *Mind, Language and Reality* (New York: Cambridge University Press, 1979), pp. 210f.

displaying an inferior ability to detect moral truth. Moral justification does not come to an end when insufficient common ground is discovered, but the failure casts a shadow within which the claim to truth plays a special role.

For example, in Canada a recent bill of rights and accompanying legislation has led to state interference in traditional Inuit practices concerning rights in childrearing and inheritance. Underlying the modern statutes are modern beliefs concerning the equal right of all women and men to advance their individual projects in ways that do not depend on the imposition of barriers to others' self-advancement. If these beliefs are true, then the intrusion on traditional Inuit family obligations is justified, though the harms of intrusion are regrettable. However, suppose that modern beliefs had no more claim to superior truth than non-Inuit Canadians' reluctance to eat blubber. Then, the regulation of Inuit family life according to modern standards would, almost certainly, be wrong. It would be wrong according to modern moral standards, which discriminate among coercively backed proposals according to whether their justifications rest on truths or mere inclinations.

The alternative doctrine that the justification of government policies is solely a search for common ground might seem a counsel of tolerance. As this case shows, the appearance is misleading, in two ways. What is counseled might be tolerance of private intolerance of others' rights. Also, if concerned with more than common grounds one can begin to discriminate between the many cases in which rationally rejected burdens ought not to be imposed, and the cases in which they should. Obviously, they sometimes should, since government should sometimes take sides when harms are privately imposed and justified by appeals to private principles. If the assessment of such intervention must be an all or nothing matter, the verdict is going to be acceptance of all interventions that are feasible means of implementing one's aversions. Mere powerfully adverse feeling becomes as good as a rational appeal to moral detection.

The search for truth also plays a distinctive role in explaining what one does when one subjects one's moral thinking to moral scrutiny. Granted, not everything one demands of one's own moral thinking entails an interest in truth. One thing which one does pursue is consistency. One hopes to be faithful to enduring moral principles, as faithful as an open-minded willingness to use some old principles to revise others in the light of surprising evidence allows. It would be irresponsible not to strive for such consistency, since people can hardly rely at all on someone who changes basic moral principles for no reason. In striving for consistency, one engages in moral justifications, seeking to fit new choices to old beliefs. But these justifications would be adequately explained by one's having a goal of basing choices on whatever principles one has embraced in the past. One seeks common ground with oneself at earlier times.

Consistency is a morally important goal. Its pursuit motivates many urgent monologues, in which we are preoccupied with moral justification. In other kinds of self-examination, we ask whether we could find common ground with others, leading them to accept costs that we impose. Still, our moral hopes for ourselves are sometimes distinctively concerned with moral truth.

Consider the anxiety induced by the anti-referential hypotheses I discussed before. Faced, for example, with the possibility that all one's moral responses are merely due to preaching and reinforcement, one is concerned with the possible loss of a capacity one hopes to have. This anxiety and the search for appropriate origins that it provokes are spontaneous, not an artificial additive, and they stand in need of explanation. Why does the debunking of the claim to truth produce its distinctive panic?

The loss that one fears is not a loss in consistency, or in right action as specified by current principles. The debunking hypothesis explains one's attachment to those principles, and need not create detachment if the hypothesis is believed. Certainly, no one who experiences moral anxiety at debunking is reassured by a mere conviction that the direction of reinforcement will not actually change. The best explanation of what we do in assessing ourselves and of why it is rational must attribute a belief in the possibility of access to moral truth, not just of psychological attachment to moral standards. Belief in this possibility explains and rationalizes our normal anxiety in the face of debunking and our efforts to discern sources of our moral responses which are appropriate to truth. Belief in the success of these efforts really is belief in the truth of moral judgments. Thus, in reflections on our lives, we encounter a worry about truth that is not a concern for common ground with others or with oneself. It is a worry that is rationally assuaged only by the justification of truth claims.

Chapter Three

LIMITLESS DISSENT

WE ARE justified in moral truth-claims. But sometimes we could not justify these claims to everyone, even if each were to respond rationally to all relevant evidence. For our justifications of some moral truth-claims depend on principles that others would reject in spite of rationality and shared evidence. How common and how important are disagreements among actual people that reason and evidence could not resolve? My few illustrative cases do not remotely answer this question. They are concerned with relatively limited disagreements dividing people in advanced industrial societies from the long-dead or the few and far-away. Later, I will offer a bigger contribution to the assessment of actual moral divides. Moral political choice is preeminently the sphere in which rational determinacy is morally important, because indeterminacy would interfere so dramatically with the morally important goal of persuading, rather than coercing, rational, principled people. So my detailed assessment of currently important divides will investigate whether there are disagreements among people in advanced industrial societies concerning justice and legitimate political action which reason and all relevant evidence would not resolve. Setting the limits of rational determinacy given the diversity of current means of moral political appraisal will turn out to depend on controversial empirical claims and long moral arguments. Because of this complexity, I will postpone further investigation of actual moral divides until the later chapters.

However, there is a further question about the limits of justification that mires us less in empirical facts and substantive moral arguments. It is the remaining item on the initial list of questions of moral realism. Are there moral judgments that could not be rejected by any possible person who possesses all relevant evidence and arguments and reflects rationally on them? In posing this question, we do not confine ourselves to frameworks actually used in answering moral questions. Any possible framework is relevant. A moral judgment which is invulnerable to such merely possible dissent will still depend on contingent facts about the object of judgment, but it will not rely for its status on any contingent fact about what standards of justification are actually applied in arriving at judgments.

Despite the absence of limits on the frameworks for dissent, it might seem that rational, informed dissent sometimes is impossible. Transparent moral horrors come to mind, here: the Nazis' "Final Solution to the Jewish Problem," assessed in light of the actual facts rather than crazy delusions about

Jews, Nero's burning Rome, assuming he ordered it for a lark, or Caligula's alleged recreational murders. The defense of the stronger claim of universal justifiability, in these cases and others, would depend on an alleged relationship between justification and meaning. The intentional causing of grave harm stands in need of a justification (so the argument begins), or else it must be condemned as wrong. If anyone does not accept this need for a justification, then, just by that token, he or she does not understand what wrongness is, and so is too confused to be a rational dissenter. There are a variety of considerations to which a possible rational person might appeal as justifying a gravely harmful act or policy. Some may be different from any that we would accept. But the variety is limited. In the case of certain moral horrors, there is no actual feature of the act or policy to which any rational person could appeal as justifying the harm. Thus, it would also constitute a failure to understand what wrongness is for someone to suppose that the simple fact of Jewish ancestry morally justifies killing, or that throwing people overboard and pushing them away with boathooks until they drown is morally justified by the fact that it leads to transient, skittish pleasure for an emperor.[1] "Now I see why it isn't wrong," here, constitutes a failure to understand that wrongness is the issue. Rational assertion of a deviant moral judgment could only be based on a false nonmoral belief connecting the harmful act with possibly relevant considerations, for example, crazy beliefs about the activities of Jews or about the need to preserve the world by propitiating a strange god.

Such constraints involving moral reasons are valid limits on the rational making of moral judgments, i.e., the rational assertion of moral properties, such as rightness, wrongness and mere all-rightness, good, evil and moral indifference contrasted with good and evil. Short of confusion or a failure to understand, someone who makes a moral judgment must recognize the need to find considerations supporting any gravely harmful acts that she judges to be right or locates in a middle ground of moral indifference in between right and wrong or takes to be indeterminate because of a tragic conflict between rival considerations. Also, she can count only a limited number of considerations as supporting moral judgments opposed to the verdict of wrongness, if she rationally reflects on the question "Is this wrong?" So, when no such consideration is actually to be found, no rational, informed person could make any moral judgment opposed to the judgment that a given act, which was gravely harmful, is wrong.—I hope that reflection on transparent moral horrors will support this conclusion, for now. In chapter five, I will reinforce it with a systematic argument that moral judges must employ certain general considerations of benefit and harm.

However, there is another possible perspective from which someone might answer "No" to a question, "Is it wrong?" Someone might answer such questions by applying a framework in which the answer to *all* such questions is

---

[1] One of Suetonius' lurid tales of Caligula; *The Lives of the Caesars*, IV, xxxii.

"No," a framework according to which there is no such thing as rightness or wrongness, or moral all-rightness in between, or moral tragedies. This person, whom I will call "the moral nihilist," is not engaged in the project of ascribing moral properties and, so, his rational options are not governed by the rules binding those who are engaged in it. Just as you and I do not presuppose that there are witches when we say that someone is not a witch, he does not presuppose that any act is wrong in denying that someone has done wrong. Indeed, just as you and I would not make a moral judgment in denying that the Statue of Liberty has ever done wrong (e.g., we are not attributing moral purity to her), he makes no moral judgment in his ubiquitous denials that acts are wrong.

More specifically, I will use the term, "moral nihilist," to describe someone with three characteristics. First, he does not think there is such a thing as moral detection, telling what is right and what is wrong, good and evil, and so forth. Second, he rejects our presupposition that some acts and policies are right, some wrong, when we ask, "Is this wrong?", and similarly for the analogous presuppositions of our other moral inquiries. He dissents from all moral characterizations of anything and anyone. Finally, he does not refuse to make moral judgments on account of some criticism he has of them, i.e., some argument that he has developed which he takes to be a rational basis for doubt in the framework of some who do start out by making moral judgments. He simply accepts no principle or process that supports any moral conclusion.

This position is much more extreme in its deviant negating than the limited nihilism of someone who denies that moral facts exist, but makes all, or all important moral judgments just as others would. Yet if the arguments of the last chapter are right, the moderate position is not available to informed and rational people. Principles of moral detection are themselves moral principles, present in ordinary moral deliberations. So someone who accepts ordinary, important moral principles, together with psychological, social or historical facts, cannot rationally deny that there are moral facts. Granted, one could still define a limited nihilism involving the rejection of principles of moral detection (the first feature of the moral nihilism I described) and acceptance of all standard moral judgments compatible with this rejection. But this position would depend on arbitrary discrimination among principles all of which play a role in the major kinds of moral assessment.—In any case, the investigation of the more limited moral nihilisms would not shed distinctive light on the question left open by the study of frameworks for moral inquiry actually employed, namely, the question of how far rational, informed dissent could extend in merely possible frameworks. Because she is engaged in moral judgment, a moderate nihilist will have to respect certain needs for justification and certain limits on the means for satisfying them.

In stipulating an understanding of moral nihilism, I also put to one side efforts to turn morality against itself, such as arguments—perhaps to be found in Nietzsche—that morality is intolerably degrading or arguments that choices and outcomes are predetermined in ways that remove everything from the scope of moral judgment. The rationality of a nihilism depending on such an argument will depend on the merits of its specific rationale for abandoning moral judgment. These rationales have always turned out to be defective. The remaining possibility is a nihilism that does not accept our principles and judgments, but does not reject our outlook as unreasonable or uninformed.

I doubt that any rational person has ever employed such a framework. But the nihilist, if he existed, could be rational and possess all relevant evidence and arguments. The task of showing that such limitless rational, informed dissent is possible largely consists of showing that the radical nonengagement in moral judgment, required for the rationality of the denials, is compatible with a grasp of the moral concepts involved, a grasp that is required if the denials are to be relevant, i.e., genuine rejections of the moral judgments that we make.

Of course, the nihilist's understanding of moral concepts does not just consist of his practice—or, rather, non-practice—in applying them. One might as well say that a person who refuses to characterize the quantum state of any system, not basing his refusal on any criticism of quantum physics, has, just by that token, achieved an understanding of quantum physics. However, the nihilist does not simply fail to engage in a practice of judgment. He fails to engage in a practice of judgment whose rules he understands. He knows that people with whom he converses take certain reasons and not others to be appropriate ultimate grounds for applying the basic terms of moral discourse. His knowledge that these conclusions apply terms of *moral* discourse partly consists of his awareness of the kinds of reasons that are countenanced by others as a basis for applying these terms, partly consists of awareness of the ways in which most people use these conclusions to regulate their further choices. Thus, we may suppose that he both knows that most people take grave harm-doing to be a basis for applying a certain term and knows that when they apply that term they think they have discovered an important reason to want others to desist from the act, even if they are not themselves endangered by these harmers. He understands the game because he knows the rules by which it is played, extremely complex rules if the "game" is moral judgment. But he does not play the game.

Each of us, confronting kinds of judgments that are alien, can combine understanding with disbelief, as the nihilist does. I understand, reasonably well, the grounds on which someone qualifies as a saint, in Catholic doctrine. I could even criticize a due-process Church finding of sainthood as an unreasonable application of Catholic doctrine. So I understand the concept of a Catholic saint. But I do not think that anyone is, literally, a saint. As it happens, I have reasons that I would use to criticize essential beliefs about the divine as unreasonable. ("The divine," of course, is another term I understand without literally applying it to anything.) But suppose I were the sort of atheist who thinks that the major religions and irreligions are all compatible with reason and evidence. I might still, myself, employ no principle that could justify identifying someone as a saint, while understanding the concept. This distance from the detection of sainthood is the nihilist's distance from the detection of right and wrong.

Although I don't believe that anyone has been a saint, I think there is a class of people who would properly be labeled "saints" by someone who makes standard Catholic assumptions as to causes of intense spiritual commitment and extreme goodness. If there were any danger of confusion as to whether I used the terms of hagiology literally to assert that some are saints or merely to single out those who would be rightly called "saints" according to those assumptions, I might indicate the second usage, in written prose, by using scare-quotes. I think that Theresa of Avila really was a 'saint', but I have my doubts about Robert Bellarmine, the canonized person who condemned the aged Galileo to house arrest for life. The device of punctuation is rarely necessary in practice, since the intended usage is usually understood. But the usage that scare-quotes would signal is common enough. Thus, the Bohannans describing the Tiv and Evans-Pritchard describing the Azande sometimes describe "what witches do" or write of someone that "he was a witch," leaving it to our good sense to tell that they do not believe in witches.

The nihilist accepts scare-quotes usages of the terms of moral discourse on the same grounds as we would accept the corresponding literal usages. As one result, indeed, the main one, his characterizations of acts, institutions and policies employing the terms of moral discourse do not entail (literal) judgments as to what ought or ought not to be done, as our moral characterizations do. The nihilist says that Bartok left Hungary because he 'realized that much evil was being done' by a government benefiting from his prestigious presence. The nihilist describes psychological processes involved in such 'realization' using morally neutral expressions that we, too, would apply. Unlike us, the nihilist does not say that these processes ought to be encouraged or that one ought to regret decisions that could not be sustained in this or some related way.

The distinction between the scare-quotes and the literal usage of moral terms is familiar from an earlier round of the moral realism controversy. Then, the distinction was used by adherents of versions of anti-realism in which people could make moral judgments on the basis of any reason whatever, so long as the utterances to which they were led played the right psychological roles. While these anti-realists thought that the normal use of a moral term was to express an attitude of the right psychological kind, they wanted to allow that someone could use terms of moral discourse current in his or her society without employing them in those psychological roles. The rational usage for such a person would be a scare-quotes usage, to single out items to which the term would be applied by people whose moral usages were typical of the community in question.

I have already argued that the doctrine of limitless variety in the contents of moral justifications is wrong. But one can reject this doctrine while allowing that it might be rational just to engage in scare-quotes usage even though people typically employ moral terms in literal usage. The point of insisting on the rationality of this practice will be to help an argument that a possible rational person could believe in the nonexistence of all moral facts and dissent from all moral judgments. In contrast to the anti-realists to whom I alluded, one would not take scare-quotes usage to differ from standard practice in the following ways: only in the former usage are justifications for proper application of a moral term limited in content, and only in the former usage are moral terms applied in order to describe states of affairs. The ordinary moral discourse of actual people, engaged in literal usage, has these two features, as well.

If, as I have begun to argue, the moral nihilist's disengagement is, in general, compatible with a grasp of relevant concepts, then he can continue rationally to reject all moral judgments no matter what evidence he acquires. Where we would have to accept a moral hypothesis as part of the best explanation of the data, he would avail himself of the corresponding scare-quotes hypothesis. Where we say that a belief is due to an exercise of moral detection, he attributes it to nothing more than 'moral detection'. He thinks his capacity to explain is not reduced by his denial that there is any state of affairs the existence of which would have literal entailments as to what ought to be done. And this self-assessment is rational. Admittedly, his self-assessment depends on ratings of explanatory need that differ from ours, for example, his finding it not to be a fluke if someone's interest in cooperation on a footing of equality should make no contribution to an accurate discernment of what is right or wrong. But the investigation of our limited disagreements with Aristotle, Chenge and other actual dissenters has already made it clear that rational frameworks may contain fundamentally different principles concerning moral insight. Nor will his explanatory practice turn out to be inferior when rated for other virtues and vices, detected without reliance on background principles specific to our moral inquiries. Scare-quotes usage is a bit more elaborate than literal usage when individual hypotheses are framed. On the other hand, it contributes to more economical inventorying of what there is. Otherwise, the two explanatory practices are on a par. In sum, the rational pursuit of the best explanation does not drive the moral nihilist to abandon his position and postulate moral facts. So he is rational to deny their existence.[2]

[2] For a slightly different case for the rationality of nihilism, see "Ways of Moral Learning," pp. 553f.

In a stimulating article, which appeared after the main text of this chapter was written, David Copp defends the rationality of a moral skeptic quite similar to the nihilist of this chapter, pointing out that the skeptic can appropriate moral concepts to pick out properties without commit-

In the next two sections, I will develop my account of nihilism as one rational response to all the evidence, looking first at the nihilist's epistemic resources, then at his capacity to reject our moral conclusions in spite of the resources he shares with us. In the course of this discussion, the coherence of nihilism will turn out to depend on an intrinsic connection between moral beliefs and reasons for choice. So my next task will be an assessment of this connection. Part of my goal will be to show that the intrinsic connection with practical reasons is compatible with my construal of our moral judgments as beliefs concerning objective facts. Certain narrow conceptions of the nature of true beliefs will have to be rejected here, as narrow constraints on their justification were, before. Finally, in light of all the limits to universality in moral justification that will have been acknowledged, I will consider the worry that belief in the truth of our moral judgments is dogmatic if our justifications fall so far short of universality.

Nihilist Resources

The rationality, in light of all data, of the nihilist's assessment of his explanatory capacity is most obvious when he and we agree that certain causal factors that can be described in morally neutral language explain the relevant phenomena, while he and we only disagree as to whether those factors constitute moral detection (or whatever) as it operates in the case at hand. How-

---

ting himself to the corresponding moral characterizations. On the basis of this similar assessment of rational dissent, he reaches some utterly different conclusions about our access to truth in moral inquiry: though morality may yield explanations in ways that would confirm scientific hypotheses, these moral explanations do not justify any moral standard, moral code or normative moral theory; the truth of a moral judgment consists of its following from a justified moral code, justified in a way having nothing to do with explanation and establishing no substantive truth-claim concerning the code itself; the truth and justification of moral judgments differ fundamentally from the truth and justification of scientific hypotheses. See "Explanation and Justification in Ethics," *Ethics* 100 (1990), pp. 237–58.

These differences in the further steps we take may be due to different assessments of current controversies within the philosophy of science. Addressing himself to all who take morality and science to be "epistemologically on a par," Copp is neutral concerning disagreements over the epistemology of science itself; he explicitly claims that "the new naturalism need not be committed to a 'realist' account of science" (p. 237). However, his immediate inference from the rationality of skepticism to the conclusion that our moral explanations do not justify us in taking moral judgments to be truths requires a distinctive view of justification, characteristic of positivist philosophy of science, in which empirical justification for a truth claim must rely on rules for connecting hypothesis and data that every possible rational inquirer would accept. This kind of philosophy of science is invalid; the approach to empirical justification that should replace it produces a realist account of science, (roughly) because empirical justification must attribute a causal role to the state of affairs described in the justified proposition. The right conclusion to reach from the rationality of moral skepticism is that moral judgments could not be justified by the relationships characteristic of scientific confirmation if the latter relationships are understood in certain prevalent ways, epitomized in positivist philosophy of science.

ever, the nihilist does not need to take advantage of such a shared neutral description to be justified in his self-assessment. Moral judges, as they would function at their most informed, reflective and rational, can themselves serve as the nihilist's means of nonmoral description. Suppose that Jim explains his neighbor Joe's repeated playing of loud music late at night as due to Joe's lack of respect for others' rights. He points out that Joe is not at all hard of hearing, and that Joe's notorious conduct toward Jill is well-explained by the same moral hypothesis. Perhaps Jim lacks the means to describe what makes for the possession of rights, in terms that are acceptable to the nihilist. Still, if Jim is justified in his explanation, the nihilist is justified in an explanation attributing Joe's conduct to Joe's lack of respect for those boundaries which Jim would impose if Jim developed his thinking as to what impositions are wrong in a completely rational response to all relevant information (rational and relevant in light of Jim's thinking). The nihilist uses Jim's thinking, as it would be at its most informed, reflective and rational, to describe a causal factor, Joe's lack of respect for a boundary that Jim would impose. But the nihilist does not share Jim's conclusion that the crossing of the boundary is wrong. Indeed, the usual intention in scare-quotes usage is precisely this use of typical judges as designators of properties less substantial than the judges suppose.

Where no further description in morally neutral terms is available, the nihilist is like an eighteenth-century scientist for whom the most definite general statement about temperature is that temperature is what thermometers measure—and we are like the thermometers. Such instrumental access is less than ideal. But wherever the nihilist lacks more direct means of describing what makes the act merit a scare-quotes characterization, we suffer from a similar lack. We must admit that we cannot give a fully adequate description of the individually nonmoral properties in virtue of which the moral ones are possessed. Like the nihilist, we rely on our moral sensibilities to remedy the lack. And we regard the lack of the fully adequate description of that in virtue of which any relevant moral term applies as a limitation in our capacity to justify and explain that it would be desirable to overcome—albeit not a lethal defect that must be overcome.

"But mustn't the nihilist admit that it is a remarkable fluke that he must rely on the responses of other people to pick out factors useful in explaining, even though these responses are affected by justifications involving beliefs that are not true? And if the nihilist makes this concession, isn't he also rationally compelled to abandon his nihilism? For he has conceded that his nihilism has an explanatory loose end that he cannot tie up, and, by definition, his nihilism is not based on any internal defect he discerns in our ways of explaining, which are not so burdened." This tempting argument involves two mistakes.

First, though the nihilist may have to start by consulting our inclinations as a basis for singling out factors he uses in explaining, he can learn to dispense with us. He can become adept at telling what we would approve or condemn in our literal moral usages, so that eventually he makes the corresponding scare-quotes distinctions on his own. No doubt, in the process of becoming adept, he imagines himself sharing in our desires, aversions, and associated genuine moral judgments. But this can remain pure imagining. He need not be converted to the making of moral judgments when, without relying on nonmoral redescriptions, he learns how we make moral judgments. In just the same way, I can gain an unavoidably nondefinitional understanding of the Italian Renaissance judgment of a person as a man of *virtù* while no more than imagining myself having the associated admiration. Or I can learn how someone applies the phrase "very nice furniture," without either discovering an adequate neutral description of what makes something nice furniture in his judgment or abandoning my conviction that this furniture is depressing kitsch.[3]

In the second place, the nihilist's need to consult inclinations of moral-judgment-makers would not make it unreasonable of him to deny that his dependency is due to the validity of the judgments distinguishing moral judges from nihilists. For the nihilist uses the responses of moral judges to locate individuals in a certain repertoire of personality types, as morally neutral as shyness or an outgoing temperament. The nihilist is interested in Jim's judgments as indicative of the inclinations of those with a certain personality structure, 'morally responsible' people. These indications help the nihilist explain conduct by attributing it to a person's having such a personality. By the same token, if someone, such as Joe, violates the judgments Jim would make, in spite of having adequate information, this will probably be due to the possession of certain abnormal traits conflicting with 'moral responsibility', traits that also serve to explain a variety of conduct.

Consider how an outgoing person might be helped in explaining conduct by observing shy people, becoming adept at imagining what a shy person's response would be. Perhaps it is essential for the outgoing person to begin with such observations, if he wants to explain shy people's conduct. Still, the outgoing would-be *Menschenkenner* need not regard the shy as having superior access to any nonsubjective truth. At most, he regards the shy as having superior access to the psychological processes governing their own conduct. Certainly, in using the shy person's access to shy psychology, an outgoing person need not make choices as a shy person would.

---

[3] Here and elsewhere in this section, in arguing that there could be adequate cognitive access to a virtuous person's way of grasping the facts despite the absence of shared moral assessments, I take myself to be criticizing John McDowell's moral epistemology, or (depending on how it is construed) setting limits to its significance. See "Are Moral Requirements Hypothetical Imperatives?", *Proceedings of the Aristotelian Society*, suppl. vol. 52 (1978), especially p. 16; "Virtue and Reason," *Monist* 62 (1979), especially p. 334.

My justifications of the rationality of nihilism do not entail that the nihilist explains the available evidence as well as we, when his explanations are distinctively nihilist. For example, in insisting that Bartok's departure is due to 'insight', not literal insight, the nihilist offers this rival to our explanation of Bartok's self-imposed exile: he left Hungary because of disgust based on equal concern and respect for those affected by the Horthy regime, but disgust based on equal concern and respect was not a basis on which he could tell that evil was being done. In fact, that Bartok's disgust, while due to equal concern and respect, was not a way of telling that evil was being done would be an anomaly, in need of explanation, and the nihilist cannot satisfy this need. He is a nihilist, not a cynic. He fails to recognize the need and the anomaly. However, his failure is not due to a lack of rationality or ignorance of evidence or arguments.

Of course, one can choose to call the nihilist's failure to share our assessment of certain processes as normally morally revealing "ignorance of evidence." But this will hardly contribute to telling how well his truth claims are justified. For consider our attitude toward Chenge's dismissal of wives' complaints or the Yanomamo husband's shooting an arrow into the thigh of his tardy wife. If failure actually to share assessments one can imagine deprived one of evidence, then our own judgment of Chenge and the Yanomamo husband would depend on such ignorance. In fact, our failure to make the judgments we might imagine making does not deprive us of relevant evidence, even though our own judgments depend on the failure. Assuming that we are anthropologically advanced, we have no less evidence to go on than Chenge or the Yanomamo husband, though we lack judgmental responses that they have. Similarly, the nihilist's position does not depend on his having less evidence than we, even though he imagines our responses without actually sharing them.

THE COHERENCE OF NIHILISM

An important objection to the possibility of nihilism is that the nihilist, as described, accepts so much that he must accept our moral judgments as we intend them. After all, in two respects, the analogy with talk of 'saints' and 'witches' is misleading. Full-fledged hagiology and witchlore include criteria for falling in the extension of the crucial term that nothing actually satisfies, in the disbeliever's view. But we think there are occasions on which moral properties are possessed in virtue of certain facts that we can describe in assertions that the nihilist would accept, as well. Caligula's having a little boy thrown overboard and beaten with a boathook until he drowned caused excruciating pain and premature death while satisfying no interest other than a desire for transient giddy thrills (assuming, as I shall, that Suetonius deserves credence in this report). A well-informed nihilist believes this, while a disbeliever in saints does not believe in the existence of the sanctifying contacts with God. In addition, most disbelievers in hagiology or witchlore do not think believers are rational to take literal saint or witch hypotheses to be the best explanations of the data. But the nihilist accepts our capacity to employ moral terms, in literal usage, to explain behavior, in explanations that we rationally take as best.—Accepting that the drowning of the boy has its salient features, accepting that no rational moral judge could regard the act as other than wrong, and accepting that those engaged in moral judgment rationally embrace moral hypotheses as superior to all rival explanations of data, how can the nihilist be said to deny that the act is wrong? Of course, it is the case that he would say such words as, "I do not, speaking literally, condemn the act as wrong." But this might be inaccurate self-portrayal, relying too much on his purely verbal inclinations.

Suppose our would-be nihilist would never take a consideration that he employs to justify his scare-quotes employments of moral terms as also, by itself, a reason for him to make a choice that we would associate with our literal employment, *even in situations in which the choice would have absolutely no costs to him.* For example, if one course of action would inflict great pain on someone else, while the only alternative would benefit everyone else but him, if he must choose between them (or can do so at no cost whatever to himself) and if neither choice would have any effect whatever on his own life, he would not choose the harmless course because it avoids great harm to another. Forced to push one button or another, he does not push the button that spares the child from torment because the pushing avoids inflicting great suffering without any compensating gain. Such a person is not just a would-be moral nihilist. He is a genuine moral nihilist. So the task of establishing the rationality of moral nihilism is accomplished if one can establish the rationality of someone who deliberates over judgments in the partly normal way described in the previous sections but never employs normal reasons for a moral judgment as reasons, by themselves, for a corresponding choice in a situation where such choice would be costfree.

Suppose that someone is not concerned in the least with harm to other people, as such. He may be concerned at harm to his pal, but only, if at all, because this person is his pal. He does not care in the least whether or not a stranger is subjected to intense and unmotivated torture. If a rational person were so radically unconcerned, then normal moral reasons would not, as such, be his grounds for costfree choices. So the question of rational nihilism depends, in turn, on the possibility of a rational person's being so unconcerned. Denials of such a possibility will turn out to confuse one reassuring impossibility with another. Moral nihilism is compatible with rationality.

Obviously, rational people differ in degree in their concern for others. So there is a burden of proof on anyone who thinks that zero degree of concern for people as such is incompatible with rationality. Given his overt rejection of standard moral judgments, such irrationality in the nihilist would consist of relevant conflict with what he would want as a result of rational, informed deliberation. If rational informed deliberation would lead one to give up an attitude or, in any case, to neglect it in one's choices, then, when one might have entered into the deliberation, one was irrational because of this attitude (for example, this desire, concern or lack of concern). The teenager who wants long life and wants to drive after heavy drinking is an example. In principle, an analogous irrationality in any nihilist might be established by an argument that assumes nothing more than desires and consequent needs for resources that any person would have in any life-situation in which moral judgment would be appropriate. Still, the argument must describe a deliberation which bases the abandonment or neglect of radical unconcern on some desires or goals of any nihilist at the start of deliberation. If someone would not have been led to abandon or neglect an attitude by rational deliberation based on some of her goals or desires, then her having that attitude does not make her irrational. Perhaps she would be better-off without the attitude, but that would be to say that she would be better-off if she were a different person, not that she would be better-off if she were a more rational person.[4]

Nihilism does, often, have its disadvantages. But they are not of the right kind to exclude nihilist dissent from the sphere of rational, informed dissent. Perhaps the life-situation of every person would provide reasons, all else being equal, to try to become a different kind of person if one were a moral nihilist, at least of the paradigmatic kind I have described. Perhaps everyone ought, rationally, to acknowledge at least a bare chance of a need for interdependence with anyone whom one's choices affect: one might, just might benefit from her future voluntary cooperation, or cooperation with someone relying on her advice, and she might be smart enough to detect deep unconcern that would lead her to avoid the alliance. The moral nihilist will reduce these risks through deception. But his stratagems are costly to him and are not apt to fool all useful cooperators all of the time. The concern for others that would remove anxieties in others preventing their beneficial cooperation does not require extreme sacrifices. So the moral nihilist already has reasons to try to become a person with that much concern for others, rather as an irritable person may have reason to try to become less irritable, reasons consisting of his present desires for companionship. This is a reassuring consequence of Hobbes' answer to the fool who saith in his heart there is no justice, an answer recently elaborated with great subtlety and useful detail by Gauthier.[5]

---

[4] I will return to these somewhat contentious topics in chapter 9. There is a concise yet extremely nuanced description of the required connection between deliberative conclusion and motivational starting-point in Bernard Williams, "Internal and External Reasons," *Moral Luck* (Cambridge: Cambridge University Press, 1981).

[5] See *Leviathan*, chapter 15, David Gauthier, *Morals by Agreement* (Oxford: Oxford University Press, 1986), chapter 6.

The Hobbesian argument is reassuring to us because, given our desires and our powers, it shows that we are not foolish to continue to be people who have some concern for humans as such. However, directed at people different from us, with special desires and powers, the same argument might not dictate such concern. Perhaps someone greatly enjoys some activities requiring harm to others and has sufficient self-protective power to forgo opportunities for cooperation beyond a limited circle of potential allies. Caligula may have been such, and so may the more eager members of the Eagle and the Jaguar clubs among the Aztecs, teams for catching human sacrifices. Despite the self-protective power, radical unconcern for people in general will still create some risk that desired cooperation might not be forthcoming. However, the abandonment or neglect of the radical unconcern would require forgoing some of the harmful enjoyments. The risk of losses of the second kind might always be serious enough to outweigh the (tiny) risk of losses of the first kind, in the rational deliberations of such a well-protected callous person.

Still, even in these exceptional circumstances, other reasons for not being a nihilist may intrude. Emperor or peasant, one's enjoyment of life depends on more than the bare undergoing of experience. One also needs the secure possession of an enduring self in the emotional sense. Through such self-possession, one can engage with one's own activity and its consequences, without being so uncentered that one loses the boundary between oneself and one's world. In secure possession of oneself, one finds it relatively easy to avoid the psychic perils of detachment and of engulfment. Very likely, the acquisition and preservation of this sense of self requires relationships of mutual concern with others. These others are, most importantly, particular intimates. But they have been accepted as intimates over the course of time. One will hardly have a secure sense of self if infantile psychological merger with one's mother is one's last acquisition of caring acquaintance. So someone who can enjoy life will be someone who has been open to new relationships in which he is concerned for another. Probably, this openness requires enough initial positive interest to make one care a bit about all whom one affects, all else being equal. So a moral nihilist would in fact have reason to try to become a person who is not a moral nihilist, viz., a securely self-possessed person.[6]

These are good reasons for us not to regret not being moral nihilists. But they do not show that a rational person could not be a moral nihilist. They fail to do so because of the difficulties of self-transformation. Even the banal analogue, the project of becoming a less irritable person, is difficult. The choice of new, initially disturbing circumstances, psychotherapy, even psychotropic drugs could contribute to becoming substantially less irritable. But

---

[6] I develop this second line of reassuring argument, with further references to the psychological literature, in "Rights or Consequences," *Midwest Studies in Philosophy* 7 (1982); see especially pp. 157–59. Peter Railton advances similar considerations at the end of "Alienation, Consequentialism and the Demands of Morality," *Philosophy & Public Affairs* (1984), pp. 168–70.

the costs of transformation may be too great to justify the eventual gains. And certain traits, say, cheery openness, may be unattainable, at any cost.

The dismal record of the best attempts to cure utter psychopaths imply enormous difficulties, at the very least, in transforming deep-seated, radical unconcern with people in general. Surely, it is conceivable that a moral nihilist who has considerable self-protective power might rationally choose not to transform himself in light of the costs and prospects. Such a person could confront our moral judgments, genuinely rejecting all of them, without irrationality or ignorance.

Thus, reflections on cooperation and on the self support the following conclusion: any possible outlook which is a clear case of understanding, informed rejection of all our moral judgments is sufficiently defective that no one who lacks it should regret not having it. Indeed, reflections on the self suggest that it would be irrational for any moral nihilist not to regret being a moral nihilist. If the issue were whether concern for others as such was desirable, these would be the relevant facts of rationality. But the question is whether every moral judgment that we make might be rejected by some possible person who is rational and relevantly informed. Here, the possible rationality of someone who is, for whatever cause, in the nihilist's state dashes our epistemic hopes, even if it preserves our prudential reassurance.

The would-be nihilist, who verbally rejects standard moral conclusions, is a genuine nihilist if the usual moral considerations are never his reasons for the corresponding choices in costfree situations. This suggests that someone who does engage in our verbal practices would, nonetheless, lack moral beliefs if moral considerations do not provide her with reasons for choice in costfree situations. The suggestion seems to be right. The ascription of moral beliefs to such a person would lack an appropriate role in explaining what she does. Her indifference in the crucial choices is explained by the absence from her motivations of any distinctively moral concern for harms or benefits. So the explanation of her utterances must rely on this limited motivational repertoire: the desires explaining why she makes the usual moral utterances are desires to conform, to manipulate, to be left alone, or the like. The beliefs combining with such desires to make her utterances rational conduct for her are not the moral beliefs the utterances standardly express but nonmoral beliefs concerning what people like to hear, and so forth. So her utterances are not to be explained as due to moral beliefs, assuming that she is rational. And, short of special circumstances absent in this case, the explanations in which belief-attributions should figure are rationalizing explanations.

Evidently, there is an intrinsic connection between one's moral judgments and one's reasons for action: one's moral judgments must provide reasons for which one would make costless choices among courses of action. This intrinsic connection is sometimes exaggerated in either of two ways, one of them hostile to the construal of moral judgments as beliefs (often true beliefs about objective states of affairs), the other hostile to common sense about human limitations.

According to the first exaggeration, there is an intrinsic connection between moral judgments and reasons for action because being committed to a moral judgment consists of having a desire, perhaps with certain further psychological accompaniments; it would follow that making a moral judgment is not a case of expressing a belief, or in any case a belief of the usual sort, asserting the existence of a state of affairs. However, this absorption of moral judgment by moral desire misidentifies the source of the intrinsic connection. Someone committed to moral judgments must have certain corresponding desires because: moral judgments are beliefs; what constitutes the having of a belief is the playing of an appropriate role in explaining conduct (or other doings and happenings on the part of the subject); in the absence of certain desires, there would be no room for moral beliefs to play their appropriate role in the explanation of what goes on with the subject. This source of the intrinsic connection with desires does entail that desires and beliefs must both figure in the explanations essential to attributing beliefs. But it does not even partially reduce moral judgments to desires.

The other exaggeration concerns the scope of the constraint that genuine moral belief imposes on choices. According to the minimal connection that I have proposed, one's moral beliefs must provide reasons for which one would make costless choices. This minimal connection is very different from another, enormous connection that has been made. It is sometimes said that someone who can justify a judgment that she ought, morally, to do something must take the moral considerations to be overriding reasons for doing it; if her moral arguments sustain her moral judgment they also make it unreasonable for her to act in opposition to that judgment. If this were so, then it would be unreasonable to confess even a small local depravity ("I knew it was wrong, but I gladly did it"), while refusing to admit that one's choice was unreasonable. But this connection between reason and right choice seems mere wishful thinking. Either every failure to care enough must itself be characterized as unreasonable or a self-conscious decision to do wrong must be said to be unreasonable on the part of the person who does not care enough about the one who is wronged. Such wishful thinking is not required by the minimal connection. Indeed, the requirement that a genuine, rational moral believer must use moral considerations as reasons for choice in costfree situations leaves it open that the mildest enjoyment of what is wrong could make the wrongful choice a reasonable one. Loss of the enjoyment would be a cost.

Similar considerations help to answer one final challenge to my attempt to describe a clear case of genuine nihilism. The challenge concerns the need to distinguish nihilism from a different position, which might be called general depravity. Most of us are guilty of local depravities, in which we do what we believe to be wrong because of our nonmoral desires. The generally depraved person does what she believes to be wrong whenever a nonmoral desire intrudes. Genuine moral nihilism must be distinguishable from general depravity. For general depravity is the condition of someone who makes moral judgments, makes them yet does not follow through.

The distinction rests on the difference between the minimal and the enormous intrinsic connections between reason and right action. The generally depraved person cannot resist the slightest temptation that comes her way. Any cost that she encounters of not doing what is wrong is reason enough for her to do what is wrong. But still, the standard moral reasons to which she appeals in her utterances are reasons which would lead her to make the standard choices in costfree situations. In addressing these situations, moral belief can engage with explanation. In the realm of psychological explanation and, hence, the attribution of belief, it makes an enormous difference whether someone yields to the smallest temptation or requires no temptation at all in order to do wrong. Of course, the moral difference between these conditions is small. And we have the same reasons for not regretting our lack of either characteristic. This makes it tempting to suppose that someone who seems to reject all moral judgments, and rationally so, actually makes them but always rationally yields to temptation.

DESIRE, BELIEF AND TRUTH

Even the minimal intrinsic connection might, still, seem the first step on a slope too slippery for anyone who thinks we have access to moral truths. Perhaps the phenomena necessarily involved in moral-judgment-making are, all told, too motivational to characterize beliefs in facts. This thought is often in the background of suspicions that access to moral truth would be a queer process. It might seem that the psychological and social facts making us the moral judges we are are not the right kinds of facts to make us believers in moral truths; some mysterious, unnatural ingredient must be added. On such grounds, one might suspect that what we do in making moral judgments is not to form beliefs, properly so called. Alternatively, one might be led to doubt that what we do believe is that our moral judgments are true. Though both suspicions are misplaced, they are a useful stimulus in the task of grounding grand semantic categories, such as belief and truth-or-falsehood, in specific, recognizable human activities.

What conditions, satisfied by us, are sufficient to make us people with moral beliefs? If the answer describes ordinary features of our lives, moral belief is unmysterious. In answering the question, it is essential, above all, to avoid one-sidedness, for example, the celebration of certain highly general functional constraints as the whole story of moral belief, when they are only part of the story. In an adequate list of conditions, reasoning, choice, content and function will all play independent roles.

Someone who has moral beliefs would, necessarily, make choices on the basis of corresponding considerations in costfree situations. So, at least to this minimal degree, someone who has moral beliefs has corresponding desires, i.e., desires directed away from what he labels wrong or bad, toward what he labels right or good. Desire is part of the story, but by no means the whole story. To add a further, ordinary ingredient: a moral believer must sometimes engage in reasoning to justify her moral conclusions, i.e., her moral utterances and whatever choices she bases on moral reasoning. Suppose, on the other hand, someone always directly and spontaneously applies the right moral label, desires the right thing and does the right thing. Such utterly nondeliberative activity is the whole story of what he does in moral matters. Though we should greatly admire him, we should not attribute moral beliefs to him. For such belief-attribution plays no appropriate role in explanation. His desire that Congress not pass a capital-gains tax reduction (for example) is due to his belief that such a proposal is being considered, together with his immediate and spontaneous desire that it should fail. His desire, I will suppose, conforms to principles of justice but, by hypothesis, he does not have the desire because he thinks it conforms to any principles of what makes a policy just. In this person's psychological apparatus, all that is moral is desire. His moral utterances are best explained, in an emotivist way, as expressions of desires.

Admittedly, as utterances become more complex, a wholly nondeliberative explanation becomes inferior. When someone adds that the capital-gains proposal *would* be just if amended in a certain way what he does is to be explained in light of moral beliefs that he employs in deliberating over alternative possibilities. That complexity justifies the appeal to belief is to be expected from the fate of emotivism, which always looked artificial when applied to utterances more complex than unconditional labelings. For complex utterances, emotivism was only supported by philosophical arguments, bad arguments depending on positivist constraints on rational true belief.[7]

So far, there has been no constraint on the content of the desires and the deliberations. As we have seen, and will see later on in clearer detail, some such constraints are needed. For example, a moral believer takes the imposition of grave harm to stand in need of justification and does not take trivial and transient pleasure to be a justification. As Philippa Foot has put it, in the course of her powerful writings on moral belief and moral reasons, there could not be a people whose whole morality consisted of the belief that it is wrong to look at hedgehogs by the light of the moon.[8] It would seem that a moral believer must take harm, even toward strangers, to be a negative consider-

---

[7] I develop this diagnosis further in "Ways of Moral Learning," pp. 510–13.

[8] See *Virtues and Vices* (Berkeley: University of California Press, 1981), p. xii. I am much indebted to the pioneering work on moral belief, evidence and meaning included in this collection, especially "Moral Arguments" (1958) and "Moral Beliefs" (1959).

ation, benefit a positive one, where harms and benefits are of certain general kinds that moral believers universally consult. To these constraints on content must, of course, be added such uncontroversial formal constraints as the requirement that a reason why an act is wrong for one person be a reason why it is wrong for another with all the same characteristics, in a situation with all the same properties.

Finally, a full-fledged moral believer must undergo some of the feelings standardly associated with moral utterances, or must engage in some of the standard uses of moral utterances in coping with others when relevant problems arise. Perhaps it is enough to have feelings of guilt when one's actions have features that one uses to label actions as wrong. Perhaps it is enough to rely on moral reasoning as the favored initial means of resolving conflicts. Suppose, however, that my otherwise standard life had no such connection with moral feelings or copings. Then even a complex, deliberated and morally justifiable aversion might seem no more than that, a mere aversion like my repugnance at punk haircuts. It would not engage sufficiently with my experience or projects to be a full-fledged moral belief.

We meet these conditions in familiar ways in our ordinary lives. Meeting these conditions makes us moral believers. So no mysterious additive is required for moral belief.

Of course, suspicious people will now object that the motivational aspect of these conditions is so distinctive, so different from conditions for belief in general, that the outcome only constitutes belief in some special sense. But in fact, the motivational aspect is a standard feature of the conditions that make us believers in ordinary characteristics of the material world. For example, someone, otherwise resembling us, who would never have any desire to displace anything (including his own body) where displacement is possible and costfree could not have beliefs concerning physical distance. Since he is utterly lacking in desires bearing on displacement, he does not, even potentially, have hopes or fears concerning placement. What happens in such a person's mental life does not involve expectations concerning placement. So he would not have expectations that one object will take longer to reach than another, or that one will get in the way of reaching another. Though initially characterized in terms of nondesire, such a person lacks a standard kind of belief concerning the material world.

Similarly, appropriate connections with motivation are part of believing among scientists. Consider the grounds on which one could establish that some nineteenth-century chemists, such as Ostwald, used but did not believe the atomic hypothesis while others, such as Berzelius, both used and believed it. As late as 1904, Ostwald wrote, "[T]he atomic hypothesis has proved to be an exceedingly useful aid to instruction and investigation, since it greatly facilitates the . . . use of the general laws. One must not, however, be led

astray by this agreement between picture and reality and combine the two."[9]
Thus, he claimed to use the atomic hypothesis as a highly economic means of
summarizing empirical regularities, and nothing more. If this was the whole
story of his dispositions to use the theory, then he was a genuine, not just a
would-be nonbeliever. As we saw in the last chapter, a hypothesis can be used
for convenience's sake when it is not believed.

Suppose that Ostwald had been in Berzelius' situation, and had seen that
atomic theory, construed as an attribution of chemical combinations to spa-
tial hookups, would imply the existence of isomers, when this phenomenon
was not to be expected on the basis of currently established empirical regularities. Would he have taken these arguments to be reasons to invest time and
resources in a project that would only be successful if it established wholly
novel phenomena, of the isomeric sort? (Note that failure to uncover such
phenomena might not be significant at all. Perhaps one was just looking in
the wrong places.) If so, the interest in economic summary is not the whole
motivation of his dispositions to use the theory, and his profession of nonbelief seems hollow. Literal belief helps to explain the costs he would have assumed. If, on the other hand, the reasoning from atomic premises would not
even be his reason for choosing such a project over others that are no less
costly, when he must choose among them, then his nonbelief is genuine, like
the nonbelief of the moral nihilist. The explanation of his indifference would
restrict his desires to employ the atomic hypothesis to desires for convenient
summary of known regularities, and the like. These desires would then explain any verbal endorsements of atomic theory, as resulting from the desire
for advantages independent of truth combined with the belief that such virtues are possessed.

Berzelius did engage in a strenuous search for isomers, which put his repu-
tation in jeopardy and encountered the usual apparent dead ends. That he
took reasons entailing the approximate truth of atomic theory to justify costly
choices is our basic grounds for attributing to him belief, not mere use. If
Berzelius had claimed nonbelief, this could be dismissed as just a false philosophical gloss on his own actual attitude. In short, testing for genuine scientific belief is analogous to testing for genuine moral belief, just as one would
expect if they are attitudes of the same kind, though directed at different
states of affairs.

The other, nonmotivational conditions for moral belief that are not tied to
specific content also correspond to conditions for quite nonmoral beliefs
about the material world. Thus, beliefs about the material world are only
attributed when they play a role in reaching conclusions. Where I live, geese
fly north in the summer, but these nondeliberative creatures do not have beliefs concerning northland summers. Also, as with full-fledged moral belief,

---

[9] Wilhelm Ostwald, *The Principles of Inorganic Chemistry* (London: Macmillan, 1904), p. 151.

full-fledged belief about the material world must play an appropriate role in feeling or coping. Imagine someone who feels no surprise at all at sudden, dramatic changes in physical color (i.e., the actual color possessed by the surface of a material object) even when he has no means of explaining the change. Suppose, in addition, that he does not use color-utterances to cooperate in finding things. He is something less than a full-fledged believer that objects have physical colors.

In general, the attribution of beliefs is part of the project of discerning the rationality in people's lives—as Donald Davidson has emphasized, with famous insight, for many years. The conditions for full-fledged believing that are common to moral and nonmoral belief are aspects of this role in rationalizing. Belief only contributes to rationality in choices if at least some choices are, or would be made on account of appropriately related desires. Belief-ascription only helps explain if it supplies reasons on which choices are based. If it did not help to explain feelings or ways of coping, as rational responses, it would not be a full-fledged belief. Because they are aspects of belief-ascription in general, these prescriptions remain valid whether or not the belief is moral.

Truth without Pictures

Reassurance that the conditions for moral belief are nonmysterious might fail to end suspicions, of the following sort, that our moral judgments are something other than beliefs in moral truths. "The facts making for moral belief are not of the right kind to make for a belief that a moral judgment is true or false, at least if it is a moral judgment like our own. The belief-constituting facts could consist of people's deliberative employment of reason-giving principles, corresponding to their desires, with contents falling in the indicated, broad range, together with appropriate connections with feelings and interactions. Those who employ these considerations in these ways might be said to have moral beliefs. However, when belief just consists of engaged deliberative employment of such standards, its truth consists of nothing more than accurate indication of what the standards dictate. This is not what we intend to convey in our moral judgments, insisting, as we do, that rightness and wrongness, goodness and badness would, in general, be as they are if we employed different reason-giving principles. So our moral beliefs are not beliefs in the truth of our moral judgments."

Certainly, engaged deliberative use of reason-giving rules does not, in general, entail belief in anything beyond the fact that the rules themselves have certain implications. Thus, those engaged in playing bridge believe that the sole trump takes a trick and, if they are rational and reflective, believe that an attempted finesse is the appropriate play in certain situations. But these beliefs are made true by the actual rules of bridge, not by a state of affairs independent of those rules. (Even the rule about finessing involves appropriateness internal to bridge. In the relevant situation it might be best, all told, not to attempt a finesse, to avoid a risk of defeating one's boss.) So if there is a nonmysterious basis for being someone who believes in the truth of moral judgments, it must follow from specific features of the conditions for moral belief, not from their generic nature as engaged, deliberate following of reason-giving standards. Since they have this specificity, constraints that limit the content of reasons or goals involved in moral belief will be especially important.

In the practice that is sufficient for moral believing, people are guided in their choices (perhaps not overridingly) by considerations of harms and benefits, even to strangers, considerations that they are willing to generalize to similar cases, by which they govern their self-development or their appeals to cooperation. Thus, they characterize an act as right or wrong depending on whether they are inclined to uphold or oppose the choice of the act on a basis involving such considerations. This way of answering a question is an exercise of a capacity to tell the difference between right and wrong. It may not be an exercise of a perfectly reliable capacity to do so. As the epistemic plight of Aristotle or Chenge reminds us, it need not even be the exercise of a capacity that would be perfectly reliable in light of full rationality and information. Still, the capacity is good enough to count as an ability to detect the difference between right and wrong—rather as Aristotle's use of "*hudor*" displayed a capacity to detect water, albeit an intrinsically defective capacity on account of defects in Aristotelian chemistry.

Someone whose moral discriminations exercise a capacity to tell the difference between right and wrong believes in the truth of her moral beliefs, not just in facts concerning the dictates of standards she happens to observe. Belief in objective moral facts is implicit in her practice of discrimination, just as belief in objective fruit facts is implicit in the normal North American six-year-old's practice in discriminating between apples, oranges and peaches. By contrast, the only relevant discriminatory capacity of the bridge players is the capacity to tell what is laid down as a rule of bridge and what follows from the rules together with the goal of winning presupposed by the rules.

This way of connecting moral belief with belief in the truth of moral judgments provokes at least two different kinds of worries. One concerns the relation between the capacities for detection that determine the actual extension of moral properties (such as those I described in chapter two) and the capacities that just resemble them well enough that their exercise attributes the same properties. What is close enough resemblance? If there are, nonetheless, fundamental differences that reason and evidence will not overcome, why take those who respond in such different ways to be referring to the same properties? For example, why suppose that Aristotle affirmed what we deny in his judgments of certain hierarchies?—These questions go deep. They do not have satisfactory answers in any current theory of content. I will try to answer them in the course of the next two chapters.

The other, very different source of anxiety concerns the highly motivational character of the processes that I have labeled processes of detection. The paradigmatic processes of reliable moral detection, to which the other, good enough processes approximate, involve someone's consulting inclinations based on appropriate desires, resources, and strivings. This claim about moral detection is not a claim that one would make about the detection of colors, shapes or Hepplewhite tables.

The motivational nature of what is relied on in detection is something special about the connection of moral judgments, and other objective normative judgments, with beliefs in corresponding truths. But there was never any good reason to expect all such connections to be the same in kind. Nonetheless, the motivational character of these moral responses seems, to many people, to conflict with the ascription of true belief in objective states of affairs to moral-judgment makers. I think that this appearance is due to a temptation to which I have already alluded, an excessive urge to assimilate true belief to accurate depiction. The responses constituting moral detection do not, as a rule, resemble the moral facts detected. Bartok's disgust did not resemble the evil at which he was disgusted. In contrast, when he remembered a memorable performance, the music going through his mind resembled the music that was played. In an important strand in the development of modern philosophy, Hobbes, Hume and many others have assumed that a full-fledged belief in a contingent fact about the world external to the believer must be grounded in something in the believer resembling the alleged contingent fact. More specifically, resemblance was supposed to determine the simplest beliefs, while others were constructible from these simplicities by utterly general processes of abstraction, conjunction and the like.

Perhaps no philosopher alive today subscribes to a theory of belief remotely as pictorial. Certainly, there is good reason not to. The projects of construction dictated by the demand for resemblance all dramatically failed—partly for reasons that will soon emerge in the criticism of positivist philosophy of science. In any case, it would be arbitrary to insist on grounding in resemblance. No episode or process is unambiguous enough to represent an object of belief purely in virtue of resemblance. The music in the mind could be part of a belief that that performance of the Waldstein was fast, or that the end of the Waldstein sonata itself is fast. A single image could stand for a color or a shape. Something other than resemblance, some cause, context or tendency, is needed to complete the connection between belief and object. This granted, there is no reason to deny that the response that constitutes belief need not resemble the object of belief at all. These are familiar criticisms of defunct theories. But perhaps these theories still haunt the debate over moral realism.

Isn't It Dogmatic?

In my answers to the many questions of moral realism, every "yes" comes equipped with a "but." Often, our moral judgments are justified truth-claims, but other people could reasonably dissent from some of these judgments despite their possessing our evidence and knowing our arguments. Many others of our moral judgments are justifiable, in light of the evidence, in every framework for moral inquiry that has actually been employed, but even these might be rejected by a possible answerer of moral questions who is rational and well-informed. . . . But, on the other hand, no possible person who responds to moral questions by making moral judgments could dissent from some judgments in light of the actual facts.

Is this a judiciously mixed verdict, or just mixed-up? Important general approaches to meaning and justification would, in fact, rule out this mixture as attempting to combine the incompatible. In the next two chapters, I will develop and defend replacements for those hostile perspectives. However, one "yes, but" can be so troubling that a more direct defense is called for, right away. Many people think they hear a confused recipe for dogmatism in the mixed proposal that some of our moral judgments are justified truth-claims that would rationally be rejected by people possessing all our arguments and evidence, indeed, by people rationally employing frameworks for moral inquiry that have actually been employed. Justified truth-claims, they think, must have a universal warrant.

One could end worries about the combination of truth with parochial justification through a deflationary interpretation of the kind of truth that is claimed in a moral judgment. Suppose that the truth claim in a moral judgment is that the ultimate reasons in the claimant's framework of moral reasons combined with all relevant data dictate the judgment in question. Perhaps it will be added, at least for certain categories of moral judgment, that this framework must be shared by some appropriately related others, for example, by participants in a shared moral culture. Then the truth claims we make in our moral judgments are psychological or sociological descriptions. There is no special problem as to our justification for making these claims. And there is no special problem of the compatibility of our justification with an adequate justification available to dissenting others—for instance, others who say that acts are all right, when we say that the same acts are wrong. The truth they claim is a truth about the dictates of their ultimate reasons, which are different from ours.

This reconciling tactic is unavailable, in light of previous arguments about moral truth and moral detection. It would force an utter misrepresentation of what we do intend in our moral judgments. Those judgments, I have argued, are truth claims in their entirety, attempts to exercise capacities to detect properties. On the "compelling reasons" analysis, the truth claim I make in judging that something is wrong is, entirely, that the ultimate reasons in my moral framework combined with relevant facts dictate that the act is wrong (or prescribe condemnation, or whatever. I shall not be bothered by any potential circularity in the analysis). If that were so, I should always be willing to add, "But were I, and everyone else in my society, to have a framework of moral reasons dictating that the act is not wrong, when combined with relevant facts, it would not be wrong." For the state of affairs described by a moral judgment is entirely a relation between premises and conclusions (by the "compelling-reasons" analysis), and the claim we make in moral judgments is entirely a claim that a state of affairs is as we describe it (by the arguments about detection). However, our moral principles rule out this much permissiveness. If our moral reasons were more Aristotelian, they might justify the oppressiveness of late-Tsarist Russia as necessary for the concentration of leisure and resources that sustained the cultural flourishing of late-Tsarist Russia. But even if I accept this relation between ultimate reasons, data and conclusions, I certainly should not accept that if I were to embrace those reasons, Tsarist oppression would be all right. No, it would merely seem all right to me, and rationally so.

Once deflationary interpretations are abandoned, the existence of justified claims about moral truths strikes many people as incompatible with the denial of universal justifiability among the rational and informed. In particular, the attempt to ground moral truths on nonuniversal justifications might seem to make too much of the existence of good fit with framework and data, in just the way that the deflationary interpretation sought to avoid. The fact that a belief is sustained by the believer's framework of inquiry combined with evidence and arguments of which the believer is aware does justify his continuing to have the belief. But if the truth in which he believes does not consist of facts about believers' reasons, then the fact that he ultimately relies on a framework which has certain consequences when combined with his data is not a justification of what he believes. This gap is just one example of a general distinction: a reason that justifies believing need not be a justification of what is believed. After all, someone might believe that he will become wonderfully thin if he keeps trying to lose weight, his having this belief might be justified by its contribution to his healthier endeavors, and yet the latter fact, which justifies believing, would not in the least justify the proposition believed. Similarly, if the deflationary interpretation is wrong, the fact of good fit with background beliefs and data, though it justifies continued believing, provides no justification of the proposition believed. If the support solely consisted of evidence together with propositions that no one could deny except on pain of irrationality, this would be adequate, by contrast. For the fact that one can only fail to believe a proposition if one neglects relevant evidence or arguments or reflects on them irrationally does justify the proposition itself.

All of these observations about reason and truth are right. But they do not affect the proposed divorce between justified true belief and universal justifiability. The justification that I have for the proposition that Tsarist repression was wrong is not that this condemnation follows from the background principles I apply combined with relevant data. The justification is that coercive violation of people's rights to basic resources for self-development is a vicious wrong, even if it specially advances the cultural development of those most favored. Of course, I justify the moral proposition by appealing to moral principles I believe, but the considerations described by these principles are not the existence of good fit with my principles. Only a megalomaniac would have in his repertoire, "Failure to fit standards I employ makes a social system unjust."

Admittedly, my reasons for condemning Tsarist repression in spite of cultural gains for an elite would be question-begging in an argument with an elitist. To accept the mixed verdict one must accept that one side in a dispute among rational people might make a justified truth-claim that could not be justified by a neutral argument, i.e., an argument which begs no question separating the two sides. By the same token, the charge that the mixed verdict endorses dogmatism assumes that the absence of neutral justification just by itself makes a belief in a truth claim dogmatic. This is the charge that I will now examine in detail.

A dogmatic person is someone who believes a proposition that stands in need of justification, a justification that the dogmatic believer is not in a position to provide. So we have to consider what needs for justification are met in the case of our moral beliefs and whether, if these needs are met, the absence of neutral justification reveals a further, unmet need.

A need for justification always arises when one has a reason to doubt the truth of a proposition. Such criticisms are provided by the evidence one encounters together with the principles which one employs in interpreting evidence. So the mere fact that someone else has a reason to doubt, solely on account of different background principles, would not lead, by this particular route, to a need for justification. (As we have seen, this irrelevance of different frameworks does not mean that incongruity with one's framework plus one's evidence is one's only reason for doubting, in the final analysis. One's reasons are those that one's framework provides.)

Many of us are reflective and responsible enough to put our moral beliefs to the test of such criticism, seeking reasons to doubt them. Some of us have done so with sufficient rigor and success that we are in a position to say that some of our moral convictions can be defended against any reasons for doubt we might entertain. This certainly could be true of beliefs that separate us from Aristotle or Chenge. I have no reason to doubt that late-Tsarist oppression was wrong, even if the contribution to the arts that I acknowledge is a reason for someone else to doubt this.

Still, the absence of negative reasons, reasons why something may be false, is not, in general, enough to fulfill all needs for justification. In part, this is because the absence must not be based on laziness, the failure adequately to pursue evidence that could provide one with negative reasons. However, there is a more basic reason why the absence of negative reasons is not enough. Often, in morality as elsewhere, belief is irrational in the absence of positive reasons. It would be a confession of muddle to say, "The proposed reduction in the capital-gains tax is unjust, but I have no idea why, not even a reason for thinking that those on whose moral guidance I rely can tell just from unjust in these matters."

Most of the ordinary work of moral justification fulfills this need for justification by providing reasons why moral properties are or are apt to be possessed, reasons in the absence of which it would be irrational to attribute those properties. Though our workmanship is often imperfect, it is often good enough to provide us with the positive justification needed for a rational truth-claim. Certainly, the fact that my reason to suppose a moral property applies is not a reason for someone with radically different standards would not put me in the muddle of the person who asserts injustice in a capital-gains reduction but has no idea why the policy is unjust.

Notoriously, justification must come to an end somewhere, or else the demand for positive reasons would require infinite work. And indeed there are moral beliefs concerning which the admission, "I have no idea why" would not be a confession of irrationality. Compare the admission about the injustice of the tax bill with this one: "Informed choices made with impartial concern and respect for all are apt to be choices of what is morally good, but I have no idea why."

"I have no idea why" acknowledges a failure to come up with any justifying derivation from further moral principles. There is, however, a sense in which justification is required, even for such basic moral beliefs. There is a possibility that negative reasons might be encountered. The injunction against laziness requires that corresponding threats be met and overcome. And this process itself constitutes a justification.

The threat arises in the following way. Our basic moral beliefs, the ones for which "I have no idea why" is not a confession of irrationality, are diverse and the ones concerned with moral detection attribute reliability to a great many diverse moral responses. Any basic belief will be too vague or qualified to stand in outright contradiction to another basic belief. Still, when situations are subjected to moral judgment, it could turn out that there is no coherent specification of a basic moral principle, definite enough to permit the resolution of questions that the principle is meant to resolve, that does not lead to claims that are false, when assessed in light of other equally basic beliefs. Then one would have a reason to doubt that moral principle.

For example, I think that there are at least two reasons that can make a social system unjust, each of them a sufficient basis for condemnation. First, a social system can be unjust because a rational person affected by it, desiring free and rational acceptability to all similarly willing cooperators, could only accept her prospects in this system on account of coercion or misinformation. Second, a social system can be unjust because, as a whole, it avoidably guarantees grave deprivation for the vast majority in ways that provide only trivial benefits for a tiny minority. Even a middle-aged professional philosopher may be unable to justify these principles by saying why each is valid. They do not contradict one another. Such terms as "free," "similarly willing cooperator," "grave deprivation" and "trivial benefit" are vague; but this does not render either principle useless if I can find an appropriate specification from case to case, picking out properties in virtue of which the principle applies. But there is this to fear: perhaps the specifications of the principle of acceptability in some normal cases will accord a veto-power to a tiny, trivially benefiting minority in other normal cases, imposing grave deprivation on the vast majority. This would be a reason to doubt the basic principle of acceptability. After all, such deliberations give me a reason to doubt that reliance on my basic principles enables me to tell the difference between right and wrong.

Responsible, reflective people seek out such threats to their basic beliefs. Having specified a basic principle, so that it provides an adequate reason for moral judgment, they often, eventually ask themselves whether other situations might merit judgments contrary to the dictates of the specified principle, according to other equally basic beliefs. In this process of testing, they are specially concerned to seek out other situations and other principles that are apt to undermine the specification if any relevant situation and basic principle would. Conflicts do arise, and new specifications are developed in response. Eventually, many responsible, reflective people achieve long-lasting stability in the face of their search for conflict. They have engaged in an adequate search for negative reasons, i.e., for deliberations that rule out all the specifications that would permit the application of a basic principle. In the end, they have discovered no such reason for doubt. Showing that a process that might have undermined a proposition does not do so is a way of justifying the proposition. So even basic moral beliefs receive justifications, in the course of normal moral deliberation. Since the demands on specification result, directly or indirectly, from one's own basic beliefs, the needs to which these deliberations answer are not generated by basic beliefs which one does not share.

The general sources of the need to justify that I have described are the only sources of needs that a nondogmatic believer must satisfy. After all, dogmatism is a defect in rationality. Defective rationality does not consist of reliance on a falsehood in inference. Indeed, reliance on a falsehood can be essential to rationality, as when one rationally relies on directions provided by an apparently normal gas station attendant who has actually given a perverse misdirection. Dogmatism is a defect in one's ways of using reasons to get at truth which does not itself consist of reliance on a falsehood. Surely, the defects of this kind that merit the label "dogmatism" are the failure to answer negative reasons, the failure to seek them out, and the failure to derive belief from supporting reasons where unsupported belief is irrational.

Obviously, one can have (and we all do have) reasons justifying a nonbasic moral belief that would not be reasons for someone with different basic beliefs. Also, if one has established that evidence and argument would not end a moral disagreement, if one has justified one's own belief (should it be non-basic), and if one has sought out the most threatening criticisms sustained by one's basic beliefs, one is not epistemically lazy. So belief combined with the absence of neutral justification is only dogmatic if awareness of that absence of neutral justification would give one reason to doubt the truth of the belief. Since general principles of nondogmatic belief do not make the absence a reason for doubt, the relevance of the absence would amount to a specific principle, moral and epistemic at once: nothing is right, wrong or all right, good, bad or morally indifferent, unless every rational person aware of all relevant evidence would accept that it is so. Such a universalist morality is conceivable. But it is false and is not our morality.

The worry about dogmatism is so common and immediate that any attempt to lay it to rest should include an explanation of how it arises among those who approach the question without philosophical prejudice. There are, in fact, two natural confusions that produce concern that a moral belief is dog-matic when there is no neutral justification for it. One is an extension of certain normal expectations into unusual circumstances. The other is a con-flation of moral needs for justification with epistemic needs.

If a rational person disagrees with one's moral judgment despite awareness of one's evidence and arguments, one usually does have reason to doubt the judgment if one cannot develop a non-question-begging response. Most moral judgments are only rational if made for reasons. The rational dissenter, then, usually has reasons for making her contrary judgment. It usually turns out that her disagreement is due to distinctive claims that are relevant both in the dissenter's framework and in one's own. In such cases, one needs to show that those claims are mistaken or overridden by further evidence or arguments. Rational dissent is usually a signpost pointing to the need for a neutral justi-fication, an argument that one needs oneself to avoid dogmatism, an argu-ment that the dissenter would have to accept on pain of ignorance or irratio-nality.

However, the very special cases of dissent that we are considering have already turned out, on investigation, solely to depend on a difference in the dissenter's framework of moral inquiry. The rational disagreement is not due to evidence or arguments of which one was at first unaware that would provide one with reasons to reject the judgment that one first affirmed. So the exis-tence of this particular kind of rational dissent is not a reason for doubt. The concern that the absence of a neutral justification makes for dogmatism is an excessive, but understandable extension of a normally appropriate expectation: the expectation that rational dissent is due to considerations that would deprive one's belief of needed justification unless one could develop a non-question-begging response.

Still, the discovery that neutral justification is unavailable might seem to reveal a further need for justification, different from any considered so far. The further need really does exist in many cases. However, it is not the right sort of need to sustain the charge of dogmatism. For it is a special need for moral justification of certain kinds of choices based on the moral belief in question. It is not a need for further justification of the belief, without which the belief will be dogmatic.

Most moral disagreements arise among people discussing choices that would affect their lives or the lives of others who share frameworks employed on at least one side of the dispute. Usually, then, if one of us discovers that a disagreement is due to a difference in framework, beyond the reach of evidence and reason, she also finds that certain choices would be protested by others on moral grounds that do not depend on ignorance or unreason. The choices are supported by her distinctive moral belief, but ruled out by theirs. The moral justification for such choices must be specially weighty. For example, interference with marriage customs based on irrational beliefs in women's inferiority is easier to justify than interference with marriage customs sustained by a way of moral learning, common to women and men in the culture, that is neither irrational nor uninformed. Similarly, if there are fully informed, rational people who do not think that the origins and consequences of unequal economic success in our society justify taxing the more successful to help the less, that makes it harder to justify redistribution. These extra burdens of justification can sometimes be met, usually by showing that inaction would have serious costs, as well. Still, the absence of neutral justification is a morally important fact, making it harder to justify choices supported by one's distinctive belief.

Since the absence of neutral justification reveals a need for justification, one might think that belief without neutral justification is dogmatic. However, the need is not a need for more justification of the contested judgment before one is justified in believing it. It is a need for more justification of the rightness of actions supported in part by the belief, i.e., more than would be needed in the absence of rational, informed complaints. The fault at issue is not dogmatism, but intrusion on insufficient grounds. One will, undogmatically, judge such sufficiency using one's own framework for moral inquiry.

So far, I have been looking at cases in which the unobtainability of rationally compelling evidence and arguments is well-established: as with Aristotle and Chenge, there is no rational hope for such means of reconciliation. Usually, however, the discovery that framework differences prevent agreement in light of present evidence leaves it open that further evidence and arguments might make disagreement unreasonable, as has often happened in science. So long as the question is open, one has a moral duty to seek the neutral justification. For the use of reason and evidence to end moral disagreement may make it possible to avoid conflict or coercion through rational persuasion. And anyone who does not prefer the path of rational persuasion is morally defective.

There is, then, a prima facie moral duty to seek neutral justification of a contested belief, even when the present disagreement is based on framework differences. However, the defect of someone who does not seek out the neutral justification is a defect of intolerance, not of dogmatism. In any case, there is no rational hope that our disagreements with Aristotle and Chenge would be ended by reason and further evidence and arguments; the diverse frameworks cope with rationally expected evidence in self-sustaining ways. So our moral duty to seek a neutral justification ends, as most or all moral duties do, with the end of rational hope that the goal can be reached. Indeed, like many moral duties, this one is best understood as requiring nothing more than trying hard enough, i.e., investing effort in proportion to the moral importance of the conflicts that might be avoided.

Quite apart from worries based on excessive requirements for nondogmatic belief, the charge of dogmatism might reflect a fear of certain epistemic consequences. Rejection of a need for neutrality seems to make it easy for someone with a capacity for faith to remove beliefs from criticism by embracing topic-specific standards sustaining the beliefs. The floodgates seem to be opened to whatever a sufficiently resourceful fanatic believes.

Fortunately, we have means of keeping the floodgates closed. A dogmatic person is someone who maintains belief in spite of the availability of relevant criticisms, i.e., arguments for doubt in the framework he employs. Though it might seem easy to protect belief if the believer's framework determines what criticisms are relevant, this is in fact very difficult. For most changes in standards of criticism that would otherwise provide immunity force one to change the subject instead, on pain of irrationality, altering the content of what is believed.

For example, given modern evidence, one cannot become a nondogmatic believer in the biblical account of speciation simply by taking what the Bible says to be, by that token, true. To understand what the Bible says, one must rely on ordinary means of inquiry, to read words, to grasp the difference between true and corrupt or forged texts, and to understand events related in the book. Responding to further evidence in these ordinary ways, one will discover that different peoples, equally apt to be good and wise, have contrary scriptures. One will also discover regularities in the stratification of fossils that contradict Genesis, when subjected to one's ordinary means of historical reconstruction. If an omnipotent, omniscient being sometimes permits deserving people to have false scripture, what reason is there to believe that the Bible is not false scripture? If one's means of causal reconstruction accurately connect currently scanned marks on paper with events in ancient Palestine, why do they go astray when they connect currently scanned rocks with ancient life-forms?—If someone declares that he does not recognize a need to answer these questions, he is either confused, or unconcerned to use the Bible as a special source of insight into past events. Rejecting the demands concerning causes as irrelevant means abandoning history as the topic of a rational dispute in which one is engaged; one changes the subject from the discernment of the past to the expression of current attitudes of piety. But accepting the demands as relevant leads to the rejection of the biblical account of natural history.

Though the connection between standards of justification and topics of rational belief is rigid enough to prevent massive immunization from rational doubt, it is flexible enough to permit certain possibilities of immunity, conferred by particular variations among standards of justification that people have used. Aristotle, Chenge and modern industrial folk are, respectively, immune from certain criticisms because they do not employ certain frameworks that they could have employed without changing the subject.

It would be extremely suspicious if such immunity were only characteristic of moral disagreements. In fact, we have encountered a variety of scientific disputes among investigators rationally responding to the same evidence in which the framework of each side confers immunity to arguments that are lethal in the other framework. In some of these cases, it was even conceivable that the rational disagreement would persist if all the evidence were in.

Indeed, the framework differences in science are of the same general kind as the ones in morality. Each side takes the considerations offered by the other as relevant but overridden in the case at hand. Thus, Maxwell wished he didn't have to attribute force to imponderable matter. His principle might best be conveyed with a regretful "even if": "a change in the state of motion of a bit of matter is always due to the state of adjacent matter, even if the latter has no mass." Similarly, the delayed-action theorists wished they didn't have to acknowledge that inanimate bits of matter could be influenced in their state of motion across a total void with a regular time delay. In the disagreement over atomic theory in the nineteenth century, both sides appreciated the speculative risks of belief in atoms, but believers gave more weight to the explanatory gains. Similarly, the crucial differences between Chenge, Aristotle and modern industrial folk are disagreements in emphasis. All accept the same general categories of goods and bads. For example, Aristotle would never approve drudgery for the many if it were not a means to excellent activity for the few, excellence that we take to be a positive consideration. But when the need for trade-off arises, he responds differently. Most if not all of the moral disagreements that would divide us from reasonable people possessing all our data would arise from differences in emphasis among ultimate considerations.

So far, in answering the charge that justified claims to moral truth require reasons that would overcome all rational dissent I have not considered indictments beginning with general accounts of the nature of genuine rational disagreement. As it happens, theories with such general scope are the most important obstacles excluding the mixed verdict as an incoherent response to the questions of moral realism. It is time to confront these obstacles and replace them—and not just to answer a charge of confusion. The mixed verdict is most useful to philosophy as a whole in provoking a new account of content which shows why the verdict is coherent.

Chapter Four

THE OBSTACLES OF CONTENT

THERE ARE many reasons to suppose that the mixed verdict on moral realism is mixed-up. According to many theories of meaning, one person cannot affirm, as a true description of objective facts, what another denies, if both are responding rationally to the same evidence. Their different responses to the evidence in the case at hand are due to fundamentally different ways of responding to evidence, and this divide (the semantic theories tell us) prevents them from addressing the same proposition, which one affirms, the other denies. Indeed, the charge of incoherence is the outcome of all current general theories that entail a definite assessment of such alleged possibilities of genuine disagreement. So the mixed verdict requires an alternative account of content, i.e., of what a person asserts in a use of words. The alternative theory of content will have to fix the limits of genuine, rational disagreement in the different way that the mixed verdict requires.

The mixed verdict creates a need to explore the nature of content for another reason, as well. It depends on certain topic-specific distinctions between what rationality permits and what it excludes in the connecting of evidence with conclusions. For example, the person who claims to affirm that some acts are wrong while denying the relevance of grave harm was said necessarily to be confused, while the nihilist was said to be rational in negating all our judgments of wrongness. These distinctions fix boundaries of content: the first denies that a certain practice of affirmation, if rational, could attribute the properties that we attribute in our moral judgments, while the second allows that the nihilist does deny what we assert. Current discussions of content provide no rationales for such characterizations. So a partisan of the mixed verdict ought to hope that the alternative account of content that establishes its coherence also shows why the underlying topic-specific demands are not arbitrary. By the same token, she should not be happy with a defense of the verdict that requires the rejection of all systematic accounts of content—however sane and satisfying such tactics may be elsewhere.

First, I will survey the main theories that would make the mixed verdict semantically impossible. Then, in the next chapter, I will develop the alternative approach to content. The survey begins with positivism, and I will sketch some reasons to reject that whole perspective. Next, I will consider two post-positivist approaches, one connecting content with an appropriate role in explaining input-output connections, the other emphasizing the causal role of environment and history. I hope to show that each of these two accounts, though part of the story of how content is determined, becomes implausible when it is made into the whole story. Both explanatory role and environmental causation are assigned appropriate, though less than imperial realms in the alternative account of content, which emphasizes rational strategies in the use of words to advance common projects.

These promises come with a disclaimer. My positive concern is to develop an account of content in a relatively narrow sense of the term, extending to what is asserted in uses of words. Almost always, the subject of my own proposals will be narrower yet, the investigation of assertions made in public discourse, using words that are means of communication. Theories of content which are also worthy of the name can, and often do, reach elsewhere. The term is readily applicable to beliefs that are not assumed to be identical with what is expressed in certain words—and to emotions, pictures and other phenomena as well. Apart from some vague suggestions in the next chapter, I will not offer an account of these matters. Indeed, I will presuppose our normal fund of uncontroversial lore concerning what beliefs others have and when they are apt to be evoked.

Still, this disclaimer imposes less of a limitation than one might think. The particular questions about what the content of something is that are live and important issues in themselves are questions about what is asserted when certain terms are used in public discourse. For example, proposals about the content of theoretical hypotheses in science or of assertions about material objects or natural kinds are not countered by offering an analysis of the results of some personal undertaking independent of public communication. The propositions at issue are conveyed to others—whatever the tantalizing difficulties in describing just what is conveyed. Certainly, questions about the content of moral judgments are questions about the reference of terms as used in public discourse. No one has ever doubted that some possible person could adopt the rule that "wrong" should solely be applied to the act of looking at hedgehogs by the light of the moon. When Foot, in a powerful essay, doubted that this could be the whole basis for some person or community's judging an act to be wrong, she was, of course, concerned with the property to which the term refers in our actual public discourse. By the same token, the urgent question about moral realism is whether someone unburdened by ignorance or irrationality could reject judgments that we would make, similarly unburdened, using such terms as "wrong" and "right" to assert truths. Our relevant uses are, of course, the normal and public ones.

In all of these cases, we know a great many facts that are relevant to whether expressions are used with the content in question. As a rule, facts about beliefs, goals, responses and social and natural environments that could be settled without first determining whether people use expressions with the controversial content seem enough to determine whether they do. It is a troubling question whether Aristotle used "*dikaios*" to refer to justice or whether what Dalton would have denied in saying, "Atoms have no detachable parts" is what a modern scientist affirms; but what philosophically unproblematic research might tell us about their beliefs and environments seems sufficient raw material for an answer, if we knew how to use the material in the right way. My main effort will be to show how certain principles that are true of linguistic content in general can be further developed so that they answer philosophically urgent questions about specific limits of content through the use of readily available means.

POSITIVISM

Classical positivism is the starkest possible example of an approach to content and justification that would rule out the mixed verdict. By "classical positivism" I mean the doctrine that the methodological appraisals most important in science can all, in principle, be made by applying a canon of general rules which have the following features: they are concerned with relations of logical form, the relations originally studied in the theory of logical entailment; they are valid in all fields at all times; no one could possibly reject them except on pain of irrationality; in principle, anyone can successfully employ them to establish a methodological appraisal by rationally reflecting on the rules and on the meanings of the objects of appraisal. This assumption motivated the powerful work of Schlick, Carnap, Hempel and their allies, who dominated the philosophy of science from the late 'twenties until the early 'sixties. For our purposes, the most important constraint entailed by their assumption is imposed on empirical justification: whenever a truth claim is justified in light of the data, the data are evidence in virtue of certain relations of logical form connecting corresponding observation-statements and the justified assertion; these relations are described by a canon of general rules, the same for all fields at all times, acceptable to every possible rational inquirer, and applicable in light of rational reflection on the content of the observation-statements and hypothesis. As Hempel put it, near the start of an important essay of 1945, ". . . it ought to be possible, one feels, to set up purely formal criteria of confirmation in a manner similar to that in which deductive logic provides purely formal criteria for the validity of deductive inference."[1]

There was much perplexity and much creative argument concerning the content of these formal rules. At least in the case of mere statements of empirical regularity, the positivists expected instantiation to be the basic tie between evidence and hypothesis: the observation of a black raven confirms the hypothesis that a raven is black just because the observation-statement affirms

---

[1] "Studies in the Logic of Confirmation" in C. G. Hempel, *Aspects of Scientific Explanation* (New York: Free Press, 1965), p. 10.

an instance of the regularity. Whatever formal rules turned out to be canon-
ical, the analysis of meaning was, also, supposed to play a crucial role, not
just in showing that the favored canon should be accepted by all inquirers,
but in applying the canon. Analyses that would be the outcome of anyone's
complete and rational reflection would make clear the underlying logical relations between hypotheses and data, as when "water-soluble," "mass" or
"equidistant" were analyzed to show what observation sequences would confirm hypotheses framed in those terms.

If classical positivism is valid, it cannot be right both to claim that a moral
judgment expresses a true belief justified by the evidence and to admit that
others possessing the same evidence and grasping the same arguments might
rationally reject the same proposition as false. In the final analysis, all fully
rational truth-judges are supposed to employ the same principles in assessing
evidence. If they seem to disagree when given the same evidence, this must
be a mere appearance. No difference in evidence was responsible for the one
denying as false the sentence that the other affirms as true. Both ultimately
rely on the same general principles to move from evidence to conclusions.
The only remaining source of difference is some difference in what each
means which has a bearing on the difference in what each finally says.
Though each is concerned with the same sentence, each interprets it in a way
entailing different logical relations to the same data. So an accurate analysis
of meanings would show that what one affirms differs in content from what
the other denies. The disagreement was merely verbal, as in James' charming
precursor to positivism, his tale of the pseudo-disagreement as to whether a
man chasing a squirrel around a tree circles around the squirrel if the rodent
always manages to stay on the opposite side.[2]

Also, nontrivial distinctions between inferences from evidence to moral
truth-claims that a rational person could make and those that no rational
person could turn out to be unjustifiable in a classical positivist framework.
Any such requirement of rationality would have to be revealed by an analysis
of meaning, together with the rules of appropriate formal relationship. For
example, any intrinsic irrationality in denying that Caligula's atrocity was
wrong would have to be revealed by a definition of "wrong" which establishes
appropriate relations between wrongness and the causation of excruciating
suffering for mild pleasure. As classical positivists concerned with morality
were glad to point out, no moral claim yet made which is general enough to
be a definition and reductive enough to reveal the needed connections is remotely satisfactory as a definition. Appealing to Moore's "open question argument," they noted that someone could always take it to be an open question
whether everything meeting the proposed defining conditions is (for example)
wrong. This entertainment of a question as open would not reveal a failure to

---

[2] See the start of *Pragmatism*, lecture 2, "What Pragmatism Means."

grasp the meanings of the terms in which the question was framed.—Of course, people do justify their moral judgments in light of empirical facts. Accepting the rationality of this practice, classical positivists concluded that moral judgments are not truth claims. Other rules of rationality, appropriate to expressions of attitude or declarations of commitment would, then, apply.

Though classical positivist assumptions are still implicit in much current work, few people these days explicitly assert them. Three kinds of challenges, in particular, have made it hard to believe that evidence is made relevant by a canon of general a priori rules concerned with logical form.

First, even in the realm of empirical regularities, where it seemed reasonably clear what rules were in the canon, considerations of logical form turned out to license hypotheses that could not be warranted by a canon of valid standards of empirical justification. Goodman noted that for every observational predicate, say, "green," there are an indefinite number of other predicates making contrary ascriptions in all cases not as yet observed, say, "grue" defined as "green if observed up until now, blue if observed hereafter."[3] Rules of confirmation are meant, precisely, to justify beliefs extending beyond what has so far been observed. But an instance of a normal hypothesis, such as "All emeralds are green" will also be an instance of hypotheses framed in the non-standard vocabulary, such as "All emeralds are grue." Rules of logical form would only make data evidence for a hypothesis reaching beyond the data while making the same data evidence, just as strong, for a hypothesis that contradicts the first throughout the realm of the as yet unobserved. Such evidence would be no evidence at all.

The pursuit of a canon of rules of confirmation was also blocked in the realm of theoretical hypotheses, the most interesting part of science and the part most often in need of philosophical clarification. Hypotheses concerning unobservable entities, molecules, for example, cannot be confirmed by observing an instance. In a positivist account of empirical justification, the relevant rule will prescribe appropriate deductive relations linking theoretical hypothesis and data. But positivists never came close to finding a rule permitting the distance from data that theorizing requires without permitting too much. Taken by itself, a theoretical hypothesis usually entails nothing about observations. If entailment when supplemented by a further hypothesis were enough, then obvious nonsense would be confirmed. "The moon is made of Camembert" would be confirmed by the observed regularities in Newton's astronomical data, since it entails them when supplemented with the three laws of motion, the universal law of gravitation and other *Principia* premises. Indeed, supplemented with the best astronomical theories, "The Absolute is made of Camembert" has the same entailments as they do among current

[3] See Nelson Goodman, *Fact, Fiction and Forecast* (Cambridge: Harvard University Press, 1983), chapter 3, "The New Riddle of Induction" (originally, 1953).

data. This permissiveness would be especially frustrating to the classical positivists, since they wanted, above all, to unclutter inquiry by showing that extravagant utterances were unconfirmable, and, hence, meaningless as truth claims.

In response, one might be tempted to restrict confirmation to what is indispensable in the entailment of data and observed regularities. But then, vast stretches of perfectly respectable theory, which rational scientists freely apply, turn out not to be confirmed. For a century, all that was logically indispensable in Newtonian derivations of data was described by Kepler's laws, Galileo's laws of free-fall and a few other empirical regularities. But scientists were surely not irrational to employ much deeper, distinctively Newtonian principles in the explanation and prediction of phenomena.[4]

Despite these and other worries about the confirmation of scientific generalizations, their disconfirmation seemed straightforward enough. If a hypothesis, perhaps combined with further hypotheses already empirically justified, has entailments that contradict what is observed, then it must be rejected as false. Reflections on the history of science, stimulated by Kuhn's *The Structure of Scientific Revolutions*, have convinced most philosophers of science that this apparent truism was untrue. It is a routine feature of rational scientific practice for hypotheses to be accepted in spite of known anomalies, cases in which the hypothesis entails what is observed to be false when combined with empirically justified beliefs about background circumstances, instruments and the like. To mention just one gross example, up until the 1960's the expectation based on the molecular theory of matter would have been that no floor could bear any weight. Of course, it was rational, nonetheless, for a scientist to take the fact that she wasn't falling through the floor to reflect an inaccuracy, so far uncorrected, in the theory of intermolecular forces rather than establishing that floors are not wholly composed of molecules. However, no rule concerned with logical form could, remotely, distinguish between the many cases in which anomalies are rationally tolerated and the many other cases in which they disconfirm.[5]

---

[4] With characteristic insight and integrity, Hempel presented especially powerful statements of such doubts concerning his original projects. See "Empiricist Criteria of Cognitive Significance" (based on essays of 1950 and 1951) and "The Theoretician's Dilemma" (1958) in *Aspects of Scientific Explanation*. Clark Glymour, *Theory and Evidence* (Princeton: Princeton University Press, 1980), chapter 2, is a recent, trenchant assessment of the classical positivists' difficulties in accounting for the confirmation of theories. In *Fact and Method*, my own detailed assessment is developed in chapter 5, which includes criticism of Glymour's neoclassical, "bootstrapping" theory.

[5] See Thomas Kuhn, *The Structure of Scientific Revolutions* (Chicago: University of Chicago Press, 1970 [first edition: 1962]), chapters 6 and 7 for discussions of scientific coping with anomalies that first made many philosophers aware that traditional philosophy of science is ill-suited to analyze this aspect of rational practice. Kuhn's emphasis is on crises in science and the urge to resolve anomalies, but Paul Feyerabend subsequently emphasized the pervasiveness of tolerance

For the last thirty years, much ingenious work in the philosophy of science has consisted of efforts to overcome these and other problems of classical positivism. Sometimes the effort has been to develop a new account of the logical relations that are crucial according to classical positivism. Sometimes, the classical perspective has been broadened. The canon pursued is still supposed to consist of a priori, topic-neutral principles, but their content is no longer confined to logical relations. Neither response has led to substantial progress in overcoming the problems I have described. Belief in the existence of the effective canon of general rules of reason remains a matter of faith, not of rational hope. By the same token, appeals to expectations concerning the content of the canon should it exist are not an appropriate basis for rejecting the mixed verdict.

For example, many defenders of positivism initially sought refuge in constraints of simplicity. This was no desperate last resort, but an unforced response that deserved to be explored. "Green" does seem simpler than "grue." Confirmed theories do seem to simplify science. The unacceptable responses to anomalies seem to complicate science. However, for reasons that I sketched in chapter two, general descriptions of the constraints in terms of logical relations always turned out to exclude too much, as unconfirmed. On the other hand, the deployment of general rules imposing nonformal constraints of aesthetic appeal, convenience or familiarity would have licensed many foolish hypotheses and would have imposed a constraint that is unlikely to indicate truths about our messy and surprising world. The simplicity that plays a fundamental role in science is causal simplicity, the elimination of explanatory loose ends. Its assessment depends, indispensably, on topic-specific principles concerning prima facie causes. None of these principles expresses a mere definition. Some, such as the principles distinguishing Maxwell from Neumann, or the Galilean telescope-users from neo-Aristotelians, might be subjects of disagreement among equally informed rational inquirers. So this third kind of appeal to simplicity would break with the expectation of a canon of topic-neutral, a priori rules, and sustain the account of confirmation as explanatory comparison on which the mixed verdict relies.[6]

In recent years, the most influential conception of the canon has been positivist only in the broad sense of reliance on a canon of topic-neutral a priori rules. The most important rules are concerned with relations studied in the

---

for anomaly, even in routine science. See, for example, *Against Method* (London: Verso, 1978 [originally, 1975]).

[6] For futher discussion of positivism and simplicity, see *Fact and Method*, pp. 245–62. As usual, Hempel perceived both the need to rely on simplicity and the perils of such reliance. See his *Philosophy of Natural Science* (Englewood Cliffs: Prentice-Hall, 1966), pp. 40–45. Elliott Sober, *Simplicity* (Oxford: Oxford University Press, 1975) presented a specially detailed and wide-ranging account of simplicity within the classical positivist framework. (Sober has since become an important critic of this framework.)

theory of probability, not the theory of logical entailment. The approach is called "Bayesian" because its central principle is an elaboration of Bayes' Theorem, in probability theory. Put roughly and qualitatively, the central principle tells us that the probability of a hypothesis is raised upon encounter with a bit of evidence to the extent to which the evidence was likely given the truth of the hypothesis but unlikely given its falsehood. At least in standard versions, the probabilities—i.e., the prior probability of the hypothesis, its posterior probability given the evidence, and the likelihoods of the evidence on the hypothesis or on its rivals—are attitudes of a rational inquirer such as might be elicited by offering bets. The constraint of rationality standardly imposed excludes sets of attitudes that would be expressed in acceptance of a bet that would result in loss, whatever happens. (In any version of Bayesianism, the basic principle is not to be interpreted as a rule of explanatory comparison, according to which the history of evidence-gathering supports a hypothesis to the extent to which that history is better explained given the truth of the hypothesis than given its falsehood. More precisely, Bayesian comparison is not explanatory comparison unless explanation has first been reduced to an appropriate probabilistic relation.) Most Bayesians impose no constraints on prior probabilities and take the rational limits of empirical justification to be described entirely by the theory of probability-raising. The basic principle rapidly gives rise to similar probability-assignments among rational investigators who initially diverge, provided that they share the same likelihoods of evidence conditional upon respective hypotheses, remain committed to their likelihoods as new evidence is encountered, and receive new evidence which all characterize in the same way.

Could a broad positivism of a Bayesian kind permit the mixed verdict? It could, if the Bayesian positivism is sufficiently permissive of divergent evidential likelihoods associated with the same hypothesis. Aristotle, Chenge and modern industrial folk could be taken to disagree on the basis of the same evidence because differences in likelihoods have blocked convergence. Aristotle takes a certain pattern of flourishing and degradation to be likely given the justice of a social arrangement, we take it to be unlikely, and so forth. However, such permissiveness would reduce the possibilities of rational criticism on the basis of a Bayesian canon. Indeed, beyond a point, the permissiveness would be intolerable in an allegedly complete account of empirical justification. Suppose that, circa 1905, someone through psychological fluke had come to regard Perrin's sort of finding concerning Brownian motion as more likely given the *falsehood* of molecular kinetic theory than given its truth. (In fact, Perrin's findings convinced even Ostwald that molecules behaving as the theory required caused Brownian motion through molecular bumpings.) The nonstandard expectation just happens to be his, and he does subsequently encounter Perrin's evidence. A theory of confirmation should explain why his claim of disconfirmation is foolish. If such demands are met by general constraints connecting hypotheses with evidential likelihoods that are part of their meaning, Bayesian positivism becomes as hostile to the mixed verdict as classical positivism. So it is useful for present purposes to test Bayesian positivism against the classical problems.

A Bayesian positivism would not overcome the most fundamental problems of classical positivism. They reappear in a probabilistic format. Thus, because of gruified alternatives, whenever one responds to evidence by changing the subjective probabilities that one attaches to as-yet unobserved phenomena, one would have been just as rational, on Bayesian grounds, to have expressed an inclination to change the subjective probabilities in just the reverse direction. This is Goodman's problem formulated probabilistically (a radical version of the case of the Brownian fool in the last paragraph), and it has no better prospect of solution in Bayesian positivism than in classical positivism. Also, Bayesian raising and lowering of probabilities would always lead to a preference for total agnosticism concerning theories, combined with a high degree of belief in some set of superficial empirical regularities. If Bayesianism has anything to say about the empirical justification of theories, it must associate the raising and lowering of their probabilities with the satisfaction and frustration of observational expectations based on the theories. Because of mistakes in fixing the theoretical parameters affecting such expectations, some such expectations are always thwarted in ways that lower the probability of the theory without lowering the probability of a catalog of superficial regularities. (If accurate description of the theoretical magnitudes were not a relatively difficult task, then the hypothesis in question would not be a theoretical claim as opposed to a statement of empirical regularity—however this much-contested line is drawn.) The need to permit confirmation of some theories, but only some, in spite of this special vulnerability is just the probabilistic version of the old problem of showing how confirmation can go beyond the observable.

Finally, drawing the line between reasonable and unreasonable tolerance of empirical anomalies is as important and as overwhelming a challenge to Bayesian positivism as it was to the classical version. The standard Bayesian assumption is that evidential likelihoods are to be held fixed as evidence is encountered. This amounts to an absolute prohibition of the tolerant response to empirical anomalies: "These aren't the data to be expected given the truth of the theory; apparently there is something wrong with the auxiliary hypotheses on which I rely in deriving expectations from theories, though I have no idea what is wrong." Prohibiting all such ad hoc adjustments would force abandonment of virtually all theories at times when they are in fact rationally held. However, without some general rule distinguishing cases in which likelihoods may be adjusted from cases in which they ought to be rigid, the Bayesian principle does not distinguish rational from nonrational changes in probabilities in light of evidence. This is the old problem of distinguishing acceptable from unacceptable tolerance of anomalies, and it is no closer to solution in a new, probabilistic positivism.[7]

Is there a nonpositivist account of empirical justification that copes with these and other problems, and provides an adequate basis for the rational criticism of scientific practice? I have already sketched one account which I developed and defended further in *Fact and Method*, a theory of empirical justification as explanatory comparison, comparison relying on a framework which, indispensably, includes topic-specific principles. According to this alternative, the normal goal in the justification of scientific hypotheses is a fair argument that the best explanation of the history of data-gathering and theorizing so far entails the approximate truth of the favored hypothesis and the basic falsehood of its rivals. Fairness, here, is the provision of an argument for superiority that is rationally compelling in all frameworks actually employed by partisans of rival hypotheses. Since this is the normal goal of scientific justification, it might as well be associated with "confirmation," the favored term of philosophers of science discussing empirical justification. However, empirical justification sometimes achieves less, sometimes more in scientific practice. Sometimes, a fair argument is unavailable yet both sides to a genuine disagreement are justified in light of the evidence. As in the disagreement between Maxwell and Neumann, each can demonstrate the superior explanatory capacity of the favored hypothesis, but not in a framework-neutral way. Finally, triumph in explanatory comparison is sometimes fair to all possible frameworks, i.e., it relies on principles (still, largely topic-specific) that no one possessing current evidence could reject without showing a failure to grasp the concepts employed in the triumphant argument.

Defending this account in *Fact and Method*, I tried to show that it does overcome the enduring problems of positivism, both classical and newfangled. I argued that a presumption in favor of color constancy, as against "cruler constancy" (e.g., an emerald's staying grue) would be part of the framework of any rational person who has color, or cruler, concepts. An appropriate discounting of grue-hypotheses would follow. I showed how background principles that play a fundamental role in rational inquiry provide empirical support for well-established theories in ways that entail no license for speculative absurdities. And I argued that anomalies are to be tolerated if they are best explained as due to an unevenness in the development of different fields of science, an unevenness in which the crucial underdevelopment afflicts auxiliary fields connecting the theoretical hypothesis in question with the data at hand.

[7] Glymour, *Theory and Evidence*, chapter 3, "Why I Am Not a Bayesian" presents important doubts about the Bayesian approach. John Earman, ed., *Testing Scientific Theories* (Minneapolis: University of Minnesota, 1983) contains responses to these criticisms by Rosenkrantz, Garber, Jeffrey and Skyrms. In *Fact and Method*, chapter 6 is an introduction to the Bayesian perspective, chapter 7 a criticism of it, both with further references.

These are bare slogans, pointing to a very long case for one alternative to positivist accounts of confirmation. I hope that my frequent analogies between moral disputes and scientific ones, in previous chapters, have already established that the mixed verdict is at home in this alternative. Certainly, there is no room for an argument that what is empirically justified for one is always justified for everyone with the same proposition in mind and the same evidence at hand. Another, similarly receptive framework is Arthur Fine's Natural Ontological Attitude.[8] What is important for present purposes is that these receptive alternatives are live options at present. In contrast, a positivist account of rational scientific inquiry would be so burdened by long-standing, centrally important problems that it would not be an acceptable basis for rejecting the mixed verdict.

THREE ASPECTS OF CONTENT

In the case for the mixed verdict, the dismissal of positivism is a bare beginning. Important criticisms of classical positivism have given rise to theories of content that would rule out the mixed verdict, just as effectively. Indeed, every current theory of content, i.e., of what determines what someone affirms or denies, which is definite enough to rule on the coherence of the mixed verdict excludes it as incoherent.

In confronting these post-positivist obstacles, I will try to show that they depend on a certain conceptual imperialism. A valid and necessary part of the answer to the question of how content is determined is made into the whole or nearly the whole answer. Such anti-imperialist tirades as mine are more believable and more useful if preceded by a vision of the right, harmonious relations, in which each aspect plays its proper, limited part.

One essential aspect of content is the explanatory role of the psychological state that is expressed. Someone only affirms a proposition if the explanation of what she does in her affirming attributes a state that plays an appropriate role in the explanation of her conduct and dispositions, overall. Far from excluding the mixed verdict, this partial answer to the question of how content is determined was essential to its defense. For in the discussion of nihilism, it was essential to showing that a rational, well-informed person with a thorough understanding of the terms of moral discourse might never affirm a moral judgment. The nihilist's states did not play a role in her conduct appropriate to moral belief.—Suppose, however, that content is said to be entirely determined by explanatory role and the standards of appropriateness are said just to describe appropriate causal relations among inputs, outputs and underlying states of an individual language-user. Then, the aspect achieves imperial

---

[8] See, for example, Arthur Fine, *The Shaky Game* (Chicago: University of Chicago Press, 1986), especially chapters 7 and 8.

status. As we shall see, the mixed verdict is excluded, as resting on an allegedly false distinction between, on the one hand, genuine disagreement, i.e., the expression of contrary beliefs, and, on the other, mere verbal disagreement, reflecting difference in the contents attached to the same sentence.

The second aspect of content is environmental causation. Someone is only attributing a property or rejecting its attribution as false if her usages are causally influenced by the possession or nonpossession of that property, influenced in a way that makes her a detector of it, though perhaps an imperfect one in the case at hand. The first aspect, internal explanatory role, is basic to someone's being a judgment-maker. This second aspect, environmental causation, is basic to that judgment's being a truth claim. This aspect of content was essential to my argument that we often make justified moral truth-claims. But, again, imperial expansion would convert support for the mixed verdict to exclusion. Suppose that the content of someone's references and attributions is said to be entirely determined by the way her usage is causally influenced, and such content is said to be fixed entirely by the existence of causal relations of the right general kind linking her usage with specific objects and properties. This causal imperialism will turn out to require a canon of general rules of right response that would make it a mystery how genuine disagreement could lie beyond the reach of reason and evidence.[9]

The third aspect of content is strategic rationality in the use of words (or other signs) to advance common projects. This aspect is the means of vindicating the mixed verdict, when all three aspects are assigned appropriate limited roles. Strategic reasoning establishes the general preferability of certain topic-specific rules for connecting utterances with beliefs in communication. The rationales are addressed to given common projects in which those utterances are useful and given common associations of those utterances. Utterances may have different environmental causes, express states that play different roles in explaining acts and dispositions, yet still have the same content because of a strategic rationale for using both to convey the same beliefs.[10]

Just as much as the other aspects of content, the role of strategic rationales

[9] Strictly speaking, appropriate *environmental* causation is only essential when the truth claim is not entirely about the subject's own internal states. If moral judgments are truth claims, they are relevantly external, so I will largely confine the discussion to cases in which insistence on appropriate relations to the environment is appropriate. The causal requirement could be generalized, however, since a truth claim about oneself requires causal interaction of a detecting kind with one's own states.

[10] Here, I assume that the terms are used to communicate with others. But the assumption is dispensable, when strategic rationales are used to individuate contents. The identity of the content of someone's private usage, employed in isolation from others, would be determined by rational strategies for communication with herself over time in enduring projects in which that isolated person engages. Since our ultimate concern is with philosophical disputes concerning moral terms used in public discourse, I will usually leave this alternative unsaid, though I will briefly explore it in a section of the next chapter.

can be exaggerated. Imperialist expansion would, as usual, produce distortion. For example, truth claims require grounding in detection in ways that are not guaranteed by the satisfaction of communicative needs. Since I see no great current danger of such imperialism, I will confine myself to using this social approach in its proper limited role, to justify limits to content, rules describing what beliefs must be associated with terms on the part of others who use them with the same content as corresponding terms of ours. Strategic rationales within our common projects will turn out to establish just the limits that are standardly prescribed in the well-studied cases of artifact terms and natural-kind terms. In the case of natural-kind terms, those limits will depend on appropriately external and causal connections, because of, not in spite of, regulation by strategic rationales. The limits of content in the moral case will turn out to be just broad enough to vindicate the mixed verdict, broad enough because of the dominant role of the pursuit of principled reconciliation in our common projects using moral words.

In sum, internal explanatory role is basic to someone's making a judgment. Environmental causation is basic to someone's making truth claims. Strategic rationales in common projects are basic to individuating truth claims, sorting out sameness from difference in content among the objects of affirmation and denial. I will develop and apply an account of the third aspect in the next chapter. The task of this chapter is anti-imperialist criticism which shows how theories based on the first two aspects alone misdescribe the conditions in which people address themselves to the same proposition, excluding the mixed verdict as one consequence of the distortion.

FUNCTIONALISM, MEANING AND WITCHCRAFT

Harman's theory of thought and language, in his book *Thought*, is an insightful and influential example of an account of content that gives priority to internal explanatory role. His account is especially plausible because of its relationship to anti-positivist arguments of Quine's. Any contrary theory of content will have to be compatible with these Quinean findings. Also, like all the best bold philosophical hypotheses, Harman's are not utterly one-sided. His account of content has a social dimension, emphasizing translation, and it admits environmental causes into the characterizations of inputs to be related to appropriate outputs. Still, internal explanatory role is given too much power in regulating legitimate descriptions of content. As a result, one would lose access to distinctions between beliefs and meanings that are important in general, and essential to the mixed verdict.

For Harman, the primary subjectmatter of ascriptions of content is the relationships, actual and hypothetical, between, on the one hand, behavioral outputs of the person to whose thought or utterance a content is ascribed and, on the other, inputs through which the environment directly affects this person, for example, in perception, frustration and satisfaction. A belief-state has its content in virtue of its role in the production of those relationships. For example, that someone believes that farmhouse cheddar is yellow helps to connect his perceptions of yellowness with his reachings into refrigerators, and this internal causal role partly determines the content of what he believes.

How should one specify the content of the particular belief that someone expresses in an utterance? As Harman is well aware, the bare functionalist theory of content does not yield a satisfactory answer to this question. One can never explicitly describe the totality of the relationships connecting a given belief-state with other states, inputs and outputs. Even if one could, there would be a need to explain why one's characterizations of the subject's inputs and outputs assign a certain content to what he says.

For Harman, the task of specifying the content of what a person affirms is a task of translation, broadly conceived so that anyone's "idiolect" stands in need of translation into that of any fellow-speaker of the language. In effect, one specifies what someone is saying by finding a sentence in one's idiolect that translates his utterance from his idiolect. According to Harman, a correct translation is the one assigned in a translation scheme that is better than any rival, "better . . . to the extent that it is simpler, preserves dispositions to accept sentences . . . in response to observations, and preserves similarities in usage. Each of these desiderata is a matter of degree and they compete with each other."[11] (Harman notes, in this connection, that similarities in environmental cause are sometimes to count as relevant similarities in usage.) An utterance in one person's idiolect translates an utterance in another person's if the two are matched in a sufficiently simple scheme which accurately and informatively answers questions of what the former would say in a certain situation given that the latter has produced an utterance in that situation.

To illustrate, with examples that are not Harman's but are in the spirit of his discussion: suppose that James would use sentences including the word "green" in response to just the observations that would produce the same respective utterances on the part of John. Then the paradigmatically simple instruction to associate "green" said by James with "green" said by John also best contributes to matching dispositions, including actual usages. Hence, the terms mean the same in the two idiolects. On the other hand, suppose that James only applies the word in response to observations that would lead John to accept the labeling "pure green," while John uses the term to label what both call "chartreuse" along with all the other surfaces that James would call "not green, but with green as the dominant part of the mix." The association of John's "green" with James' "either green or a color dominated by green" is not as simple as the identity-translation. But it does a better job of accurately

[11] Gilbert Harman, *Thought* (Princeton: Princeton University Press, 1973), pp. 107f.

matching dispositions to accept sentences in response to observations. The simplest association, the identity-translation, sacrifices some accuracy in matching dispositions, so the meanings of the color terms, though similar, are not exactly the same. "Two people can be said to mean exactly the same thing by their words if the identity-translation works perfectly to preserve dispositions to accept sentences . . . and actual usage" (p. 109). But the dispositions to accept given sentences and the situations actually eliciting the employment of given words are never just the same for any two people. There is bound to be some observation, for example, that would evoke reluctant assent to a color-term on your part which I would, after some hesitation, withhold. "To the extent that the identity-translation does not work perfectly, people do not mean exactly the same thing by their words . . . The only sort of sameness of meaning we know is similarity in meaning, not exact sameness of meaning" (ibid.).

In its emphasis on translation, Harman's account of content is highly social. Indeed, he proposes that communication be taken to be the whole subjectmatter of theories of meaning. However, given his account of translation, utterances have their content solely in virtue of individual language-users' dispositions to accept words in response to observations and their actual usages. In effect, one's specification of the content of someone's utterance is a commentary on the resemblance between these input-output relationships on the part of the other (or oneself at another time) and these relationships in oneself, i.e., their resemblance when utterances are correlated in simple ways. The appropriateness of the commentary is not due, in part, to some fact independent of the input-output relationships, any more than James' being taller than John would be due to some fact independent of James' height and John's. In contrast, in the account of content that I will ultimately develop, sameness of content will be due, in part, to facts about common projects and strategic advantages that are independent of individuals' linguistic dispositions in response to observations and their actual usages.

That different people never mean exactly the same thing, in using the same words, does not challenge any characterization to which someone would be strongly committed, philosophical inclinations to one side. For the matchups that we would ordinarily regard as cases of sameness of meaning will still be cases in which meanings are practically the same. The troubling conflicts with important characterizations are a further result of the underlying claim that linguistic dispositions in response to observations together with actual usages are the whole story of sameness and difference in content.[12]

[12] Harman usually employs the term "meaning," not "content," in the relevant passages in *Thought*. But he has in mind a very broad use, including "reference, meaning and understanding" (p. 59). My emphasis on questions of content marks off whatever aspects of meaning determine when people genuinely disagree or agree, so that one affirms (say) what the other denies. I hope

Routinely, people differ in their dispositions to assent to a given utterance in response to the same observations because of differences in background beliefs. If one person believes that there are Tasmanian devils in the neighborhood, the other not, or one believes that some dogs look like bears, the other not, the difference in belief will give rise to different dispositions to accept the sentence, "There's a dog." So sameness of dispositions in response to observations and sameness of usage cannot be the whole story of sameness of content if the following distinction is real: the distinction between differences in acceptance of a sentence due to differences in belief and differences in acceptance due to differences in the content that the sentence has for different language-users. Harman welcomes this consequence. He emphatically denies that there is any real distinction between underlying differences in content and underlying differences in belief. "There is no real distinction between change of language and change of view" (p. 106). The dictionary-entries established in a translation scheme are not to be distinguished from encyclopedia-entries in a catalog of someone's beliefs (p. 97).

It follows that there is no real distinction between a genuine disagreement reflecting a difference in beliefs and a purely verbal disagreement solely due to a difference in the content of what is expressed using words that are the same or that would be associated in the simplest translation-schemes. This is the troubling consequence of Harman's sparse apparatus for identifying content.

If the denial of a real distinction is correct, the mixed verdict is muddled. In our disagreements with Aristotle and with Chenge, each side was said to affirm what the other denies, rather than differing on account of partial differences in the meanings of terms that are only roughly translatable as "right" or "wrong," "just" or "unjust." In this characterization, and in the characterization of analogous cases in science, I made a distinction that is excluded by Harman's theory, and, it would seem, by any account of content in which input-output relations are the whole or nearly the whole story.

This distinction between genuine and mere verbal disagreement seems to mark a major, qualitative difference. So it cannot be explained as due to normal neglect of questions of small degree, like our characterization of most adult speakers of English as using "green" with the same meaning. Still, the disagreements that I discussed in the previous chapters are rare and extreme. One might suspect that any concern for a particular characterization of them would have to reflect some philosophical predisposition. But the conflict with imperialism about internal explanatory role affects ordinary cases, as well. The distinction between genuine and merely verbal disagreement is made in

---

that my shuttling between the two terms will cause no confusion, now that our different preferences have been explained.

ordinary cases, where it marks out an important difference which a satisfactory theory of meaning should allow.

John says, "George wore a green blazer and brown shoes Wednesday night." James says, of the same person, "George wore brown shoes Wednesday night, but did not wear a green blazer." We know in advance that John and James do not respond to observations in precisely the same way in their utterances of "green." But this leaves unsettled the question of whether their disagreement is genuine or merely verbal. Presumably, it is genuine if due, say, to James' relying on the report, "Wednesday night, George wore a truly revolting combination, a red jacket and brown shoes." It is merely verbal if solely due to John's using "green" to mean a broad range of colors including chartreuse, while James does not.

If the distinction between the genuine and the verbal only arose in connection with superficial classification of properties that we perceive in the most direct ways, perhaps the distinction could be explained in a correspondingly limited way which would not conflict with Harman's theory. But the same characterizations are important where the properties are not superficial or immediately apparent. Consider the trio, John, Heinrich and Jacques. John says, "Jacques is a marquis." Heinrich says, "*Jacques ist kein Margraf.*" Since the structure of the German nobilities was not quite the same as that of the English or the French nobility, a highly precise dictionary will agree with Harman's theory in assigning the respective predicates different meanings. But this hardly settles the question of whether John and Heinrich genuinely disagree. They do if the apparent conflict (the contradiction produced using a crude dictionary) is based on John's believing that Jacques is the direct descendent of Louis XIII's favorite marquis, while Heinrich thinks Jacques is descended from a long line of nonaristocratic con-men. They don't really disagree if the apparent conflict is due to the fact that the possession of superior political power is part of what Heinrich means, and John does not, in attributions of aristocratic status. Similarly, when I once said to a colleague (of someone in a very different department and field from ours), "He is a buffoon" and my colleague said, of the same person, "He is not a buffoon," it took real sorting out to discover that our disagreement was purely verbal.

In such sorting out, people often search for a single utterance which both are disposed to accept, which one takes to be equivalent to his or her initial utterance. Finding such an utterance, they assess the original disagreement as verbal; failing to, they assess it as genuine. As I have described the case of John and James, they could have found such further equivalents, and this would probably have been their means to a common assessment of their disagreement. The case of John and Heinrich is helpful in showing that such a process is not always available. For John and Heinrich might each be monolingual. And even if two people would normally be regarded as speaking the same language, the search for a shared equivalent cannot be assumed to be decisive without begging the questions about idiolect-translation that Har-man raises. If my colleague and I agree on "Prof. X is not bright" and I take this as equivalent to my charge of buffoonery, do we mean the same thing by "not bright"? If we can't find a sentence to agree on, does this reflect genuine disagreement or only a failure of our idiolects to be rich enough in paraphrases to supply this means of reconciliation?

The view that the distinction between the genuine and the verbal marks a real difference in the cases I have described hardly depends on philosophical predispositions. Presumably, an adequate theory would explain the distinc-tion in a way that makes it real and important. But a theory in which internal explanatory role is the whole or nearly the whole story cannot do this, with-out reintroducing just the distinctions between meaning and belief that such theories must deny.

It might seem that an appeal to background experiences distinguishes the two kinds of disagreements without distinguishing meaning from belief: John and James' disagreement about George's blazer is real just in case it is due to a difference in their experiences. But this will not do. Presumably, the differ-ences in the handling of "green" that result in purely verbal disagreement also result from different experiences, in particular, different experiences in early childhood. A relevant distinction involving experiential causes would have to distinguish different kinds of experiential causes. And the differences in kind cannot just be a difference in timing. If James is governed by lore he acquired in early childhood about Uncle George's horrid taste for red blazers, he really does disagree with Jim. To respond by distinguishing experiences that constitute language-learning from experiences that constitute acquiring beliefs about the world would obviously involve the resurrection of just the distinction that was supposed to be dead.

Of course, someone wondering whether the John/James difference reflects a difference in experience would not normally have any childhood experience in mind. She would be concerned with some limited relevant part of their experiences, directly relevant to the case at hand. Suppose relevance is de-fined in terms of some general epistemic relation, say, being the evidence whose possession explains and justifies the presence of the particular belief in question as opposed to its absence in a total belief system that is otherwise the same. One might be able to distinguish John from James on the ground that the experience directly relevant to what one of them affirms is different from the experience directly relevant to what the other affirms.—But then one must not insist that genuine disagreement be due to a difference in directly relevant experience. For difference in background belief could be enough. Perhaps hearing George saying, "I wore my favorite blazer" is the directly relevant experience for John and James, but each has different background beliefs concerning George's wardrobe and his attitude toward it.

Finally, note that Harman's taking similarity of causes as an aspect of similarity of usage does not help in accounting for these distinctions concerning content. In all of the cases that I have described, one party's linguistic dispositions and usage are governed, in general, by a different, though not wholly different, set of external properties from those governing the other's. In all of these cases, the particular disagreement to be assessed involves different responses to the same external situation.

CONTENT AND ANALYTICITY

On the face of it, a theory of meaning is defective if it does not allow important distinctions commonly made by practiced language-users. But the charge of defect can be rebutted. To deny this is to sing the praises of naïveté. The rebuttal consists of showing that the distinction presupposes a falsehood. Harman does defend his conflation of meaning-difference with belief-difference in this way. He takes reliance on the distinctions he rejects to entail the classical positivists' assumption that meanings are specifiable in analytic sentences, i.e., specifications of meaning that are, in a certain sense, incorrigible: any rational person could ascertain the truth of such a sentence by introspection; once introspective reflection on meanings has established such a truth, no further data, whatever its bearing on contingent nonintrospectible facts, could make it reasonable for her to reject her conclusion as false. Harman argues that there are no such incorrigible sentences. Analyticity, like witchcraft, does not exist, even though many are sure they can detect it.

The nonexistence of analyticity, in the indicated sense, is a lethal problem for classical positivism. The canon of rules was supposed to be sufficient to determine whether given observations confirmed a given hypothesis. But meaning-analyses were often needed to connect a hypothesis with observations stated in a different vocabulary. The positivists explained away this further necessity as superficial, on the grounds that meaning-analyses added nothing to the inquirer's stock of beliefs. This could hardly be said of fallible commitments about the course of nonintrospectible reality. Also, if there are no incorrigible propositions, to be revealed by introspection of meanings, then the status of the canon of ultimate methodological principles is itself incomprehensible. One is supposed to rely on these principles to connect any hypothesis with any data, confident that any possible rational person would, similarly, rely on them. So these principles must themselves be guaranteed by findings available to every rational person. What else, besides introspection, could be such a universal source?—Looking at positivism from a perspective slightly different from mine, but quite compatible with it, Harman emphasizes the centrality of the analytic in much the same spirit, at the start of his book. He notes that the appeal to analyticity was essential to the positivists' attempt to answer various forms of skepticism by showing that the skeptic assumed the corrigibility of what were really truths in virtue of meaning.

In all their projects, the positivists relied on semantic characterizations as the secure foundation for inquiry, prior to the tumult of empirical argument and immune from rational dissent. Elegantly and forcefully, Harman shows that the positivist assumption of semantic incorrigibility was wrong. With the collapse of this foundation, their other structures, which he characterizes as answers to certain philosophical doubts, I characterize as the search for a certain kind of canon, collapse as well. However, the existence of a real distinction between genuine and verbal disagreement, which was not introduced to advance the positivists' projects, is not affected by this collapse.

The distinction between verbal and genuine disagreement would be semantic witchlore if it were the distinction between differences that arise when people are guided by different incorrigible principles and differences arising in other ways. But distinctly semantic guidance need not rest on incorrigible principles. Consider this statement of meaning, which the positivists accepted as paradigmatic because of their respect for physics and because of their tactics in explicating relativity theory. Early in this century, a scientific congress established, by stipulation, that "one meter long" meant being just as long as a certain bar of iridium kept at constant temperature in a laboratory in Paris.[13] Though the stipulation did fix the meaning of "one meter long" for the scientific community, it was corrigible, in principle, from the start. It was corrigible, and not merely changeable by canceling this stipulation and setting up a new convention. For it might have been discovered that a previously unknown form of magnetic fluctuation afflicted Paris, affected the length of iridium bars, and could not be screened out. In that case, as everyone knew from the start, it would have been reasonable to deny that "one meter long" meant just as long as the iridium bar.

Suppose a second, breakaway scientific association had met in congress early in the century and associated "one meter," by stipulation, with a different iridium bar, kept at constant temperature in Buenos Aires. When Prof. A writes concerning a wavelength, "It is .16 m.", Prof. B writes back, "It is .17 m." If this apparent disagreement is solely due to A's being committed to the breakaway convention, B's being committed to standard fare, then their disagreement is merely verbal. It is merely verbal, not a conflict of beliefs, because it is due to different specifications of meanings. But those different specifications are not, either of them, incorrigible. So one can distinguish merely verbal from genuine disagreements without subscribing to the witchlore that meanings are specified in introspectible, incorrigible truths.[14]

[13] See, for example, Hans Reichenbach, *The Philosophy of Space and Time* (1927) (New York: Dover, 1957), p. 15.

[14] Harman accepts, indeed emphasizes that explicit definitions in science can be overturned by empirical discoveries (p. 100). Our disagreement concerns the relation between this shared judgment and his view that dispositions in response to observations together with actual usage wholly determine sameness and difference in meaning. This view, I have argued, dictates the

That the distinction does not depend on the witchlore is one moral of the story of how "meter" got its meaning. There is also another moral—or rather, a further clue to the nature of content. The actual stipulation only fixed a meaning as a result of social authority within a community. Its effect on the meanings of people's utterances might have depended on their participation or nonparticipation in relevant cooperative institutions, as in Prof. A's hypothetical attachment to the Buenos Aires Congress. Specifications determining what people affirm or deny may have that role on account of common projects in which those people participate, projects that the specification itself advances in relevant ways. This is the clue I will follow in developing a theory of content which has a place for the mixed verdict.

The rejection of analyticity is an important insight that ought to be preserved in any account of content, even though Harman's own account ought to be rejected. Yet it is easy to convert the insight into a denial of distinctions that are important to a valid account of content and essential to the mixed verdict. Some preliminary sorting out of advances from blind alleys is needed.

The rejection of semantic incorrigibility suggests that the following statement is valid.

1. A characterization of what meanings someone associates with words is, entirely, a characterization of a subset of his or her beliefs. In every case of meaning-association, the beliefs are not entirely linguistic, and are corrigible on extralinguistic grounds.

The "meter" example shows that linguistic characterizations are sometimes concerned in part with extralinguistic beliefs. Harman defends the general principle in arguments of great elegance and power. I agree with Harman that the principle is valid.

Principle 1 might be summed up in the statement that there is no real distinction between specifications of meaning and statements of belief. This is a good short summary, as such slogans go. But it is potentially misleading. It might also summarize:

2. There is no difference between the specification of the beliefs on which someone's acceptance of a sentence depends and the specification of what someone means by the sentence.

Principle 2 leaves no room for distinctions on which the mixed verdict relies. But the arguments against analyticity support 1 without supporting 2. The "meter" example suggests how 1 might be valid, 2 invalid. Specifications of meaning attribute a quite particular kind of belief, in which strategies for using words in common projects play an essential role along with extralinguistic beliefs presupposed by those strategies.

---

denial of a real distinction between genuine and merely verbal disagreement. Scientific ways of specifying meaning show that this distinction need not presuppose outmoded myths of incorrigibility.

"The Causal Theory of Reference"

The classical positivists thought that the semantic foundations for the rest of inquiry were discernible by introspection, and incorrigible once linguistic introspection had done its work. Quine's attacks on the assumption of incorrigibility, criticisms that Harman adapts to defend his theory of meaning, did much to destroy confidence in the whole positivist project. The old foundations were also devastated by arguments that assertions do not possess their content just in virtue of introspectible states of the language-user—or, indeed, just in virtue of any state that could exist regardless of the nature of the world external to the language-user. In these powerful and enormously fruitful arguments, Kripke, Putnam and others showed that the content of someone's assertion can depend on what external causes give rise to his or her use of words.

The pioneering discussions revealed the essential contribution of external causes in fixing the reference of natural-kind terms. That the contribution is essential is neatly evoked by describing certain counterfactual possibilities. Aristotle did, in fact, use "*hudor*" to mean what we mean by "water," even though he sometimes used the term to make statements about the essential nature of stuff with which we disagree in our "water" usage. Thus, according to his chemistry, water could not be the result of putting a spark to two gases.[15] So different beliefs about essential properties need not be a barrier to shared content. However, it is essential that what he labeled "*hudor*" was actually the same kind of stuff, in standard cases, as what we call "water." If ancient Greek seas, lakes and streams had been full of a special form of clear, nonintoxicating alcohol, tasteless and odorless in water's way, then Aristotle would not have used "*hudor*" to mean water. As one consequence, he would have not used "*hudor*" to deny what we assert in saying, "Water results from putting a spark to two gases."

Putnam, Kripke and others put the notion that reference depends on the facts of external causation to powerful uses, in inquiries into meaning, truth, communication and necessity. So their approach deserved a distinctive label, and "the causal theory of reference" was the one applied. For present purposes, the label is a misfortune. It suggests that some general description of a way in which a linguistic usage is causally determined is the whole story of what makes a use of language refer to something. More precisely, in such a causal-imperialist account, some general causal relationship is the whole story of how reference is determined among those who use language to express beliefs. (The latter, belief-expressing status might be possessed on the basis of

---

[15] Water is the cold-moist element in Aristotle's chemistry. A spark, hot and dry in its essence, cannot make two gases (two varieties of air, for him) cold and moist. See *De Generatione et Corruptione* II, 2–4.

functional role, as in Harman's theory.) The reference of an utterance could always in principle be identified by applying the general causal recipe to particular facts about the utterance in question.—The pioneering "causal theorists" never, remotely, made this claim. But it will prove useful to assess this second imperialism, which also excludes the mixed verdict.

The dependence of reference on external causation, for which the "causal theorists" did argue, hardly entails that some general kind of causation is the whole connection between utterance and referent in every case, even in every case in which a natural-kind term is employed. Still, the imperialist urge might lead one to pursue such a general causal recipe. The simplest recipe would be: someone (i.e., someone who is using terms to express a belief) uses a term, t, to refer to X just in case the presence or absence of X determines whether or not she applies t (i.e., whether she accepts, at least implicitly, an affirmative answer to some question, "Is it t?"). But this simplest proposal cannot cope with the elementary facts of sincere falsehood. Supposedly, I use "dog" to refer to dogkind when the presence or absence of dogkind determines whether I apply the term or withhold it. But I can, in fact, misidentify, using "dog" to refer to dogkind when I apply the term in response to a large shaggy cat under the table or when I deny a dog is in the room, overlooking the dog curled up in the corner.

Evidently, an imperialist causal theory cannot rely on the actual causes of an utterance to determine its reference—even in cases of reference to natural kinds, the home territory of the causal approach. Two different resources are available for fixing the theory, idealization of the actual causation and appeal to past history. Both tactics would exclude the mixed verdict. Neither works.

The first option appeals to causal molding of usage as it would affect the language-user should she function ideally. This is a tempting response to standard difficulties with the crude version. After all, my application of "dog" in a dog's absence and withholding in the dog's presence reflect defects in coping, if I use the term with the usual reference. According to the idealizing theory, term t is used to refer to X just in case any application of t would be due to the presence of X if the language-user was not ignorant of relevant evidence, was rational and (perhaps) satisfied other general norms of right response, as well. When I misapply "dog" to a cat, I would not have done so if I had responded in the ideal way.

Of course, it is trivially true that misapplication is a defective response. However, because it is offered in the context of causal-imperialism, the proposal says much more. Violation of the norms must be what makes the use a misapplication, and the norms must be appropriate to all terms that refer. This topic-neutrality is needed to satisfy the imperialist demand for a general causal recipe describing what it is that makes any usage have its reference. Thus, possessing nonretractable claws is a zoologically respectable criterion of dogkind, which might be used to determine that a doglike cat is not a catlike dog. But reliance on the criterion is only an aspect of ideal response in a particular case of language-use if it is already established that the language-user is referring to dogkind. So the relevance of the topic-specific criterion must be a further consequence of some general recipe for ideal causation, applied to the facts of the case at hand.

The requirement that such a recipe work would rule out the mixed verdict. According to the mixed verdict, Chenge, Aristotle and we all refer to rightness in genuine disagreements in which one side says something false, yet neither side is ignorant of relevant evidence or responds irrationally. In general, neither side falls short of the topic-neutral ideals required by the imperialist causal theory.—But this combination is an impossibility, according to that theory. If both sides responded ideally, the affirmations and denials of each would have to track the presence or absence of the respective referents. For the only explanation of mismatch is departure from ideal causal molding. But if both tracked referents correctly, neither would say something false.

Though the imperialist causal theory is an extrapolation from important anti-positivist insights, it excludes the mixed verdict in much the same way as classical positivism. And it should be rejected for similar reasons: it imposes excessive constraints on scientific practice.

According to the imperialist causal theory, there is an ideal way of responding to one's environment that guarantees referential tracking, so that the property to which one refers in applying a term is actually present. In short, ideal molding guarantees truth. No doubt, the ideal way of responding will include ideal access to evidence, not just our actual limited access. (As one consequence, this theory is opposed to the part of the mixed verdict that denies all rational hope of reconciliation by evidence and argument. Indeterminacy in light of actual evidence may not be a problem.) However, the ideal way of responding to that ideal evidence will be governed by norms that rational people actually consult. For there is no other way that we limited beings could comprehend a way of responding and take it to be ideal. And the attribution of reference is one of our actual achievements.

We are approaching familiar territory. Allegedly, topic-neutral norms which we now consult guarantee truth, when applied to ideal evidence. Why suppose that there are such norms? An answer is essential, since no amount of evidence leads to truth unless it is interpreted correctly. But otherwise plausible answers require relapse into positivism. Thus, it might be said that the norms are rules determining the truth claims of every possible rational inquirer, and truth just is what every possible rational inquirer would assert in light of all evidence. But this is a bad answer (perhaps among other reasons) because it appeals to a myth, the positivists' canon of rules.

To avoid this myth about rationality, one might forgo topic-neutral norms for current response in favor of the second option, reliance on historical origins. Presumably, I was taught how to use "dog" through linguistic instruction in which the term was applied to dogs. Perhaps the crucial causal molding is causal molding by the past. One uses t to refer to X just in case that use derives, through an appropriate causal process, from the introduction of t in an appropriate causal connection with X. Once again the mixed verdict is excluded. The differences in response of Aristotle, Chenge and us can be traced to different connections established earlier (in personal language-learning and, before that, in cultural development) between the use of the terms in question and various human phenomena. Causally, these differences are as substantial as in other cases where referents are different in spite of substantial overlap in extension. And the initial differences are transmitted to later usages in quite standard ways.

So long as the standards of appropriate introduction and transmittal are topic-neutral descriptions of causal processes, the imperial ambition is satisfied by the historical proposal. But the result is bound to be another myth, constraining change in reference.

There are important problems about which early events to count as part of an origin determining content. Perhaps in my language-learning days some slapdash adult pointed to a hyena in a zoo and called it "dog." That hardly affects the reference of "dog" as I use it now. But perhaps these problems can be solved by some non-question-begging requirement of typicality or of causal dependence in a learning process. The more obviously lethal problems directly concern the intermediate process that is supposed to make the introductory cause the referent of the current utterance. In general, causally continuous use can involve departure from first reference. No one has come close to providing a topic-neutral standard distinguishing the kinds of continuous evolution that maintain reference from those that change it.

In his pioneering work, Millikan used "electron" to refer to the kind of particle that bears unit negative charge, and current usage, influenced by his work, uses the term to refer to the kind, even when the term is applied, by mistake, in the absence of relevantly situated electrons. This is the sort of fact that makes the appeal to origins tempting. However, as Arthur Fine has noted, Millikan's eventual usage of "electron" had a different referent from that with which he and other scientists of his youth began. The term was introduced by Stoney in 1891, referring not to a particle but to the magnitude of charge, negative or positive, equal to that of a hydrogen ion in electrolysis.[16] Similarly, physicists continue to use the phrase, "centrifugal force," but not with the same referent as pre-Newtonian physicists, because of disagreements reflected in the modern truism, "A centrifugal force is not a force." Both continuity and discontinuity of reference can be sustained by the continuous usage of a term after it has been successfully invested with reference.

It might seem that these linguistic evolutions lack a causal ingredient that

---

[16] See Arthur Fine, "How to Compare Theories," *Nous* 9 (1975), pp. 24f.

is generally required, for an original event to regulate the content of subsequent usage: there is no continuous chain of intentions to conform to past usage. Of course, *successful* intention cannot be required here. Successful intention to use a term with the same reference as it had on another occasion is what the causal theory is supposed to explain. But is some mere attitude toward the past the missing part of the process, in these examples from the history of science? No, or not necessarily. Perhaps Millikan, or the physicists who persisted in using the phrase "centrifugal force," had conformist attitudes which are adequate elsewhere for continuous reference, as their usage drifted to a new referent. This would just be a quicker version of the centuries-long drift in the use in English of "villain" from a term referring to a serf entirely subject to an overlord to a term referring to someone of low moral character; presumably, parties to this drift had the usual English-speaker's intention to conform.

In any case, there would be a need for a further causal recipe describing a kind of intention required for transmission, if intolerable circularity is to be avoided. There need be no intention to conform to all aspects of past usage. I need not use "snake" to express the same alarm as my parents did, in order to use the term with the same referent. Adequate connection does not even require an intention to use a word to refer to whatever the word was used to refer to in all past uses of which one is aware. On every occasion in which I use "bank," I use it with purely topographic or purely financial reference, sometimes conforming to some past uses, sometimes to others. The relevant intention must be an intention to use a word to refer to the same thing as it was used to refer to on some occasions. A theory of reference should help to explain what makes an intention an intention of this kind. And all causal theorists do have this goal.

In response to the semantic discontinuities, an imperialist might combine the historical approach and a certain degree of idealization. He might insist that genuine continuity of reference involve applications that are forced on the language-user by the rational encounter with new evidence. Mere permissible continuities are not enough. But this would produce excessive discontinuities, constant shifts of reference such as the pioneering causal theorists meant to deny. Dalton thought that heat phenomena were controlled by atoms of caloric. Daltonians could have responded to the downfall of caloric theory by declaring that atoms did not exist, and introducing a new coinage (rather as taxonomists periodically neaten their terminological stables). The actual continued application of "atom" is merely permissible. But it involves genuine continuity of reference, nonetheless.

In sum, there is no way to fulfill the causal imperialist ambition. Actual current causal molding does not determine the content of what is said. One remedy, norms of ideal molding, requires positivist myths constraining rationality. The other, standards for molding by the past, requires post-positivist myths of ancestry, false constraints on change of meaning.

CAUSALITY AND MORAL REFERENCE

Is anyone imperialist about the causal aspect of content, or is this just a possible mistake, with no actual distorting force? Those who developed causal insights into reference certainly were not guilty of such excesses. Thus, Putnam's most detailed description of causal mechanisms of reference, a sketch of mechanisms by which "electricity" is connected with that physical magnitude, gave an independent role to speakers' intentions to describe a physical magnitude and conceded that an independent role may also be played by speakers' intentions to describe a physical magnitude capable of flow or motion.[17] Elsewhere, he suggested that the determination of reference is largely described by an account of social cooperation.[18]

Still, an attraction to causal imperialism seems to exercise important influence on both sides of the moral realism dispute. Granted, the worship of origins is not very influential, since it looks so artificial to single out a phase of moral learning or moral history as the mere introduction of reference, as opposed to teaching about the nature of the referent. But it is a frequent working assumption that moral reference would be established by a causal process guaranteeing truth in ideal circumstances, and hence, guaranteeing improved access to truth as more and more evidence is taken in by those who satisfy topic-neutral norms.

On the anti-realist side, the charge is often made that literal moral insight would be a mysterious process, since moral terms are not made to register objective moral properties by the processes that generally produce conformity

---

[17] "Explanation and Reference" (1973) in his *Mind, Language and Reality* (Cambridge: Cambridge University Press, 1975), pp. 199f.

[18] "The Meaning of 'Meaning' " (1975), ibid., p. 246. See also "Explanation and Reference," p. 205. The theory that I will develop also appeals to roles in social cooperation. Putnam's own investigation of linguistic cooperation has centered on the role of stereotypes, socially recognized prerequisites for minimal competence in the use of a term. Despite its usefulness elsewhere, the notion does not resolve our questions about the limits of content—and was not meant to. In late twentieth-century English-speaking communities one can, as Putnam notes, meet minimal requirements for linguistic competence in using "elm" by knowing that an elm is a tree, without being able to tell an elm from a beech. But perhaps in eighteenth-century English-speaking communities features distinguishing elms from beeches were part of the elm stereotype. Whether or not this might be called a change of meaning, Alexander Pope and a barely competent "elm" user such as I would have been agreeing with one another in saying "Squirrels sometimes live in elms." The suspicion that Aristotle and we, Chenge and we, or, for that matter, Maxwell and Neumann talk past one another would not be confirmed by establishing the presence of different stereotypes—which would be compatible with the same shared content as Pope and I enjoy in our "elm" talk.

of predicate-use to property-presence.[19] The charge presupposes that there is a general norm describing the processes producing conformity of applications and withholdings to presence and absence. The ease with which this assumption is made suggests that an attraction to causally imperialist views of reference is at work, no doubt among other distorting forces.

The temptations of causal imperialism sometimes influence the other side, as well, prompting commitments concerning the grand sweep of the history of moral belief which are wishful thinking, if my arguments in chapter one are right. Consider the vision of progress in Richard Boyd's influential and stimulating essay, "How to Be a Moral Realist." Boyd takes moral realism, which he resourcefully defends, to commit him to the claim "that there is a general tendency for our beliefs about the good to get truer."[20] This tendency, he says, "is guaranteed by basic evolutionary and psychological facts and it is just such a tendency which we can observe in the ways in which our conception of the good has changed in light of new evidence concerning human needs and potential."[21] In context, these claims about the good are claims about all important moral properties, including rightness and wrongness, justice and injustice. Boyd is defending a realism that extends to all these properties. He emphasizes general progress in knowing the good because he takes a version of nonutilitarian consequentialism to capture the truth about morality as a whole.

It would be nice to believe of our species that our basic nature guarantees a tendency to get closer and closer to the truth in moral matters. But even gross trends in actual belief are often not so nice. The flickerings of morally insightful concern for democratic cooperation in classical Athens were snuffed out by the Macedonian conquest. Outlooks endorsing extreme subordination characterized the Greco-Roman world for the next millennium. More generally, what we know about the moral outlooks of hunter-gatherer societies and technologically primitive agricultural societies indicates that Mediterranean societies more morally insightful than the Roman Empire were extinct by the time of the Empire or extinguished by it. The same considerations suggest that the Aztec empire, the Mayan empire (which itself became more brutal over the course of centuries) and pharaonic Egypt constituted moral retrogression. These are not little kinks in the overall trend.

Boyd is well aware of sad facts about the history of moral belief. His strategy is to explain departures from moral progress as due to the influence of factors of a kind that generally interfere with the pursuit of truth, in moral and in scientific inquiry.[22] Suppose the times of moral error were due to inadequate

---

[19] See, for example, J. L. Mackie, *Ethics: Inventing Right and Wrong*, p. 39.

[20] See "How to Be a Moral Realist" in G. Sayre-McCord, ed., *Essays on Moral Realism* (Ithaca: Cornell University Press, 1988), p. 210.

[21] Ibid.

[22] See pp. 210–13.

evidence or to interests which directed thinking away from available evidence and rational argument: were it not for these factors, the impact of moral properties on the usage of moral terms would have made the latter track the former more and more accurately. If so, then the tendency for people to gain insight might well be taken to be more basic than the phenomena of retrogression, even if the times of error are long-lasting.

This does seem to be Boyd's assessment of our history. It is just a more subtle form of wishful thinking, if the arguments of chapter one are right. The moral errors of Aristotle and Chenge did not depend on their departure from topic-neutral norms. If they had been fully aware of relevant evidence and arguments and responded rationally in light of this awareness, they would still have disagreed with us concerning truths that we assert.

Boyd offers strong assertions of moral progress as claims a moral realist must make. He offers no evidence to support them. Yet he takes moral realism to be valid. Why would an insightful partisan of moral realism burden the doctrine with such baggage? A causal account of reference is the basic reason.

"The reference of a term," Boyd writes, "is established by causal connections of the right sort between the use of a term and (instances of) its referent. . . . *Roughly*, and for non-degenerate cases, a term t refers to a kind (property, relation, etc.) k just in case there exist causal mechanisms whose tendency is to bring it about, over time, that what is predicated of the term t will be approximately true of k . . ." (p. 195). Governance by a common mechanism is what makes it the case that there is "a single moral property that we're all talking about" even when "moral concepts differ profoundly" (p. 186). Otherwise, "it will not be possible to assign a single objective subject matter . . ." One is left with "divergence of reference of a sort which constructivist relativism is best suited to explain" (p. 210. The passage leads to Boyd's strongest assertions of moral progress).

The denial that the troubling appraisals of Aristotle, Chenge and other apparent rational deviants are moral judgments is sufficiently strained that a moral realist does well to avoid it. Yet a contemporary moral realist will certainly say that the deviant moral judgments are false. So she will want to ascribe coreferentiality where the usages of others have the standard moral translations (just as Boyd recommends). But this preference has a troubling outcome if reference is taken to be a matter of causal molding. The troubling outcome is the epistemic wishful thinking in which important deviance is supposed to depend on departures from general relevant ideals of response or evidence. To have our moral truth without this wishful thinking, we need a means of establishing coreference that is not a matter of causal molding, a means I will try to provide in the next chapter.[23]

---

[23] Boyd's description of moral learning is guided by a moral theory, "homeostatic consequentialism," as well as by a theory of reference. I think that the moral theory also requires wishful

Detection and Charity

But is it really possible to avoid this wishful thinking given the account of moral truth to which I am already committed? The defense of the mixed verdict relied, in part, on a claim about detection that resembles Boyd's causal theory of reference. It might be objected that the resemblance is so close that the same wishful thinking emerges.

In arguing that we are justified in taking our moral judgments to be true, I took a true assertion about the possession of a property to consist, in typical and nonaccidental cases, of the successful exercise of a capacity to detect the property. Otherwise, I could hardly have said that one is in a position to make a truth claim just in case one is justified in taking oneself successfully to have exercised relevant capacities for detection. However (as someone might note in trying to turn the tables on me), Aristotle, Chenge, and all rational informed inquirers who have made false moral judgments have made true ones as well. It follows that Aristotle, for example, successfully exercised capacities for detecting moral properties. If he also made false moral judgments involving some such property then, it would seem, in such a judgment he exercised a capacity for detection under unfavorable circumstances. After all, he is exercising the same capacity as in his true judgment—otherwise *his* judgments would not have the same subjectmatter. So were obstacles in inquiry removed, he would arrive at the truth, employing his capacities; this seems to be just the conclusion that I rejected as too nice to fit the facts.

The misstep is the last step in this tempting argument, in which the unfavorable circumstances are interpreted as obstacles to inquiry without which Aristotle would have judged truly in the case at hand, as a result of his method of detection. Consider the crucial cases for the mixed verdict, for example, the cases in which Aristotle compared a constitution promoting a better life

---

thinking, in this case wishful thinking concerning conflicts of interests. If homeostatic consequentialism merely entailed that one ought to promote an objective interest when other objective interests are thereby advanced, and none is thwarted, then the doctrine might well be acceptable to all rational inquirers. But it would be wishful thinking indeed to suppose that an adequate morality needs only to cope with such homeostasis. Inquiry lacking the means to resolve trade-offs in which one objective interest requires the frustration of another would hardly be moral inquiry at all. I see no way to make the theory he sketches adequate to these tasks without making it a false moral theory. If homeostatic consequentialism deals with the trade-offs by enjoining promotion of some greatest aggregate of goods that are typically mutually reinforcing (typically, but not in the case at hand), then it will sometimes wrongly impose large burdens on a few for the sake of gains for many that are much greater in sum but small on the part of each beneficiary. I will return to this objection in discussing utilitarian accounts of justice. If, on the other hand, homeostatic consequentialism requires the promotion of fully cooperative social relations, over the long run, then it does not confront trade-offs between ultimate results and immediate impositions which may affect people who do not benefit from the nice end-state. Also, either form of consequentialism would be too demanding in matters of personal choice, for reasons that I will discuss in the final chapters.

for the elite with one promoting a decent life for the vast majority. The unfortunate circumstance for Aristotle's exercise of his detection capacity was simply the fact that a certain question was posed. The circumstance was not unfavorable because Aristotle's means of detection would have led to a true answer if obstacles to inquiry were removed. Rather, this is the sort of inquiry in which Aristotle's means lead him astray in the absence of obstacles. He has an intrinsically imperfect way of learning about right and wrong, and this is one of the cases in which the imperfection makes a difference.

Here, content has been determined by the assessment of an imperfect capacity for detecting something as good enough to be a capacity for detecting it, nonetheless. In all philosophically interesting cases, the task of setting limits to content (of determining when people address themselves to the same subjectmatter) is the task of determining when such charitable treatment is appropriate.

The recommendation of charity toward Aristotle's and Chenge's imperfections is reminiscent of Neil Wilson's and Donald Davidson's "principle of linguistic charity," which is sometimes understood in a quantitative way, as a commandment to find the interpretation maximizing the number of truths that the subject believes. But in fact, such a mechanical understanding of linguistic charity would rule out the mixed verdict, once again. To maximize Aristotle's truths, one would interpret his "*dike*" not as justice but as conformity to the arrangement devoting the most resources to the most virtuous activity, and so forth. What seemed genuine disagreements turn out to be purely verbal, in a way that makes Aristotle's statements more frequently true than they seemed, though less frequently addressed to our primary concerns.

This mechanical, quantitative understanding of linguistic charity is wrong, not just in the controversial cases of radical moral disagreement, but in other, less controversial cases as well. Perhaps the vicious falsehoods of an extreme racist could be reduced by taking "black" often to mean stupid, lazy or savage black, in his usage. We do not prettify his usage in this way, choosing instead the interpretation that helps explain his constant returning to questions of color when he is concerned with matters of political choice. We could reduce the incidence of falsehood in the statements of Laplace, Carnot and other users of caloric theory by taking "caloric" to refer to internal molecular motion. Instead, we interpret them as making claims about an incompressible fluid, increasing the incidence of falsehood, but preserving the rationality of their arguments for positing caloric.

The quantitative, mechanical recipe for linguistic charity fails, as one should have expected to begin with. We are seeking a basis for judgments that a means of labeling is close enough to our means of detecting something to be a means of detecting the same thing, though an imperfect one. On the face of it, "close enough" means close enough for relevant purposes, purposes which will, presumably, vary depending on the projects in which our usages and theirs occur. Limits of content depend on the charity appropriate to the various goals of our word-using projects. Let this be the final clue leading toward a more adequate account of content. It is time to convert clues into solutions.

Chapter Five

MEANINGFUL PROJECTS

FOR ALL their enormous differences, the theories I have surveyed rely on similar conceptions of content. The ascription of content is taken to be a way of
explaining how individual language-users arrive at their verbal conclusions
when their processing of information satisfies general standards of good functioning. The differences among the theories are differences in the kind of
explanation of processing that is thought to be revealing. For the positivists,
it is the description of a chain of inferences of the appropriate standard form.
The goal for Harman is a description of the internal states producing input-
output connections; further questions about content concern more or less
convenient ways of sorting these descriptions. In a purely causal theory of
reference, the environmental causes that would explain usage, if the user met
general standards for good detection or for guidance by authoritative past interaction, are the subjects of ascriptions of content.

These are all ways in which one might also describe a computer. Indeed,
each of these approaches commonly elicits analogies with computers (or, in
the precomputer heyday of positivism, related analogies with rules for calculation). In all of these very different theories, the ascription of content is part
of the description of how we would operate as well-functioning individual
computers, connecting inputs from the great keyboard of observation with
outputs on the great monitor of behavior.

There is another approach, in which content is determined by appropriate
use in projects involving communication. In the past, this approach has given
rise to Wittgenstein's emphasis on "language-games," appropriately structured
communicative activities, as the source of meaning. Grice's account of meaning in terms of intentions to convey beliefs through the recognition of such
intentions is part of the same communicative approach, for all the difference
in style. More recently, Burge has emphasized the role of the social environment and social norms in determining what individuals refer to, even in their
individual thoughts and even when they refer to nonsocial aspects of their
environment.[1] Such theories naturally lead to analogies with other cooperative activities, rather than effective computers.

I will be developing an account of content that is in this tradition. As an
alternative means of identifying the content of what people say, this account

[1] See Tyler Burge, "Intellectual Norms and Foundations of Mind," *Journal of Philosophy* 83
(1986); "Individualism and the Mental," *Midwest Studies in Philosophy* 4 (1979).

is a rival to the more computer-like approaches, fixing different limits on genuine disagreement. It will base these limits on strategies for advancing common projects involving the use of words. Instead of analyzing the processing of an idealized individual language-user, the crucial strategic rationales are directed at common projects in which interacting people use words and take as raw material for pursuing these projects shared associations of responses with utterances. Such rationales are intrinsically cooperative, and are often concerned with superficial obstacles to linguistic success that would disappear in the idealizations of the other approaches. (If, as is almost always the case, the projects are common to more than one person, then the rationales are not just intrinsically cooperative, but intrinsically collective. In the rare case of a wholly private linguistic project, content is governed by strategies for cooperation with oneself, over the course of time. I will usually neglect private discourse, since the most pressing questions about content concern words in public discourse.)

In this chapter, I will try to show that these rational strategies for advancing common projects fix the limits of content. They are the missing ingredient in the imperialisms that I criticized in the last chapter—or, in any case, a missing ingredient that is adequate to answer the most pressing questions about sameness and difference of content. It would be a tragedy, of a familiar kind, if on the basis of such success the old imperialisms would be replaced by another. This is not, remotely, my intention. We *are*, very broadly, computers, and descriptions of processings and their causes *are* the best way of answering many questions about content. Thus, talk of explanatory role is a way of describing what the state of an asserter consists of, the best way of combating the appearance that asserting involves some mysterious addition to action, the stream of consciousness and their causes. Similarly, talk of detection sheds distinctive light: it demystifies the ascription of true assertion; moreover, facts about the actual nature of what is detected play an essential role in determining the content of important kinds of assertion.

Still, the accurate, causally perspicuous description of our processings often has this limitation: it does not tell us when different processings are the same in ways that are of interest to us. For these interests are not, on the whole, interests in the accurate, causally insightful discernment of our processings. Thus, a true description of the neuromuscular processes in which Pollini's playing during a certain period of time consists would not provide a description of what makes that playing a performance of the last Beethoven sonata, a performance of the same thing as Schnabel played in his neuromuscular transactions decades before. In the description of language-use, there is an analogous need to answer questions of what makes different assertings and denyings assertings and denyings of the same thing. What fills this gap does not tell the whole story of assertion and denial, any more than our usual nonphysiological tactics of performance identification establish the irrelevance of physique to performance. But in both cases, interests in something other than processing dominate the identification of the content of the processings.

First, I will present an account of the connections between content and communicative strategies, an account that is rich enough to be useful in determining the limits of genuine agreement and disagreement. Then, I will test this account by applying it to obvious or well-established findings concerning such limits, including the causal view of natural-kind terms that sometimes expands into a causal-imperialist theory of content. Once these tests are passed, I will use the strategic account to vindicate the mixed verdict on moral realism. Finally, I will take advantage of the clearer view of moral discourse that the strategic approach provides, to describe the similarities and differences between science and morality.

COMMUNICATION AND CONTENT

In seeking help from the alternative tradition, Grice's account of meaning is a good place to begin. Adapting some of his proposals to our purposes (and ignoring the virtually infinite complications that his proposals acquired over the years), we can connect content with communicative intentions in the following way. In uttering the sentence S, a person asserts that p just in case she intends her saying S to be a reason for any relevant hearers to believe that p, a reason in virtue of the hearers' grasp of certain linguistic conventions and their recognition, relying on these conventions, of her intention so to induce belief that p. It is important, here, that the intended recognition rely on linguistic conventions. When I tell my little girl, "This is the messiest room I have ever seen," I intend that my words be a reason to believe that I am angry and intend that they provide this reason through the listener's recognition of this intention. But I do not use those words to assert that I am angry. This is not part of the very content of those words, when I use them, even though I am using the saying of those words to convey that message as well. It is not part of the content because I do not intend that my daughter recognize the belief in my mood, which I do intend to convey, by applying linguistic conventions to my words. (Grice would identify the content in question as "the timeless meaning in a language of a sentence-type, applied to a particular token utterance." Elsewhere—though not in this particular case—he tended to avoid appeals to conventions in his theory of meaning, but his reasons need not detain us.)[2]

What is the source of our prolific access to conventions, when we communicate? Such authoritative performances as a scientific conference's fixing the

---

[2] For Grice's basic account of meaning see H. Paul Grice, "Meaning," *Philosophical Review* (1957). For the elaborations see his *Studies in the Way of Words* (Cambridge: Harvard University Press, 1989).

reference of "meter" are rare. And, in any case, the source of their linguistic authority remains to be explained.

Granted, one is often aware of a certain consensus among all those with whom one expects to communicate. There are features, say, that every such person takes typical bearers of a term to have and expects others to ascribe. Such a consensus may provide raw materials for linguistic conventions. But much of this material is discarded or modified along the way. I believe and expect others to believe that all elephant populations derive from either Africa or Asia. But in saying that Jumbo is an elephant, I do not assert African-or-Asian-ancestry, even if I intend to convey such belief about Jumbo in virtue of recognition of my intention to do so by my utterance. For example, if the circus quiz-master challenges you to find something in the room whose ancestors came from Africa or Asia, I might helpfully whisper, "There's an elephant sleeping in the corner," intending to produce the ancestor belief through recognition relying on common knowledge. Still, the belief conveyed exceeds the content. Linguistic convention determines what part of the consensus, if any, is relevant to content.

With very few exceptions, the conventions that fix content do not depend on explicit public declarations of common loyalty to rules. So we had better take advantage of the rich philosophical discussion of tacit commitments and uncodified conventions, starting in seventeenth- and eighteenth-century political philosophy, and most recently advanced by Lewis and Gauthier.[3] As Locke and Hume emphasize, people engaged in common projects can have a tacit commitment to follow a certain rule because of the evident instrumental rationality of the practice dictated by the rule. Suppose that people are engaged in a common project, committed to its goals and aware that others are similarly committed. Suppose, moreover, that the following conditions are satisfied: each can see that conformity to some practice would advance the goals of the project if (nearly) everyone conforms, each can expect (nearly) everyone to be aware of that advantage, and each can expect conformity to that practice to be more advantageous under the circumstances than any alternative. Then, without any explicit declarations of loyalty to the practice, each is tacitly committed to conform to it provided that too many others do not indicate unwillingness to do the same. If, in addition, conformity would be advantageous if most others also conform but disadvantageous if they don't, then actual general conformity to the rule motivates those committed to the common project to continue to conform in the same way as a general declaration of loyalty to a codified convention would. Each seeks to do what others count on her to do, avoiding free-riding that would put common undertakings in jeopardy. One may speak, in such cases, of regulation by a tacit

---

[3] See David Lewis, *Convention* (Cambridge: Harvard University Press, 1969); David Gauthier, "David Hume, Contractarian," *Philosophical Review* (1979).

convention. In short, a tacit convention is a practice, burdensome if not generally observed, which each participant in a common project can justify as the best means of advancing the project should others be willing to do the same.

Majority rule is one of Locke's examples of a convention to which people can have a tacit commitment. People who have set up a government as a trusteeship to protect their common interests will each regard it as irrational to require unanimity in the passage of laws or to accord veto power to small minorities, since such voting rules would end their common project through paralysis. On the other hand, they will appreciate the irrationality of law-making by individuals or small minorities, since this is apt to subordinate the common good to private interest. It is urgent that there be some voting rule in legislation (i.e., in voting for legislators and in legislators' voting), and that the general rule be between the two extremes. So, if there is an in-between rule that will be most salient to all among otherwise acceptable arrangements, everyone should accept it, in the absence of agreement on another. That it is the first to come to everyone's mind makes it the most effective coordinator in the absence of explicit agreements, even if its salience only depends on simplicity. "Majority wins" is such a rule. In the absence of alternative voting rules explicitly authorized (by at least a majority of those who have joined in citizenship), someone is disloyal to a commitment implicit in citizenship if she refuses to obey legislation approved, directly or indirectly, by a majority of her fellow-citizens. She is disloyal even if she disobeys on the grounds that a rule requiring 60% approval would be the best compromise between paralysis and tyranny.[4]

Means for determining limits of content are now at hand. The content of someone's assertion consists of beliefs she intends to convey which are connected with her utterance by linguistic conventions. Genuine disagreement is the rejection of some of the beliefs intended to be recognized by means of linguistic conventions, while genuine agreement is the acceptance of the beliefs intended for conveyance in the appropriate, convention-based way. The conventions giving beliefs this status are practices of basing belief on the utterances of generally competent and trustworthy people, practices which have an appropriate rationale: if generally observed they are known to be the best means of advancing common projects using the words in question. Even in the occasional case of explicit linguistic convention, the explicit rule will have its authority in virtue of the instrumental connection with common

---

[4] This is a loose construal of Locke, *Second Treatise of Government*, chapter 8, sections 95–99. It is loose because Locke also takes the priority of majority rule to be a "law of nature and reason," offering a glib appeal to an analogy with a body's movement by "the greater force." Hume, in contrast, is clear about the sufficiency of a vivid purchase on everyone's imagination, when all have reason to seek a coordinating principle. See the discussion of the rules of property, Hume's prime example of principles of justice, in *A Treatise of Human Nature* III, ii, 3.

projects, rather as explicit voting rules, in the Lockean argument, derive their authority from an appropriate relation to the shared goal of a "political society." In short, questions of whether someone else affirms or denies the same thing as one affirms or denies in an utterance are settled by strategic reasoning: one finds a rule for associating utterance and belief which would best advance the common projects in which one's words are used. If similarly grounded rules for the other's practice assign the same beliefs to the relevant part of her utterance, then the contents are the same.

Seen in this light, the limits of content are a solution to a practical problem of how best to promote given goals using given raw materials. The given goals are, of course, the goals of the common projects in which the words in question are employed. For example, we expect others to use "table" to advance various projects of learning about furniture: describing how interiors look, finding furniture to make life comfortable, finding attractive furniture. The raw materials deployed in the practical solution are, above all, spontaneous associations and beliefs that are typical and believed to be typical among those engaged in the projects. "Table" would have a different referent if most people took the term typically to apply to objects with a back, seat and legs, built to be sat on.

The consensus is no more than raw material because learning would rarely be advanced by a practice of making all the routine evocations into beliefs whenever someone uttering the associated words is so trusted that his saying is a basis for believing. To determine what attributions are best connected with a term and, hence, how much belief is best connected with sentences involving the term we must balance a variety of considerations, some pointing toward less belief, some toward more. Convenience points toward meagerness, avoiding complexities in the accumulation and revision of beliefs and needless complexities in testing for competence. Though "table" evokes the thought of a four-legged object in most people, the complexities of employing additional terms in basic furniture inventories to record the presence of non-four-legged things with legs and flat tops built to sustain inanimate objects would not be justified by a corresponding advance in our projects. As an example of our avoidance of needlessly complex testing for competence in using a plain term, consider how someone who doesn't know about elephant ancestry may still be a useful contributor to basic projects of animal-classification.

In addition, a practice of taking on relatively few beliefs sustains efficient learning in the face of surprises. As time goes on or as the number of cooperators increases, someone who meets all conditions for trust that are readily applicable may have good reason to believe that the current consensus is wrong. If too much of the current consensus is taken to be conveyed by current means of utterance, he will be unable to contribute to the advance of learning by means of the old words, without clumsy hedges or confusing new coinages.

If each of us could instantaneously and effortlessly signal the totality of our observations and observational expectations, there might be no need to avoid clumsiness and confusion by using conventions to distinguish content from underlying belief. That is why the distinction looks like witchlore in computational theories that ignore our actual limitations and their impact on our need to rely on one another.

As always happens in complex and important activities, solutions often require striking a balance among competing considerations. Although the above considerations are reasons to reduce uptake, others justify practices of increased uptake. For example, employment of a term should convey beliefs substantial enough to produce discriminations that are useful in advancing common projects in which the term is used, i.e., used along with other, contrasting terms. If our plain furniture terms conveyed nothing more specific than "an object that is normally moveable," this consideration would be, disastrously, violated. The right limit on the scope of the term is the one that narrows the scope in ways that make it an effective discriminator in the tasks of learning in which it is employed, but no narrower.[5]

Emphasis on linguistic convention was a common tactic of positivists seeking to answer skeptical doubts. But that emphasis is not being put to this use. So there is no need for rigid claims of nonrevisability. Indeed, revisability in principle is guaranteed. Obviously, encounters with new facts can make it irrational to continue a practice that was, before, the rational means of advancing a project. The discoveries motivating the change need not themselves be concerned with language or cooperation, even when the strategies are linguistic means for advancing cooperation. So in general, such revision is not a matter of change in meaning as opposed to change in view of the world. It is a kind of change in view that is a change in meaning.

That the limits of content are the limits that would best advance our projects is a hypothesis that I will mainly defend by showing that it draws recognized limits correctly. In addition, a general argument from analogy supports these piecemeal claims of confirmation. Largely as a result of other work of Grice's, it is universally accepted that conversational implicature, what someone means by saying something in a conversation, is determined by tactical rationales addressed to the immediate conversational project of helping others through the use of words in that conversation.[6] People know and expect others to know that such projects are advanced by adherence to certain maxims, for example, "Stick to the point." One's saying what one does is rightly interpreted on the assumption of conformity to those maxims, unless one explicitly

---

[5] As Rosch and her colleagues have emphasized in their illuminating account of our basic classifications. See, for example, Eleanor Rosch et al., "Basic Objects in Natural Categories," *Cognitive Psychology* 8 (1976).

[6] See H. Paul Grice, "Logic and Conversation" in G. Harman and D. Davidson, eds., *Semantics of Natural Languages* (Dordrecht: Reidel, 1972).

cancels the background assumption. So, if you say, "How can I get to Marble Arch?", and I say, "You can go around Highbury Corner and down Holloway Road," in saying the sentence I mean that this is the way to Marble Arch— even if I say to myself that it isn't—since otherwise a maxim of relevance would be violated. Though this maxim governs the semantic characterization of my behavior, its justification is pragmatic. It is a way of achieving economy in discourse and avoiding miscues without elaborate stipulations.

What one means through saying something in a small-scale, immediate linguistic project is determined by these tactical rationales. What one asserts in one's utterance is different. But the difference, on the face of it, is a matter of scale and permanence. One's assertion seems to be the part of one's meaning that could be identified on the basis of general knowledge of what goes on in one's linguistic community, not special knowledge of the conversational context. If this is, indeed, the difference, then what one asserts ought to be determined by analogous strategic considerations addressed to general and enduring linguistic projects.

A NAUTICAL ILLUSTRATION

As a first test of the hypothesis about content and strategic rationales, I will apply it to a question that will cause no philosophical earthquakes. The ancient Greeks thought, and expected one another to think, that objects to which the term "*naus*" applied were objects made of wood, reeds or leather constructed to transport people or cargo across stretches of water on which those objects were meant to float. They would have denied that anything that is a *naus* is made of iron. In such utterances (whose specification I leave to those whose Greek has not disintegrated), would the Greeks have denied what we would affirm in saying, "Some boats are made of iron"? Of course, they would. Being made of wood or reeds or leather was not part of the very content of a *naus* ascription itself. So we can test the hypothesis about strategies and content by seeing whether their "*naus*"-related projects would have fixed appropriate limits of content.

The ancient Greeks used "*naus*" to communicate in ways that advanced projects of finding, improving on, and preparing for transportation. It advances such projects if plain and common classifications are relevantly discriminating yet otherwise broad. A term referring indifferently to boats and to wagons would not be a useful basic term for classifying means of transportation. But a conventional specification of composition might inhibit the project. The object answering to one's need for water transport might have an unforeseen composition. The object approaching the harbor might have a surprising composition, but call for the usual preparations. Other language-users might turn out to have different beliefs about composition and yet to be capable of playing a useful role in conveying beliefs with a direct bearing on transportation. The use of *"naus"* to refer only to wood, reed or leather boats risks inconvenience, confusion or the need for novel word-coinage in these cases, and has no compensating virtues.

Suppose, on the other hand, that the Greeks had been extremely concerned to tear up old boats and use them for firewood. If this wreck and burn project were important enough, then the limited understanding of *"naus"* *would* serve their concerns. In speaking of iron boats, we would be addressing ourselves to a different content. In this scenario, ancient beliefs in the internal properties of *nautes* need not be different from those in actual history. Moreover, *nautes* might still be built for the purpose of transportation—it is just that nautical scavenging for firewood has become much more important. Finally, though the thoughts and images evoked by *"naus"* would be different from those actually evoked in antiquity, the difference would be no greater than that separating the thoughts and images actually evoked by *"naus"* among the ancients from the congeries evoked by "boat" among English-speaking moderns. The crucial change is a change in ancient projects.

Natural Kinds and Social Needs

Unlike the analysis of talk of artifacts, the analysis of talk of natural kinds has been earthshaking. Once an adequate formal logic was established, by Frege and Russell, the question of what makes the use of an expression its use to refer to something became the leading question in describing how the content of a sentence is determined. In recent years, answers concerning reference to natural kinds have been a major source of illumination. A further test of the current proposal about content and projects is whether it can account for the best-established findings of these inquiries. If the test is passed, this will remove the suspicion that the proposal fits artifact talk for the special reason that artifacts are themselves means devised to serve people's projects. Most important of all, if the recent analyses of natural-kind talk can be based on strategic rationales, then this basis for setting limits to content can be reconciled with the insight that content often depends on the actual nature of external causes, regardless of whether their nature is recognized by the asserter or her community. For the analyses of natural-kind talk are the prime examples of such assertions of externality.

Putnam's discussion of "gold" in "The Meaning of 'Meaning' " has been highly influential, and is characteristic of detailed, insightful accounts of the reference of natural-kind terms that emphasize external causes. Putnam persuasively argues that we use "gold" to refer to whatever has the underlying structure typical of bearers of certain superficial characteristics commonly associated with the word, among objects naturally possessing those properties in the local environment of our linguistic community. Someone uses a term with the same reference, making assertions of corresponding content, just in case he (1) uses the term to refer to whatever has the underlying structure typical of bearers of certain commonly associated superficial characteristics among naturally occurring samples in his community, (2) those superficial characteristics are the same as the ones we associate with "gold," and (3) the underlying structure is the same as that typical of our samples, viz., being composed of the element Au perhaps with some impurities. Thus, Archimedes would not have been talking about gold if the only minerals that he and other Hellenes labeled "*khrusos*" were some stuff wholly lacking in Au, yet sharing all the superficial characteristics and indistinguishable from Au by ancient means. However, nature did not actually play this trick. Under the circumstances, Archimedes did use "*khrusos*" to make assertions about gold, even when he applied the label incorrectly as a result of his beliefs about nature.[7]

I will try to show that these limits of content are part of the rules for using plain, nontechnical natural-kind terms that best advance the common projects depending on the use of such terms as a basis for cooperation. These projects are projects of learning about nature, above all, of learning how to make nature useful.

If strategic rationales determine reference, then the reference of a plain and common natural-kind term will bear some significant relation to easily detectable properties that people in a community generally associate with the term, naturally occurring properties which have a direct bearing on the common and important projects advanced through the use of the term. So "gold," for example, will bear some significant relation to such properties as a glittering yellow look, malleability and heaviness. After all, our plain terms play an important and distinctive role in quickly and simply conveying beliefs among the broadest circle of language-users.—This emphasis on common usage is not the prelude to some philistinism in which unusual interests and associations are dismissed in general. A technical term such as "deuterium" will be connected with associations and interests of experts or aficionados.[8]

---

[7] See especially, "The Meaning of 'Meaning,' " pp. 235–38. This summary is a mixture of Putnam's phrases and mine. For example, I have noted, in a vague sort of way, the role of certain commonly associated superficial characteristics where he adds certain strictures about linguistic "stereotypes." As noted before, this part of his theory seems too constraining to fix limits to content, though it may be relevant to other important aspects of meaning. In general, I intend this paragraph as an outline that captures what is relatively uncontroversial in a line of inquiry in which controversy is still vigorous and fruitful.

Notoriously, common usage of "meaning" is too slippery for use in settling philosophically important controversies. Yet one liberating effect of "The Meaning of 'Meaning' " and related work by Putnam and others has been to cast doubt on traditional ways of carving up this terrain. On the whole, the subjectmatter of Putnam's essay is referential intention, what a term is used to refer to, the aspect of reference that is one way of answering the question "What did he mean by that term?" I will often speak of this phenomenon as "reference," for short. I think no confusion will arise, so long as attention is ultimately focused on what makes it the case that one person affirms or denies what another affirms or denies.

[8] To avoid suspicion of professorial naïveté, I had better acknowledge that being expensive in its pure state is the single most important property of gold for most purposes. Still, it is an aspect

What is the relevant relation between the reference of the term for a natural kind and the possession of the superficial features? It might seem that here, as in the case of artifact terms, the term ought to indicate the possession of the commonly associated, easily detectible features that are part of the most useful and economical scheme for making distinctions when taken together with contrasting terms. But such superficial communication would in fact interfere with our most important projects in learning about natural kinds. Those projects are not primarily directed at nature-shopping, in which we look for useful superficial properties already present in nature's store. They are, in the most important and complex cases, projects of transformation. Some of the transformations are relatively passive (i.e., they make the latent manifest). We find ways of working up parts of nature until the superficial properties of interest emerge. Some of the transformations are relatively active (or, more properly, artificial). We change something which may already have one of the clusters of superficial properties most usefully distinguishing things found in nature; we change it in ways that put it to new uses. Our learning to transform nature in these ways would be inhibited if natural-kind terms were a means of attributing superficial properties. It is advanced by the limits to content set by the causal account of these terms.

Consider, first, the interest in passive transformation. As any layperson knows, finding what falls under a natural kind commonly involves finding what does not have the easily detectible properties of common interest, but can be made to have them if put in an appropriate state. People who did not individuate searches for kinds of things in nature in this way would miss much that is useful, for example, gold in rocks which must be smelted before it is malleable. Knowing our interests and our basic rationality, each of us knows that terms for kinds of things found in nature should be extended to items that do not have the commonly associated features, but can be made to have them through a change in state. Here, we are not interested in the mere capacity to acquire those features. In particular, we are not interested in acquisition that adds to nature rather than developing what is actually there. Gold in low-grade ore is gold but lead is not gold even though it can be gilded. Without this restriction to potentials unleashed by new circumstances or by rearrangements, the criterion of susceptibility would be too broad for our pur-

---

of "gold" 's being a natural-kind term that the features relevant to the reference of the term occur naturally, i.e., do not depend on human acts and preferences. That we do treat "gold" in this way reflects a further strategic consideration, implicit in the work of Rosch and her colleagues. It is in our interest to have wide-ranging classes of contrasting plain and common terms, i.e., this advances the corresponding generic projects. "Gold" is one of the many contrasting terms used to make ordinary basic discriminations in the investigation of nature, and this generic function is what governs its reference. Accordingly, in discussing natural-kind terms I emphasize the generic projects and interests that guide us in dealing with gold, water, corn or any other natural stuff, and the clusters of superficial features which are salient in each case to people who are guided by those generic projects and interests.

poses. Anything found in nature can be given any cluster of properties by addition, so it is pointless to convey the information that such transformation is possible.

In the relatively passive aspects of our interest in the workings of nature we want to appropriate the products of nature or to unleash the workings of nature. This is an interest that is advanced by having simple and common means of reporting the results of searches. The terms serving this interest best will extend both to items having the easily detectible commonly associated natural properties with a direct bearing on our projects and to items having underlying properties, harder to detect, giving rise to the former upon appropriate change of state.

In a sense, these relatively passive interests are primary, since the general task of taking advantage of nature must be based on knowledge of what nature provides. But of course, we are also interested in the workings of nature because of the possibility of putting natural products to further use. Taking nature as our fellow-worker, we employ a natural product in unnatural ways as in manufacture. Quite untheoretical laypeople have a basic interest in learning that advances these interests in manipulation. As a consequence, they ought to prefer a restriction in the basic means of categorizing natural kinds.

The project of finding useful ways of manipulating nature is enormously advanced by means of communication that facilitate its coordinated pursuit among far-flung people in many generations. In this complex common project, the findings of some must be effectively coded in ways that provide helpful guidance to distant strangers, whose total belief system is quite unpredictable. Suppose that a person or group discovers that a certain operation will have a certain effect on some things that have the easily detectible properties, P, commonly associated with the plain term C. For example, someone discovers that some stuff which is heavy, malleable and glittering yellow in nature can be hammered into extremely thin sheets. The discovery of the transformation is apt to provide useful guidance to others, provided that the bearers of P that are encountered by the cooperating language-users can typically be transformed in that way to that effect. If the effects are themselves useful, the guidance is apt to be useful directly. Even if they are not, the storage of rational conclusions that P's can typically be transformed to a certain effect enormously enhances dealings with nature. Later, others will often find the means of putting such an effect to use.

If the proviso is not met, and the transformation typically does not work for P's, then those who are guided by the initial result in their dealings with P's are apt to waste their time at best. Disasters may befall them. Of course, it would be ideal if the initial finding were universally relevant, so that the same operation would have the same effect on any P. But such universal claims are virtually never true for clusters of easily detectible properties.

Because she is sensitive to these risks, a trustworthy cooperator in the task of making nature useful is not apt to make a report that doing X to whatever is P brings about a change to Y. Indeed, if she has good sense and basic knowledge of nature's wiles, she will be reluctant to claim that doing X to whatever is P usually brings about Y. The clusters of easily detectible, commonly associated properties are often associated with different underlying structures, making it unpredictable how results can be extrapolated, even approximately, to the general case. Moreover, useful cooperation in manipulating nature is far-flung, and other useful cooperators may well base their beliefs on inquiries into a local environment where a different underlying structure, producing different transformation-tendencies, is typical of P's. On the other hand, reasonably energetic investigation of her local environment sometimes puts a trustworthy cooperator in a position to report that an operation on whatever has the underlying structure typical of local instances of P leads to a certain result. This report is useful far and wide if those in other environments have reason to believe that the structures underlying their typical local P's are the same; yet the report does not encourage dangerous extrapolation. So it will advance our far-flung, agelong cooperation in learning how to manipulate nature if plain and common terms refer not to whatever is P, but to whatever has the underlying structure typical of local instances of P.[9]

The two basic kinds of cooperation in learning about nature are reports of the findings of searches and reports of the results of manipulations. Both tasks turn out to be advanced by plain and common usages that are not addressed to easily detectible, commonly associated properties, but to the underlying structures giving rise to them. Consideration of manipulation reports supported a narrowing of referent to what has the structure typically underlying local instances (loosely: "all that glitters is not gold"). Consideration of search reports supported a broadening of reference to encompass stuff that acquires the superficial properties when put into an appropriate state (loosely: "all that is gold does not glitter"). Fortunately, it is easy to combine these two demands on plain and common natural-kind terms. To reduce the riskiness of simple manipulation reports, we count only what has the underlying structure (nature, natural essence, basic constitution) controlling all kinds of transformations among most local instances of the superficial properties. To increase the usefulness of simple search reports, we count everything that has that structure, including items that only manifest the superficial properties when put in an appropriate state. The best rule, all told, in using plain and common natural-kind terms is to use such a term, for example, "gold," to refer to what-

---

[9] If there is such a typical underlying structure. Sometimes it turns out that there is not. Thus, as Putnam notes, "jade" comprises two different kinds of minerals, jadeite and nephrite. Upon such a discovery, one abandons use of the term in extrapolating results of manipulations, and takes it to mark possession of what has or can be worked up to have the superficial properties of interest. And, if one is engaged in abstract semantic characterizations, one will conclude that the term fails to refer to a natural kind.

ever has the underlying structure typical of bearers of certain easily detectible, commonly associated properties—in the "gold" case, say, glittery yellow, heavy and malleable—among instances encountered so far in one's linguistic community.

Would a rational user of plain and common natural-kind terms, then, want it to be standard practice for her attributions using such a term to be treated as abbreviations of attributions of the form "has the underlying structure of typical instances of properties P in the environment of my linguistic community"? Not quite. Statements employing natural-kind terms are means of coordinating extremely far-flung and long-enduring projects embracing many linguistic communities. It would be an enormous complication if the simplest attributions were treated differently just because they came from different linguistic communities responding to different sets of samples. In accumulating the simplest lists of alleged facts about kinds of minerals the compiler would have to record a report differently whenever it came from a different linguistic community. This burdensome procedure is bad strategy.

Instead, the rational cooperator's intention will be satisfied if the audience for her report associates the term with whatever underlies their local samples of the same superficial common properties, provided this structure is the same as that underlying the reporter's local samples. Thus, in using "gold" with the reference I do, I single out a certain underlying structure as whatever underlying structure controls transformation potentials of typical instances of yellow, glittery, heavy, metallic stuff in my linguistic community, and I use the term to produce beliefs in others concerning whatever structures underlie typical instances in their communities provided that structure is the same. In this way, the rational strategy for cooperation dictates the limits of content fixed by Putnam's (and Kripke's) analyses of natural-kind terms. Note that this account of content gives a decisive role to mere questions of convenience at the level of rationale, even though the description of content established by the rationale singles out deep, hard-to-detect aspects of objective reality: the mere difficulty in practice of keeping track of locale removes locale from content. [10]

These rules for the reference of plain and common natural-kind terms are also rational strategies for another reason. They best advance the coordina-

[10] Since "gold" is part of the standard English vocabulary everywhere, and has a single reference, as a natural-kind term, in common usage, it is tempting to paraphrase it using the expression "typical samples currently encountered by English-speakers." But this would leave one helpless to decide whether reference has changed as the language evolves. Even more disastrously, paraphrases referring to actual community encounters rule out obvious identities of content with utterly different communities. To their current sorrow, the Yanomamo of the Amazon live amidst gold. Presumably, they used a term to refer to gold in precontact days, when their local instances were utterly different from those encountered by English-users. Note that in this case, the effort to derive coreference from common origins would also be quite hopeless.

tion of expert and nonexpert usage. On the one hand, experts are more apt to be right about the nature of what falls under a natural-kind term. In achieving greater and greater power to explain, predict or manipulate, they increasingly rely on jargon to describe nature. So it is good cooperative strategy to let the practices and needs of experts determine the content of their special terms and usages. Yet nonexpert usages are indispensable, as well. Experts start out as nonexperts, and take their first steps toward expert understanding through the employment of plain and common talk. (At least they do if their expert understanding is genuine!) Experts rely on observational reports and manipulations carried out by nonexperts. An expert is an expert in relatively few fields; in advancing learning in her field of expertise she often finds expert usages in other fields too fine-grained for her purposes. For example, the lepidopterist is not interested in the technical description of the alloy in the rim of her butterfly net. Finally, technical findings are often made useful through practical applications by nonexperts who do not grasp jargon.

In learning about nature we need to maintain common usage, encourage fluent and economical interaction between common usage and expert usage, and, at the same time, avoid avoidable tendencies to perpetuate the false beliefs that are often associated with common usage. We can do all this most effectively if plain and common terms for natural kinds are used to refer to whatever has the underlying structure, etc., while technical terms are used to describe those underlying structures themselves.

Given that rich background of permissive but not inaccurate common usages, it will make sense to be less permissive concerning the limits of technical content. After all, the experts in a field are relatively few and relatively well-positioned to coordinate their interactions with new coinages and explicit conventions. Thus, the precise meaning of units of magnitude, a matter best left to experts, undergoes frequent changes. For similar reasons, a theoretical term introduced in connection with a novel explanatory strategy should be more easily deprived of reference by scientific change than a plain and common natural-kind term. Thus, if the explanatory strategy is abandoned as a result of empirical discoveries, the theoretical term is taken to refer to nothing. For example, "caloric" was taken to be an empty category when the strategy of explaining thermal properties in terms of the distribution of an incompressible fluid was abandoned.

I have described a number of ways in which strategic rationales advancing our common projects in dealing with nature would set limits to the content of our natural-kind talk. Since these matters are at once dauntingly complex and dauntingly elementary, I am sure that my description of those limits and rationales has not been accurate in every detail. Still, perfect accuracy is not required to defend the claim that the limits (whatever they are) are due to strategic rationales (whatever they are). It is essential, though, that the limits of content depend on the common projects in which we use our words. So I must show that changes in our goals or our resources could, in principle, break the connections between reference and underlying causes described by the recent analyses of natural-kind terms.

Suppose that all who live in a certain wholly isolated community are lazy in their dealings with nature. Their only interest is in the direct consumption of things as found in nature, on the basis of immediately evident properties. Their only communicative need is for terms by which to report to one another where nature is freely providing certain goods. Like shoppers in a furniture store, their rational means of classification would be terms indicating possession of easily detectible properties of direct interest. Such people would be very different from us, not least in the luck their survival requires. When we imagine their lives and communications, it does seem that their terms would have the superficial reference suiting their projects. If they happen to be descendants of ours, lotus-eaters who have forgotten the strenuous existence of their forebears, then they might speak truly, as we do not, in labeling gold-like lumps wholly lacking in Au "gold."

Or consider people who differ from us in supreme intellectual resources, rather than the simplicity of their needs. Each possesses and knows that all possess infallible knowledge of the specific structures typically underlying easily detectible clusters of properties that are of practical interest. Indeed, such knowledge is part of the first lore that their children absorb while learning language. If they are epistemically blessed descendants of ours, they might still use our plain and common terms. But their rational practice would be to take these terms as abbreviations for the universally known, infallible theoretical specifications. These new rationales would yield new meanings. When, on the basis of their specifying technical theories, they say "Gold is . . . ," the specification is an empty tautology. Archimedes' "*khrusos*" attributions never have just the same content as attributions of "gold" in their usage. The old meaning has become obsolete because open-mindedness and tolerance of the inexpert have become obsolete virtues.

Beyond Communication

One familiar strategy in philosophical approaches to content is to start at the bottom, describing processes that could determine the content of mental states of isolated beings who use no language at all. Instead, my whole discussion has aimed near the top. I have described the determination of the content of terms in public discourse, taking for granted the identity of many beliefs and intentions. This avoidance of the foundations seems to permit useful exploration of live controversies concerning philosophically important identifications of content. But it might be undermined from below. Expressions can be used by one person, unconcerned to communicate. Such private uses can have content, serving to express beliefs. Moreover, beliefs themselves have content, which are not possessed just in virtue of the fact that a certain sentence would be affirmed with a certain public role. After all, evoked beliefs are the raw material for public sentential content, not the other way around.—If either of these different bearers of content had content because of facts quite unrelated to communicative strategies, this would cast doubt on my analysis of the content of terms as used in communication. For asserting that p in public discourse, noting for one's own private purposes that p and believing that p are surely connected with the proposition that p in broadly similar ways. At least a brief plea for a strategic and communicative approach to private usage and mere belief is in order.

In fact, private assertion is described by the communicative approach, broadly understood. Strictly and literally understood, communication re-quires interaction among two or more people. But there is a broad understand-ing in which communication is any coordination of belief-states in a process of learning. In this sense, the referential use of a term in a one-person lan-guage also consists of its use in communication, i.e., this person's communi-cation with herself in advancing her own ongoing projects of learning. One uses the referential terms of a one-person language to record or retrieve find-ings, use or provide premises for further deliberations, and otherwise to coor-dinate one's past, present and future activities in the interest of one's own learning. If, to the contrary, one just had a tendency to print a particular shape or make a particular sound in response to something of a certain kind, without any intention of influencing one's future beliefs by this means, then one would not be using a sign to refer to that kind of thing. If I only say "Gork" in response to the sight of a certain kind of horrid beast, this is a mere response. But if I also write down "G" on a map that I use to avoid horrid beasts, my response refers to something. And if writing down "G" 's on the map, consulting where the "G" 's are and avoiding the corresponding place is my strategy for avoiding meeting up with tigers, then I use "G" to note a fact about tigers. (Presumably, the fact is where a tiger has been seen—but other learning strategies will determine this, and nonlinguistic content can be es-pecially indeterminate.)

Unlike utterances and writings, beliefs are not chosen—apart, perhaps, from a few exceptional cases. So talk of strategy is bound to be loose. Still, broadly speaking, a belief, too, is part of a project, and its content is deter-mined by its strategic role in communicating with oneself in this project. For a belief that one has must be a resource to be employed in learning, should the need arise. Otherwise, having that state may constitute a response to something, or an experience undergone, but one will not have a belief about something.

Moreover, roles in learning are what makes one's mental state the particu-lar belief it is. For consider what a person S does or would now do in problem-solving in which she makes use of access to mental state M, remembering it, imaginatively manipulating it, employing it in deliberation, or whatever. If her believing that p, when she gains access to M, is part of her rationale for solving problems as she does, then she believes that p when in state M. On the other hand, if identifying access to M with belief that p provides no such rationale, she does not possess the belief that p in virtue of being in state M. Possession of a belief is a matter of appropriate explanatory role, and roles in problem-solving conduct are decisive.

The deep question remains of what roles in learning are required to make one's state the belief that p. After all, people (or the same people at different times) can have different ways of learning, yet have the belief that p. Now, I use noticing greenness to detect finocchio, and conclude that a garnish will look green because the recipe calls for finocchio, but I did not learn in these ways thirty years ago. Yet thirty years ago I often had the belief that something was green.—I would suggest that this familiar-sounding problem should be solved by familiar means. In communicating with one another, each of us counts on certain broad similarities in learning strategy, as conditions for taking others seriously, using their assertions as if they were one's own findings. The similarities have to be broad, or else the reliance on them would either be foolish or uneconomical. (One might have to neglect too many reports by others or spend too much time discovering whether others learn in the required way.) The broad strategic roles that are definable in this socially useful model are the ones that distinguish content among beliefs, even the beliefs of noncommunicators.

If this speculation is right, then communicative strategies fix the limits of content directly, so far as belief is concerned. But even if it is wrong, the determination of content in the case of belief is not of a kind to undermine a communicative and strategic approach to content in public discourse. For one's belief could not have a different content from its actual content, given the actual functions of access to it as a resource for learning. If philosophically controversial questions about the content of terms in public discourse depend in part on communicative goals, this reflects our further need and intention to rely on one another in the more complex tasks of learning.

From this point on, I will assume that the strategic approach to content is well enough tested that it is fit for use. Its use is urgent, because of the outstanding questions of moral realism. Are the framework-dependent differences genuine disagreements in which one side asserts what the other denies? What are the conditions for making moral assertions?

JUDGING THE MIXED VERDICT

The application of a moral term in literal (non-scare-quotes) usage would not advance any project of a moral nihilist. After all, the applicability of such a term in such a usage is never in the least a moral nihilist's reason for making a choice that he would not otherwise make. However, this fact, combined with the nihilist's grasp of content, creates no barrier at all between moral content and strategic rationales. For the moral nihilist is a semantic parasite. His grasp of the content of moral judgments wholly consists of his understanding of the basis on which others who do sometimes attribute moral terms intend to attribute them. Those others will, at least to some extent, be guided by moral attributions in their projects. As one consequence of this semantic parasitism, there could not be a self-contained community in which someone used terms to refer to moral properties yet no one took the applicability of a moral term to be, in any circumstance, a reason to make a choice. In such a community "wrong" might be used to refer to hurtful acts, acts which we would judge wrong, but the ascription will no more be an ascription of a moral property than "Delicious" as used to classify apples by agronomists ascribes delicious taste if it happens to be applied to a delicious fruit.

This much priority for the projects of those who engage in moral judgment was already assigned in chapter three, in the defense of the rationality of moral nihilism. In light of the strategic account of content which I have advanced, there is a much more definite and useful connection, as well, between moral content and the projects of those engaged in moral judgment. We modern industrial moral-judgment makers use moral terms in assertions that all, or virtually all, of us can understand. The approach to content, which has passed some strenuous tests, implies that the content of those assertions is fixed by the rules connecting utterance and conveyed belief that best advance the common projects in which we use those terms.

Do the people in other cultures who seemed, in chapter one, to deny what we affirm in our moral judgments without suffering from unreason or ignorance of relevant evidence really deny what we affirm? (Of course, those others were not semantic parasites relying on our practices, nor were they would-be nihilists.) This question about genuine disagreement can now be answered by seeing which beliefs would be conveyed by our moral utterances according to the rules for conveyance best advancing *our* common projects. If the utterances in which they seemed to disagree were intended—on the basis of analogous strategic rationales of theirs—to negate the beliefs that our strategies connect with our utterances, the disagreement is not just verbal, but genuine. This ultimately functional basis for content would be an instance of an utterly general relation between content and verbal projects, not part of a functional semantics that is special to moral talk and other forms of evaluative discourse.

In the crucial cases of apparent moral disagreement, our local projects and the raw material provided by our elementary beliefs about the extensions of our terms are the basis for our local meanings; and their local projects and beliefs are similarly basic for their meanings; and the respective projects and beliefs are different. Still, the previous inquiries suggest that these may be cases of genuine disagreement. Such virtues as open-mindedness and simplicity, which were so important in fixing the limits of content elsewhere, might justify sufficiently broad limits in the moral case as well.

To show that what is rational strategy for us is indeed broad enough to establish common moral content with others in the absence of neutral justification is the first task in vindicating the mixed verdict. Of course, the content ascribed to moral judgments had better make the latter a fit subject for the exercise of detection, as described in chapter two.

In addition to these findings of appropriate breadth with room for detection, a defender of the mixed verdict must hope that the investigation of the content of moral ascriptions will produce a specification definite enough to explain why any non-nihilist must accept certain moral judgments, on pain of ignorance or irrationality. In the case of natural-kind terms, it turned out that anyone who ascribes a natural-kind term is committed to the existence of underlying structures giving rise to easily detectible properties. Similarly, whatever the limits of moral content may be, they will specify the commitments of any maker of moral judgments, i.e., anyone who thinks that some acts are wrong, or right or morally good or evil. Once these intrinsic commitments are established, the rest of the case for the mixed verdict would, then, consist of the observation that the moral nihilist is not constrained by such commitments, together with the defense of the rationality of nihilism in chapter three.

The vindication of the mixed verdict begins, then, with a search for relevant projects. The projects in which we use moral terms are, most importantly, projects involving practical reasoning, in which moral ascriptions are reasons (not necessarily overriding reasons) for choice. But of course, not every kind of practical reasoning is moral reasoning. Among us modern industrial folk, reasoning that is moral serves certain distinctive functions. Broadly speaking, these functions can be divided into the social and the personal.

To begin with the more specifically social function: by offering moral reasons, we persuade one another to accept actions, practices and institutions infringing on narrow self-interest. The justified measures can make disadvantageous courses of action that would otherwise be advantageous and might be desired apart from their effects on others. Of course, only someone who is excessively pessimistic (and probably a masochist, as well) would insist that moral reasons always constrain in this way. Sometimes what they justify would, in any case, be to the advantage of some who are affected and to the disadvantage of none. Still, practices of justification that could only promote acceptance when no one is disadvantaged would lack a major function of moral discourse.

As a further reflection of their persuasive role, moral reasons can provide a persuasive underpinning to acts and institutions that are, themselves, coercive: the force of moral reasons in the social realm is strong enough that they can, rationally, lead people to accept coercion, including punishment, even in cases in which those people are the targets. Socially, then, moral reasoning is a principled basis for preventing through rational persuasion fights that would be generated by narrow self-interest; as part of this function, it is a basis for the willing acceptance of coercion and threats of coercion (which is to say, in part, that it can justify political institutions).

In the personal realm, moral reasons guide conscientious reflection on one's actions and oneself. They justify avoidance of actions one would engage in were it not for effects on others or on one's own development. They provide reasons to try to become a different sort of person. In the course of reflection on oneself, moral reasons are strong enough to justify burdensome choices of actions one would strenuously avoid were it not for effects on others or for the kind of personality that those actions would express and reinforce.—Though directed inward rather than outward, this function of moral talk is quite as communicative as any other. Moral talk in the personal realm is the vehicle for advice. Moreover, conscientious self-reflection is a prime example of communication with oneself in which, employing records of one's past, one seeks to influence one's future deliberations.

So far, the description of what moral reasons do for us has been virtually devoid of content. People might guide choices in these ways on the basis of the consideration that the number of blue things in the world should be increased or that moonlit hedgehog-watching should be avoided. Certainly, we do not use moral reasons to end discord and regulate preference on just any basis. In content, the regulative reasons that we actually employ in our moral reasoning are of certain kinds. The positive reasons include the advancing of the interests of people who are affected, the attaining of their willing participation or consent, and the enhancement of their capacities. The infringement of people's interests, their coercion and their stultification are all negative reasons, morally speaking.

Such a catalog of uncontroversially positive or negative considerations is not nearly enough to justify many moral choices that are right. Right moral choice often requires striking a balance, balancing burdens to some against benefits to others, or ranking different kinds of benefits and burdens. The framework differences that seemed to sustain moral disagreements that do not depend on ignorance or irrationality were all of this kind. A catalog of the basic considerations serving to justify social and conscientious choices for Aristotle or Chenge would be the same as ours. But Aristotle and Chenge balance those reasons differently. Aristotle judged social arrangements by their tendency to enhance the development of the most advanced citizens—even when the cost was stultification for the less advanced majority, which he did regret. He judged character, above all, by the presence of traits sustaining accomplishments of a self-sufficient kind, condemning avoidable dependence that drained resources from such accomplishments, even though he recognized the genuine, if lesser, value of concern and mutuality. Balancing social costs and benefits differently, we think that serious conflicts between the interests of different people should be assessed with equal concern and respect for all, so that the severe deprivation of some is not less serious just because their accomplishments are less worthy of admiration. And we take concern and respect for others, regardless of the worth of their achievements, to be an important goal of personal development, which can override the pursuit of self-sufficient excellence. Similarly, Chenge gives overriding weight to the maintenance of the given network of interpersonal ties, while regretting the burdens imposed on recalcitrant individuals, where we think the given network should only be supported at serious cost to some if support is justifiable from a standpoint of evenhanded concern for all affected.

In using "right," "wrong" and other basic moral terms, each of us modern industrial folk intends to convey that choices are justified by moral reasons balanced in the right way, whatever way is right in the case at hand. If this were not so, we could not use the basic terms of moral discourse to convey that something was morally justified on balance when there is a need to balance rival moral considerations. Such a gap would stand in the way of our basic projects of persuasion and self-development. In any case, our basic moral assertions obviously are meant to describe where the appropriate balance is struck.

In addition to beliefs as to where the balance of moral reasons lies, each of us also has certain beliefs concerning what particular way of balancing considerations is right in the case at hand. Are these also beliefs that we intend to convey, i.e., intend to convey by a recognition of our intention which is governed by conventional linkages between words and beliefs? This is the crucial question in assessing the crucial apparent moral disagreements. If there is anything to the previous discussions of content, the answer to this question will depend on the rationality of the stricter standards as means of advancing the projects in which we use the basic terms of moral discourse. I will now argue for the following answer. Just as in the ascription of a plain and common natural-kind term we make an assertion about an underlying structure without describing the structure, in the ascription of a basic moral term we make an assertion about the right way of balancing moral considerations without describing that right way. As in the natural kind case, this modesty expresses not agnosticism but pursuit of the rules for communication best advancing projects using the words in question.

Since the immediate issue is the content of *our* moral talk, the most important strategic considerations are reasons for us industrial moderns to observe relaxed rules for acceptance in moral communication with one another. To begin with a relatively simple case in which the relaxed procedure is wise, suppose that you take the balance of reasons to be determined, in a broad class of cases, by a theory of the sort that philosophers advance. You are a hedonistic utilitarian. Or (to mention a theory that I will be defending), you resolve basic questions of institutional choice by seeking arrangements that all affected could freely and rationally accept, understanding freedom in an appropriately determinate way. You may, then, want everyone to balance moral considerations in the particular way that you think is the right one. But of course, others, lacking one's theoretical commitments, do not use the basic terms of moral discourse to convey the satisfaction of one's theoretical standards. Does this defect in the making of moral judgments, as one sees it, constitute linguistic incompetence as well, a failure to grasp the content of moral assertions?

The moral theorist should answer "no"—not because linguistic competence never depends on accurate extralinguistic belief (it does, the positivists were wrong), but because a more relaxed rule for connecting utterance with communicated belief is better strategy. For example, if you are a hedonistic utilitarian, you will not want "right" to be used to convey the belief that an action or policy is morally justified on balance because it is a means of maximizing net pleasure in the long run. To advance the main social function of moral talk, you will want the basic terms of moral discourse to be used in ascriptions by which others, including non-hedonistic-utilitarian others, would voluntarily constrain themselves. If content is too narrow, the scope of rational persuasion, including the reach of one's own arguments and judgments, is avoidably reduced. After all, the arguments of a hedonistic utilitarian often point to considerations that would rationally persuade others to accept choices, even when those others reject hedonistic utilitarianism as a whole. Indeed, others may take the utilitarian to be a wise moral judge from case to case, trusting in her particular moral judgments so long as trust does not require embrace of her general theory, which they take to be unwise. And similarly for any determinate and general theory of broad scope. From the standpoint of a moral theorist engaged in the common project of rational persuasion, it would be a loss if basic moral ascriptions entailed acceptance of the true theory, the right way of balancing. The theorist would then be faced with pervasive, avoidable rejection of the claims that she advances using the plain terms of moral discourse. Note that this would be a loss even if everyone in the theorist's society would embrace her doctrine if they reflected long and well enough on relevant facts and arguments. It is sufficient that they don't. The right linguistic convention is the one that each would accept on rational reflection—but each must be supposed to take the typical state of awareness of others as raw material in such reflection.

Of course, the moral theorist wants others to employ her theory in striking the balance, and wants to persuade others of the rightness of that theory. Like everyone else, she thinks that some ways of striking the balance would be moral disasters, and she has her own convictions as to which ways are disastrously wrong. But the relaxed standard does not inhibit in the least the project of arriving at the right way of striking the balance and persuading others that it is right. In ascriptions of basic moral terms one conveys that something is the result of the right way of striking the balance, without conveying a description of that way. Through empirically informed moral reflection and moral argument, the theorist justifies her description of that right way.[11]

Of course, people often balance rival, relevant moral considerations without appealing to a general, determinate principle with the broad scope that philosophers usually pursue. Still, what makes it good strategy not to use basic terms of moral discourse to convey philosophers' ways of striking the balance also makes it good strategy not to use those terms to convey that one's modest and piecemeal way of striking the balance has been satisfied. Perhaps I think that tax policies in advanced industrial capitalist societies ought, overridingly, to reflect concern for the most disadvantaged. Still, I will not want there to be a generally accepted rule by which the ascription of "just" is used, in part, to convey belief that something has satisfied the overriding concern for the most disadvantaged that justice requires in such cases. For then, "just" would not be available as a signal of my agreement with someone who accepts the same tax policy, in response to empirical facts in which I believe as well, because she thinks that tax policies ought to promote the general welfare. Rational political persuasion is best advanced by the use of basic moral terms to convey the correct balance of conflicting considerations. I should, of course, be concerned that the other balance interests in the right way, not just in the way that comes out right in the case at hand. Her getting it right in this case is something of a fluke, from my perspective. The relaxed rule does not make my efforts to correct her any less effective or relevant.

So far, the reasons for relaxed conveyance of the right balance whatever it is have involved our typical, local differences in ways of striking the balance, i.e., differences such as one would expect to encounter in principled arguments within a modern industrial society. In addition, there are similarities uniting the vast majority of modern industrial folk capable of self-constraint on the basis of principled argument, for example, commitment to balancing processes governed by the vague requirements of equality that I introduced in describing fundamental forms of moral detection. Still, having gone so far as to require neutral content in response to typical local differences, there would be no point to attaching a proviso requiring adherence to our local similari-

---

[11] "Balance" may suggest some quantitative procedure in which effects weighted by intensity are added, and these sums compared. This is the procedure of hedonistic utilitarianism. But "way of striking a balance" is meant very broadly, here, to include any principled way of coping with conflicts of interest. Such a procedure need not be based on the summing up of effects from an impartial perspective. It need not assess the seriousness of an individual effect in terms of an impartially applied scale as opposed, say, to the choices of the individual victims. It need not even base accurate judgment on any uniform, distinctive, all-encompassing basis for deliberation, i.e., on any perspective comfortably labeled "the moral point of view."

ties. In atypical local cases, relevantly dissimilar people will encounter one another, since there are radically dissenting minorities within modern industrial societies. Moreover, we are still in contact with other kinds of societies, contact giving rise to morally significant conflict according to our morality. And who knows what moral divides may open up in the future of our societies, in response to new situations and new conflicts? The project of rational persuasion extends to all of these presently atypical encounters. So, as in the case of plain and common natural-kind terms, the neutrality of specification should be general.

This thinning out of the beliefs conveyed does make our moral ascriptions less informative than they would be otherwise. However, the reduced economy in moral reporting is not a serious enough loss to override the increased effectiveness in rational persuasion. Our typical ways of balancing moral considerations are not esoteric. People know what the pervasive modern ways of moral learning are—i.e., they know what to expect and when to be surprised in the course of moral argument. So one can, on the basis of common knowledge, infer that a moral judge has balanced considerations in certain ways, rather as one infers that an "elephant" ascriber probably thinks that the ascriptee has African or Asian ancestors.

Our basic common projects employing moral terms are best served by a rule conveying belief in where the right balance of certain general considerations lies, but not describing how they are to be balanced. But of course, the basic projects that I have described are not special to us. In every society, people have used terms, which would normally be classified as moral, in pursuit of these projects of persuasion and self-development. It is rational for them to set the same limits to the content of their corresponding assertions. So, as the mixed verdict requires, we are in genuine disagreement with Aristotle, Chenge and others even if they differ from us on account of fundamental differences in their frameworks for inquiry.

All the strategic reasoning so far has supported broad limits to content. Yet in one way, the mixed verdict was narrow even in drawing the limits of content. Someone engaged in making moral judgments was required to accept the relevance of certain considerations on pain of showing a failure to grasp the content of those judgments. In effect, those relevant considerations were the items in the general catalog of goods and bads that I sketched in my rough description of basic moral considerations. If the mixed verdict is right in this narrowness, then there had better be reason to avoid a treatment of what is balanced in a moral judgment which is as neutral as the treatment of how the balance is struck. The content of a moral ascription must include the claim that the considerations balanced include, as important items, substantial gains and losses in the general catalog. Otherwise, someone could engage in moral judgment by accepting that the appropriate considerations, balanced in the appropriate way, are reasons for making a choice—yet deny that the avoidance of excruciating pain is an appropriate consideration, even prima facie.

It would be pointless to make moral content that neutral, because such open-mindedness would contribute nothing to the social function of moral talk. The goods and bads in the catalog, as I intended it, are things which any human seriously cares to have (the goods) or to avoid (the bads) in her own case, if she cares about herself at all. Someone who does not take any of the corresponding benefits and deprivations in others to be, even prima facie, reasons for choice will not impose the smallest sacrifice on himself in order to permit goods or prevent burdens that another would seriously care about and that he would seriously care about if his interests were so affected. (That is, he would seriously care about these benefits and burdens for himself, unless he does not care about himself at all, in which case the enterprise of persuading him to accept constraint is moot on account of the depth of his depression.) One cannot persuade such a person to make choices otherwise disadvantageous to him, on the basis of rational appeals to principle. So nothing is gained by thinning out the beliefs conveyed by moral ascriptions so that what is conveyed can be what he intends to convey, as well.

Before, the specification that the way of balancing is one of our highly typical ways turned out to be too discriminating for our purposes, like the specification that "table" refer to a four-legged object. Now, omitting specification of certain relevant considerations turns out to sacrifice discriminations relevant to our projects, like a plain and common furniture term referring indifferently to objects with backs made to be sat in and objects with flat tops made to support inanimate objects. If people generally respect the rule connecting moral attribution with certain considerations, there is no loss to the project of persuasion and there are gains. Less time is wasted in doomed efforts at persuasion. More information of a kind that bears on relevant choices is conveyed with maximum economy. As usual, a grand semantic limit depends on humble strategic advantages.

The conclusions so far might be summed up in the same style as the account of plain and common natural-kind terms. A basic moral term, for example, "just," refers to what is justified by appropriate considerations balanced in the right way, whatever that right way is, a justification capable of constraining self-interest on the basis of general principles, and giving serious consideration to gains and losses about which everyone cares who cares about himself (perhaps along with other, nonuniversal concerns). Someone only makes a judgment with the same content if he has corresponding intentions concerning the same domain of objects of justification and includes these universal concerns among his serious considerations.

In addition to these parallels, one further similarity is probably required for another to use terms with the same content as we do in our moral judgments. The other's way of striking a balance, together with any considerations on which she fundamentally relies, must dictate the morally correct choice in a variety of important cases in her situation, and this must be no accident. Otherwise, it would be irrational to spend time seeking to persuade her on the basis of our moral arguments, or seeking to persuade her to trust our moral judgments as bases for her choices.

Aristotle, Chenge and all other actual people who rely on goods and bads in the basic catalog satisfy this criterion as well, for two reasons. There is substantial overlap between their ways of balancing considerations and ours. Moreover, our fundamental moral concerns often affect their deliberations in an instrumental way, even when their fundamental moral premises are relevantly different. Thus, the nonaccidental relationship between social instability and deprivations imposed by social circumstances often leads Aristotle to conclusions of our egalitarian sort, despite premises of his hierarchical sort. Still, one can imagine violations of the further requirement. At least in philosophical fiction, a culture might resolve all conflicts within the basic catalog of goods and bads by the rule that the tallest wins. A bit less fantastically, there might be creatures with Aristotelian ways of deliberating among whom the promotion of Aristotelian virtue pervasively conflicts with considerations that we rightly take to be overriding, in circumstances creating no systematic link between social feasibility and relative equality. Their applications of their main terms for deliberation do not overlap our applications of moral terms in diverse important cases. Then they do not affirm or deny what we do in our moral judgments.

I offer this last requirement tentatively, as an attractive construal of the demand for at least imperfect detection, understood in the strategic perspective on content. Note that in spite of this requirement, it could still be true that nearly all our moral judgments could rationally be rejected by one or another non-nihilist. The most that could be claimed is that a single non-nihilist could not do all of this rejecting.

The mixed verdict was mixed, above all, because permissiveness about rational disagreement was combined with assertiveness about truth. Certain ways of moral learning were said to be ways of finding out the truth in moral matters, and, on the basis of such ways of learning, moral judgments were rejected as false even though they did not depend on ignorance or unreason. A more detailed rehearsal of the parallels with natural-kind terms should make it clear that such assertiveness about truth and detection is compatible with the relatively relaxed understanding of moral content that I have been defending.

We take Archimedes to refer to gold in his use of *"khrusos"* even though he was an unreliable detector of gold in that use, sometimes labeling nongold *"khrusos."* Similarly for Aristotle (and, very likely, Archimedes) labeling institutions *"dikaios"* which are not just.

Granted, we think that if Archimedes had rationally responded to our arguments and evidence he would have become as reliable a detector of gold as we are. However, as we saw in previous chapters, there may be other differences in scientific response that cannot be resolved by evidence and reason. Perhaps the evidence and arguments available in the case of gold, "gold" and "*khrusos*" are not, actually, rationally evadable. Still, it is intelligible to ask whether Archimedes would have referred to gold even if reason and evidence could not have made him as good a detector as us—say, because his framework of inquiry was relevantly, rationally unreceptive to arguments for atomic theory.

The answer to this question is "yes." Despite the imagined radical difference, Archimedes would still intend to convey, by means of linguistic conventions, beliefs about whatever structure underlies typical local instances of stuff with certain superficial properties. Our intentions are the same with respect to our local environment. And Au would still underlie his typical local instances even if reason and evidence were not sufficient to reveal this fact to him. We use our detection capacity to determine the extension of his term even if observance of general norms would not lead him, at the ideal limit of evidence, to detect that extension. In effect, a criterion for sameness of content, based on a strategic rationale, tells us how imperfect a detector of gold Archimedes can be and still refer to gold.

Similarly, Aristotle uses "*dikaios*" to refer to whatever results from the right way of balancing certain considerations in a certain domain of choice. The domain is part of the domain of our term "just." His considerations are ours. His way of balancing them, though different from ours, is a basis for principled constraint on self-interest, and leads him to make judgments that things are to be accepted as "*dikaios*" in many important cases in which we think those things would be just. So, though an imperfect detector of justice, he is good enough to refer to justice, good enough by a criterion based on a strategic rationale. Neither criterion nor rationale entails that Aristotle's ways of detecting moral properties would lead him to answer any given moral question rightly if he responded reasonably to all relevant information. We should use our capacity for moral detection to assign extensions to his terms, even though reason and evidence would not lead him to assign that extension. The mixed verdict is vindicated.

Literally vindicated, but there is one further implication of the verdict that deserves to be stated and justified. Those who think there is such a thing as moral truth and moral detection do not think this just one feature of valid moral judgment, like the existence of morally binding fiduciary responsibilities. We think that truth and detection are centrally important aspects of morality, so that a total practice of justification would barely constitute a morality if there were not even tacit commitment to truth and detection. It isn't just that commitment to moral truth and moral detection is consistent with an accurate fixing of the limits of moral content. The utter absence of such commitments would be a radical change in the nature of moral judgment. Why?

Someone who was so uncommitted to truth and detection would determine success and failure in the two great moral projects in very different ways from us, so much so that it is unclear whether he is engaged in the same projects. In the case of the social project, the difference is most striking in the justification of coercion. We take it to be an important criterion of success in the moral justification of coercion that the imposition be based on true premises, not mere inclinations. Someone unconcerned with truth is not guided by that criterion in his efforts to cope with conflicts of interests.

It is in the personal project, however, a project to which I have only implicitly appealed so far, that the concern for truth and insight is most pervasive. It would misstate our total goal in conscientious reflection to say that each of us wants to base action on a coherent, determinate set of ultimate convictions. It is an additional goal, reflected in additional anxieties, that our convictions serve as means of detecting the difference between right and wrong. If all that we sought were determination by actual convictions, we would have no reason to be troubled by the thought that our reasons might be due to mere inculcation. Nor would we have deep reasons to prefer moral education based on enlarged experience to brainwashing and other shortcut methods of changing beliefs.

Thus, when we seek the right way of balancing moral reasons we seek the way that gets at the truth. So does everyone else actually engaged in the projects that make discourse moral. A moral judgment maker who is not, even implicitly, a moral truth pursuer is, at best, an imaginable borderline case.

MORALITY AND SCIENCE

Is morality like science? Asking this question is a timeworn way of beginning and organizing a discussion of truth and justification in moral matters. Recently, the technique has become worn-out, as a way of starting. It tends to disorganize discussions because there are now so many relevantly different conceptions of science itself. (The most thoroughgoing moral realist I know once spent three months of painstaking argument convincing a seminar of the deep resemblance between morality and science, only to discover that everyone among them had made the further inference that science is fundamentally subjective.) However, a bad way to start such a discussion can be a good way to end it. These five chapters of discussion of truth and justification in morality and in science have, I hope, established important similarities and important differences between science and morality. A summary of these comparisons depicts many conclusions already drawn, seen from a new angle. What is more, the investigation of the limits of content helps to explain the differences between science and morality, and to do so in ways that do not cast in doubt the existence or importance of the similarities.

The timeworn question of whether morality is like science presupposes that morality and science are either fundamentally similar or fundamentally different. But the arguments since the start of this book entail, more modestly, a number of important similarities (none of them the fundamental similarity) and a number of important differences (none of them the fundamental one). A judgment that similarity is more important than difference, or vice versa, would reflect nothing more than the temperament of the person who does the comparing.

Here are the three most important similarities and the three most important differences.

Similarities:

1. In science and in morality, we are often justified in making assertions about facts, assertions not made true by our beliefs and sentiments. In both kinds of inquiry we are justified because the best explanation of relevant data entails the truth of the assertion in question. A characterization of the features in virtue of which data, explanations, detection processes and framework principles are relevant to justified truth-claims in science as a whole would characterize moral inquiry, as well.

2. The broadest goal of justification that is typically of interest to scientific inquirers is the development of arguments making it unreasonable for any actual person to dissent from a truth claim should he or she possess all currently available evidence. This goal is often attained in moral inquiry, as well as in scientific inquiry.

3. Sometimes, scientific inquiry would make it unreasonable for any possible person who makes any positive assertion in the field in question to dissent from the particular hypothesis in question. Some moral judgments are also rationally compelling in this way.

Differences:

ι. In the case of any scientific disagreement among actual inquirers, it is always at least a rational hope that further evidence and argument would end the possibility of rational disagreement. In morality, this is not always a rational hope.

ιι. In most fields of science, on typical occasions, the main goal of someone justifying a hypothesis to someone else is to offer evidence and arguments making it irrational for him to deny that the hypothesis is part of the best explanation of the history of data-gathering and theorizing so far. The typical goal of moral justification to another is to offer evidence and arguments including reasons which the other must accept, on pain of irrationality, as reasons for making a practical choice, which is not a choice of an explanation.

ιιι. Sometimes in science evidence and argument would make it irrational for any possible person to reject a hypothesis as false; the negative answer would entail ignorance of data or a failure to understand the arguments or the question posed. In morality, reason and evidence never have this power. Negation need not show a failure of information or understanding, so long as it is sufficiently universal. Moral nihilism is a possible rational position in the face of all data, but a similar nihilism concerning all of science is not.

In short, morality resembles science because in both kinds of inquiry truth claims are justified, they are often confirmed (i.e., justified to all relevant actual inquirers), and sometimes are rationally compelling for any possible person who sometimes ascribes the properties in question. Morality differs from science because there is sometimes no rational hope for confirmation, the interest in common ground for choice dominates justification, and there is always a possible position (the moral nihilist's) from which the truth of an assertion can be denied without ignorance or unreason. I have already argued for these conclusions, especially the claims of resemblance. However, the new account of content, emphasizing strategies for communication in pursuit of common goals, helps to clarify the basis and importance of the differences. This task of clarification has often launched anti-realist treatments of morality denying at least some of conclusions 1–3. I will end the metaethical part of this book with an alternative assessment and explanation of differences.

Even though we are often justified in claims as to moral truth, the rational hope for evidence and argument that would be compelling for all actual inquirers, which does pervade science, does not pervade morality. Why? A combination of two factors creates this special limit to reason in moral inquiry. On the one hand, people's basic moral principles are rational responses to parochial problems, differing from one human setting to another, to a far greater extent than the principles at the basis of scientific justification. On the other hand, the goals of our moral discourse sustain broad limits to content, at least as broad as the scientific ones, making morality the common topic of diverse local inquiries.

Almost everyone's fundamental moral beliefs (i.e., beliefs held without deeper justification which are classified as moral when the limits of content are fixed) directly or indirectly reflect his or her society's solutions to the local version of a certain problem. The problem is to find a stable, enduring basis for fluent and productive interaction in the face of conflicts of interest. The solutions will depend on the content and distribution of interests and resources, resources which include both coercive powers and inherited attitudes affecting one's capacity to grasp one's interests. Against this background, fundamental moral beliefs evolve either as common premises in deliberations through which conflicts are resolved or as shared responses to formative life-experiences which are themselves governed by local tasks of coping with conflicts.

I have argued at length that such explanations of moral beliefs are sometimes truth-justifying, not debunking—for example, if the stabilizing solution is determined by equality in the distribution of coercive resources. But many other processes of challenge-and-response have also characterized human communities. For example, the utterly unequal coercive resources of feudal overlords and serfs gave rise to stabilizing responses different from ours, as did the life-histories of people advancing themselves through a network of personal loyalties in many decentralized agrarian societies, such as the Tiv. To put the point in the most banal way: the problems of human conflict and the possibilities of solution have taken diverse forms in the course of history, giving rise to different first principles for coping with conflict.

Scientific inquiry is also based on beliefs that people acquire early on and normally regard as truistic. In science, too, the fundamental beliefs are largely formed in the development of solutions to problems, above all, children's problems of getting, moving, and communicating. These problems and their rational solution are universal. The great sensorimotor sagas of Piaget's *The Origins of Intelligence in Children* can be told of any physiologically normal child, not just Laurent learning how to reach for the rattle. The relevant resources and interests are the same. But later, Laurent will learn how to compete in a quite nonuniversal context of interests and resources. Even the tales of resolving conflicts over the game of marbles in Neufchatel, the initial theme of Piaget's *The Moral Judgment of the Child*, cannot be extrapolated, as one realizes when Erickson reports childhood games among the Sioux. [12]

Granted, it is an open question in the philosophy of science to what extent these primordial starting-points determine the ultimate outcomes of scientific inquiry when combined with data and rational reflection. Since the seventeenth century, new problems have given rise to important new background principles. Perhaps an alternative response might sometimes have given rise to a very different basis for inquiry, equally rational and enduring. For present purposes (though not for purposes soon to come) we need not reflect on such possibilities. The more radical novelties in background principles arose in one relatively homogeneous cultural circle. Once evidence and argument do their further eliminative work, relatively little diversity in actual frameworks remains.

Suppose that the principles normally arising in response to local problems of coping with humans are addressed to a nonlocalized moral subjectmatter, and the principles normally arising in response to problems of coping with nature are, similarly, addressed to a common, scientific subjectmatter. Then rational moral disagreement, as distinct from scientific disagreement, will sometimes involve evidence and background principles that make it unreasonable to hope that new evidence and argument will end the possibility of

---

[12] See Jean Piaget, *The Origins of Intelligence in Children* (New York: International Universities Press, 1952); Piaget, *The Moral Judgment of the Child* (New York: Free Press, 1965), chapter 1; Erik Erikson, *Childhood and Society* (New York: W. W. Norton, 1950).

rational dispute. In the case of moral inquiry, inclinations are important evidence, if one takes them to have arisen in morally revealing ways. The solutions to the different problems of social coping will give rise both to characteristic inclinations and to principles of detection according to which these data are morally revealing. Different ways of moral learning are self-sustaining, as I put it in chapter one. So there will be cases in which there is no rational hope that new evidence would overcome a disagreement due to different ways of learning. In the case of scientific inquiry, the evidence of sense perception is decisive if interpreted as appropriately revealing. Because of similar bodily equipment, most people, despite differences in belief, do respond to the same circumstances with similar sense-perceptions. And their frameworks for interpreting evidence are relatively similar. So it is always reasonable to hope that more data, combined with the largely, though not entirely similar background principles, will give rise to a single rational scientific response.

This argument for different hopes has depended on a certain supposition, namely, that the responses in each respective realm are concerned with a common subjectmatter. If everyone fundamentally relying on significantly different principles from those which we consult in moral matters addressed himself to nonmoral matters, then genuine moral disagreement might always be ended by evidence and argument. So the difference in hopes also depends on the permissive limits of moral content. The point is not that the limits are broader for basic moral ascriptions than they are in science. As we have seen, our understanding of plain and common natural-kind terms is similarly permissive. Rather, the limits to content in moral discourse, which are broadly fixed there, as they often are in science, qualify the different social solutions as divergent ways of learning about a common subjectmatter.

The second major difference concerned the different interests that people typically pursue in justifying propositions to others. In scientific justification, the typical main interest is persuading the other side to explain in a certain way. In moral justification, it is persuading the other side to take moral reasons as justifying certain choices, which are not choices of explanations. The strategic approach does not help to explain this difference, but it does help to assess its importance.

Anti-realists have traditionally emphasized the fundamental importance of this difference in goals for the interpretation of moral discourse. They have, then, gone on to develop an interpretation incompatible with some of resemblances 1–3. Though the anti-realist inferences are wrong, the difference in goals is important. The content of moral utterances depends on the main typical goals of moral discourse. If the explanatory project were primary, then it would, perhaps, be rational to make typical modern ways of balancing moral considerations part of the very content of our moral utterances—for the main reasons for breadth have to do with the nonexplanatory project of reconciliation. We might even let social scientists fix limits to moral content, rather as curators and major antique dealers resolve fine points about the meaning of "chair." For in these ways, we might more economically convey discriminations relevant to our explanatory practice.

Greater semantic charity is rational and, hence, determines the limits of content, because the avoidance of conflict through principled persuasion that can constrain self-interest is so much more important a goal in moral justification than persuasion that an explanation is the best. But acceptance of the relative urgency of the first goal in our enterprise of justifying moral judgments to others hardly entails that the second is unattainable (contra 1 and 2). Moreover, the other main project of moral discourse, concerning, as it were, the justification of oneself to oneself, is guided by an urgent interest in distinguishing what is just coherently accepted from what is accepted in ways explainable on the basis of insight. The search for common ground and the desire for appropriate explanatory ground both play crucial roles in semantic characterization, in different ways.

Finally, in previous arguments I have assigned a special universality to certain scientific beliefs and denied that moral beliefs ever attain it. This difference in resistance to skepticism remains to be explained.

In both realms, it would sometimes be unreasonable for any possible person, possessing all current evidence and aware of all current arguments, to reject a given property-ascription as false if he ever ascribed that property. But only in science can we ever drop the if-clause and claim that dissent in light of the evidence and arguments would be unreasonable for any possible inquirer. In moral inquiry, such universal reach is blocked by the nihilist who, though aware of our evidence and understanding our arguments, rejects all ascriptions of moral properties as false.

In quick, initial summary, this difference in resistance to wholesale disbelief depends on different possibilities of successful semantic parasitism. The moral nihilist understands our practices well enough to address himself to our moral affirmations in negating all moral ascriptions. But a rational person who negates all ascriptions of scientific properties would have to negate all ascriptions of properties to matter and to other minds. Such a person could not believe enough to grasp our ascriptions indirectly, by understanding our practices. And there is no other way for her to address herself to the properties whose ascription she would have to negate as a condition for rational disbelief. So she cannot in fact negate all ascriptions of scientific properties, while rationally reflecting on all data and arguments.

Here is a somewhat longer version of the argument. (A full-fledged version would require at least a long book.)

The special universality of certain scientific beliefs, i.e., their universal force given the evidence actually available, depends on the special universality of framework principles connecting them with the evidence. These principles are extremely well-hedged truisms, claiming nothing more than that certain phenomena are, prima facie, evidence in favor of certain propositions. Thus, that someone is screaming and grasping her limb is, prima facie, evidence that she feels pain in the limb (obviously, only prima facie, since she might, for example, be acting in a play). With similar hedges: if something makes the vaguely visible clear and distinct, that is a sign that it makes visible what would otherwise be invisibly present; if something nonliving erratically changes course that is a sign that something else has moved it off-course.[13] These and other topic-specific principles of relevant evidence concerning ordinary material properties and psychological characterizations are in the framework of all actual rational inquirers. As we shall see, they also limit the rational disbeliefs of all possible inquirers with experiences such as ours.

In the nontechnical inquiries into matter and mind that are part of science in the broadest sense, familiar sorts of evidence directly combine with these topic-specific truisms to justify beliefs, for example, a belief that a screamer is in pain, that a dead leaf is being pushed to and fro by something, or that squinting and peering reveals something new. Sometimes in technical science, as well, a hypothesis could be justified, in the final analysis, on the basis of such truistic principles, though this would require initially surprising evidence and, often, ingenious arguments establishing technical principles along the way. Belief in microbes in light of microscopic evidence and belief in molecules in light of the evidence and argument culminating in the Einstein-Perrin-Smoluchowski investigations of Brownian motion are two such cases, whose outlines are at least dimly suggested by truisms just presented.[14]

Disbelief in all of science would require nonreliance on the underlying truisms. But such disbelief could not be rational without reliance on the truisms.

Negative belief is an achievement, a greater accomplishment than nonbelief. When I was six I did not believe in the Copenhagen interpretation of quantum physics. But I was not so precocious as to believe that the Copenhagen interpretation was false. Even if I had said, to impress my elders, "The Copenhagen interpretation of quantum physics is false," I would not, at the time, have believed this. Negative belief requires some significant relationship to the propositions or practices of positive believers.

Normally, rational negative belief depends on criticism, actual or potential, of positive belief as relying on too little evidence or tainted by irrationality. But the first criticism, in which the naysayer advances additional evidence, is excluded by hypothesis, in the case of the nihilist concerning all of

---

[13] The hedges are always crucial. In the last case, the discovery that an erratically moving thing has internal, appropriately erratic cogs and wheels would meet the burden of proof and end the evidence of external interference. The strenuous arguments for spontaneous discontinuity in the development of quantum physics are a fancier example. Compare Arthur Fine's criticisms of my treatment of truisms in his article, "Piecemeal Realism," *Philosophical Studies* (1989).

[14] See *Fact and Method*, chapter 8 for more details.

science. The dissenter in question is relying on the same evidence as we. Also I shall suppose that the second charge, the charge of internal incoherence, could not be made by our rational negater. Skeptics have offered such arguments, but none has turned out to be good.

How, then, could the nihilist achieve his negative belief? In his disbelief in all scientific ascriptions, he must grasp the respective causal roles that the ascribed properties are supposed to serve, and deny that anything plays such a role. However, such understanding normally involves guidance by relevant topic-specific truisms. One knows what a cause of a change in state of motion would be through reliance on the principle that erratic changes in course of a nonliving thing are prima facie a sign of external interference. One knows what possession of pain by another would be through reliance on the principle that behavior such as screaming is a sign of pain in the screamer. But such reliance is not available to our disbeliever. Granted, the positivists tried to define causation abstractly and generally, in terms of regularity. But this was one of their spectacular failures.[15] The basis for the abnormally total naysaying remains to be found.

There is one other route that rational naysaying sometimes takes. Unlike the others, this one requires understanding of what yeasayers do, not just an operation with concepts that actually resembles theirs in relevant ways. Without having acquired reasons, even prima facie, one is sometimes well aware that others make inferences on the basis of them. Could the naysayer believe of us who do engage in banal ascribing, that we are wrong in our conclusion, specifying that denial, by a kind of ostension, as denial of whatever conclusion we reach? No, he believes too little to believe this. Rejecting the truisms, he lacks a rational basis for beliefs concerning what others think, even how their bodies move. Yet, by hypothesis, he forms beliefs rationally.

This argument—or rather the full-fledged argument of which this is a fragmentary sketch—is not meant to be that much-sought philosophical gimmick, the all-purpose linguistic argument against skepticism. For one thing, I have simply assumed that internal criticisms of the normal framework of inquiry are no good. Skeptical arguments consisting of such criticism will have to be countered on their own terms. (Usually, these days, they neglect the basic distinction between an alternative explanation and a rival explanation.) Also, an argument for the impossibility of rational negative belief hardly establishes the impossibility of mere rational nonbelief, a topic to which I will soon turn.

There are also moral truisms, sufficiently compelling to make rational, informed rejection of certain moral judgments impossible for anyone except a

---

[15] See ibid., chapter 1 and 2, with references to the abundant literature on this theme. Of course, the reasons acquired in the process of understanding causation might subsequently be criticized as incomplete, or even wrong. Such criticism motivates the introduction of new kinds of causation. But this is certainly not our naysayer's project.

moral nihilist. For example, anyone except a moral nihilist would be irrational not to condemn the paradigmatic horrors in which only serious suffering results from an act. But rational moral nihilism is possible. Granted, the standard routes to negative belief are missing, since the moral nihilist lacks negative evidence or undermining arguments. Moreover, there is no reductive definition in nonmoral terms of what moral positive believers intend to convey that the moral nihilist can use to give appropriate content to his denial. Still, he can, by the last route, achieve belief that no moral property exists. He can believe enough about us to understand how we arrive at moral attribution. Employing this understanding he can believe that none of our moral assertions is due to detection of anything.

Thus, nonmoral beliefs about matter and mental life can achieve a universality to which no moral belief can aspire. This conclusion has often led to the denial that moral beliefs are justified true beliefs. But really, the difference in universality has a much humbler significance. Certain sources of nonmoral belief are so elementary that their abandonment leaves no room for semantic parasitism. Elementary nonmoral beliefs are needed, as it were, for a grasp of their own content. Moral beliefs are not needed to grasp their content. So one can negate all moral ascriptions, but not, say, all beliefs about matter, while possessing all the evidence there is and responding to it rationally.

The topic of nonbelief is significantly different from the topic of disbelief. Of course, the latter attitude includes the former. The rational moral nihilist, believing in the falsehood of all moral ascriptions, does not believe in their truth. But there can be nonbelief in the absence of disbelief, as in my relation to Niels Bohr's interpretation when I was six years old. Is there a possible rational person who takes in all the sense experiences on which we base ascriptions of properties to matter but does not believe in the truth of any of these ascriptions—without believing in their falsehood? Here, the relation between the rejection of moral facts and the rejection of material facts is more complex.

Someone who takes in our sense experiences, is rational, but has none of our beliefs concerning material objects also has virtually none of our desires. If, for example, she ever desired food, then the desire for food would have to play an appropriate role in the explanation of her actions. But the desire could only play that role if her actions, on appropriate occasions, were due to the desire for food together with some belief as to what would provide it. And, by hypothesis, she has no such beliefs. So, when she feels the pangs that are intense pangs of hunger for us, and a nice breakfast is spread out before her, she does not want to have a bite, even though she takes in the same sense-experiences as we. In general, the wholesale nonbeliever must have virtually no desires (or perhaps none at all. But a few bare desires directed at inner states will not affect the argument). Moreover, her barrenness in this regard is not due to her awareness of a radical incapacity to get her way. She has the usual sense-experiences and, in any case, has no such substantial beliefs.

Could there be such a person? Presumably, a drug or trance could put some-one temporarily in such a state, taking away both desires and beliefs concern-ing matter, but permitting intake of sense-experiences and access to memories of them. Such a person would not seem to be irrational. So here, wholesale nonbelief about matter seems on a par with wholesale nonbelief concerning morality. Both are rational in possible people, whom no one would want to be for long.

However, there is a difference, as well. A being permanently bereft of de-sires, as a permanent nonbeliever in material properties would be, would not seem to be a person at all. In contrast, the radical unconcern characteristic of a wholesale moral nonbeliever makes for a monstrous person, whose attitude toward others is one he would want to change if inner change were not so difficult. But he is a possible person nonetheless, even if his radical unconcern for others characterizes his whole life. In the face of standard evidence, wholesale material nonbelief, unlike wholesale moral nonbelief, cannot char-acterize the whole life of a being who is a person.

Taking all the differences and similarities together, is moral inquiry, on the whole, like scientific inquiry? I can think of no principled or interesting way to sum up the differences and similarities. I hope the reader is now inclined to reject this final grand question as itself misguided, like the initial grand question of whether moral realism is valid.

For these first five chapters, I have been concerned with the conflicts among sets of basic convictions that are most important for resolving general questions about truth and justification in morality. These conflicts have in-volved dramatic differences in frameworks for moral inquiry, the differences that most decisively establish the limits of reason and evidence in moral judg-ment and the relation of those limits to moral truth. Yet, for all their impor-tance in resolving general questions about morality, these conflicts of belief, characterizing very different societies where they contrast outlooks that are both actual, are not the most morally urgent problems of conflict for us. Moral responsibility requires, above all, a morally acceptable response to potential harm that one's choices might inflict on others. The existence of interests and beliefs among long-dead people has no bearing, here. And most of us, most of the time, have little interaction with people in utterly preindustrial soci-eties.

In the rest of this book I will be concerned with typical modern conflicts. First and at greatest length, I will describe how the institutions of a modern industrial society should be judged, in the face of intrasocietal conflicts that make such assessment a moral judgment. This is the most intensively worked terrain of theories of justice. Then, I will consider whether the standard that I defend ought to be applied to conflicts of interest across the borders of modern societies, arguing that it should. Finally, I will turn from questions of justice to questions about the burdens of moral conscience in general, assessing conflicts, alleged and real, between one's interests and the demands of morality. Although none of these problems is mainly a difficulty in responding to the existence of different beliefs, the perspective on moral truth and justification summed up in the mixed verdict will contribute to each solution.

Chapter Six

JUSTICE AS SOCIAL FREEDOM

THE INSTITUTIONS of a society are just if and only if they could not be rejected, freely and rationally, by anyone living in the society who desires such acceptability on the part of all who share this desire. The requirement of rational acceptability is met only if rejection is precluded by some relevant rationale that does not depend on ignorance. In the moral defense of a social system, it would be no better than a vicious pun to say, "They are in no position to complain. For they are taught that what they do is virtually worthless—which is, of course, quite false." The requirement of free acceptability is meant, in part, to guarantee that the crucial rationales do not depend on the force available to others or on one's own incapacity to defend one's interests. It would be just as vicious a joke to propose that the burdens of living under a system are relevantly acceptable just because the alternative to bearing them is to be locked up.

These statements might be summed up as declaring that justice is social freedom. Though my particular formulation is deeply indebted to recent contractarian work, Scanlon's in particular, this outlook, which I will call "justice as social freedom," is very widely shared. At least since the seventeenth century, most major political philosophers have embraced it. In advanced industrial societies, most people are implicitly committed to it—and (as I shall argue later, largely by criticizing utilitarianism) virtually everyone would be so committed after rational reflection on relevant facts. Yet this appearance of agreement is deceptive, and the consequences of disagreement are deeply troubling.[1]

The appearance is deceptive because the agreement in demanding free and rational acceptability is accompanied by disagreement as to the proper interpretation of the demand itself, i.e., as to the nature of the goals on which relevant acceptance and rejection are grounded. Alongside the uncontroversial conditions for free and rational acceptance mentioned above, other, deeply controversial ones are imposed. Rawls famously insists that the commitment to free and rational choice for all excludes any attempt to benefit

[1] T. M. Scanlon, "Contractualism and Utilitarianism" in A. Sen and B. Williams, *Utilitarianism and Beyond* (Cambridge: Cambridge University Press, 1982) is a powerful, concise discussion of the requirements of acceptability whose political implications I will be exploring. See also his "Liberty, Contract and Contribution" in G. Dworkin et al., *Markets and Morals* (New York: John Wiley, 1977).

from special advantages, including advantages in natural endowment. Though a rational choice among basic social arrangements responds to their benefits and burdens, a choice governed by one's pursuit of advantages depending on traits other than willingness to cooperate is (he claims) doubly opposed to free acceptability: it imposes a burden on the less advantaged, and it reduces the autonomy of those whose fundamental choices are mired in such contingent advantages. Arguing from his specification of social freedom, Rawls famously concludes that basic institutions should be of maximum benefit to the worst-off. In Nozick's specification of justice as social freedom, the relevant goal of free and rational acceptability is only pursued by those who respect side-constraints extensively protecting the honest and nonviolent employment of results of honest nonviolent self-advancement. In this view, a choice of institutions violating these boundaries must express a departure from the goal of free acceptability. The only special provision for the needy is a low threshold required to compensate for exclusive control of raw materials and land. Some further lines in this wide spectrum of alternative specifications are the requirements of mutual advantage which Gauthier advances as dictates of the pursuit of free and rational agreement and specifications which exclude the neglect of the urgent needs of some when the remedy is of small cost to others.[2]

How should one argue that justice as social freedom is the right basis for assessing fundamental institutions and important policies in advanced industrial societies? Partly, by criticizing rival perspectives, among which utilitarianism is the main systematic alternative. Partly, by connecting reliance on justice as social freedom with processes of moral detection. In addition, there is one other essential part of the argument, by far the most demanding, which will take up most of this chapter and the next. One must show that justice as social freedom, combined with relevant facts, would generate coherent answers to the most basic questions of social choice in an advanced industrial setting, not contradictory answers due to diverse specifications which survive critical reflection.

So far as civil and political liberties are concerned, the diversity of specifications is not very threatening. The outcomes of the different specifications all seem to include strong emphasis on equal civil and political liberty in the advanced industrial setting. (Of course, it would be useful to clarify the common rationale and to show that it supports just one of the variants of the shared, strong emphasis. I will do this, in chapter eight.) In contrast, the course of recent philosophical controversies makes it a live worry that the diversity of specifications might block informed and rational agreement on a

---

[2] See John Rawls, A *Theory of Justice* (Cambridge: Harvard University Press, 1971); Robert Nozick, *Anarchy, State and Utopia* (New York: Basic Books, 1974); David Gauthier, *Morals by Agreement* (Oxford: Oxford University Press, 1986); T. M. Scanlon, "Contractualism and Utilitarianism," p. 123.

standard specific enough to determine the basic economic institutions and policies of advanced industrial societies—i.e., to determine them in light of relevant facts. The project of answering this doubt will be my main defense of the adequacy of justice as social freedom—i.e., its adequacy for answering the institutional questions that are urgent for advanced industrial folk. For reasons that will emerge later on, important noninstitutional questions and important institutional questions in settings that are less technologically advanced may have no single answer in all defensible specifications. This is no general refutation of the claim that justice is social freedom, though it could lead to moral tragedy.

One might seek to achieve rational agreement on a modern economic standard by a process of elimination at the level of moral first principles, arguing that only one specification of justice as social freedom survives well-reasoned and informed reflection on the part of any partisan of the generic demand for social freedom. But now, more than thirty years after the debate over Rawls' theory of justice began in earnest, anyone surveying the luxuriant crop of survivors has reason to despair of the hope that fair criticism will weed out every specification save one.

I will be pursuing a somewhat different strategy, in which facts specific to advanced industrial societies will play a fundamental role. The economic standard that I will ultimately defend is egalitarian in the same way as Rawls'. In modern industrial societies, in the most important social choices, justice requires economic arrangements under which the typical lifetime expectations of those in the worst-off situations are greatest; in short, inequalities must work in the interest of the less than equal. Even though this is a currently controversial standard, which would determine the most basic choices of economic institutions and policies, the moral principles employed in defense of this standard will be a minimal specification, centering on a demand for equality of opportunity, which every partisan of social freedom would accept on adequate reflection. In this chapter, I will present this minimal specification and try to show that every partisan of justice as social freedom would be unreasonable to reject it. I will have occasion to criticize influential proposals as rationally indefensible specifications, so a priori elimination will play an important role in this phase of the minimalist project. Still, the minimal specification will be compatible with a variety of further differences as to the nature of the demand for social freedom, differences reflected in present-day controversies in philosophy and in politics.

Then, in the next chapter, I will try to show that the minimum is enough, i.e., enough to provide a means of judging institutions and basic policies in an advanced industrial economy. People in such an economy can maintain those remaining differences concerning justice as social freedom without being divided by them when they construct a moral yardstick for assessing their own society. The yardstick all partisans of social freedom would choose, on the basis of thorough moral reflection and relevant economic knowledge, is the egalitarian standard previously described.

The modern adequacy of the minimal specification depends on two kinds of facts about the advanced industrial setting. On the one hand, people are, pervasively, victimized by social barriers to advancement in any reasonably efficient capitalist economy. The minimal specification entails that the barriers are only acceptable as an unavoidable outcome of processes benefiting the disadvantaged. Otherwise, their knowing acceptance of prospects lowered by those barriers would not be free. On the other hand, in an advanced industrial setting, some reasonably efficient capitalist system is best for everyone who is constrained by commitment to justice as social freedom. In short, the adequacy of the minimal specification will depend on facts that would sadden most observers of the modern industrial scene, saddening different observers for very different reasons: central planning does not work, yet traditional socialists were right in most of their charges of capitalist inequality.

We are used to hearing that the demands of freedom conflict with the demands of equality, especially in economic arrangements. Actually, in the modern economic setting, freedom when properly understood requires as much equality as a rational egalitarian would demand.

In this chapter's long journey from a generic demand for free and rational acceptability to a basis for demanding economic equality, I will begin by connecting justice as social freedom with the basis for claiming moral truth that I have been defending. Then, I will describe certain circumstances of unequal opportunity and argue that any defensible specification of justice as social freedom will condemn such circumstances as unjust if they can be changed in the interest of the disadvantaged. The argument that this is so will largely consist of a critical survey of Nozick's arguments for a narrower understanding of social freedom.

My defense of the prohibition concerning unequal opportunity will suggest an even broader, yet still minimal construal of social freedom, "the Hobbesian interpretation," as I will call it. In part, my description of it is intended as a basis for resolving questions outside the sphere of economic justice, in chapter eight. However, the immediate sequel, in this chapter, will be the investigation of a further disagreement, clearer against the background of this shared position. The disagreement is a version of the familiar split concerning whether advantages of superior natural endowment have any special standing when economic justice is pursued. The description of the rival positions will set the terms of the reconciling project in the next chapter: justice in modern industrial circumstances must be determined by considerations stemming from the minimal prohibition against unequal opportunity, and the split over the relevance of natural endowment must have no important impact on the application of these considerations.

Finally, in defense of justice as social freedom itself, I will turn to its main modern rival, utilitarianism. I will argue that utilitarianism violates the requirement to treat people evenhandedly, in choices of social arrangements. Because the requirement is so widely shared, the violations provide almost everyone who is now a utilitarian with compelling reasons to abandon this position, in favor of justice as social freedom.

JUSTICE AND TRUTH

Even without the metaethical framework of the first half of this book, the project of reconciling different specifications of social freedom would be important. Any decent person has a preference that measures seriously affecting people be accepted by them, or, in any case, would be accepted if they possessed relevant information and rationally reflected on relevant arguments. Rational persuasion is to be preferred to force. So one ought to have a specially strong preference for arguments with broad potential to persuade, provided that they depend on moral convictions that one shares. Commitment to justice as social freedom is very common in advanced industrial societies, yet it is not clear initially that it provides a basis for common judgments of the main effects of social choices. So someone who shares the commitment must regard it as morally urgent to determine its adequacy as a basis for rational persuasion among its many partisans.

In addition, the metaethical context of the previous chapters justifies an even deeper interest in the reconciling project. In chapter two, I argued that the main fundamental source of insight into facts about justice was the adjustment of bases for rational political deliberation to equality of coercive power. This process gives rise to the belief in justice as social freedom. Indeed, it is hard to see how any contrary belief could result—especially once one realizes that the greater power of someone in a stable majority to gang up with others and impose measures on the whole of society is, as such, an inequality in coercive power. On account of its ultimate origins, endorsement of a political measure that is based on commitment to social freedom together with relevant data and rational reflection constitutes justified true belief. What is more, most partisans of rival commitments either do not claim that their alternatives arise from processes of detection, or make claims about detection that are dogmatic or irrational.

For these reasons, someone committed to justice as social freedom will take this commitment to be the most promising means of finding truths about justice. (I hope that chapter two has made it clear that this last sentence is not at all tautologous.) This search for truths is of much more than intellectual interest. Along with our strong moral preference for rational persuasion, we have a strong moral preference for basing coercively enforced measures (for example, any measure enforced by a state) on truths rather than mere strong convictions. Yet it is not clear that there are truths enough to justify basic political choices. The divergence in specifications of social freedom might stand in the way. Sufficient success in detection will depend on the usual process of specifying and testing, starting with first findings that are vague or narrow. This is the way to uncover sufficiently determinate truth, if it can be found. And it is morally urgent to pursue the truth in this way.[3]

"Inheritance"

Those who have different general specifications of free and rational acceptability often agree, nonetheless, that an economic system imposing fundamentally unequal opportunities for self-advancement would be relevantly unfree. A version of the demand for unequal opportunity is the core of the minimal specification, the part that plays the leading role in deriving identical judgments from different interpretations of social freedom. Family-based differences are the most common threat to such equality, and might, then, seem a good means to explore the content of the minimal demand. Yet thought about the family is easily distorted by sentiments or obscured by unexamined assumptions. So I will begin with a highly artificial example, in which the objectionable nature of certain kinds of barriers to self-advancement is especially clear.

Imagine an isolated economy in which every adult works, no parent cares specially about his or her children, and current optimal technology calls for a certain mix of jobs. Nine-tenths of jobs, the alpha-type jobs, are generally interesting, rarely exhausting, and require considerable training. One-tenth, the beta-type jobs, consist of unskilled drudgery.

The alphas, who, of course, include the teachers and administrators, de-

---

[3] I will end these preliminaries by attempting to assuage a worry about words that my formulations might create in some readers, namely, a worry about the words "rational" and "reasonable." In the central formulation of his proposal in "Contractualism and Utilitarianism," Scanlon speaks of "any system of rules for the general regulation of behaviour which no one could reasonably reject as a basis for informed, unforced general agreement" (p. 110). In characterizations of what people do, the use of "reasonable" rather than "rational" sometimes marks an important difference. I will present these differences in detail in chapter 10 (although the alternative terms are generally equivalent in the usages I myself employ). However, there is no difference between what Scanlon intends by his reasonable rejection criterion and what I mean in speaking of free and rational acceptability to all who desire such acceptability on the part of everyone sharing this desire. For Scanlon notes, "The intended force of the qualification 'reasonably' . . . is to exclude rejections that would be unreasonable *given* the aim of finding principles which could be the basis of informed, unforced general agreement" (p. 111). My different phrasing is only meant to bring to the fore potential disagreements in the interpretation of the generic principle, by connecting it with debates over freedom and over the moral interest in rationality. Similarly, though my failure to emphasize Rawls' distinction between "the Reasonable" and "the Rational" hints at a different underlying metaethics, it reflects no disagreement in moral principles. (In contrast, Scanlon's proposal that his central formulation is a valid general account of moral wrongness is a point of disagreement, which I will also discuss in chapter 10.)

cide on a scheme that avoids the inefficiency of a system in which unneeded skills are taught and labor is expended in the impartial administration of competitive tests. Having established that there are rarely any significant innate differences with a bearing on alpha-competence, they randomly assign babies to the alpha or the beta track at birth, in the technologically appropriate proportion. More precisely, they implement this plan through a contract between the alpha educators and the alpha noneducators. Because only alphas have the energy to accumulate a surplus beyond urgent and immediate needs, because only they have the skills to do so, because of luck in a lottery, or for some other noncoercive, nonfraudulent reason, alphas and only alphas can make a mutually satisfactory bargain with teachers and educational administrators. In the interest of gains in efficiency and on account of their bargain, alpha teachers will only teach the special skills to those with an alpha on their birth certificate.[4]

These educational decisions are protected, in ways familiar to us, from deceitful or coercive intrusion, on the basis of laws passed by a democratically elected legislature, enforced by the familiar apparatus of courts and jails. For example, presentation of an altered birth certificate is punished as fraud, and an angry mob of betas occupying Alpha High School could expect eventual arrest for criminal trespass.

Once children emerge from the educational system, they freely compete for jobs, with predictable results. If a beta (i.e., someone who was beta-assigned) applies for a desirable job, she can expect alpha-assigned competitors to get the job instead. And she cannot comfort herself with the thought that if the better-trained competitors were not hired, she would not have been hired anyway. In Alphabetaland, as in our land, firms need not passively deploy whatever labor happens to be on offer, any more than they passively deploy the current output of iron mines without smelting or prospecting. Were there fewer alpha-assigned applicants, the beta's chances of success would improve, since firms are prepared to overcome skill shortages through on-the-job training and support for their employees' pursuit of further education. If there were a long-term general shortage of people with alpha skills, then investors, managers and others who depend on the prosperity of firms would willingly pay extra taxes for state-provided training in addition to that provided through Alphabetan assignment.

In sum, Alphabetan assignment does not merely give rise to better prospects for some than for others, it guarantees that situations arise in which some do worse than they otherwise would because others have been provided

[4] "Birth certificate" is a bit of a misnomer. Maternity nurses and other alphas involved with neonates privately manufacture certificates of alpha-assignment, which are filed, distributed and examined at strategic times.

with superior resources. Alphabetan assignment is not just a system of inequality, it is a system of competitive advantage and disadvantage.

The educators of Alphabetaland do not employ wrongful coercion; they teach. The characteristic discrimination reflects benign concerns for material gain, not vicious desires to treat some less well than others. The coercive apparatus of the state is only used to protect the noncoercive nondeceitful employment of resources acquired by nondeceitful noncoercers. Yet few who insist on free and rational acceptability to all would count this arrangement as just, in the absence of strenuous further justifications, which are unlikely to be available. A beta who was born into this system would be right to call for change, and an alpha would be wrong to resist.

Even those who would generally protect the results of nonviolent, nonfraudulent self-advancement have reason to withhold protection here, since alphan bargaining and teaching is in the same troubled moral terrain as productive activity that pollutes: it gives rise to harmful side-effects, viz., betan disadvantages in competing for rewarding work. The victim of a harmful side-effect is not, in general, wrong to interfere with its production. This is especially clear, even to the most laissez-faire, when the harmful side-effect is catastrophic. If Friday is dying of emphysema because Crusoe stubbornly insists on making his canoes by the traditional hot coals method on the adjacent beach, Friday is not wrong to move the workshop by force. But the consequences need not be catastrophic. If Friday is simply made to cough and hack, he may forcibly move the workshop if other methods are of no avail.

Moreover, a harmful side-effect can justify interference when it is part of a whole process that is beneficial, on balance, to the one who is harmed. Farming in the state of nature, Mr. Alfalfa lets all his effluents flow downstream to Ms. Grey's farm—both beneficent fertilizers and noxious sewage. Ms. Grey, who is helped on balance, may still intervene to stop the discharge of sewage. She might have been reasonable to choose both effects if Alfalfa, asking for her consent, had offered her the choice of both or neither. But Grey didn't contract for the water service, so she has a right to move Alfalfa's privy if persuasion fails.

Perhaps such victims as Friday and Grey should, if possible, make it worth the polluter's while to eliminate the harmful effect, by offering him compensatory payment as part of a process eliminating the effect. Still, this rule of compensation would have no direct impact on the harmful side-effect we are considering, namely, the creation of a competitive disadvantage. Betan compensation of alphas for refraining from the unequalizing bargains would drain competitive resources from betas, re-creating competitive inequalities rather than removing them. In this respect, inequality of opportunity is a stricter constraint on traditional capitalist rights than pollution, at least if the victims' whole life-prospects are lowered and they live in a society in which all resources available for compensation are resources for competition, as well. It is as if there were a diabolical form of pollution in which compensation for nonpollution magically turned pollutant.

Broadly speaking, the Alphabetan system is unjust because it imposes on some barriers to their self-advancement which they did not choose, would not have been rational to choose, and only endure on account of vulnerability. The reasons why moral condemnation would be the response of so many moral judges can be made more precise by specifying certain features of the system that might be essential to condemnation for some partisans of social freedom, and jointly dictate condemnation by virtually all. ("Virtually all" is not the same as all. In subsequent sections, I will discuss objections from some partisans of social freedom, arguing that all such dissent from the following standard for condemnation depends on insufficient reflection.)

1. *Entrapment.* The system of assignment is not chosen by betas, and they cannot evade its consequences (or can only do so by costly, risky ventures in emigration).

By way of contrast, suppose an analogous system was part of the internal scheme of training and promotion within a certain factory, surrounded by other factories, regularly taking on new employees, with a variety of significantly different schemes. Then, many partisans of justice as social freedom would refuse to condemn the scheme.

2. *Restriction.* In the Alphabetan system, betas are burdened by inequalities in competitive resources, due to others' choices.

In some specifications of justice as social freedom, it is crucial that the inequality of opportunity results from human activity. By way of contrast with Alphabetan activity, consider a politically unified archipelago with islands of widely differing fertility, rough seas impeding movement, but no humanly created impediment to movement from island to island. Could the luckless ones, born on the less fertile islands, reasonably reject arrangements that had no geographic subsidies? Partisans of different versions of justice as social freedom will answer in different ways, corresponding to different understandings of the impact of natural inequality on the moral recognition of equal freedom. Some (Nozick and Gauthier, for example) would regard insistence on subsidies as desertion of the goal of free and rational acceptability to all.[5]

For many partisans of justice as social freedom, the fact that some have lesser prospects than others over the course of their whole lives, due to humanly created causes which the worse-off did not choose is, by itself, a powerful indictment; it creates a moral demand that the entire situation be justifiable from the standpoint of those worse-off. In this view (Rawls', for example), it is enough that the betas, who did not choose to be born into the Alphabetan system, have lesser prospects given equal willingness to try, not

---

[5] The example of the archipelago is adapted from Nozick, *Anarchy, State and Utopia*, p. 185 and Gauthier, *Morals by Agreement*, pp. 218–21.

as a result of some natural necessity, but as a result of human choices. The system benefits betas less than alphas for reasons that have nothing to do with betan choices, but much to do with avoidable choices of others.

Still, we are pursuing a minimal specification. So it is important that others would not be so impressed by the humanly avoidable creation of unchosen unequal life-prospects. In their view, it is always a token of envy, not justice, to complain of a superior outcome for others, even if the outcomes reflect confinement to humanly created lifelong inequalities in prospects given equal willingness to try. What does impress them about Alphabetan assignment is the feature that makes the provision of superior resources analogous to pollution once the graduates compete. Alphabetan assignment gives rise to situations in which some are worse off than they would be if others had not been given superior resources, even if the extra resources were not given to them instead. Because of competition, advantages for some create disadvantages for others. Very few would regard consequent complaints as mere envy.—"Restriction" stipulates that such worsening effects, as well as human causes, are part of the system of inequality.

3. *Coercion.* The choices whose effectiveness gives betas less opportunity to advance their interests than others are protected by the coercive apparatus of the state.

For some, relevant violations of freedom must include outright coercion, which is confined to the political realm in Alphabetaland. Note that the condemnation of Alphabetan arrangements including such coercion is apt to block the justification of otherwise similar arrangements lacking this feature. Unless the characteristic choices are protected by coercive public means from private intrusion, their disruption is apt to be so severe that no one, alpha or beta, would lose through the replacement of the system by another whose public coercive protection is justifiable. As Hobbes noted at the start of modern political philosophy, economic rights are virtually worthless unless forcibly guarded by the great Leviathan, the state.

4. *Undesirability.* The betas have reason to prefer to have been born into a different system, on account of benefits under that alternative that would not depend on the entrapment, restriction and coercion of others who are themselves willing to forgo benefits depending on such unfreedom for others.

There is a certain division of labor between this last condition and the first three. If a system creating unequal opportunities is characterized by entrapment, restriction and coercion, it is not morally protected, i.e., change to another system could rightly be imposed on the basis of an appropriate comparison between its effects and the effects of the alternative. The undesirability described in condition 4 is the comparison justifying such change.

Suppose that the equality of opportunity required to evade the first three conditions is highly inefficient. Then, the desirability required to justify Alphabetan assignment might provide betas more than what they would receive in conditions of equal opportunity. Still, so long as alphas benefit from unequal opportunity, they are in no position to complain of changes under which they would lose benefits depending on such inequality. For example, an alphan teenager is in no position to complain of the reduced chance of rewarding work that less inequality would inflict on her, and an alphan teacher could not complain if the abolition of Alphabetan assignment makes teaching less rewarding.

According to this strong requirement of desirability to the disadvantaged, advantages depending on entrapment, restriction and coercion are a kind of moral credit in the social account of the disadvantaged: so long as the credit is not used up, the system creating it must be preferable to all otherwise acceptable alternatives from the standpoint of the disadvantaged. A weaker requirement of desirability would only require that the system be preferable to any which wholly removes the imposed inequality, preferable, that is, from the standpoint of the actually disadvantaged. Reliance on the second standard, but not the first, would make it good reasoning to argue, "The elimination of this source of unequal opportunity would be a disaster in the way of intrusion and inefficiency from everyone's point of view. So, alas, we must accept the source, together with all its outcomes."

In the next section, I will describe how the first, stronger standard results from an understanding of the terms for free and rational acceptability. Even without such deeper reasoning, the strong standard of comparison is supported by good fit with other judgments of interactions and inequalities, not just polluting interactions but also the great inequality that was the first subject of political philosophy. In any political system that is not on the verge of collapse (and some that are), some relatively small group of officeholders possess legislative and administrative powers, individual or collective, far in excess of those available to others. It is easy enough to show that some such inequality of power is better, for virtually everyone, than its absence. But no one takes this general advantage to justify any particular inequality of power. An inequality of power which improves everyone as compared with the state of nature might still be rejected as too despotic. Any systematic concentration of power in officials must be shown to be of maximum benefit to ordinary citizens. Similarly, any socially based, coercively protected concentration of economic opportunity must be shown to be of benefit to those disadvantaged by it—not just as compared with equal dispersion of opportunities but also as compared with alternative arrangements in which they are somewhat disadvantaged. Thus, even if a system of equal opportunity turned out to be worse for everyone born in Alphabetaland, the justification of an economic system including Alphabetan assignment would have scarcely begun. Perhaps, in the interest of betas, the education of betas should be improved or the impact of betan assignment mitigated through social insurance, a progressive income tax or a minimum wage.

THE COOPERATIVE GOAL

The strong standard of desirability to the disadvantaged results from adding requirements of relevance to a starting-point that is so subminimal that it is more of a warning against stupidity than a standard of justice. If an alternative set of institutions would be a net improvement for some and a net loss for none, then, of course, the potential gainers can reject the status quo in favor of the alternative while seeking arrangements that are freely and rationally acceptable to all. The corresponding basis for rejection is horridly permissive, with no effect on systems of slavery so long as they benefit any slaveholder. One imposes sterner specifications by excluding as irrelevant benefits and losses to which someone could not appeal if his choice were guided by the crucial goal of free and rational acceptability to all, "the cooperative goal" as I will sometimes call it. The description of such constraints is a way of adding content to the goal, going beyond the bare avoidance of rationales based on force, misinformation or muddle. The utterly weak "no loss" standard is then enormously strengthened by adding a requirement of relevance. A system is freely and rationally rejected by some who seek free and rational acceptability to all if a change to an alternative would benefit some and harm none when only relevant gains and losses are counted.

One, uncontroversial constraint on relevance excludes benefits depending on uses of coercion whose justification rests on discriminatory premises, i.e., premises entailing that the acceptability of institutions to some who have the cooperative goal is relatively unimportant because of the kind of people they are. Even if an anti-Semite cared more about avoiding Jews than any Jew cared about associating with gentiles, justice would not require, indeed it would forbid compensating the anti-Semite for the absence of ghettos.

Another obvious exclusion concerns gains that are ill-gotten by individuals. Someone will not relevantly reject arrangements because they deprive her of advantages that she obtains through the wrongful coercion or deception of others. It is not a relevant ground for rejecting the institution of courts and police that they deprive one of gains from highway robbery.

The first three conditions in the fourfold principle also describe a causal taint that makes benefits irrelevant. That is why transfer to the disadvantaged is required so long as competitive inequality is imposed. A loss of benefits which depend on entrapment, restriction and coercion of others is not a relevant basis for rejecting a proposed alternative, i.e., an alternative which is preferable to those who suffer from the corresponding competitive disadvantage and who pursue the cooperative goal.

The irrelevance of benefits from unequal opportunity is especially clear in light of a previous judgment: betas would not be wrong to resist the imposed inequalities by presenting phony certificates or staging high school sit-ins. Such permission should be part of any outlook in which free and rational acceptability to all is a fundamental demand. For the betas are responding to dangers of competitive loss which are imposed on them by the choices of others, in processes independent of betan choices. However, in the face of betan resistance, the system will not work for anyone unless it is protected coercively. And someone pursuing the cooperative goal will certainly exclude benefits depending on superior capacity to coerce exercised against people advancing their interests in ways that are not wrong.

So long as benefits are tainted by entrapment, restriction and coercion, their loss is not relevant for those who have the cooperative goal. If the loss or transfer of such benefits is necessary to improve the situation of the disadvantaged, this will create relevant benefits for some and relevant losses for none. So the change will be just. As the strong standard of desirability requires, advantages from entrapment, restriction and coercion are a kind of moral credit on which pursuers of justice will draw for changes benefiting the disadvantaged.

In the real world, in modern times, have entrapment, restriction and coercion combined to taint benefits that would otherwise influence the determination of justice? Alphabetaland is just a horrid fiction. Legal prohibitions of access to goods and opportunities, as in de jure racial segregation, are horrid nonfictions, but they are a special case, since coercion is specifically and intentionally directed at imposing barriers to self-advancement. The fourfold principle also excludes systems in which state coercion protects processes whose actually discriminatory outcome is not required by law. To uncover an obvious case in which such indirect imposition has tainted benefits in the real world, one has only to clarify a certain ambiguity in the third condition that made Alphabetan assignment objectionable, the one I labeled "restriction."

It was objectionable that betas had fewer competitive resources because of choices that others had made. It might seem that the crucial worsening choice must be the fateful marking that leads to discrimination—here, the entry of the fateful letter on a birth certificate. But on second thought, a basis for discrimination produced by nature could be just as objectionable. Suppose that 10% of babies are black, and, to save effort in record-keeping, this natural fact is used to assign babies to the beta category. The moral equivalence of the alternative systems implies that a competitive disadvantage is objectionable (i.e., lacks moral protection if sustained by coercion and entrapment) if it results from a certain combination, the combination of other people's choices with a feature of the person disadvantaged by those choices which is beyond his or her control. A seeker of justice, pursuing the cooperative goal, will not insist on competitive advantages depending on entrapment, coercion and this restrictive combination of burdensome choices and unchosen features giving rise to the choices. More precisely, he will not insist on such benefits when an alternative would remove them while providing relevant improvements from the standpoint of the disadvantaged. He is willing to put these benefits to one side, even if the discriminatory choices are not his own.

This side of Alphabetaland, certain systems of racial discrimination vividly illustrate this general rule. Consider the situations of blacks in many towns in the southern United States, at least as recently as the 1960's. Quite apart from any legally enforced segregation, they could not dwell, dine or open businesses as they would have chosen because of decisions made, on account of their race, by realtors, renters, house-sellers, restaurateurs and bankers. The worsening decisions not to transact with blacks were not necessarily motivated by racist repugnance for the transactions with blacks as such. Rather, the bankers, restaurateurs and others often were seeking to avoid net financial loss stemming from desertion by customers who preferred not to transact with businesses serving people without racial discrimination.

Laws prohibiting such discrimination (as many laws now do) prevent sellers from making choices that they otherwise might. In considering whether these laws are just, could frustrated racists relevantly reject them on account of the coercively created mental distress they suffer in eating at the same restaurants as blacks? In the pursuit of justice, could *nonracist* whites relevantly reject the new arrangement because of their coercively created burden of longer lines at the best restaurants, or their greater difficulty in finding a mortgage due to less discrimination by banks? Virtually everyone committed to justice as social freedom would answer "no" to these questions. The irrelevance of such benefits makes the prohibition of such racial discrimination a demand of justice.

Justice and Discrimination

"Virtually everyone" does not mean everyone. Readers of a certain age will remember a time when a sizable minority argued that the legal prohibition of racial discrimination by restaurant-owners, realtors and bankers was an assault on freedom. These appeals to freedom were often accompanied by declarations that the racist choices, though morally protected, were deeply abhorrent. Not all of these protesters—in effect, dissenters from the fourfold principle—were hypocrites.

These days, the legitimacy of anti-discrimination statutes is not the subject of live political controversy, despite heated debate over particular proposals. Still, in political philosophy, the importance for justice of unequal opportunity is not uncontroversial. It is time to consider whether dissent from the fourfold principle is rational for any partisan of social freedom.

There is a burden of proof on such dissenters. They give standing to benefits derived from the competitive burdens of others in the choices that determine justice. In the interactions giving rise to the benefits, some people are blocked by unchosen properties in pursuing their goals, and the block is due to the choices of others. No doubt, political measures correcting this state of affairs will themselves block some other choices. But no one who approves of any law at all regards such interference as intrinsically wrong. In seeking just institutions and social measures, why should one care when someone complains that he stands to lose a benefit of advantages which depend on the entrapment, restriction and coercion of others? This is a good question, for any partisan of social freedom. I will now consider, in turn, three answers that have been offered: Nozick's appeal to the unobjectionable character of actions exploiting unequal opportunities, his claim that all interference with noncoercive, nondeceptive uses of the result of one's noncoercive nondeceptive activity is wrong, and an assimilation of social settings of inequality to morally unobjectionable natural settings which is suggested by certain passages in both Nozick's and Gauthier's writings. These are, I hope, the main issues avoided so far.

In the section entitled "Equality of Opportunity" in *Anarchy, State and Utopia* (pp. 235–38), Nozick acknowledges "feeling the power" of appeals to equality of opportunity, but denies that such considerations can justify institutions or public policies reducing the benefits enjoyed as a consequence of the advantages (p. 237). In support of this denial he appeals to the benign aspect of certain private activities in which people routinely benefit from unequal opportunity. If the future Ms. Nozick rejected a suitor because of Bob Nozick's superior intelligence and good looks "would the rejected less intelligent and less handsome suitor have a legitimate complaint of unfairness? Would my thus impeding the other suitor's winning the hand of fair lady justify taking some resources from others to pay for cosmetic surgery . . . ? *No such consequences follow.* (Against whom would the rejected suitor have a legitimate complaint? Against what?) Nor are things different if the differential opportunities arise from the accumulated effects of people's acting or transferring their entitlement as they choose. The case is even easier for consumption goods [as opposed to competitive resources]. . . . *Is* it unfair that a child be raised in a home with a swimming pool, using it daily even though he is no more *deserving* than another child whose home is without one? . . . Why then should there be any objection to the transfer of the swimming pool to an adult by bequest?" (pp. 237f.).

If the swimming pool is just used for fun, it does not create a competitive burden on others. Yet if one thinks of advantages in swimming competitions, or changes the swimming pool to a home library or prep school, the example becomes relevant to the fourfold principle. For this principle certainly can dictate changes in institutions in order to reduce the competitive burdens of those whose parents are less well-off. And, with these changes in the example, Nozick's rhetorical questions still have much power—as his claims require. (That the benefit involves a consumption good is just supposed to be a specially obvious instance of the larger truth about transfers.) Giving competitive resources to one's child is surely unobjectionable. Similarly, in the more romantic example, who could blame Bob Nozick for employing his good looks and intelligence in romantic competition? The suitor could not justify taking from Nozick by any sane complaint about Nozick, and any complaint he might make about anyone else would be spiteful or bizarre. To put Nozick's penetrating questions in our current framework: if private acts in which people create and exploit unequal competitive resources are so unobjectionable, why can't people who are concerned with justice seek to preserve access to such advantages in their acceptances and rejections of proposed institutional arrangements?

Because the private acts are so obviously unobjectionable, an answer must appeal to some difference between private choices made against a background of given institutions, on the one hand, and, on the other, public choices, i.e., votes and other actions that ought to reflect approval or disapproval of those institutions. Once the challenge is described in this way, it soon loses its force. I will begin with what parents give to their children, since the romantic example raises a special question, to which I will turn, of how the disadvantaged are expected to benefit from institutional change.

Given background institutions and policies, just people may certainly show great partiality toward family members. It would be absurd to claim that a just person cannot be partial to her child, and such a parent will be reluctant to withhold parental benefits that she can offer, given the background. However, these truisms do not imply at all that a just person deciding whether to accept or reject alternative arrangements as the background for solicitude will reject alternatives because they sacrifice unequal competitive advantages accruing to her children (or accruing to her from her parents). To remove social arrangements giving rise to entrapment, restriction and coercion, a just rich parent would support heavy taxes on inheritance if they benefited people in poor families. She would not reject such proposals on the grounds that her children would receive less. Yet the same parent, if she loves her children, may well show that love, in part, by leaving them her property, i.e., leaving them as much as the actual laws allow. She is like the millions of relatively well-off parents in the United States today who support the improvement of less well-endowed school districts, voting for corresponding transfers of public resources, and also prefer to live in the best-endowed school districts.

Through such distinctions, the rich parent avoids appeals to benefits of unequal opportunity in her choices of institutions and policies, while deploying those benefits in choices within institutions. Her responses are not symptoms of liberal guilt, but a decent separation of different spheres. For those institutions and policies, unlike her private measures, are involved in entrapment and coercion, and she respects the need to reconcile such imposition with the freedom of others. These chains must be rendered legitimate, in Rousseau's golden phrase. Conversely, systems of inherited disadvantage that harm the disadvantaged depend, not on unjust choices to give to one's children, but on unjust political choices, the choices of voters and politicians that sustain the background institutions and policies.

In addition, until a threshold of lavish competitive resources is reached, freelance withholding of competitive advantages from oneself or those one loves would require a strange kind of saintliness (as steely as most saintliness so far as the loved ones are concerned). Up to a high threshold, the withdrawal of competitive advantages might make a seriously injurious difference in future competition. So one puts one's future in jeopardy, or jeopardizes someone who expects loving support, very likely jeopardizing affection as well. Yet it is, of course, by no means guaranteed that anyone who triumphs through one's withdrawal will be among those who suffer from burdens one refused to exploit. One's daughter's loss may be a benefit for a product of Armonk, St. Mark's and Yale. One's dangerous unilateral withdrawal from the full use of permitted competitive resources at best creates a slight increase in the odds that some disadvantaged person on some occasion may suffer less from background injustice.

For these reasons, a private choice not to give up full use of permitted competitive resources is not, in general, morally irresponsible. But these reasons do not apply to the political choice of new background institutions which reduce the lifelong competitive advantages of oneself or those one loves. Such changes are specifically directed toward extensive improvement of the disadvantaged. They also create less jeopardy, since they do not make the forbearing advantaged person (in this case, one who votes for the change) more vulnerable to other advantaged people as private unilateral forbearance would. Here, one's commitment to equality of opportunity does not give those less committed a free ride at one's own expense.[6]

Admittedly, when we turn to Nozick's more romantic example, we do not rush from the insight that public choices can be objectionable where private uses are not to the conclusion that public policies should reduce or mitigate the inequality of opportunity. Suppose that the gorgeous have a better chance than others, with the same effort, of finding and keeping a satisfying mate. (The gorgeous of my acquaintance strenuously deny this, but perhaps they

---

[6] The private and political do intersect somewhat in the morality of social transition. Often, it would have required a kind of saintliness not to derive benefits from competitive advantages produced by a system of unequal opportunity. And people should have considerable security that their morally responsible pursuits will not be rendered pointless. So justice requires a preference for nonconfiscation. It is preferable that a policy promoting equality of opportunity be financed from income earned by the advantaged after the policy is adopted. Increases in inheritance taxes are preferable to confiscation of previously inherited assets. In the absence of strong reasons to the contrary, a qualitative increase in inheritance taxes should be phased in so that morally responsible accumulation for the sake of bequeathal in the past is not made pointless. Perhaps the generic discussions of state-enforced taking in *Anarchy, State and Utopia* inspire more fear than they should because of the absence of such distinctions.

underestimate their luck.) This consideration does not strike us as a serious reason why a gorgeous person should support public policies reducing the advantage of the gorgeous over the rest of us.—But this is as it should be, according to the fourfold principle and the interpretation of the cooperative goal. For the minimal specification requires that policies backed by coercion relevantly benefit some, and it is hard to imagine what the relevantly beneficial policies would be. Thus, the burden of proof is on the equalizers.

Certainly, the nongorgeous won't be helped by random assignment and forced marriage. As described, they want romantic attachment and marriage based on love. Some would be helped if cosmetic surgery is freely available to make anyone gorgeous. But in the absence of this institution, the nongorgeous can find nongorgeous mates, on any sane version of our supposition. The innovation is only needed to satisfy a special interest of some in finding a gorgeous mate, or being attractive to others with a special interest in great looks. If these desires are unalterable and important then they do define a goal in a system of imposed competitive burdens. But such desires are too exotic and demanding for public alleviation. Someone with the cooperative goal insisting on such subsidy would have to recognize that similarly exotic and demanding desires also require satisfaction; but he should then see that the system of institutions will collapse under the weight of these demands.[7]

Suppose, however, that these special reasons for skepticism about romantic equalization do not apply. One such atypical circumstance is the complaint of those who are not just nonhandsome, but repulsively ugly. Through no choice of their own, some people have physical features that lead so many others to avoid close relationship that they have serious difficulties finding an enduring loving relationship. They are as willing to find and sustain such a relationship as others but lose because of what others choose to do in response to the unchosen feature. Their frustration is based on normal desires for love, not on exotic and demanding desires.

Do they also suffer from the state's protection of those intimate choices, as the minimal specification requires? This is not so clear, since different protections for the private choices would not obviously benefit the ugly. But perhaps the coercion is employed in a way that brings the fourfold principle into play. Then, the repulsively ugly ought to receive cosmetic surgery if such measures work to the benefit of the most disadvantaged—a question which would involve familiar controversies over the right vehicle for meeting medical needs. Reflection on romantic competition was supposed to reduce to absurdity the admittedly powerful appeal to equal opportunity. Once the appeal is properly understood, it requires nothing more than routine attentiveness to needs of nature's victims.

[7] For a similar view in a different context, see Scanlon, "Preference and Urgency," *Journal of Philosophy* 72 (1975).

Equalization also becomes plausible if the consequence of winning fair lady or gentleman's hand is changed. Suppose that marriages are arranged, with the consent of the affianced, which is almost always forthcoming. The most important consequence of marriage is access to scarce resources which are only readily available to married couples. Despite the unromantic goals of marriage, prospective grooms and brides are preferred or dispreferred by matchmakers and prospective in-laws partly on the basis of unchosen features. In this very common system of unequal opportunity, the disadvantaged might be better off under an alternative arrangement. And in such a system, complaints of victimization are hardly absurd. (It would also be relevant if crucial processes are coercively protected by strong sanctions against adultery, barriers to divorce, and enforced compensation for breach of promise to marry.) In a somewhat similar situation, a paragon of beauty and grace in Jane Austen's England had better favor improvements in the lot of spinsters, if she thinks herself a paragon of justice, as well.

ENTITLEMENT

So far, the minimal demands for equal opportunity have retained their power, for partisans of social freedom, in the face of examples specifically designed to show that victimization by unequal opportunity generates no relevant complaint. However, such specific criticism of demands for equality is unnecessary if Nozick is right in his general view of entitlement. He proposes that it is wrong to interfere with nondeceitful, noncoercive uses of any holdings that solely result from people's nondeceitful noncoercive activities, above all, their deployment of their own natural assets in production and exchange. If this principle, "the free enterprise principle" as I shall sometimes call it, is right, then the regulations or mitigations that the betas might demand could only produce gains dependent on wrongful taking, so that their demands would be incompatible with the cooperative goal. For the only legitimate use of the state's enormous power to interfere would be protection against people's acts of deception or coercion. Quite generally, though the fourfold principle might describe a state of affairs that ought to be regretted, it would not describe a sufficient justification for taxation or other interference. Yet such intrusions are part of any political intervention that rectifies situations of unequal opportunity—at least in a world in which available goods are largely the result of human endeavors.[8]

[8] See *Anarchy, State and Utopia*, pp. ix, 31f., 149, 160, 225f. Nozick acknowledges that what humans use is not entirely the result of human activities. Usually, nonhuman Nature has provided the raw materials. When this initial material is scarce, benefits from exclusive control of it are only protected if the so-called "Lockean Proviso" is satisfied: the exclusion of others from access to raw materials must make no one worse off than she would be if there were no such exclusion, but the general imperative to leave people free to transact using the benefits of their

Nozick sometimes suggests that this robust protection for free enterprise is justified, in part, by its fit with our firm pretheoretical judgments of "micro-situations," interactions involving a few individuals at most, considered apart from controversial assessments of the social setting (pp. 204f.). But in fact, the principle forces judgments that are very far from anyone's repertoire of pretheoretical convictions. Suppose a selfish genius invents a cure for cancer, but refuses to divulge it until paid the financial assets of Japan. As the anguished international negotiations slowly unfold, even after the selfish genius receives a secure guarantee of five million dollars for life once the formula is public, it would be wrong (by the free enterprise principle) for someone dying of pancreatic cancer to take the formula from his desk.[9] A woman whose baby is screaming from hunger, through no fault of either of them, happening upon a dozen bottles full of milk on the back steps of the house of a self-made millionaire, knowing that she will have no other way to get food that day, would be wrong to take a bottle for her baby. Friday, dying of emphysema in the previous tale of canoe smoke, would be wrong to move Crusoe's workshop if persuasion fails.[10]

A partisan of social freedom needs to justify reliance on the free enterprise principle in assessing proposed changes in situations of unequal opportunity, i.e., situations embodying the same four conditions as Alphabetan assign-

own internal natural assets were respected. I will follow Nozick in assuming that this mixed system would be quite inefficient, imposing a very low threshold. See pp. 174–82.

[9] Assuming that the genius' research does not exclude people from access to scarce raw materials, the Lockean Proviso does not apply. See p. 181.

[10] Since Crusoe is not seeking to benefit from exclusive control of Friday's beach or air, the intrusion is not covered by the Lockean Proviso. In any case, the variant in which Friday is just made to cough and hack would leave him above the low Lockean threshold, even though it does not seem wrong of him to force a slightly less convenient location on Crusoe should persuasion fail. Note that Friday may lack the means to persuade through compensation, and Crusoe may be too stubborn to accept compensation, in any case.

In his brief discussion of pollution (pp. 79–81), Nozick does in fact accept forced compensation for pollution damaging others' "property, such as their housing, clothing and lungs" (p. 79). But his rejection of state-imposed remedies for unequal opportunity is much more important in his larger argument. And there is no plausible understanding of the free enterprise principle that excludes these remedies without prohibiting forced compensation for pollution as well. For example, the remarks on pollution may reflect Nozick's previous acknowledgment that one may interfere with a "party who is a threat, even though he is innocent . . . who innocently is a causal agent in a process such that he would be an aggressor had he chosen to become such an agent" (p. 34). Smoking up Friday's beach out of spite, not as a by-product of innocent canoe-building, might be counted as aggression, unprotected by the free enterprise principle. But spitefully lowering someone else's prospects by competing with superior resources just in order to make him lose is aggression by the same token. At any rate, there is plenty of room for counterexamples drawn from the cases that Nozick specifically excludes from his discussion of compensation for pollution (p. 79), cases in which there is no damage inflicted on something another owns. Consider sewage disposal whose only adverse effect is to make it impossible for a downstream fisherwoman to catch fish in unowned waters that are an essential basis for her livelihood.

ment. For in such situations the disadvantaged suffer from unchosen, humanly created burdens on self-advancement. Why doesn't this justify corrective interference, if such interference is appropriate, for example, when deception is used to impede someone's self-advancement? Evidently, the justification cannot consist of otherwise good fit with pretheoretical considered judgments. Many of those judgments make the need for a deeper argument more pressing. But the only deeper argument that Nozick offers cannot fulfill this need.

According to Nozick, "Side constraints upon actions reflect the underlying Kantian principle that individuals are ends and not merely means" (pp. 30f.). In insisting on this status for individuals, he does not intend, any more than Kant did, to require each of us to act for the sake of the others we affect. Such concern is violated in virtually any commercial interaction. Nor does he mean that we should regulate our conduct by rules that we approve from a standpoint in which we regard everyone's interests as demanding equal concern. Rather, his fundamental principle is that individuals "may not be sacrificed or used for the achieving of other ends without their consent" (p. 31). Of course, mere acceptance, whatever its origins, does not count as consent, here. The choice must be relevantly free and informed. The robber does not treat us as ends, when, at gunpoint, we agree to hand over the money. If someone interacts with me, but wouldn't if he knew my intentions I do use him as a means (ibid.).

Suppose that those advantaged by a system of unequal opportunity maintain their competitive advantage, by votes or other politically effective acts. Then they sacrifice the interests of the disadvantaged for the achieving of other ends. Moreover, the disadvantaged do not consent to the sacrifice, i.e., their choice is not relevantly free if it is relevantly informed. The disadvantaged may be rational in accepting circumstances of disadvantageous action on the part of others, because those circumstances are protected by the state. But this is acquiescence, not free consent—like the agreement to hand the wallet to the robber. The burdensome actions respond to features of the disadvantaged which they did not choose. The actions constitute circumstances that the disadvantaged did not choose and can only leave at great cost. Their unwillingness to accept those circumstances, apart from coercion, is compatible with a desire that all have equal inducement to cooperate. In this process, the disadvantaged are sacrificed for an end not of their choosing.

GOOD FENCES AND GOOD NEIGHBORS

Although the free enterprise principle does not fit all widely shared considered judgments of microsituations, it takes some ingenuity to construct microsituations leading to judgments conflicting with the principle. Special considerations need to be introduced, such as pernicious side-effects of production or extreme unavoidable deprivations whose sole remedy is a mere inconvenience to another. We are reluctant to approve of taking results of noncoercive, nondeceptive activity. Moreover (as Nozick has emphasized), our reluctance extends to interactions in an imagined nonsocial state of nature. So it cannot just consist of an assumption that relevant institutional protections will have certain benefits. If, in their precooperative days on the island, Friday spotted a fresh-minted canoe outside of Crusoe's workshop, then, we would initially suppose, it would be wrong for Friday to take what Crusoe made, and wrong because he made it. Perhaps the rest of the story will turn condemnation to acceptance: Friday only uses the canoe for a day, with infallible knowledge that Crusoe won't even think of using the canoe and that the canoe won't be a bit worse for wear, and Friday has serious need of it; or Friday uses it for a day's fishing when he will starve without it, knowing that he will inconvenience Crusoe at worst and that he has no prospect of gaining Crusoe's consent. Still, such details are not dispensable.

A partisan of social freedom who rejects the free enterprise principle needs some other means of justifying her predisposition to condemn interference with noncoercive, nondeceptive uses of results of honest toil and exchange in microsituations. More precisely, since this is a shared predisposition of partisans of social freedom who differ in their specifications, the minimal specification should motivate it. In fact, two central features of the rational pursuit of the cooperative goal support the predisposition.

First, anyone who pursues the cooperative goal in choices among institutions will have a certain strong preference for making and voluntary exchange over taking as a means of advancing her interests. In choices among institutions which seriously affect her life prospects, she is prepared to sacrifice benefits that would be sustained by coercively enforced advantages if others, burdened by those institutions, could freely and rationally reject them. Such concern for cooperation in social cases will, in all consistency, require a preference for nonaggression in nonsocial cases. She will prefer to advance her interests through production and exchange that does not impose harms on others, even when she could advance those interests somewhat more efficiently by taking from others instead. If she were indifferent between making and taking in the nonsocial case, she would be indifferent between uncoerced and coerced benefit in the social case. Still, the prejudice against taking in the nonsocial case need not be absolute. In the social case, she insists that the others take her interests into account. In the nonsocial, where mutual adjustment does not yet take place, she need not endure extreme burdens when interference is the only alternative.

Presumably, Friday could engage in canoe-making without doing much worse than he would as a canoe-snatcher, and snatching Crusoe's canoe would threaten Crusoe's interests. Responding to this assumption, we partisans of social freedom would condemn his snatching, supposing that Crusoe has reason to protest it while Friday could only commit it out of preferences that would not motivate a person with an interest in social freedom. But special stories can be told, canceling the assumptions, and these stories remove the condemnation, just as the minimal specification implies. These are, for example, the special stories I told before, in which Crusoe is utterly protected from loss of benefits or Friday must snatch the canoe to cope with dire needs, at trivial cost to Crusoe.

The second factor explaining our prejudice against taking involves a deep-rooted need of any rational person capable of social cooperation. Every such person needs to be able to choose, on frequent and significant occasions, to confine his or her activity to certain spheres in which achieving one's goals depends on one's uncoercive efforts and choices and in which one is reasonably well-assured that the results will not be taken on account of claims of others that one does not wish to satisfy. If there is not substantial room for such interaction between one's choices, one's efforts and one's enjoyments, one is deprived of a sense of self and of activity in the world—beyond a sense of oneself as combatant, which is hardly satisfying. As one striking reflection of this need, one would rather not live a whole life as an utterly passive consumer of goods delivered at the bedroom door every morning. Though this is hardly the worst fate imaginable, it is a bad fate despite the consuming. And in the real world, the loss of a zone of free activity is not usually compensated with free deliveries.

In a nonsocial state of nature, any intrusion into a zone where activity would otherwise be free is a serious matter, which should give pause to anyone who cares about the rational acceptances and rejections of others. In the absence of definite, enforceable rules defining the spheres of undistracted self-advancement, any incursion is apt to justify corrosive anxieties and pervasive defensive activity that radically reduces the zones of peaceful self-advancement.

In a real society, for example, a modern society including a state (to which I shall confine the discussion from now on), these demands of personality take a different form. Everyone needs there to be important spheres of activity that he or she can choose to enter with reasonable assurance that ultimate enjoyments will depend on noncoercive efforts and choices. But these spheres do not have to be all-encompassing for the sense of self to survive. Through definite, enforceable laws, specific, sufficiently important spheres can be protected. If a reasonable measure of due process is observed and publicly acknowledged standards guide political deliberations, changes in the zones will not justify corrosive anxiety or pervasive defensiveness. The shared need for a sense of self and activity will not dictate that currently established zones protect this or that particular kind of self-advancement.

Thus, in 1830, British manufacturers could choose to enter a sphere in which they could employ anyone of any age for a working day of any length in pursuit of profit. If one chose to confine oneself to current rules for contracting, one could pursue one's goal without undesired distractions. By 1860, the sphere had shrunk, since British manufacturers could no longer employ, say, ten-year-olds for sixteen-hour days without a significant likelihood of undesired distraction by factory inspectors, police and courts. It would be stupid to suppose that their sense of self was placed in jeopardy.

Anyone committed to the minimal specification will try to keep the spheres of freedom extensive, and will insist that there be a serious reason for seriously shrinking them. After all, a society in which shrinkage is treated lightly will be one in which people will never have a reasonable expectation of nondistraction should they commit themselves to a currently protected sphere. This explains our demand for strong justifications of interference with making and voluntary exchange. But the minimal specification can provide serious reasons for substantial shrinkage, for example, the goal of reducing or mitigating imposed competitive burdens.

In the choice of institutions and policies, what are these valid reasons for restricting individuals in their pursuit of material gain? Different specifications of justice as social freedom will provide different general answers. But all can be summed up in the generic principle that people are to be free to pursue gain unless there is a measure restricting their pursuit that no one can freely and rationally reject who has a goal of free and rational acceptance by all. The different specifications will, then, interpret free and rational acceptability in their different ways. The validity of this generic principle also helps to explain the appeal of the free enterprise principle. For the generic principle can give undue support to the free enterprise principle, via a philosophical pun.

In an extended sense, an act in pursuit of economic gain is coercive if the agent relies on benefits from others' lack of freedom. In a similar extended sense, an act is deceitful if the agent relies on benefits from others' lack of access to relevant information. Of course, these acts themselves are not all literally coercive or literally deceitful. Still, if the unfreedom and lack of information are incompatible with the choices on which justice depends, the acts are so tainted with coercion or misinformation that they lack moral protection, as surely as literally coercive or deceitful acts.

Such extended usage in talk of coercion or deceit is common among people who have no interest in twisting words to advance political goals. As a part-time antique dealer, I know the fabulous complexity of determining when selling is as honest as a morally protected economic act should be. If a retail dealer knowingly sells to a typical retail customer without telling him of a repair that may affect resale value, he has made a deceitful sale, even if he has said nothing false and even if this customer is too naive to know that retail dealers are expected to reveal such flaws to retail customers. Even if the seller did not know of the repair and did not provide a guarantee, we antique dealers think he is engaged in the equivalent of literal deceit if he refuses to refund the money the next day when the angry customer returns. Indeed, we shrewd ones are aware that dishonest antique retailers usually pursue gain dishonestly by keeping themselves ignorant of certain kinds of facts. On the other hand, a dealer buying from a dealer is on her own, and only kindness compels the seller to give up what is not the result of literally lying. Relevantly acceptable practice, not state of mind, is primary. When we say that no one has a right to gain from fraudulent sales, we usually intend all of these distinctions.

If terms are so stretched in principles governing the buying and selling of old chairs, they will be stretched in similar ways in the judgment of other practices. So long as someone's gains depend on the entrapment, restriction and coercion of others, his pursuit of those gains is coercive, in an extended sense. Yet his pursuit may be noncoercive and nondeceptive in the literal sense of those words. It would be protected by the free enterprise principle.

The same words can state what every partisan of social freedom must say about freedom to pursue economic gain or state the free enterprise principle, depending on whether they are used in an extended sense or literally. Our interest in spheres of free activity leads us to seek a simple statement of the basic protection on economic activity. So the free enterprise principle has a more plausible sound than it deserves, through a philosophical pun.

So far in this section, I have been arguing against the free enterprise principle. However, it may also be possible to develop these same considerations into an argument for a significant strengthening of the fourfold prohibition concerning unequal opportunity. There may be a minimal argument for omitting the reference to competition in the "restriction" clause, so that inferior life-prospects are subject to challenge when they do not involve competitive burdens.

Suppose the plight of betas were simply that they are less able to advance their interests than others, because of circumstances they did not choose that others choose to create and sustain. If it would not be wrong for betas to use certain forms of coercion or deception (the sit-ins or forgeries, for example) to force sharing of the alphan advantages, then their inferiority would be unjust. For actual alphan superiority would depend on superior coercive power in dealing with those whose actions are not wrong.[11]

However, interference with mere humanly created inequality in life-prospects does seem wrong to some partisans of social freedom. It appears to be wrong because it involves interference with people's mere choice not to give as much to some as to others.

In spite of such first appearances, the examples of the cancer patient and of

---

[11] Gauthier thinks that benefits depending on the successful coercion of those who do no wrong are not subject to moral criticism in a wholly asocial situation. But even he insists that coerced gains and losses not be counted when people assess the acceptability of rules governing socially regulated interaction. See *Morals by Agreement*, pp. 198f., 214.

the mother of the starving child would provide many with reasons to with-draw their initial endorsement of this protection of lesser giving. The selfish discoverer of the cure and the self-made millionaire who will not part with one bottle of milk are nongivers, not takers. Moreover, if principles of non-interference are to be a basis for assessing actual social arrangements, there must be permission for third parties to interfere with attempts at prohibited interference. Otherwise, essential uses of state-coercion would be wrong. That the selfish scientist takes nothing from others must not simply make it all right for the scientist forcibly to stop the cancer patient; this same fact must make it all right for anyone forcibly to stop him.

Many find *this* conclusion hard to accept. Nonetheless, they will want to be able to do justice to the obvious importance, on the whole, of respect for others' choices. Other investigations in this section suggest a way of satisfying this demand. One should confine coercively protected rules for interaction to those that everyone has a noncoercive reason to accept if she seeks equal noncoercive inducement for all; such inducement must reflect the profound need of everyone for extensive spheres of unimpeded self-advancement. The requirement of a noncoercive rationale and the centrality of zones of free activity give choice a central role, here. But there is no fundamental protec-tion for all choices to give less to some than to others, any more than there is a fundamental protection for a choice to institute eighteen-hour shifts. Com-petitive burdens to one side, betas are in a position to complain of confine-ment to a system which they have less inducement than others to accept.

These considerations establish the coherence of a version of justice as social freedom in which humanly created confinement to lesser prospects stands in need of justification from the standpoint of the worse-off, competitive bur-dens to one side. Perhaps it can be shown that no contrary version survives rational reflection. But perhaps not. In the face of examples such as those I presented, some are still prepared to take it as fundamental that a choice should not be blocked unless it would block another's choice, if unimpeded; and they sharply distinguish blocking from nongiving. As part of a commit-ment to justice as social freedom, their position is not clearly arbitrary, though contrary positions have turned out to be defensible.—In contrast, it would be arbitrary to insist on a fundamental principle that one may not resist imposed adverse effects. In a position requiring free acceptability, there would have to be some further justification for the claim that those hurt by pollution or competitive losses through no choice of their own may not interfere with the imposed worsening. (This explains why Nozick's ultimate principle is that no one may be sacrificed or harmed without his or her consent.)

Lacking a minimal basis for excluding the prohibition against being the first to impede, I will continue to include competitive blockage as part of the four-fold prohibition, and argue for the inevitability of such blockage under capitalism. If this proves unnecessary, so much the better for my egalitarian conclusions.

JUSTICE FOR TERMITES?

The final objection to the minimal specification of equal opportunity rests on an alleged similarity between unchosen social situations and mere misfortunes in natural situation. Consider an isolated Robinson Crusoe, stranded, through natural calamity, on a barren desert island. She could, rationally, bemoan the fact that her barren external circumstances make her unable to get what she wants while expending the same effort as other, more fortunate Crusoes. However, even though her circumstances are unchosen, she would have no rational moral complaint of unfreedom. "Crusoe is free to use her capacities in whatever way will best fulfill her preferences given the external circumstances in which she finds herself."[12]

Now, consider the life of someone who is not at all an isolated Crusoe, someone engaged in standard economic activities of work, exchange and investment. Her prospects of achieving her goals will certainly be affected by the resources, preferences and choices of others. But, it might seem, "these limitations are the interpersonal analogues of those experienced by Robinson Crusoe alone on her island."[13] Crusoe's locale was unchosen and undesirable, but this fact only justified her in bemoaning her misfortune compared to more happily shipwrecked Crusoes. Similarly, it might seem, for someone restricted by unchosen and undesirable location in the network of economic activity. She has grounds for bemoaning, but no grounds for a moral complaint.

The attraction of the analogy reflects the temptation to adopt this underlying principle, assimilating natural and social settings: misfortune in location within a network of economic activity is no more a basis for moral complaints than misfortune in location among natural settings. This plausible general principle, combined with the observation that Crusoe has no legitimate moral complaint when she bemoans her relatively barren environment, would certainly conflict with my specification of justice as social freedom. The betas, after all, are simply people who have an unfortunate relationship to the preferences and resources of others.

The assimilating principle contributes to impressive anti-egalitarian arguments of Nozick's, and is suggested by at least one argument of Gauthier's. It is attractive, yet utterly question-begging.[14]

---

[12] See ibid., p. 90.

[13] Ibid., p. 91.

[14] See Nozick, *Anarchy, State and Utopia*, pp. 185 f., 263. As my borrowings indicate, there is also a parallel with Gauthier, *Morals by Agreement*, pp. 90f., where the alleged analogy is used in an important argument that certain processes of exchange are not subject to moral complaint. I should add that other passages in the book make it clear that Gauthier is not really committed to

The principle that assimilates unfortunate natural locations and unfortunate social locations is wrong because it reflects only the passive aspect of the misfortunes. In this aspect, the misfortunes are analogous. Being a victim of the one mislocation involves suffering just as serious as being a victim of the other, sometimes suffering of just the same kind. However, if my misfortune is my location in the natural environment, I am morally free to respond in certain distinctive ways. Putting niceties of conservation to one side—I may freely use death, destruction and stealth to change undesired features of my natural niche. If I am stuck in a termite-infested island and want to build a house of wood, I may stealthily kill termites, and do no wrong thereby.

If I have an unfortunate social location, I am not, in general, morally free to remove undesired features of my social environment by treating its constituents as if they were termites. The moral constraints are important, since such attacks may be in my power. Individuals with relatively few resources can, nonetheless, go on the offensive by sneaking up or ganging up, as Hobbes notably observed.[15] A major task of political philosophy—in effect, the task of describing justice—is to characterize systems of institutions and rules such that whenever everyone else conforms anyone would be wrong to advance his interests by violence or stealth, and wrong because of their conformity.

No doubt, there can be other reasons why it is wrong not to attack others— they are humans too, they are not seriously to blame for one's suffering, one will not accomplish much by the aggression, and so forth. But these are not reasons of their conformity to appropriate institutions and rules. Those who thought it wrong to kill police informers under apartheid usually did not suggest that aggression was wrong because of the nature of what the informers did. The latter sort of reasoning makes the subjectmatter one of justice.

Conversely, institutional injustice does not, generally, license individual coercion and stealth. Those who oppose the welfare state as unjust do not say it would be all right for the put-upon rich to steal food stamps from the poor

the general assimilating principle, though it is suggested by the quick claim that market situations are interpersonal analogues of Crusoe's island. Gauthier's sole use of the robinsonade is to argue that no one can complain of a process of exchange in which everyone receives no more or less than the least that he would accept for what he provides in exchange. He goes on to allow the legitimacy of complaints about outcomes of free exchange in which some, benefiting from scarcity of that with which they are endowed, extract more than the least that would lead them to part with what they provide. The general moral irrelevance of burdens depending on the preferences and resources of others would make it illegitimate to complain when someone else extracts this rent from the scarcity of his talents; yet this is a complaint that Gauthier does allow. The consideration that really underlies Gauthier's argument concerns a more specific analogy between desert islands and rent-free markets: in either circumstance, one will, if rational, pursue one's goals until the last unit of gain is worth no more than the cost of obtaining it (see ibid., p. 92). As we shall see later on, the moral force of this analogy is, also, unclear.

[15] "For as to the strength of body, the weakest has strength enough to kill the strongest, either by secret machination, or by confederacy with others . . ." (*Leviathan*, chapter 13).

and fraudulently use them. Those at the opposite end of the spectrum do not say it would be all right for victims of inadequate welfare to remove their burdens freelance by robbery in the better neighborhoods. Yet one often has some notion of coercive or deceptive action that could be all right if established political channels prove inadequate. Suppose someone admits that it *would* be all right for people to interfere in those ways with practices protected by a particular system of institutions . . . and then goes on to call the system just: "The betas do no wrong in blocking the entrance to Alpha High, but there is nothing wrong with Alphabetaland." This is an absurdity.

An identification of natural and social mislocation as having the same moral standing would make it impossible to set these limits on aggression correctly. Anyone with mere cause to wish that he were differently located in the social network would be free to advance his interests by treating others like termites. An adequate political philosophy will describe the features of the social environment which are reasons not to engage in the violent, stealthy methods that are in general perfectly acceptable means of changing an environment. In the absence of these features, someone may or may not be morally free to respond aggressively. But if there are reasons why aggression is wrong, they will not consist of the potential victims' conformity to the right sorts of institutions. So, if those worsened by the absence of the crucial features have moral or prudential reasons not to go on the attack, they will still be in a position to complain, i.e., to complain of injustice.

Suppose that the defect which removes institutional reasons for not engaging in aggression involves an unchosen source of reduced ability. In such cases, a victim has grounds for complaining that her ability has been reduced through no choice of hers and unjustly. Such complaints of injustice were out of place on the desert island not because of some deep fact about the general irrelevance of unchosen differential misfortunes, but because of the obvious, superficial fact that the hostility of the local environment does not consist of any undesired acts of other people. Restrictions on aggression against other humans are always part of the topic of justice.

THE HOBBESIAN INTERPRETATION

These distinctions between natural and social misfortunes and between natural and human targets conclude my minimal defense of equal opportunity. They also suggest a unified general specification of justice as social freedom, what I will sometimes call "the Hobbesian interpretation." Though only the piecemeal arguments offered so far are needed to establish the modern adequacy of justice as social freedom, the Hobbesian interpretation is minimal, as well. It describes most of the common moral premises to which partisans of social freedom would be led by sufficient reflection. By the same token, it helps to reveal the most important disagreements, against this common background.

Briefly put, the Hobbesian interpretation identifies a just system as a system that gives everyone a noncoercive rationale for setting aside her right to resist or rebel provided that she would agree to any arrangement yielding a similarly noncoercive rationale to all. More specifically, a system of institutions and policies is unjust if and only if:

a. someone's sole basis for rational, informed willingness to conform would depend on her knowledge of her lesser capacity to use coercive force in ways that are not wrong, even if

b. she would willingly uphold any system acceptable to all affected provided that no one's acceptance depended on ignorance, unreason or the balance of power nonwrongfully to coerce and provided that everyone were governed to the same degree by this goal of general acceptability.

As in the previous section, wrongful coercion should, more precisely, be understood as coercion that is wrong because of the nature of the rules to which the victim was conforming. We put to one side the many other reasons not to interfere, which, as we have seen, might apply in unjust circumstances. Also, as usual, "coercion" should be taken as short for "coercion or deception."[16]

This account of justice corresponds, roughly, to the part of Hobbes' project of political justification that has broad current appeal, the argument culminating in the description of commonwealth by institution in chapter seventeen of *Leviathan*. In this justification, Hobbes is recommending a system as acceptable to people who are, to all intents and purposes, equal in coercive power, each seeking peace based on generally accepted principles provided that others are willing to do the same. More properly, I am offering a "semi-Hobbesian interpretation," because there are other, less appealing aspects of his project of justification, above all, the rationale based on "despotical dominion" in chapter twenty. In this passage, he takes the rationality of submission to an overwhelming coercer as establishing the justice of any nonle-

---

[16] I am indebted to Scanlon's "Contractualism and Utilitarianism," especially p. 111. However, while Scanlon is presenting a general account of moral wrongness, my proposal is only concerned with justice and introduces considerations of wrongful and nonwrongful coercion without specifying when coercion is wrong. At these junctures, the Hobbesian interpretation leaves open a variety of questions that I attempt to close through piecemeal arguments, so far as modern industrial societies are concerned. Later, I will argue that Scanlon's general account of moral wrongness is invalid. Also, when he introduces construals that are definite enough to resolve questions of justice, his account would exclude some specifications that are rationally defensible. My piecemeal and, often, empirical arguments are meant to show that my less demanding account is determinate enough to resolve modern choices on common moral grounds.— If, however, his account were confined to justice, made vague enough to be minimal, but definite enough for determinacy in a modern social setting, the Hobbesian interpretation or something much like it would result.

thal arrangements the coercer imposes in exchange for the subordinate's survival. And here, where unequal coercive power is intrinsic to the rationale, we find Hobbes' argument quite unappealing—as did nearly all of his contemporaries. The standard modern mixture of acceptance and repugnance in the face of the whole, great argument is the minimal demand for justice as social freedom.

It is hard to satisfy the demand for social freedom in the Hobbesian interpretation, since those who want to avoid reliance on the balance of coercion also want there to be a coercive state apparatus enforcing rules that govern many important interactions. According to the Hobbesian interpretation, the complete justification of a system has two aspects. First, there may be moral principles accurately identifying as wrong any interference with certain activities, i.e., identifying interference as wrong because of the nature of those activities. The system will not be unjust because it effectively uses coercion to protect against such intrusion. For people can only complain if their vulnerability limits their capacity for coercion that is not wrong. Indeed, if those who seek advantage in morally protected ways encounter interference, their only basis for accepting such victimization will be their lack of adequate power to respond with countervailing force. So a just system will provide safeguards for their morally protected activities.

Suppose that the coercive apparatus of the state does more than protect activities with which it is wrong to interfere. It must engage in such further action, if only to extract salaries to pay police and judges. There must be some further, noncoercive rationale for conformity, addressed to each subject, if the system is not unjust. The only source of such a rationale would be everyone's presumed preference for arrangements acceptable to all. Each will want there to be net benefits to others inducing cooperation. Each will want the inducement to be equal for all, since all are presumed to desire cooperation to the same degree. No one, in other words, is expected to be a social saint, sacrificing more than others in the interest of cooperation. Net benefits measured from baselines produced by the intrinsically protected activities should, then, be equal, unless inequalities are essential to arrangements benefiting the less than equal.

Moreover, the total net benefit to each should be as great as possible consistent with this rule of equality (so that the least net benefit, measuring from the baselines, is as great as in any alternative). For suppose a system imposes no inequality that does not benefit the less than equal, but another system would be of greater benefit to some without producing inequalities of which any could complain. Then those potential beneficiaries would not be wrong to force a change to the alternative system. For example, suppose everyone benefits equally from certain social arrangements even though the arrangements include no public works programs and the transportation network is sparse because of this lack. Then, those who need canals would not be wrong to force a change to public works if the benefits to them would not be part of an objectionable inequality. Presumably, in the acceptable new arrangements, those in need of roads and seaports are properly benefited, as well. (More precisely, any wrongness in bringing about the change would only have to do with the means chosen—say, premature resort to sit-ins on private highways.) The only reason why the canal-needers would acquiesce in their canal-deprivation would be their lack of sufficient power to force a change that it would not be wrong to force. And such a situation is unjust, according to the Hobbesian interpretation.

In sum, the system that all could accept for reasons untainted by the balance of force provides maximum equal inducement to cooperate for those who need no inducement to avoid wrongdoing and who put to one side any advantages in coercive power. Though the constraints on inducement and coercion make this, broadly speaking, an egalitarian conception of justice, a variety of important inequalities might, in general, be allowed. Inducement is determined by net benefits of cooperation measured from the baselines, baselines which might be unequal. And, in any case, equal maximum inducement does not require equal benefit. Someone who is relatively worse-off has no less inducement to cooperate if the relative worsening is a necessary feature of an arrangement that is absolutely better for the worse-off than any more equal arrangement. So, in general, arrangements are just if they are relevantly best for the worst-off, and, should they satisfy that demand, best for the next-worst-off, and so on up the line.[17] In addition, even when equal benefit is required, benefits should not be identified with goods possessed. Arrangements under which Ms. Ant and Mr. Grasshopper acquire the same goods, the one by working three different jobs fourteen hours a day, the other by showing up for free provisions, are hardly of equal benefit to burdened Ant and carefree Grasshopper.

These potential departures from equality are sufficiently complex that it will often simplify exposition to ignore them. Thus, I will sometimes investigate "the requirement of equal benefit" without adding: "except for inequalities that help the less than equal." I will sometimes speak of the prior claims of "the worst-off," sometimes of "the worse-off" sometimes of "the less than equal," since the precise specification of graduated priority from the bottom up is so ungainly. I hope that these abbreviations do no harm in light of the preceding warning and the investigations of relevant equality that follow.

The Hobbesian interpretation leads to the three independent features that I introduced as characteristics of the cooperative goal. First, someone's accep-

---

[17] This is the general formulation of the difference principle which Rawls presents in A Theory of Justice, p. 83. Note that this standard will often require discounting of idiosyncratic desires. The eccentric would himself be worsened by institutions permitting the complex, unpredictable, discretionary measures required for equal net benefit to all, no matter how idiosyncratic their desires.

tance or rejection of institutions is not to be treated as relatively unimportant because of the kind of person he is. This feature is part of the rule of equal inducement for all. Second, no one is to insist on gains dependent on wrongdoing. This feature reflects the fact that inferior coercive power in *nonwrongful* action is the only coercive rationale for acquiescence that is to be avoided. Third, no one is to suffer from coercion, restriction and entrapment in interactions with others. Even if it is not wrong for those advantaged by such arrangements to defend the arrangements coercively, it is not wrong for those disadvantaged to attack those arrangements. Acceptance of such coercively protected rules would only be rational as a concession to superior force, unless they are part of the best system for the disadvantaged. So arrangements violating the fourfold principle are unjust.

THE GREAT DIVIDE

Even if partisans of social freedom agree on the Hobbesian interpretation, they will have many disagreements. Of course, they will disagree over empirical claims that have an important bearing on the application of their common moral demand. Also, at the level of moral first principles, they may differ in their ways of measuring gains and losses—some, for example, attending to preference-satisfaction, others to the possession of all-purpose resources, others to well-being. Still, if it does not affect the protection of liberties that some take to be fundamental, such a disagreement seems unlikely to give rise to widely different appraisals of a total system. Presumably, the outcome will be relatively minor disagreements, which every partisan of social freedom would willingly resolve on the basis of democratic deliberations. I will return to this question in the course of the next two chapters, offering detailed support for this optimistic assessment of the scope of disagreements over relevant goods among partisans of social freedom.

It might seem that basic disagreements are bound to arise from the employment of different, rationally defensible principles in the aspect of social assessment in which one determines whether certain activities are morally protected as such, as opposed to the aspect in which one determines whether the system provides equal benefits measured from the protected baselines. Such disagreements would, indeed, loom large if the system of institutions to be assessed governed activities in which no one's production and use had an adverse effect on anyone else's. Suppose that each person engages in a cycle of activities in which each makes nature useful, consumes some of the output and, energies replenished, makes nature useful again. And suppose that one person's cycle has no adverse effects on another's. In some perspectives, it would, then, be wrong for anyone to interfere with anyone else's cycle of activity; the different respective outcomes of each person's activity should be taken as different baselines for equal inducement. From other perspectives, each producer ought to be willing to submit to a system equally benefiting all, with respect to a common baseline.

Suppose, however, that institutions backed up by force protect activities through which some get ahead at cost to others, who also conform to the imposed rules. In contrast to the system of insulated production, which lacked adverse effects, this sounds like the world of advanced industrial capitalism, in which people compete for desirable jobs, desirable investment opportunities and shares of desirable markets. On minimal grounds, the difference between such a system and a system of insulated production is important. Activities responding to people's unchosen characteristics that give rise to imposed competitive losses lack moral protection. The competitive gains and losses are subject to change in the interest of equal inducement. In addition, suppose that economic life in the system in question has this further feature. Any socially enforced rules for self-advancement under which it is harder for some to get ahead than others will make it harder for those worse-off to acquire competitive resources. Then, so long as the larger system is maintained, institutions and policies that make it harder for some to get ahead than others are always subject to rectification in the interest of the worse-off. The nature of the acts by which advantaged people get ahead does not prohibit interference.

Postponing further argument until the next chapter, I will assume that we are in a system in which self-advancement has all these reverberations, and that alternative systems ought to be rejected on minimal grounds. Still, anyone reasonably experienced in current disputes over economic justice has the impression of a great divide that could lead partisans of social freedom to very different assessments of social choices with these features. This impression of great potential difference is correct. However, in competitive settings such as ours, the great divide concerns the phase of equal benefit, not an independent phase of baseline drawing. According to one of the two rationally defensible competing perspectives, there is relevantly equal benefit when everyone has the same prospects of success given the same degrees of willingness to make sacrifices to achieve success. According to the other, there is relevantly equal benefit when everyone has the same prospects of success given the same degrees of willingness and the same innate productive capacities. In this second perspective, but not the first, equal benefit affords people with superior innate productive capacities extra success depending on their employment of their capacities in the system. Despairing of labels that are both vivid and fair, I will sometimes call the first perspective "the situational perspective" (because it appeals to a certain context of interaction on which self-advancement depends), the second "the restrictive perspective" (because it imposes an extra restriction on equalization).

The two perspectives depend on different construals of the goal of equal benefit in the Hobbesian interpretation. According to the restrictive perspective, a system is of equal benefit to all if what each gains from the participation of the others is the same; gains from another's participation are identified with benefits depending on her willingness to deploy her capacities together with any innate productive superiority of her capacities. The difference that these two aspects of an individual make to subsequent benefit is entirely credited to her, not to the system. On this understanding of equal benefit, equal prospects for equal degrees of willingness to try mean unequal benefit among those with different innate productive capacities. If equal prospects are provided, then less talented Smith gains more from joining with the rest, including more talented Dale, than Dale gains from joining with the rest, including less talented Smith. Each tries as hard and gets as much, so Smith gains from Dale's superior contribution to total output. The restrictive perspective tells us that the superior talents of some who take part are themselves inducements for others to join, as in the spontaneous formation of softball teams.

According to the situational perspective, the less talented may claim benefits depending on the superior innate capacity of others as exercised under a system, when the former insist on equal benefits as a condition for submitting to the system. This is a defensible perspective if (as in all modern societies) each, no matter how superior her innate ability, depends on the network of interactions governed by the system for virtually all she has. If someone has chosen to stay in a system and virtually all her output depends on interaction with others governed by the system then the others need not attribute gains due to her innate talents as deployed in the system to her as against the system itself. Superior prospects based on equal willingness to try are always extra benefits of participation, so long as the superior outcome depends on participation in the social system; this is how gains look from the situational perspective.

Despite the social dependence of virtually all benefits of any trait, there is a basis for taking the restrictive perspective, a rationale that a partisan of social freedom might accept, but need not. The first step in this rationale is uncontroversial. It is not rational to require, as a condition for participation, that one receive the genetic endowment of another instead of one's own. If one had received her endowment, one would have been her. But this first step takes us hardly anywhere, since bare possession of a genetic endowment yields hardly anything without interaction with other people. In the second, controversial step, one considers the consequences of forcing someone with this superior endowment to conform to rules providing everyone an equal prospect of success for equal willingness to try, as a condition for her staying in the system. Under these arrangements, the innately superior are forced to benefit others more than others benefit them. After all, this is the only way in which degrees of success could be equal when productive capacities are unequal. Such coercion might be rejected as wrong on the grounds that it is always wrong to use coercion to extract a transfer in which what someone gains is worth more than what another gains in return. More precisely, this might be taken to be wrong if the endowment employed in producing the benefit is not itself subject to moral criticism—which was the outcome of the first step. Thus, the appropriateness of the restrictive construal of equal benefit might be based on a prohibition against forced unequal exchange.

Such a defense is possible, but not inevitable. As the partisans of the situational perspective emphasize, the provider of greater benefit was not forced to stay, and the greater benefit only results from her endowment as exercised in interactions governed by the system of institutions. (Here as elsewhere, I assume that the less gifted do not use coercion to prevent the more gifted from leaving.) Admittedly, the rules of the system are coercively enforced and leaving is difficult. So a kind of prohibition against forced inequality does apply. But it is the situational requirement that net benefits to each depending on interaction with others be equal, not the restrictive requirement that each benefit in equal proportion to contributions depending on endowments that are not subject to moral criticism.

I can think of no way to resolve this controversy at the level of moral first principles, even among those already committed to justice as social freedom in the Hobbesian interpretation. After all, we do not first learn to assess fairness in transfer, then learn to assess the fairness of rules in light of outcomes—or the other way around. We learn the difference between justice and injustice by receiving piecemeal instruction of both kinds, in no particular order, and trying to make sense of this confusing mess of warnings, demands, praises and blames.

The contrast between the two perspectives is also a reminder that important controversies as to the moral protection of holdings ("Would it be wrong to take from one such as him in the interest of one such as her, given the causes of their holdings?") need not concern a stage of baseline drawing independent of and prior to the assessment of equality measured from the baselines. So long as the better-off benefit from imposed disadvantages of the worse-off, the nature of their self-advancing acts does not locate their holdings within a protected baseline. Nonetheless, transfer from the better-off might go too far in the direction of equality, for reasons depending on the causes of the difference. Thus, in the restrictive perspective, superior outcomes due to superior innate productive talent would be protected—as sources of relevantly equal benefit, not as entitlements prior to a requirement of equal benefit.

The restrictive perspective protects advantages due to superior innate productive capacity in a system that is justified apart from these differences. It might seem that yet more restrictive perspectives are also available, protecting differences due to superior resources that are not innate. But such requirements are not acceptable as moral first principles.

Suppose that you have a desperate need for shoe repair because no one can

competently cobble without being taught and the cobblers' guild limits instruction. If you must pay for repairs, you are rational to pay the going exorbitant rate. If you agreed to pay an exorbitant price for new soles, perhaps you
should keep the bargain. But suppose that an itinerant cobbler sees your shoes
outside your back door, and, out of confusion with another customer, makes
the repair by mistake. What you ought to pay for the unchosen service need
not be the exorbitant price made rational by the cobblers' guild. It is the price
one would rationally pay under just arrangements as defined by some specification that does not protect all productive advantages. Similarly, one is not
wrong to impose arrangements under which someone receives less benefit
than before from wholly productive activity if that extra benefit was due to
transactions to which one did not consent, conforming to rules that are not
independently justifiable.

Just as the restrictive perspective is the least egalitarian specification of social freedom which is defensible in a competitive setting, the situational perspective is the most egalitarian. For suppose that arrangements provide equal
prospects of success for those who are equally willing to try. Then if the total
outcome of someone's activity is less than another's, this fact has one of two
causes. It may reflect social randomness, the inevitable departure of some actual outcomes of efforts and choices from those made likely by social arrangements. In that case, the lesser outcome was too unpredictable for purposes of
social design. Otherwise, the lesser outcome results from less willingness to
try. In this case, it results from the choices of the less successful person, based
on preferences among courses of life untainted by the need to avoid coercion.
So the lesser success is not grounds for free and rational rejection of the underlying arrangement.—Of course, I assume (as I shall in general) that the
arrangement does not give rise to irrational unwillingness to try, which the
less successful would regret if they reasonably assessed relevant information.
Since acceptance must be free and rational, such arrangements are ruled out
(all else being equal) on minimal grounds, as well.

I have concentrated on the great divide that the two perspectives might
create in the employment of the Hobbesian interpretation. These perspectives also affect the interpretation of more specific principles, above all, the
fourfold principle concerning unequal opportunity. This principle, after all,
amounts to the Hobbesian interpretation applied to systems regulating economic competition. The fourfold principle removes moral protection when
some suffer from others' superior competitive resources. But do the innately
productively inferior suffer when the innately superior receive more, for the
same trying, solely because they can produce more with the same trying? From
one perspective, this should be said. The inferior suffer from a worse deal than
they could exact without doing wrong, since they do not force the superior to
stay and the superior derive virtually all gains from the system of interaction.
From the other perspective, the inferior do not suffer any morally relevant

loss, since a more equal deal for them would impose an unequal exchange of benefits.

Because it provides a defensible interpretation of worsening, the restrictive perspective is not overridden by considerations of unequal opportunity; in this it differs from the free enterprise principle. That laissez-faire principle appealed to the moral superiority of noncoercion but neglected the role of coercion in the imposition of unequal opportunity. But the prohibition against imposing unequal exchange admits that social arrangements can impose barriers to self-advancement. Rather than competing with the fourfold principle, it accepts and interprets it, with an appropriate understanding of what is involved in suffering from unequal opportunity.

Though the two perspectives survive rational reflection, perhaps the difference between them does not matter, in the end. It does not if each perspective, given its own interpretation of relevant principles, dictates the choice of capitalism and, within capitalism, dictates the choice of an arrangement of maximum benefit to the worst-off. That will be my argument in the next chapter.

SOME COMPARISONS *

In the renaissance of political philosophy that began with Rawls' theory of justice, the writings of Rawls, Nozick and Gauthier have exemplary status. They all believe that justice is free and rational acceptability to all relevant choosers. So, if the specification that I have developed really is minimal, either the situational or the restrictive version of it should lead to demands that are also prominent in each of their theories, so far as the theory survives appropriate criticism. It might seem that the discussions of social freedom so far correlate with their positions in an obvious way: when the Hobbesian interpretation in the situational perspective is applied to a system of competitive losses and gains, the result is the requirements for justice that Rawls imposes; the restrictive perspective yields Gauthier's demands; Nozick's position must be rejected as a wholly inappropriate specification. But the actual relationships are, on the whole, less simple. The more accurate comparison helps in the always rewarding task of characterizing and assessing these writings.

The simple correlation is truest in the case of Rawls. The Hobbesian interpretation in the situational perspective does, on the whole, yield his requirements for justice, at least when differences in life-prospects involve differences in competitive resources. Rawls takes justice to be conformity to terms of social cooperation acceptable to all who share a highest-order interest in regulation by rules that they would choose in conditions that "must situate free and equal people fairly and must not allow some people greater bargaining advantages than others. Further, threats of force and coercion, deception and fraud, and so on, must be excluded."[18] This conception of justice is offered as the appropriate response to the inescapable impact of basic institutions, including the state with its coercive enforcements. In particular, Rawls emphasizes the impact of this basic structure on life-prospects. "The primary subject of justice . . . is the basic structure of society. The reason for this is that its effects are so profound and pervasive, and present from birth. This structure favors some starting points over others in the division of the benefits of social cooperation. It is these inequalities which the two principles [i.e., Rawls' favored principles of justice] are to regulate. Once these principles are satisfied, other inequalities are allowed to arise from men's voluntary actions in accordance with the principle of free association."[19] The right response to the socially imposed differences in prospects has, as its quickest slogan, "Injustice . . . is simply inequalities that are not to the benefit of all."[20] In making this slogan specific, Rawls insists that the free and equal participation which the just pursue precludes discrimination on the basis of innate differences in capacity.

I have drawn a crude map of the most familiar territory in recent Anglophone political philosophy to mark the approximate truth of the association of Rawls' work with the Hobbesian interpretation viewed from the situational perspective. Admittedly, Rawls takes his principles of justice to follow from his stringent yet general description of the moral personality that should govern all decisions about justice. In my minimalist style, I have only insisted that the situational version of the Hobbesian perspective is one of two perspectives that might properly determine justice in specific circumstances of unequal opportunity. Still, the outcome for us of Rawls' theory, on the one hand, the situational perspective applied to such circumstances, on the other, is approximately the same if our economic world is the sphere of unequal opportunity described in the arguments of the next chapter. Also, in a world of this kind, arguments from the Hobbesian interpretation in the situational perspective are often more concrete, more widely persuasive analogues of Rawls' appeals to general characterizations of moral personality.

Nonetheless, there are at least two areas of apparent disagreement. The distributions Rawls tends to emphasize concern the primary goods apt to be possessed over the course of a lifetime, while I have associated the more demanding equality with degrees of expected success conditional on degrees of

[18] "Justice as Fairness: Political, Not Metaphysical," p. 235. The phrase "highest-order interest" occurs in the parallel passage in "Kantian Constructivism in Moral Theory," *Journal of Philosophy* 77 (1980), p. 525.

[19] *A Theory of Justice*, p. 96. There is a parallel passage in the initial outline of his theory; see p. 7. Similarly, Rawls specifies that the goods whose distribution is regulated by justice are "social primary goods," whose distribution is directly determined by the basic structure, not primary (roughly: all-purpose) goods of every kind. See ibid., p. 62.

[20] Ibid., p. 62.

willingness to try. Also, Rawls insists on the absolute priority of maximum equal civil and political liberty in modern circumstances.

In the course of the next two chapters, I will try to show that these apparent differences amount to little or nothing. Even though the ultimate goal of justice in the situational perspective concerns the likelihood of success conditional on willingness to try, the pursuit of this goal will turn out to require maximizing the lowest expectations among typical occupants of social positions, as Rawls proposes. And the Hobbesian interpretation requires enormous emphasis on civil and political liberty, as absolute as Rawls' own rationales for priority permit.

The relationship of Gauthier's *Morals by Agreement* to the Hobbesian interpretation is more complex. To begin with, Gauthier's treatment of coercive inequalities and interpersonal interests is different. In his initial statement of his project, he says, "We are committed to showing why an individual, reasoning from non-moral premises, would accept the constraints of morality on his choices" (p. 5). The constraints are to be justified by showing that they serve the interests each agent has, in the situation in which the agents interact. In contrast, what I have called the Hobbesian interpretation is farther from Thomas Hobbes' outlook. Rationales based on actual differences in coercive power are discounted and choices are only relevant if they would be compatible with a prescribed, fundamental interest in equal inducement.

Though Gauthier does reject these idealizations, the rejection is ultimately based on premises concerning rational moral inquiry which are too weak to bear this weight. As he acknowledges, the special liability of attempts to base morality on actual self-interest is a risk of identifying might with right in situations of unequal power. The horror of Hobbes on despotical dominion is that the rationality of abject submission to a conqueror is held to establish the justice of the concession of despotic power. To avoid this horror, Gauthier relies on a distinction between "wholehearted acceptance" and the mere "acquiescence" of those who conform on account of weakness but look forward to rebellion if the balance of coercive power shifts (p. 230). Only the rational wholehearted acceptance by all of terms for cooperation makes the terms valid moral principles governing their situation. If coercive inequality prevents such accord, no moral principles apply. "Morals arise in and from the rational agreement of equals" (p. 232. I will neglect some apparent admissions of injustice, on pp. 286f. and 294, for example, which seem to conflict with Gauthier's larger program).

The connection between actual interests and morality that avoids the horrors of Hobbes introduces distortions of its own. Around 1900, Europeans in British East Africa would have been rational to accept (wholeheartedly) terms under which Europeans' control of farms, mines and taxing power was assured regardless of how it was imposed on native people. The latter were rational to acquiesce if the terms included such safeguards as prohibitions of floggings without due cause. They would have been rational to acquiesce because they did well to take seriously a verse sung by British soldiers in East Africa, "They are brave, but we have got / The Maxim gun, and they have not." It is a relief to be told that an arrangement that some only accept on account of such knowledge is not morally justified. But surely the East African arrangements were morally defective. Gauthier at one point suggests that interaction between those whose powers are not approximately equal has the same extra-moral status as interaction between people and horses (p. 17). But whatever their coercive impotence, it surely matters, morally, that the native peoples were, after all, human beings.

Gauthier's restriction on the scope of morality can hardly be justified on the grounds that it relies on "a weak and widely accepted conception of practical rationality" (ibid.). For the restriction is itself less plausible than more robust conceptions of the rationality that should guide moral choice (for example, Rawls' or the Hobbesian interpretation). But there is another epistemic justification that could work, the denial that any alternative provides any basis for rational moral inquiry. ". . . [O]nly within the context of mutual benefit can our condemnation appeal to a rationally grounded morality" (ibid.).

But why suppose that grounding in the rational pursuit of constraints suiting participants' actual interests is the only rational basis for moral judgment? Admittedly, there are reasons to prefer this grounding to emotivism and similar alternatives, in which a justified moral judgment expresses the judgment-maker's attitude but not a truth claim. For decisions that can justify coercion should not be based on mere inclination, if this can be avoided. In contrast, rational wholehearted acceptance by all, based on the actual interests of each, is preferable. But there is another alternative. The identification of what would be acceptable to all given certain resources and interests that need not actually be theirs might be a means of detecting moral truth. The closest Gauthier comes to considering this option is a brief sketch of reasons, of Harman's and Mackie's kinds, for denying that ascriptions of objective value could play an appropriate explanatory role.

It is surprising to discover that a moral difference in responses to coercive inequality depends on a disagreement about truth and justification in which the philosophy of science plays a leading role. But this does seem the ultimate basis for Gauthier's exclusion of relevant idealizations from moral rationality. This basis is not justified in detail in Morals by Agreement. If the metaethical chapters of this book are right, the basis for exclusion is wrong.

A second difference between Gauthier's theory of justice and the Hobbesian interpretation is his general, fundamental reliance, in fixing baselines, on gains from market activity, corrected for certain inappropriate causes of gain and loss. Because of its minimalism, the Hobbesian interpretation does not impose general principles for assessing net cooperative benefit. The principles embodied in the restrictive and the situational perspectives are requirements imposed specifically on processes of interaction in which resources inferior to others' make one vulnerable to competitive loss. Still, when such interactions are noncoercive—in effect, when people advance themselves through competitive market activity, Gauthier's principles turn out to be close to the Hobbesian interpretation in the restrictive perspective. (Admittedly, a full appreciation of the closeness of the two approaches depends, in part, on investigations of the effects of markets and of alternatives to them, which I must postpone until the next chapter. A morally minimalist case for some form of market economy will emerge, while Gauthier's distinctive techniques of baseline drawing will turn out to neglect inevitable effects of market activity that are relevant in his larger framework.)

Gauthier's standard for just terms of cooperation is a version of the demand that net gains from participation in a cooperative arrangement be as great as possible for those least benefited by participation. The gains are to be measured from baselines adjusted to account for participants' rights. In particular, in determining these baselines, we are supposed to adjust actual gains from self-advancement to eliminate advantages due to violation of a prohibition against "worsening the situation of others except where this is necessary to avoid worsening one's own position" (p. 203). This rule is roughly equivalent to the prohibition against forced unequal exchange that generated the protection of gains from innate productive superiority in the previous section. And Gauthier does take his prohibition to entail that everyone has a right to certain benefits due to "her *basic endowment* . . . what she can make use of, and what no one could make use of in her absence" (p. 100). He claims that differences in basic endowment from person to person would justify differences in the baselines from which a just cooperative system provides equal inducement to cooperate—differences that might be quite substantial, yet disallowed by Rawls' theory of justice (see pp. 218–21).

This approach would depart from the restrictive perspective if differences in basic endowment were not confined to differences in natural endowment. Sometimes, Gauthier does speak of one's basic endowment as if it consisted, quite generally, of one's physical and mental capacities, available and useful in the absence of other people. This might include all results of training, instruction and other help in the past which contributes to one's present capacities. But elsewhere, he identifies one's basic endowment with one's natural capacities (for example, p. 273: "the proviso, in giving each person the right to his basic endowment—his natural capacities—gives him . . ."). This construal is also implied by his discussion of inheritance. There, he concludes that a practice of inheritance must be justifiable in light of its expected benefits to all (p. 302).

In associating basic endowments with natural capacities and associating substantial differences in natural capacities with substantially different base-lines, *Morals by Agreement* supports similar assessments to those that emerge from the restrictive perspective. But some of Gauthier's discussions of individual contribution and social dependence come close to entailing the situational perspective. This is true, in particular, of his rationale for excluding rent from baselines, in the very broad sense in which the term "rent" is used in economic theory.

Someone who receives rent, in the relevant, broad sense, "receives more than is needed to induce her to bring her factors to the market; rent is by definition a return over and above the cost of supply" (p. 98). Gauthier's paradigm of rental income is the difference between the least amount that would induce Wayne Gretzky to play hockey and his actual remuneration. Benefit from factor rent is not protected in baseline drawing. Otherwise, if rental income is retained, some people whose economic self-advancement is based on market activity could reasonably complain that they have not been treated impartially by the market process. A fan (say) could protest that she could not rationally assume the current costs to her of what she sells if she did not receive her current gains, while Gretzky could rationally assume his current burden for less than the benefit the market actually yields him.

To accept the legitimacy of such complaints, Gauthier must show that the exclusion of rent does not violate his prohibition against worsening someone (say, Gretzky or someone else with a scarce talent) when this is not required to avoid one's own worsening. Part of his demonstration is an argument that there is no fundamental right to terms of cooperation yielding factor rent. "The benefit afforded by factor rent . . . arises only in social interaction. . . . Gretzky's talents command factor rent because they are scarce, but their scarcity is not a characteristic inherent in his talents . . ." (p. 274).

These reflections on social dependence are reminiscent of the rationale for the situational perspective. To restate the rationale, with emphasis on apparent parallels with Gauthier's discussion: what each of us could produce in the absence of social interaction with others is virtually nothing compared with our share of the further product afforded by a specialized interdependent division of labor deploying a technology produced by and adapted to that division of labor. Benefits from lonely deployment of one's basic endowment are a sub–Stone Age minimum that one can safely ignore in drawing baselines and assessing net cooperative gains. That a person who is generally clever does better than someone who is generally rather dense may be intrinsic to her talent. Perhaps she would do better alone in the woods—assuming, of course, that she has been helped to survive when young. (Perhaps, however, the brute strength of the one who is rather dense would be more useful. Really, we neither know nor care about tendencies to flourish in isolation.) Still, what is not intrinsic to the talent of the clever one is the capacity to convert the talent into goods as desirable as a Nissan Infiniti, while the dense one must make do with public buses. The size of the difference a difference in raw talent makes is, certainly, socially determined.

Gauthier's own conclusion, the exclusion of rent from baselines, stops well short of the situational perspective. Someone who has greater innate productive talents can extract more than others from deploying her talents without receiving rent; she is able to extract more from market activity before she reaches the point at which the cost to her of the last commodity she provides barely equals the gain to her from providing it. But why stop short of this further conclusion: no one has a precooperative right to benefits depending on the deployment of a superior natural endowment in markets and the other facilities (for example, a specialized division of labor) that markets sustain? These benefits, like benefits from rent, are due to opportunities for self-advancement by interaction that the beneficiary did not create. She did not create the market, a specialized division of labor, or the background of technological knowledge. Even if no factor rent is earned, the less able will have to work harder than she to extract the same gain from market activity. If rent from the natural scarcity of someone's endowment is subject to rectification on the basis of legitimate complaints, why are not mere market-dependent advantages of superior natural endowment?

The answer must be implicit in the other part of Gauthier's case for excluding rent from baselines. This is an argument that no right to free choice would be violated by the confiscation of rent. Presumably, any further leveling would violate this right to freedom. But it is not clear why only the first leveling would be allowed.

Sometimes, Gauthier seems to deny that the exclusion of rent has any impact on choice. "A tax on rent cannot affect the preferential ordering of alternative courses of action and so cannot affect one's freedom" (p. 273). But surely there is no general, literal absence of impact. Were Gretzky to be deprived of rent for his scarce skills he might well be rational to make different choices concerning his activities apart from hockey-playing. With less to count on after retirement, he might, reluctantly, engage in somewhat undignified product endorsements. Any change in the schedule of returns typically, but not invariably, affects choices. (Similarly, the neglect of indirect effects of changed returns can create the false appearance that redistribution to the less able benefits no one in a rent-free market: the more able, who benefited just enough to induce their providing, will simply provide less. In fact, though the more able might, indeed, choose more leisure when their work pays less, they might, instead, provide at least as much as before, to satisfy desires for consumption goods in the face of the new schedule of returns.)

Putting the broad denial of impact to one side, Gauthier's arguments from freedom are appeals to the natural freedom of an isolated Crusoe which is preserved in market interactions provided that no one extracts rent. Whether she is on a desert island or in a rentless market system, we can say of someone that if rational she will satisfy her preferences up to the point at which the value to her of the last good obtained equals the cost to her of obtaining it. Since the different prospects of self-advancement of different Crusoes are not violations of impartiality, neither are the different prospects of their rent-free market analogues. (See pp. 90–92.)

However, we have discovered that the absence of legitimate complaints from Crusoes has too simple an explanation to support such large morals. Complaints are out of place because they lack an appropriately human target. This is quite compatible with the utterly plausible view that the protection of human interactions giving rise to similar unchosen differences would not constitute impartial treatment of those who do less well despite a sacrifice at least as great.

Finally, Gauthier might simply exclude the latter complaint as words without meaning (or in any case, without morally relevant meaning), on the basis of certain strictures against robustly interpersonal comparisons of costs and gains, strictures which he observes in his own utility theory. He does offer powerful arguments against general techniques of interpersonal comparison which would violate these strictures. But there is no argument against a more piecemeal claim: our usual reliance on rough, topic-specific, prima facie truisms concerning, for example, empathy, effort, groans and sighs gives us access (when we are lucky) to the fact that one person has sacrificed more to obtain a total benefit no greater than another's, even when the benefit to each is just enough to make her total effort rational for her. If arguments in the first half of this book are right, rejection of such piecemeal inferences would be no better than a positivist prejudice.

As a whole, the arguments of *Morals by Agreement* seem to point in two directions. Some are powerful appeals to the view of contributions and benefits that generates the restrictive perspective. But some are powerful appeals to the considerations of social dependence that yield the situational perspective. It is urgent to resolve this conflict. But reflections on rationality, cooperation and value, even as rich and penetrating as Gauthier's, do not meet this urgent need.

Turning to the third and final comparison—Nozick's principles of entitlement violate the demands of justice as social freedom in the Hobbesian interpretation, if previous criticisms are valid. According to those criticisms, the victims of imposed competitive disadvantages are not wrong to respond coercively to the imposition if this suits their interests. So the Hobbesian interpretation can require the violation of Nozick's side-constraints. Still, if one gives more weight to Nozick's deepest principles than his ultimate conclusions and if one applies his work to situations of imposed competitive inequality, it leads to the Hobbesian interpretation in the restrictive perspective.

Nozick's deepest justification of the free enterprise principle appeals to the Kantian consideration that one's interests may not be sacrificed for the achieving of another's ends without one's consent. This underlying consideration has turned out to be inadequate to justify the free enterprise principle when it conflicts with equality of opportunity. Then, enforcement of the free enterprise principle would sacrifice the interests of some through imposed terms for self-advancement benefiting others. Still, the Kantian considerations to which Nozick appeals might be taken to justify a different principle restricting equalization of prospects in competitive circumstances. In particular, the prohibition against forced unequal exchange which yields the restrictive perspective is one available specification of the Kantian prohibition. This specification would justify differences in prospects depending on differences in innate productive capacities. It is not the only defensible specification, but, unlike the free enterprise principle, it is defensible in circumstances of unequal competitive advantage. For, with appropriate refinements, it yields a rationale for denying that anyone is worsened when differences in outcomes can be explained by differences in innate productive capacity. In short, the restrictive perspective is the most plausible adjustment of Nozick's argument to circumstances of unequal opportunity.

What about situations in which the free enterprise principle would protect substantial differences but would not conflict with the fourfold principle requiring equal opportunity? This might be the case, for example, in the archipelago of unequally fertile islands on rough seas. The fertility differences together with the rough seas produce unequal prospects of success for those with equal willingness to try, even if everyone's innate productive capacity is equal. Yet the fourfold principle is not violated, because coercion and restriction are not sources of the inequality. Moreover, if the rough seas prevent interisland coercion, the Hobbesian interpretation creates no pressure toward equality. Here, then, the free enterprise principle might be imposed, so far as the minimal specification shows. So Nozick's Kantian foundation can support the free enterprise principle for mutually insulated economic agents, together with the restrictive version of the Hobbesian interpretation for agents who get in one another's way.

The free enterprise principle *might* be applied to the archipelago, but rival principles might, instead. Perhaps someone objects that a just person on a fertile island should seek motivations to cooperate independent of contingent advantages. Such disagreements cannot be resolved on minimal grounds. The only way to eliminate this indeterminacy, so far as we modern industrial folk are concerned, is to show that it does not concern us, because our actual setting is relevantly different from the archipelago. In systems that are preferable on minimal grounds, the actual impact of unequal opportunity puts holdings within the scope of the fourfold principle. The fact that we get in each other's way contributes to the case for equality, here, as the fact at the other pole, that we depend on one another in a specialized interdependent division of labor, contributed to the case for equality in the discussion of Gauthier.

In the next chapter, turning from robinsonades and archipelagos of subsistence farmers to the real world of advanced industrial production, I will try to make a case for equality on minimal grounds, without bias among the specifications of social freedom that survive critical reflection. But first, to reduce the need for bias among all moral standpoints, I will take a brief look at a standpoint foreign to justice as social freedom.

UTILITARIANISM

So far, in arguing against this or that moral claim, I have meant to show that no sufficiently reflective and informed partisan of the generic demand for social freedom would embrace it. In addition, many of those who are initially uncommitted to justice as social freedom share specific judgments on which I have relied, and will, I hope, be led to adopt the minimal specification. But none of my arguments so far is apt to persuade someone committed to a rival systematic basis for assessing institutions. And there is at least one rival to justice as social freedom which is currently advanced by important political philosophers, namely, utilitarianism. I will conclude these arguments about moral first principles with a sketch of reasons that should lead virtually all utilitarians to stop being utilitarians.

As I shall understand the term, a political philosophy is utilitarian just in case it takes the sole reason, in the final analysis, for implementing an arrangement to be the fact that the implementation would give rise to the greatest net sum of positive impacts over the long run. In speaking of a greatest net sum, I mean the highest ranking assigned by some single general procedure capable of ranking all alternatives which has these three features:

a. The inputs to which the procedure is applied are individual incremental (or decremental) impacts on lives. The effect of each input on the ranking is independent of whose life is affected or how the input was produced.

b. In giving importance to an input, by itself or in comparison with other inputs, the procedure weighs inputs in some manner that could be appropriate in a rational person's self-interested choice. As one consequence, although being under threat of coercion may be assigned negative value, the disvalue will always be overridable by benefits. For one often chooses to enter arrangements in which one will be under threat of coercion, because of consequent benefits. Indeed, every enforceable contract is of this kind. Because of condition a, the benefits which override for purposes of utilitarian ranking can, indifferently, be those of the one coerced or those of another.

c. An alternative can always be assigned top rank because it has a positive impact on sufficiently many people, no matter what the negative impact on individual others and no matter how small the positive impact on each benefited individual. It is because of this feature that talk of a "greatest net sum" is in place, at least as an evocative metaphor.

I have framed these conditions vaguely, so that they are receptive to the great variety of utilitarian political philosophies. Relatively classical utilitarianisms take the inputs to be experiences, positively or negatively weighted as an individual might in self-interestedly choosing a course of conduct in light of its effects on her experience. For purposes of convenience, I will largely confine myself to these relatively classical versions. Their difficulties will entail corresponding problems for any version. Moreover, as utilitarianisms become radically nonclassical, they become arbitrary standards in the eyes of most who are initially attracted to the generic project.

When the atomism about inputs in a and the individualism about their weighing in b are combined with the aggregation required by c, the results are sometimes judgments that virtually everyone would reject, even virtually everyone initially sympathetic to utilitarianism.

Suppose the National Institutes of Health could relieve a million people of mild, three-minute attacks of hives, but only through an excruciating, three-hour-long procedure in which an anti-hives elixir is extracted from the liver of one, fully conscious person. Suppose that no one is a good enough utilitarian to volunteer. Then (as virtually everyone would agree), kidnap and torture would not be the procedure of choice, even if relief of transient itchiness in enough more people is the consequence.[21]

This example is typical of the anti-utilitarian literature in purchasing clarity at the price of fantasy. But other examples, to the same effect, are both realistic and concerned with current political choices. Suppose that government measures eliminating the dire deprivation of the very worst-off in the United States today, say, the homeless, would inevitably reduce the welfare of most others a bit, say, on the order of having or not having a portable CD player. Enough are deprived of a bit for aggregate welfare to be reduced. This happens because of effects on inflation and the balance of trade. Suppose there are these further facts about the trade-off: suffering of the worst-off as compared to the relative success of most others tends to reflect their lesser life-prospects, in the sense of lesser initial likelihoods of successes given equal willingness to strive and equal innate capacity; a system of upbringing, education and employment eliminating all inequalities of life-prospects would be a disaster for all, e.g., because of consequent inefficiencies; but the impact of the present system on those worst-affected by the inequalities can be mitigated in the indicated way, despite reduction of aggregate welfare. Almost everyone initially attracted to utilitarianism would regard this as a situation

---

[21] According to reliable sources, Onora O'Neill once asked a very eminent Australian utilitarian whether he approved of feeding Christians to the lions provided enough people in the Coliseum were sufficiently entertained. "No," he answered, "but I'm not a good utilitarian."

in which the enormous deprivation of the minority should be alleviated in spite of the many small losses to the rest. This is also the dictate of justice as social freedom, as we will see in more detail in the next chapter, in an argument implicit in the discussion of unequal opportunity in this one. But according to utilitarianism, whether the measures should be adopted will depend on how many people would suffer the equivalent of the loss of a portable compact disc player. If enough would, that is reason enough not to eliminate the distinctive misery of the homeless. This is torture-for-hives writ large.

Torture-for-hives was based on a fantastic supposition. Though homelessness-for-portable-CD-players was not, I did not show that the supposed connection between benefits and losses exists. Perhaps, for all I showed or intend to show, the relief of enormous deprivation in a worst-off minority of the population never requires losses for vastly many more, as a result of macroeconomic effects, losses that are real but not remotely as serious for any individual as the suffering of the deprived individuals. Perhaps no one can establish, with reasonable certainty, the existence of such a structure of gains and losses in any actual situation of political choice. Some defenders of utilitarianism would take this uncertainty to defeat the criticisms of the doctrine. Utilitarianism, they think, is only to be abandoned if it yields invalid judgments of actual cases.

This defense fails for two reasons. First, in order to make a valid case for abandoning a moral doctrine, it is enough to show that it is overwhelmingly likely that it fails in some actual cases, without specifying which. The burden of proof is on the utilitarian to show that, despite the great variety and flux of social interactions, the relief of acute suffering for relatively few is not likely ever to require tiny deprivations for so many more that the aggregate would be reduced over the long run.

The other, more revealing defect in the appeal to actuality concerns the special burdens of a theory of the sole basic reason why an arrangement should be chosen. To adopt some ugly but standard jargon, possessing the top ranking assigned by the utilitarian procedure is being optimific. Utilitarianism is the claim that being optimific is a sufficient reason, and the sole reason in the final analysis, why an arrangement should be implemented. Such a claim, that possessing a characteristic is the sole and sufficient basic reason why a property is possessed, is much stronger than the claim that whatever actually possesses the characteristic possesses that property (and vice versa). As it happens, the difference is nicely illustrated by some discussions of what makes arrangements optimific. Perhaps an economist has the belief that the optimific economic arrangements are, precisely, those that most effectively promote GNP. This belief of his is based on relevant generalizations, for example, an alleged fact that most people care more for increments in goods than for any increase in leisure they might have under minimally efficient economic arrangements. Still, he knows that others, who are pretty well-informed if not thoroughly informed, advance alternative hypotheses, relevant to discerning the optimific if true, according to which the promotion of GNP would sometimes be nonoptimific, because of reductions of leisure. Surely, then, he cannot claim, in all consistency, that the fact that an arrangement maximizes GNP is the sole reason, in the final analysis, why any actual economic arrangment is optimific. He accepts that GNP maximization is optimific, at least in part, because of further characteristics of GNP maximization, when he admits that situations which pretty well-informed participants in current debates take to have a significant probability of occurrence would be ones in which GNP was maximized by a nonoptimific arrangement. So the further characteristics (whose presence makes GNP maximization optimific in his view and whose absence would make it nonoptimific) are an independent part of the reason why an economic arrangement is optimific in the final analysis.

For purposes of distinguishing what is and what is not a sole and sufficient basic reason, plausible hypotheses are good enough. Being F is not the sole and sufficient reason why anything is G, in the final analysis, if an F would not be a G on some plausible hypothesis. Reasons, after all, are means of promoting agreement among people who do not agree on all the facts—for example, people engaged in absolutely every political dispute.

Similarly, being optimific is not the sole reason, by itself and in the final analysis, why an arrangement ought to be implemented, if pretty well-informed participants in current debates entertain empirical hypotheses about the trade-offs between benefits and burdens according to which optimific arrangements ought not to be chosen. That social programs required to eliminate the distinctive misery of the homeless might have pervasive though individually small negative effects, through increased inflation and a worsened balance of trade, is one such plausible hypothesis. The corresponding "What if . . ." question is a good test of the claim that optimificity is the sole reason, in the final analysis, justifying the choice of an arrangement.

In my argument that the minimal specification of social freedom is determinate enough I will appeal to controversial empirical claims about actual circumstances, an appeal to actuality which I have just criticized as misguided in the defense of aggregative reasoning. But there is no double-dealing, here, because the two defenses are directed at different kinds of assessments. The empirical arguments in the next chapter are not meant to defend the primacy, as a source of reasons, of the generic principle of justice as social freedom. (This defense is the task of other parts of the book, for example, the present discussion of utilitarianism and the demonstration in chapter eight that social freedom gives the weight of numbers an appropriate role in choice.) Rather, the empirical arguments are meant to show that the differences between alternative specifications of a generic reason for choice, justice as social freedom, are irrelevant to the outcome in actual circumstances. The analogous project concerning utilitarianism would be the attempt to show that the differences between the general ranking procedures proposed by different utilitarians are irrelevant to the outcome in actual circumstances.

So far, the uses of trade-offs between the many and the few have been directed against utilitarianism, the doctrine that being optimific is the sole fundamental reason why a choice is right. These arguments do not overturn the following, more modest proposal favoring utilitarian considerations, as against utilitarianism: being optimific is a fundamental moral reason and, so, is capable of overriding other considerations, made relevant by independent fundamental standards, in at least some cases. For the examples discussed so far might just be different cases from the latter, cases in which the other, independently relevant considerations are powerful enough to override optimificity.

The modest proposal is bold enough to challenge justice as social freedom, on the grounds that free and rational acceptability to some might sometimes be neglected to maximize utility. However, the trade-offs illustrated by torture to relieve hives and homelessness to provide portable CD players are part of a further argument that ought to dissuade virtually all initial partisans of the modest proposal. Most of the latter, like most people in general, accept the following general constraint on morally acceptable ways of resolving conflicts of interest: if some people win but some people lose (or win much less) depending on which total social arrangement is established, then the right choice must be justifiable in a way that treats all people concerned evenhandedly. They must be treated as equals, even if each does not receive an equally valuable bundle of goods and opportunities.[22] This requirement of evenhanded treatment of people is extremely vague. The generic demand for social freedom is, itself, one way of specifying that even vaguer principle. Most of those attracted to utilitarianism take it to be the right way of specifying the constraint. Most of those who claim, more modestly, that utilitarian considerations are fundamental take the achievement of optimificity to be one way of satisfying the constraint. They impose the requirement of evenhandedness and think that utilitarianism would provide one way, but perhaps not the only one of satisfying it. This is why they think that a way of resolving trade-offs in which optimificity plays a fundamental, sometimes overriding role is a means of treating people evenhandedly.

The cases in which the enormous deprivation of a few people is a means by which a great many more people each enjoy trivial gains show that this judgment of utilitarianism is too gentle. The right interpretation of these cases is that utilitarianism treats experiences (or, more broadly, impacts) evenhand-

[22] This is Ronald Dworkin's way of putting the demand in a series of powerful essays. See, for example, *Taking Rights Seriously* (Cambridge: Harvard University Press, 1977), especially "Reverse Discrimination."

edly, but does not treat people evenhandedly. And evenhanded treatment of people is what is required. Virtually all of those inclined to impose the requirement that people be treated as equals in case of conflict of interests would accept that the one tortured for three hours to relieve hives in others has not been treated as an equal of the beneficiaries of itchiness-relief, and similarly for the homeless and those who trivially gain. (Note that the use of these examples purely to clarify the difference between evenhanded treatment of people and evenhanded treatment of experiences does not even depend on their being plausible hypotheses about the real world.)

The fact that the total sum of positive impacts is increased is not even *a* reason why someone is made to suffer deprivation without injustice—unless its relevance in the particular case at hand can be grounded on some consideration other than optimificity. It is not an independent fundamental reason, since this would produce a deliberation in which the one deprived is not treated as an equal.

This stark rejection follows from the demand that people be treated evenhandedly even if experiences are not. But what of the position that impacts should be treated evenhandedly, even if people are not—or, more or less equivalently, that evenhanded treatment of impacts is all that the requirement of evenhanded treatment of people need amount to, in morality? The number of makers of moral judgments who would accept this position without a supporting argument is negligible—not surprisingly, since moral judgments are made by people, not bits of experience. However, some classical utilitarians do try to provide such support, through an argument depending on an alleged analogy with self-interested rational choice. When one is only concerned with impacts on oneself and makes a rational choice, then (the argument begins), one gives no more or less importance to a possible experience according to whether it is experienced at the time of choice or in the more or less distant future. Rational self-interested choice now involves evenhanded treatment of experiences regardless of whether they are experienced now or in the future, including the distant future. More specifically, ideally reflective rational self-interested choice assesses each alternative by ascertaining the experiences it might produce, determining the desirability each experience would have at the time of occurrence and adjusting for probabilities. The rational choice is the one that is apt to produce the greatest sum of desirabilities. But one's future experiences are no more one's experiences at the time when the choice is rational than the experiences, future or present, of another person. So it would be arbitrary to deny that the rational choice when one is concerned with effects on everyone, not just oneself, is the one that treats all possible experiences produced evenhandedly, assessing, adjusting for probabilities and summing in the same way. However, this process of choice just is the rational pursuit of optimificity. So evenhanded treatment of all relevant experiences is the right constraint of evenhandedness on any rational process of choice—including the rational choice that singles out the social arrangement that should, all-told, be chosen in the face of trade-offs.[23]

In fact, this argument depends on a false characterization of self-interested rational choice. Such choice need not be, and rarely, if ever is, the pursuit of a sum of experiences each important in proportion to the desirability of experiencing it. Unless it is the only escape from dire circumstances, few, if any, rational people would accept a secure offer to plug them into a machine which produces extremely desirable experiences, via electrodes, for the rest of one's expected life-span, as one lies limp and oblivious to one's actual surroundings.[24] Moreover, most, if not all, rational people care about the patterning of experiences. In self-interested choices, they distinguish, for example, between certain athletes' fates of a peak of success in late adolescence followed by a steep, unreversed downward slide, and the pattern in which success is consolidated and enjoyed, perhaps at a lower peak, in late middle age. In sum, rational self-interested choice generally involves the pursuit of a goal embracing much of one's life, which gives importance to alternatives that is not measured by the sum of the independent desirabilities of having each component experience.

If rational self-interested choice can depend on whether an alternative promotes a certain kind of life, irreducible to a sum of desirable experiences, then, when one is concerned with all effects on interests, rational choice of an alternative can also depend on its being a means of pursuing a life-goal—for example, a goal of cooperation among all with whom one interacts. Requirements of evenhanded treatment of people that do not reduce to evenhanded treatment of experiences demand that some such cooperative goal be pursued. So abandoning the false characterization of rational self-interested choice means losing the means to override the appearance that evenhanded treatment of people, irreducible to evenhanded treatment of experiences, ought to constrain the rational choice of social arrangements.

My arguments are not addressed to everyone imaginable. Suppose that someone thinks that evenhanded promotion of desirable experiences is an independent consideration, sometimes overriding all differently grounded considerations, which stands in no need of further justification. In particular, while distinguishing this consideration from evenhanded treatment of people, he does not impose a requirement of evenhanded treatment of people, despite the possibility of optimificity via trivial benefits for many at the cost of enormous deprivation for a few. Such a person has no reason to be persuaded by my arguments. But I wonder whether such a lover of optimificity exists.

[23] See, for example, Henry Sidgwick, *The Methods of Ethics*, seventh edition [1907] (Chicago: University of Chicago Press, 1962), III, xii, pp. 381f.; J.J.C. Smart, "Distributive Justice and Utilitarianism" in J. Arthur and W. Shaw, eds., *Justice and Economic Distribution* (Englewood Cliffs: Prentice-Hall, 1978), pp. 108f.

[24] See Nozick, *Anarchy, State and Utopia*, pp. 42–45.

It is still a serious worry that justice as social freedom is itself too one-sided, because it does not permit sufficient attention to numbers. The promotion of the common good is a routine aspect of just politics, and in this process numbers often do count.

One way in which justice as social freedom actually requires attention to numbers is through insistence on adequate access to better prospects for those currently disadvantaged. When systems of unequal opportunity are justifiable, they must maximize the life-prospects of the most disadvantaged. A system will not do this if current provision for the most disadvantaged is always maximized, whatever the serious individual costs to a great many others. There will be too little room higher up, to attain later on. In any case, this total neglect of numbers will reduce the chances of access to a better life when justice as social freedom dictates both significant inequalities in current situations and significant reliance on private strivings. The discussion of zones of free activity earlier in this chapter suggests that this will be so in general, and the connection will be strengthened through the case for capitalism in the next chapter.

Still, concern for access to chances is too vague and too infrequent in just political deliberations to explain the pervasiveness of appeals to the general welfare. In chapter eight, I will describe why social freedom requires such pervasive attention to numbers, while setting limits to it. Of course, attention to numbers is also an important feature of many nonpolitical choices. In chapter ten, I will connect questions of wrongness with self-constraints that morally responsible people impose, in a way that leaves room for attention to numbers without the implausible demand that it take just the same form in the political and the personal spheres.

Chapter Seven

INEQUALITIES

SUPPOSE THAT in any capitalist economy inequalities of lifetime economic success typically, substantially exceed differences in contribution due to different degrees of willingness to work and different innate productive capacities. Suppose, in addition, that the different prospects of those with the same willingness and innate talent are typically due, to a significant extent, to inequalities in competitive resources. Finally, suppose that those who do suffer the most serious competitive burdens would, typically, suffer the most serious competitive burdens if any feasible capitalist alternative were instituted. Then, at least among capitalist alternatives, the difference between the two perspectives concerning innate ability has no basic impact on social choice. The minimal specification of social freedom defended in the last chapter dictates preference for institutions and basic policies making the worse-off as well-off as possible, starting with those worst-off. The benefits of competitive advantage are, as it were, a fund for arrangements improving the worst-off economic situations, a fund that is never exhausted under capitalism. (By "capitalism," I mean an economy in which the main influence on resource-allocation is the decisions of firms hiring people who must sell their labor, firms ultimately forced to satisfy the expectations of investors solely interested in returns. On this broad definition, a capitalist economy need not be—and, in fact, has never been—a laissez-faire economy, in which the state only serves to protect individuals in all nonviolent, nonfraudulent uses of results of nonviolent, nonfraudulent transactions.)

So far, the argument using the minimal specification would only show that a just economic arrangement, if capitalist, is in the interests of the worst-off. As a final step in a minimal argument, suppose that any defensible specification of social freedom dictates the choice of the most just capitalist arrangement, in an advanced industrial setting. Even those who insist on equality among people with different innate capacities unless an unequal arrangement benefits the worst-off have reason to dismiss all noncapitalist alternatives in favor of some capitalist option. Then, without further controversial specifications, social freedom, combined with the social facts, dictates a single determinate standard for advanced industrial economies. They are just if and only if they are best for the worst-off.

When a thick bundle of empirical data and theoretical arguments is used to supplement a relatively thin moral standard, argument becomes elaborate and detailed. Here is a more detailed description of the main steps I will take, deriving a demand for economic equality from the minimal specification and the facts of modern economic life.

In most of this chapter, I will make a case that capitalism does inevitably give rise to unequal opportunities that justify insistence on desirability to the disadvantaged. The case will have three main parts.

1. First, I will draw on a variety of empirical findings, mostly from the contemporary United States, to argue that in actual advanced industrial capitalist societies family-based differences in competitive resources have an enormous impact on prospects of success, independent both of differences in willingness to sacrifice and of differences in innate productive capacity. It is important that the effects of the unchosen competitive disadvantages be large and systematic, since otherwise all feasible measures to reduce such losses would create more serious imposed losses than they alleviated, at least on some defensible specifications of social freedom. This first set of facts, combined with the demand for justice as social freedom, requires some significant change in the interest of the disadvantaged in actual societies, if such improvements are possible.

2. Then, I will argue that the situations that actually generate family-based competitive disadvantages would do so, to some quite significant extent, in any reasonably efficient advanced industrial capitalist economy; morally important inequalities are guaranteed by the rational organization of education and production. Since the worst-situated are always specially liable to imposed competitive losses in this setting, any feasible change in the interest of the worst-situated will be a demand of justice. Any other setting for capitalist production would be so inefficient that it would not be in the interest of the worst-situated, or anyone else. (This is a more powerful conclusion than the outcome of the first step, which only dictated some improvement, if possible, for the worst-off in actual capitalist economies. But the rich data about actual lives deployed in the first step are essential to responsible argument. Hypotheses about the workings of capitalism need to be grounded on facts about observed consequences of those workings. Above all, real data are needed to justify claims about the size of the impact of economic mechanisms.)

3. In the course of these arguments about capitalist disadvantage, I will often speak of a need to improve the situation of the worst-off. But this way of speaking is only justifiable if policies directed at reducing the competitive burdens of the disadvantaged are, in the main, policies directed at maximizing the lifetime economic success of typical occupants of situations giving rise to the lowest likely success. I will argue that this attention to outcomes is part of the pursuit of justice, given the information available to us, even though the (minimal) goals of justice concern the reduction or mitigation of imposed competitive burdens.

As it happens, some of the reasons why important imposed inequalities of opportunity are inevitable under capitalism suggest that unmitigated dominance of economic life by market processes would impose objectionable risks, even if opportunities were equal. I will conclude my analysis of capitalism by showing how the dangers of imposed risk create an argument for a quite demanding social minimum, independent of concerns about effects of unequal opportunity.

These arguments about capitalism cannot establish the adequacy of the minimal specification in advanced industrial circumstances. To show that the minimum is enough, one must extend it to noncapitalist alternatives. This will be my final major task. I will argue that alternatives to capitalism, in a modern industrial setting, are worse than the most just attainable version of capitalism, for everyone, so that the latter should be preferred on minimal grounds. In the present age of capitalist triumphalism, the empirical data telling against actual alternatives to capitalism are celebrated enough, without repetition here. So I will mainly be concerned with the general reasons why central planning and workers' management are bound to be intolerably inefficient. These reasons for preferring some form of capitalism will not be reasons for preferring relatively laissez-faire versions of capitalism, in which people's economic lives are almost wholly dominated by markets. Some form of ordinary, non-laissez-faire capitalism will be just—but, like any sane brief argument about important social choices, the minimal case for capitalism does not say which specific set of institutions and policies must be chosen. Rather, it completes the minimal case for the demand that must be satisfied, in light of further empirical inquiry, namely, the demand that an advanced industrial society be best for the worst-off.

INHERITANCE

This side of Alphabetan assignment, some sources of unequal economic success obviously are violations of equal opportunity. If previous arguments are right, they justify intervention in the interest of the disadvantaged, even at cost to the advantaged. Discrimination on the basis of race, ethnicity, religion or gender are examples. If these inequalities were rectified, would any form of unequal opportunity pervade an advanced industrial capitalist society, substantially contributing to inequalities of outcome in typical cases? The most evident modern candidate for this role is unequal inheritance, in the sense of the transmission of unequal nonbiological competitive resources along family lines. People are born into families headed by others (whom I will assume for simplicity to be the parents) who differ in resources, leisure, skills and interpersonal ties. Future prospects of self-advancement can be affected by disadvantages in this background, as a result of the actions of others, for example, potential employers, on the basis of choices coercively protected by the state. On the whole, the disadvantages lower prospects by reducing resources for competition—for example, competition for desirable jobs. So inheritance, in the broad sense of such transmission of family advantages and disadvantages, is an instance of entrapment, restriction and coercion. By definition, it does not consist of the transmission of genetic advantages in productive capacity. So in either perspective on social freedom, unequal inheritance ought to be eliminated, or its effects should be mitigated in the interests of those who are disadvantaged by it.

Of course, real people, unlike Alphabetans, do, as a rule, care specially about their children, actual or adopted. And real people always suffer if those who bring them up do not display such partiality. It would, then, be irrational for anyone to favor the total abolition of inheritance, on the present broad construal. Still, the general acceptability of some process of inheritance by no means frees actual processes from stringent regulation by the demand for desirability to the disadvantaged. The impact of unchosen disadvantages in initial resources ought to be reduced until the disadvantaged have no reason to prefer a relevant alternative.

Suppose that the typical impact of unequal inheritance on life-prospects is small and unpredictable. Then there is no minimal case for changing economic arrangements in the interest of the worst-off, since change is apt to give rise to impositions that are at least as serious. Perhaps those not favored by government action would find it harder to succeed, given the same willingness to make sacrifices, or, in any case, would suffer from more loss due to the choices of others. Or perhaps differences in innate productive capacity will not be allowed to contribute to eventual success to the extent to which they should in the restrictive perspective. However, inequalities of inheritance do have a large and systematic impact in the United States and other advanced industrial societies, in spite of equalizing institutions already in place, for example, inheritance taxes, free public education and what extra-familial support there is for entry into higher education. In the next three sections I will present some data sustaining and further specifying this verdict of inequality.

UNEQUAL OUTCOMES

Certainly, the outcome of economic activity is very different for different people. The difference is stark when measured in the usual way, quantitatively precise but conceptually crude, by noting inequalities in income. According to Bureau of the Census figures, the best-off fifth of families in the United States in 1988 received 44.0% of total family income, the worst-off, 4.6%.[1] This pattern has not changed substantially since 1910.[2] Skewing toward the

---

[1] *Current Population Reports (U.S. Bureau of Census)*, Series P-60, 167 (1990), p. 16.

[2] See Samuel Bowles and Herbert Gintis, *Schooling in Capitalist America* (New York: Basic Books, 1976), p. 85.

very top is even more extreme. In 1986, the top 1% of taxpayers in the United States received 14.6% of reported income.[3] The degree of overall inequality is broadly similar, despite significant variations, among the major advanced industrial nations. The Gini coefficient for income distribution, the standard measure of the departure of the actual distribution curve from total equality, varies among these nations within a range from about 32% to about 45%, taking typical surveys in typical years.[4]

Granted, these distributions might be a bad guide to the extent of inequality in economic outcomes in the course of whole lives. For example, an accurate estimate of net inequalities would take into account special costs of achieving eventual outcomes. When greater income requires costly training, the cost that is borne by the high earner should be discounted. Friedman and Kuznets found, in the most widely cited empirical study, that the differential required to compensate for the extra expense of training of skilled self-employed professionals ranged from 55% to 70% in the communities they studied in the United States. Still, the actual earnings differential ranged from 85% to 180%.[5] In addition, the cost of training of skilled self-employed professionals is typically much greater than the appropriate discount on eventual earnings in assessing high earners' net economic success. Even among skilled professionals in private practice, costs to the professional of entering the profession are often reduced by others' contributions. Perhaps the future lawyers' parents helped her out in law school, or their availability as a financial last resort kept loans from being too risky. Among managers and other high earners outside of the professions, many training costs are likely to be borne by a firm in which the earner pursues his or her career.

One further doctrine of the costs of success, extremely popular among my students in one of the best and most expensive universities, is that great rewards are compensation for extreme stress and fatigue. It is excruciating to be an investment banker, but someone has to do it, and some do it for a com-

---

[3] From a Brookings Institute study by Joseph Pechman, cited in Kevin Phillips, "Reagan's America: A Capital Offense," *New York Times Sunday Magazine*, June 17, 1990, p. 26. The corresponding figure for 1981 was 8.1%. Part, but by no means all, of the change reflects gains from a stock market boom.

[4] See Royal Commission on the Distribution of Income and Wealth, "The International Comparison of Income Distributions" in A. B. Atkinson, ed., *Wealth, Income and Inequality*, second edition (New York: Oxford University Press, 1980), pp. 82–95.

[5] See Milton Friedman and Simon Kuznets, *Income from Independent Professional Practice* (New York: National Bureau of Economic Research, 1946). The co-authors, one of them the future co-author of *Free to Choose*, conclude, "[T]he actual difference between the incomes of professional and non-professional workers seems decidedly larger than the difference that would compensate for the extra capital investment required . . . [T]here is nothing surprising about this finding. It is clear that young men are not, in fact, equally free to choose a professional or a non-professional career. . . . First, the professions require a different level of ability from other pursuits; second, the economic and political stratification of the population leaves only limited segments really free to enter the professions" (pp. 84, 88).

pensating price. Perhaps the following, nearly Victorian words of wisdom are
an adequate response to large claims for these costs. If the burdens of the best-
paid jobs were proportionately great, wrote Cannan in 1914, "We should find
well-to-do parents in doubt whether to make their sons civil engineers or
naval stokers, doctors or road-sweepers."[6]

When mere income distributions are supplemented and interpreted to create a more complete assessment of the distribution of economic outcomes, the
adjustments toward greater equality—based on training costs, for example—
ought to be accompanied by other, equally well-motivated adjustments toward greater inequality. Thus, the satisfaction of many virtually universal
goals in economic life is much more unequal than income distributions would
suggest. Job security is one example. In the United States, in 1981, the unemployment rate among blue-collar workers was two and a half times greater
than the rate among white-collar workers.[7] In Britain in 1978, half of those
entering unemployment came from the bottom fifth of earners.[8] Similarly,
typical differences in income are reinforced by the tendency for higher-paid
jobs to be more interesting, to offer more scope for control, ingenuity and
pacing by the doer, and to be chosen on the basis of temperamental fit. Professors, lawyers, and doctors are sometimes unhappy with their work, but few
voice the routine observations of the production workers in Beynon's study,
working at British Ford in a period of rising wages. " 'It's strange this place.
It's got no really good points. It's just convenient. It's got no interest. You
couldn't take the job home. There's nothing to take.' . . . 'The point about
this place is that the work destroys you. It destroys you physically and men-
tally. The biggest problem for people is getting to accept it, to accept being
here day in and day out.' "[9]

When all the needed adjustments are taken into account, the inequality of
outcomes is at least as stark as the raw income distributions suggest. Indeed,
Jencks, Perman and Rainwater have recently presented impressive evidence
that the distribution of income substantially underestimates the total inequality in economic success. In a series of nationwide surveys, their team asked
people to rate their own jobs for desirability and to characterize their jobs in
a variety of ways, monetary and nonmonetary. On the basis of these data,
Jencks et al. constructed an index of job desirability in which each characteristic was weighted according to its average effect on job ratings. As they note,
this average effect is the most revealing measure for the study of capacities to
succeed in the job market, since average desirability determines the interest
in a job of one's potential competitors. In the surveys, people were asked,

[6] Edward Cannan, *Wealth* (1914) (London: Staples Press, 1928), p. 207.

[7] *New York Times*, January 11, 1982.

[8] See A. B. Atkinson, *The Economics of Inequality*, second edition (New York: Oxford University Press, 1984), p. 89.

[9] See Huw Beynon, *Working for Ford* (London: Penguin, 1973), pp. 121, 188.

among other questions, "What chance do you think there is that you will lose your job completely in the next two years? . . .", "In your present job, do you get dirty?", "What percentage of the time do you do the same things over and over?", "About how many times . . . does a supervisor check up on your work?", "Does your boss have a boss?" The independent direct impact of *each* of these considerations of security, menialness, intrinsic interest, autonomy and rank, and several others as well, was at least half as great as purely monetary considerations, in some cases greater, when assessed by standard statistical techniques.[10]

When desirability was measured by the whole index, the level of inequality was 2.8 times larger than when it was measured by monetary characteristics alone.[11]—These findings, it might be noted, are powerful confirmation of Cannan's worldly wit. If advantages in earnings were, on the average, even in part, compensation for net burdens endured, then the shift to an overall index would reduce the degree of inequality.

THE PROCESS OF INEQUALITY

Of course, dramatic differences in economic outcome can result from competition in which everyone has equal initial access to competitive resources. Many poker games combine eventual significant difference with initial equality in just this way. However, the competitions that dominate economic prospects in advanced industrial societies consist of the more troubling combination of dramatically different outcomes and unequal initial advantages in pursuing the best outcomes. Some people are dealt more cards than others. Above all, those with certain family backgrounds have importantly different odds for success than others.

For example, the effect of initial difference has been profound in the United States in recent years. Bowles and Gintis report the strong linkage between the socioeconomic status of a man's parents and his likelihood of ending up in the top income fifth. The bar graph expressing the likelihood of ending up on top from families in ascending socioeconomic tenths rises steeply and uniformly to the right, with a likelihood of top arrival from the bottom tenth of 4%, from the fifth tenth of 16%, and from the top tenth of 44%.[12] Summarizing two decades of studies of the relation between family background and earnings or occupational status, Jencks and the co-authors of *Who Gets Ahead?* conclude, "These estimates imply that those who do well economically typically owe almost half of their occupational advantage and

[10] See C. Jencks, L. Perman and L. Rainwater, "What Is a Good Job? A New Measure of Labor-market Success," *American Journal of Sociology* 93 (1988), pp. 1322–57.

[11] Assessing inequalities by the standard deviations in measures that are themselves logged ratio scales. See ibid., p. 1353.

[12] See Bowles and Gintis, *Schooling in Capitalist America*, p. 121.

55 to 85 percent of their earnings advantage to family background. . . . If
. . . an omniscient scientist were to predict the economic standing of sons
from different families, he would find sons from the most favored fifth of all
families had predicted Duncan scores [a widely used measure of the status of
occupations on a scale from 0 to 96] of about 64, while sons from the least
favored fifth of all families have predicted scores of about 16. This is the difference between a social worker or the manager of a hardware store (both 64)
and a construction painter (16), a farmer (14), or an auto mechanic (19). If
we rerank families in terms of their predicted earnings, the sons of the most
advantaged fifth could expect to earn 150 to 185 percent of the national average, while the sons of the least advantaged fifth could expect to earn 56 to
67 percent of the national average."[13]

Striking as it is, the frequently observed impact of family background on
earnings and on occupational prestige underrates the impact on economic
success, according to Jencks, Perman and Rainwater's study of job desirability. Effects of parental status on nonmonetary aspects of job-desirability are
much greater than effects on monetary aspects. "Seven-eighths of the effect
of parental education and two-thirds of the effect of having a white-collar
father are traceable to the fact that these characteristics influence the nonmonetary characteristics of children's jobs." Substitution of the job-desirability index for ratings of occupations by (unstandardized) Duncan scores also
doubles the effects of family background and schooling.[14]

If we lived in a subsistence economy with no scarcity of the best land, then
family-based superiorities in means to get ahead would not consist of superior
resources for competing with others. But in the United States, as in other
industrial capitalist economies, important means to economic success are,
pervasively, resources in competitions for desirable positions, for example,
good jobs and education increasing the prospects of a good job. Of course,
growing up in one family rather than another can provide competitive advantages in many different ways: literal legacies, having books at home, being
read to as a child, going to a good neighborhood school, being sent to a private school or college, associating with families who can be helpful later on,
learning to talk, dress or eat as better-off people are expected to, starting out
in a prosperous, cosmopolitan region and so on. Suppose that typically important family advantages are like the ones that I have just mentioned in the

[13] Christopher Jencks et al., *Who Gets Ahead?* (New York: Basic Books, 1979), pp. 81–83.
These overall estimates are largely derived from comparisons of variance of earnings among
brothers with variance of earnings among men in general. Jencks et al. also discuss thirteen
specific demographic characteristics—for example, father's education, being raised on a farm,
race and ethnicity—finding that these characteristics by themselves account for about half of the
variance in Duncan scores of occupational status and about one-third of the variance in earnings.

[14] "What Is a Good Job?", pp. 1352, 1349. Most variation in job-desirability occurs within the
occupational categories which are rated by such standard measures of status as Duncan scores.

following respect: they do not consist of superior innate productive capacities due to the transmission of genes within the family or greater willingness to make sacrifices for future goals instilled in children by their families. Then rectification or mitigation of unequal opportunity would be required by justice as social freedom in all defensible specifications. The disadvantaged, through no choice of their own and regardless of differences in innate talent, compete less effectively even if they are equally willing to make sacrifices, failing to do as well as a result of choices that people make in virtually inescapable institutions protected by the state.—Evidently, a society like that of the United States, in which family advantages do have great impact, can only evade this verdict of unequal opportunity if the advantages largely consist of innate productive superiorities or superior willingness to try.

Since innate manual dexterity would not contribute much, on average, and since highly specific cognitive skills are not apt to be innate, the relevant innate productive superiority would, presumably, consist of some general intellectual capacity specially contributing to economic success when combined with available training. At least in the restrictive perspective, unequal prospects would be protected because they reflect the unequal distribution of this capacity (provided that it is innate). If there is such a capacity, childhood I.Q. would be a reasonably reliable measurement of it in the population at large. If those on top are there because their I.Q. was tops, one would expect differences in childhood I.Q. to be a great, independent unequalizer of prospects, similarities to be a great, independent equalizer. This is not remotely the case. When the bar graph for arrival in the top income fifth from a family in ascending socioeconomic tenths is constructed for men who all have average childhood I.Q., it is nearly identical in its stark inequality to the graph for the population at large. For example, the bottom tenth of average-I.Q. men have a 5.5% chance of arrival on top as compared to 4.2% for the bottom tenth of all men. For the fifth tenth, the corresponding figures are 17.1% and 16.4%, for the top tenth, 40.8% and 43.9%. Even assuming Jensen's controversial, high estimate of the heritability of I.Q., the contribution to unequal prospects of the genetic component of I.Q. would approach triviality.[15]

The other trait which is sometimes celebrated as the disproportionate possession of those on top is a special willingness, at any given level of current resources, to postpone immediate rewards in the interest of long-term economic goals, chosen through a rational assessment of probabilities and payoffs. What is possessed by those on top is supposed to be disproportionate because variations in eventual success largely depend on variations in such Weberian heroism. If so, then the lesser prospects of some would be due to an unwillingness to do as much or risk as much for success, an unwillingness that turns out to be perpetuated, to a substantial degree, along family lines.

[15] See Bowles and Gintis, *Schooling in Capitalist America*, pp. 120–22.

Though their probability of success is lower, it is not at all clear that their opportunities are less. They are simply less prepared to exploit them. They do less well on account of their own choices.

If this neo-Weberian hypothesis were right, then inequalities in wealth among different age cohorts would be very different. Since the rewarded virtue is a virtue of postponement, the degree of concentration of wealth in the wealthiest fractions would be much greater as older cohorts are considered. It is not. In fact, in the United States, the degree of inequality in wealth is the same for those 65 years and older as it is for the general population.[16]

Moreover, Bowles and Gintis found that the likelihood of arrival on top from the fifth decile was little more than a third of the likelihood from the top decile. No one supposes that the children of the struggling middle class typically strive far less vigorously than the children of the rich.—Of course, if local schools are good and parental homes and bank accounts are big, people may rationally invest in their future in ways that are irrational or unavailable in less well-off families. That hardly shows that the machinist's child has lower chances of material success than the investment banker's because of choices as opposed to given circumstances. What counts is the sacrifice that each would make for the future given the same resources.

In addition to facts about familial causes of success, I have relied on a characterization of the crucial processes of selection for success which needs more justification. These processes, above all, hiring and promotion, are not merely processes of selection, in which some hopefuls succeed but some do not because of assessments of what they offer. They are competitions, so that the chances of success of those who fail would have been greater if the resources for success of some who succeed had not been superior. If I make a bona fide offer to buy every lovely piece of country Queen Anne furniture that is brought to me, and buying such goods is all I do, then some who truck their heirlooms will be disappointed to discover that I don't find them lovely or authentic, but no one who is disappointed would have succeeded had less good stuff arrived. Hiring, I have supposed, is not like this.

One reason why is that firms in modern capitalism (like the firms in Alphabetaland) do not passively confront the labor resources on offer. Frequently, they hire at their standard level of compensation for the kind of work in question and provide training on the job for those applicants who were attractive enough to be hired. Often, if as many applications of that much attractiveness were not at hand, firms would have lowered the threshold for hiring, coping with any consequent differences through further training. Indeed, this is just what many firms do when an upturn produces a labor shortage. So, in many cases, an unsuccessful searcher for a desirable job is more likely to have succeeded if successful searchers had not been more attractive candidates. In-

---

[16] See Atkinson, *The Economics of Inequality*, p. 177.

deed, if educational processes sensitive to family advantage had led to a long-run shortage of applicants of the more attractive kinds, those who benefit most from the prosperity of firms would, in many such cases, have willingly paid more taxes to support the extension of the more advantageous kinds of education to the less advantaged.

Also, employers lack precise knowledge of whether hiring one person rather than others would actually work out best. Personnel departments' responses to the features that applicants present are, in large part, mere educated guessing. They take certain credentials and aspects of speech, dress and general appearance to be signs that an applicant has or will develop desired attitudes or skills. But they are well aware that this is just a shortcut avoiding disastrously costly trial-and-error experiments. So hiring someone who would have been sent away if more attractive applications were at hand need not even create greater training costs or lower productivity. The less advantaged applicant may work out fine. Conversely, the availability of more advantaged applicants can be a reason not to take the extra chance in hiring others that would otherwise, rationally, be taken.

Finally, competitive losses are specially great when factors other than technical needs for skills play an important role in determining the prevalence and desirability of positions. Organizational rationales are one such factor. If there had been no applications as attractive as the winning ones for the first rung of the management ladder or the winning one for the senior supervisor opening, there would be a need to fill these positions. And even if a position was filled with someone whose personal traits promised less addition to profits, there would be a need, independent of the winner's personal traits, to make the position relatively desirable. For the total effectiveness of people's work in the actual job-structure depends on expectations, attitudes and inducements created by status differences. A senior supervisor's skills may be no greater than the norm in the department; still, if her salary is normal, she will have less authority, and the prospect of eventually becoming senior supervisor will not provide an incentive for others to stay with the firm.

I have introduced two themes that will reappear later in this chapter. One is the pervasiveness and rationality of differences in job-desirability that are not the product of the skillfulness of each typical job-holder. The other, related theme is the moral importance of the distance of actual capitalism from models sometimes used in neoclassical economic theorizing, models in which an individual's gains from her efforts are the marginal product of her kind of effort and the marginal product depends on the talents whose use she sells in the context of current technology. These themes will receive the elaboration they deserve. Meanwhile, I hope that the realism of my description of how people compete is obvious enough to motivate concern with unchosen disadvantages in this process.

A Genetics of Earnings?*

So far, empirical findings have concerned relatively specific hypotheses about productive capacities or attitudes toward sacrifice, hypotheses that might reconcile family advantage with justice as social freedom. A different type of study, which might help such reconciliation, seeks to establish a link between innate differences and differences in success through inferences that are unburdened by specific accounts of advantageous traits. The variation in earnings is established among subjects paired by various categories of known biological relationship. On the basis of further assumptions, including assumptions about the typical variation in environment accompanying the known genetic relationship, the study infers the heritability of earnings in the whole society in question, i.e., the amount of variance in earnings that is due to variation in genetic endowment. On this basis, a further conclusion is often reached (but rarely distinguished from the former) as to the amount of inequality in earnings that would occur in circumstances of equal opportunity.

The inferences to heritability that are actually made in these studies always and inevitably depend on a variety of assumptions, genetic and environmental. In this respect the studies are no different from any interesting empirical inference. However, the quality and impact of the assumptions is utterly different from the background of any empirical inference on which one should rely. Some crucial assumptions are just as likely to be false in ways that would yield dramatically different conclusions. In these cases, there is no feasible way to tell which basis for inference is right. Other assumptions are false in ways that exaggerate heritability. Properly assessed, the studies of the large-scale genetics of earnings cannot override the more specific investigations of mechanisms of advantage, in which family advantage does not seem to consist of innate productive superiority.

One study of the genetics of economic success is universally regarded as the most important evidence for a large genetic component. It is representative of the rest in its techniques and defects. In this study, Paul Taubman and his colleagues compared earnings among 1,900 pairs of white male twins, some fraternal, some identical, born in the United States between 1917 and 1927, who responded to a 1974 survey which reached them through addresses derived from Veterans Administration records. A heritability figure can be extracted on the basis of certain assumptions about genetic and environmental variation. The variation in environment among all individuals in the study was assumed not to differ in any statistically distorting way from the variation in the population at large. In addition, there must be some assumption about the similarity of environment among those paired by one genetic relation as compared to the similarity among those paired by another. Here, as in analogous arguments for the high heritability of I.Q., Taubman and his colleagues assumed that the similarities of childhood life potentially relevant to earnings among fraternal twins are precisely the same as those of identical twins.

Finally, one must make certain assumptions about genetic resemblance, beyond the known genetic identity of identical twins. To compare the overlap in genetic material among fraternals with the total identity of identicals, one must have an assessment of the genetic resemblance of parents, assessing the extent of what comes under the undignified but reasonably self-explanatory label of "assortative mating." In addition, in order to compare the extent to which the genetic overlap in fraternals affects earnings with the extent to which it does in identicals, one must answer a question about interactions within genetic material, the question of "additivity" in the jargon of genetics, "To what extent do variations at different genetic loci interact, so that the total influence of genetic similarity on economic outcomes is not the sum of each individual genetic identity, i.e., of its influence in isolation?" In effect, Taubman and his colleagues assume that genetic effects are entirely additive and mating entirely genetically random.[17]

On the basis of all these assumptions, Taubman and his colleagues inferred heritability of earnings of 48%—an uncontroversial calculation, if the assumptions are accepted. This figure is about the same as the total proportion of variance in earnings due to difference in family background, genetic or nongenetic. So, if the heritability estimate is right, if genetic differences make a difference via productive traits and if general economic success is heritable in the same way as earnings, then actual family-based inequalities in economic prospects create no moral pressure to increase equality, in the restrictive perspective on social freedom.

Taken together, the purely genetic assumptions resolve by stipulation questions whose true answer could, just as well, dramatically change the estimate of heritability. The assumption of genetically random mating is, by itself, fair enough in defending the claim that heritability is at least as high as Taubman's figure. If parents tend to resemble each other genetically, then, all else being equal, Taubman's calculations underestimate the extent to which similar outcomes for fraternals are due to genetic resemblance. On the other hand, if effects of genetic overlap are more than additive, Taubman's calculations exaggerate heritability, all else being equal. The greater similarity of outcomes for identicals would be due to their greater sharing of genetic material to a larger extent than Taubman supposes. So the proportion of variance due to genetic difference in the population at large would be overestimated by projection from the impact of the fraternal/identical difference as Taubman assesses it. Within the range of utter plausibility, the combined impact of the facts concerning assortativity and additivity could dictate any of a wide range of heritabilities, some dramatically lower than Taubman's estimate.

[17] See P. Taubman, "The Determinants of Earnings," *American Economic Review* 66 (1976).

Putting aside the genetic assumptions, whose validity is utterly uncertain, one can assess the standard environmental ones. When twins are identical—but not when they are fraternal—most people with whom they grow up can only tell them apart with great difficulty, if at all. Parents, teachers and the twins themselves testify to the profound importance of this environmental similarity, and the enmeshing of childhoods to which it can give rise. One characteristic investigation of young twins found that 43% of the identical twins studied had never spent a day apart, as compared to 26% of like-sexed fraternal twins.[18] The assumption that fraternal twins are exposed to environments as similar as identical twins' is certainly false, yet the inferred heritability is exquisitely sensitive to changes in this parameter. Suppose that the average influence of common childhood environment on earnings among fraternal twins was 56% of the influence of the common childhood environment of identical twins. Then the inferred heritability would decline to 0.[19] Any warranted definite comparison of the impacts of shared childhood environment in the two cases would have to be based on the detailed hypotheses about causes that the studies are meant to evade. All that we can say, without such inquiry, is that the 48% figure is inflated by a wide margin through the false assumption of equal environmental similarity, if the other assumptions are right.

Any inference to heritability in the population at large requires some hypothesis linking environmental variation in this population to that in the subpopulation surveyed. Provided that all else is in order, the 48% figure can be inferred if the subpopulation of surveyed twins contains, as a whole, the same distribution of environmental features relevant to lifetime earnings as the population at large. But this is certainly false. In any process of data-gathering that has been employed in any twin study, economically unpropitious environments reduced the probability that twins would enter the data base. In this study of twins' earnings, failure to serve in the armed forces, dying before most of one's cohorts, failure to respond to questionnaires, and being unemployed[20] were some of the reasons why 96% of all male white twins born in the United States between 1917 and 1927 were not part of the basis for assessing heritability. Those who were included had an average income 52% higher than white male veterans in their age group in the population as a whole.[21]

Relying on Taubman's data and methods, there is no way of determining whether this special feature of the data-base distorts the estimate of heritability in the population as a whole. Does the reduced variation in success among the data-base, as compared with the population as a whole, reflect reduced

[18] See Leon Kamin, *The Science and Politics of I. Q.* (New York: Erlbaum, 1974), pp. 97f.
[19] See A. S. Goldberger, "Heritability" in Atkinson, *Wealth, Income and Inequality*, p. 166.
[20] See Taubman, "The Determinants of Earnings," p. 865.
[21] Ibid., p. 864.

variation in their environments? To the extent that it does, high heritability of earnings among the twins will coexist with low, perhaps virtually zero, heritability in the population at large. Among the twins, the amount of variance due to genetic variation will be relatively high because the amount of relevant environmental variation is unusually low. Consider how, in an isolated Appalachian village, the behavioral trait, speaking English by the age of three, is 100% heritable, because all variation is due to the presence or absence of birth defects.

To answer the question of the extent to which reduced variation in earnings among the twins in the survey is due to reduced variation in environments, one would have to know, already, a great deal about the genetics of economic success, just the sort of question that the study of the twins is supposed to resolve. One would have to know the relationship between the heritability, in the population at large, of the factors affecting inclusion in the data-base (factors which obviously do involve economic success and failure) and the heritability of earnings within the data-base. In effect, Taubman assumes that the two heritabilities are roughly the same. But this assumption stands just as much in need of justification as any of its rivals.

Suppose these barriers to the accurate assessment of heritability could be overcome. The actual heritability of earnings would still be an overestimate of the extent to which variations in earnings are untainted by unequal opportunities whose rectification is required on minimal grounds. Whenever an inborn difference affects earnings, heritability is increased, regardless of whether the advantageous genes help by yielding a superior capacity to contribute productively. The more racism there is, the higher the heritability of earnings. Taubman and his colleagues studied white males, avoiding the direct registration of racial differences (but not of economic similarities due to shared advantages of being white). Still, any inference concerning equality of opportunity would be tainted by a variety of responses to inborn features, affording some competitive advantages over others in ways that the minimal specification would exclude from moral protection. Identical twins are more apt than fraternal twins either to both look very southern-Italian or both look not at all southern-Italian. (Recall that the twins studied established their basic earning-patterns between the two world wars.) Apart from ethnic discrimination, earnings appear to be influenced, to a shocking extent, by job-unrelated traits of physical appearance, for example, height, which is highly heritable (90% in the United States at present), and weight, which is moderately heritable (66%). In one study of University of Pittsburgh graduates, height was more important as a predictor of earnings than either grade point average or an honors degree.[22]

Suppose we could develop a narrower heritability assessment, measuring

[22] See Bowles and Gintis, *Schooling in Capitalist America*, p. 97.

the variance in earnings due to genetic variation affecting traits which actually constitute skills. This measure might still overestimate the extent to which unequal competitive prospects are protected from rectification on minimal grounds. Perhaps some change in the setting of economic institutions and basic policies is required to fulfill the fourfold principle concerning equal opportunity, or some other demand of the minimal specification. The benefits of an inborn trait to which a chooser of justice could appeal must be benefits that would arise in the just alternative. But the bundle of innate properties that are skills in the present situation might yield fewer benefits to the possessor in a just situation. Thus, a talent for cajoling bureaucrats can add a great deal to productivity in the South African film industry, on account of baroque regulations and subsidies meant to sustain apartheid. But those who dismantle apartheid are hardly obliged to preserve advantages due to this capacity, even if it should have an important innate component.

In particular, the reduction of characteristic inequalities of capitalist societies is apt to reduce the benefits of certain talents and traits, for example, the talent for quick calculations of advantage, the love of rapid material gain and the tolerance for frantic, lonely, risky yet peaceful confrontation displayed by heroines and heroes of leveraged buyouts. If heritability of earnings is high, then the distribution of these traits probably has a significant genetic component. If the benefit of these traits depends on institutions imposing competitive burdens on others, then the advantage of genetic properties promoting the competitive-individualist talents and inclinations need not be preserved when justice is pursued. If the competitive burdens are not side-effects of improvements for the worst-off, the benefits of the genetic properties depend on injustice. The benefits depend on injustice even though they are the outcome of pursuing unobjectionable economic goals, once the unjust choice of institutions is made.

Uncertainty and Justice

I have used a variety of studies to vindicate the judgment of most non-experts: the education, skills, leisure or drudgery, social connections, neighborhood ties and financial resources of a baby's family have a substantial impact on the prospect of the baby's eventually advancing her interests in her interactions with others. One's family background usually makes a considerable difference to one's prospects of competitive success, quite apart from any superiority or inferiority of innate productive talent or willingness to make sacrifices.

In any case, this is the drift of the best empirical studies, appropriately interpreted. There are also arguments to the contrary in the enormous literature. In our moral assessments, however, we ought to be guided by a certain special concern for the worst-off which is based on our conditions of ignorance, i.e., our real ignorance, not the product of a hypothetical veil of ignorance. In conditions of uncertainty, one should choose with some special concern for those who will suffer the most if hypotheses on which one relies turn out to be false. Here, of course, the absolute level of suffering is decisive. That an unjust tax on high income and inheritance contributes to someone's becoming a bricklayer who would have been a millionaire may be a cause for moral regret. It is also a cause for regret if an unjust distribution of childhood advantages contributes to someone's raising her three children in one room without a working toilet in a disintegrating welfare hotel in a red-light district, when she would otherwise have had a secure blue-collar job and a neat two-bedroom apartment. However the potentially unjust loss of benefits is measured in each case, the second possible cause for regret is more to be avoided when one is uncertain of crucial empirical hypotheses affecting the justice of alternatives.

Opportunity Gaps

Evidently, people in advanced industrial capitalist societies suffer from unchosen disadvantages in competitive resources. The origins of this inequality are not mysterious. The unequal outcomes of competition among parents become unequal resources for their children as the children compete for education, jobs and wealth. Unchosen disadvantages in resources for social advancement are associated with generally inferior economic situations. It is as if the gamblers with the least funds were also dealt the fewest cards. In actual capitalist societies, there is a gap in opportunities which must be filled either by equalizing opportunities or by improving the prospects of those in the worst economic situations. Though I believe that much more should be done to fill the gap in the first, direct way, I will now argue that such efforts (so long as they suit anyone's just interests) would be inadequate to fill a gap as large as reasonably efficient advanced industrial capitalist economies require.

The traditional front in the drive to equalize opportunities is education. No doubt, much more should be done to equalize educational opportunity. But the gap cannot remotely be filled by this means. Suppose that equally valuable resources are devoted to the education of each child through high school, whether in the poorest village in Mississippi or the richest district in San Mateo County. If the provision of skills is good enough for efficiencies on which all rely, this equalization would already require an enormous shift of resources into education. In addition, are high school graduates to be given whatever further education they want, of as high a quality as they want, so long as they will be helped to learn? If so, the shift in resources to education would be too great for reasonable efficiency. In an economy in which jobs dependent on special qualifications are specially interesting and specially lucrative, people chronically overestimate their chances of succeeding by pursuing such careers. That we are so afflicted with "the presumptuous hope of success" is one of Adam Smith's many enduring truths, and it would be all the truer if all higher education were free.[23]

Suppose, then, that higher educational institutions continue to screen applicants, accepting only some of those who could benefit. The screening would rely on what differences there are, even though the differences are less important in themselves than they used to be. Aspects of social inheritance—growing up with one parent or none, growing up without books at home, growing up in a tiny, noisy apartment, growing up with a family who rely on income from the work of children—will still contribute to differences relevant to this screening. And the effects of this screening will be reproduced and magnified by screening for jobs later on. So, as at present, years of education will be well-correlated with eventual success, while years of education are well-correlated with socioeconomic background.[24]

Finally, suppose, just for the sake of argument, that everyone actually does receive whatever desired education would add to her competitive abilities. Firms will still screen job applicants, i.e., management will order a certain number of hirings from personnel at levels of compensation that are largely standardized for the positions in question and personnel will sort out applicants according to signs of how more or less profitable their hiring is likely to be. In this sorting out, firms will still be interested in differences in grade point averages and test scores—to a large extent as predictors of appropriate self-discipline, loyalty, and self-assertion.[25] And the differences in grades and scores, even if smaller than at present, will still reflect, to a substantial extent, differences in family background. Also, employers will be all the more concerned with non-educational predictors of whether an applicant will work out—for example, the styles of speech, behavior and dress that indicate whether an applicant will fit into a work environment. So long as unequal outcomes lead to differences in family life and residence, such screening will often turn difference into disadvantage.—Partly because of firms' lust for screening, the substantial reduction of inequality in years of schooling in the United States since World War II has had very little impact on inequality of economic success.[26]

Even if the opportunity gap could not be eliminated by changing initial resources, it might be eliminated through a vast reduction in the importance

[23] Adam Smith, *The Wealth of Nations* (London: Penguin, 1986), p. 211.

[24] Summarizing their classic study of occupational structure and mobility, Blau and Duncan write, "A man's chances of occupation advancement depend on his education (zero-order correlation, +.61), which, in turn, depends to a considerable degree on the socio-economic status of his father (+.41)" (R. Blau and O. Duncan, "Some Preliminary Findings on Social Stratification in the United States" [1965] in M. Abrahamson et al., *Stratification and Mobility* [New York: Macmillan, 1976]).

[25] See Bowles and Gintis, *Schooling in Capitalist America*, pp. 134–40.

[26] See Lester Thurow, *Generating Inequality* (New York: Basic Books, 1975), pp. 61–66.

of the differences in resources (vast because the gap is so big). To some degree, the policies of most advanced industrial economies have such an impact—for example, through progressive income taxes and social insurance. However, in a reasonably efficient capitalist economy, there is a pervasive limit on the reduction of the difference that differences in competitive resources make, namely, the rational organization of work by the capitalist firm.

Firms require various kinds and degrees of loyalty, deference, self-discipline, initiative (or the absence of initiative) from various kinds of employees. Stable hierarchies imposing large differences in income, job security, working conditions and independence are essential to firms' pursuit of the right attitudes. These differences are not means of compensating individuals for cost to them of training and for the special burdens of their work. So they result in net inequalities when all benefits and burdens are taken into account. As a further consequence, these hierarchies guarantee that the amount of difference in ultimate success of those with the same innate productive capacities will not typically be explainable as due to differences in willingness to sacrifice for success. Nonetheless, without these structures of inequality, production and training in a modern capitalist economy would lack the orderliness and the limited, well-harnessed initiative on which reasonable efficiency depends.

To begin at the middle of a modern capitalist work force, the dominant firms have an interest in dissuading blue-collar workers of some skill from searching for better jobs and an interest in persuading them to train other workers in their skills. These firms implement long-term, complex plans involving advanced production techniques. With these goals, which are essential to advanced industrial capitalism, the frequent replacement of such workers is much less efficient than maintaining a reliable work force whose skills are largely acquired on the job. Among other considerations, the direct and indirect costs of finding and hiring workers with training suitable to current production are substantially reduced.

If such a firm were frequently to renegotiate individual wage-contracts in response to current economic circumstances, workers would certainly scan the want-ads, and would be foolish to train their own competitors. So the dominant firms cope with their need for reliability among relatively skilled blue-collar workers by offering a long-term package of expectations. After a probationary period, workers can look forward to movement up a job ladder, if they are reasonably obedient and stay with the firm. The jobs at the higher end are relatively well-paid, as an incentive to stay and as support for respect toward workers who supervise and teach others. (Partly because of the Smithian tendency to overestimate one's chances, the actual proportion of novices who eventually reach the top rungs can be small.) One may be laid off, but one will be rehired, according to seniority, unless the factory is closed outright. So in training others, one does not create one's own replacements. The dominant firms reward employees in this regular work force at a level that dissuades them from forsaking seniority and engaging in a search for a higher bidder. The system benefits the firms because of the advantages of a stable, internally trained work force. Once it is generally established on the basis of these mutual benefits, the system can be further enforced by personnel departments. A trained blue-collar worker who is eager to sell skills acquired on the job to a higher bidder will find that other firms' personnel departments interpret this eagerness as undesirable disloyalty, not commendable entrepreneurship.

This arrangement produces better economic conditions for relatively skilled blue-collar workers than what they could obtain in short-term wage bargains conducted in the normal capitalist circumstance in which a significant number of competing applicants have been unemployed for a significant amount of time. Others are not so lucky. In some branches of production, demand varies widely, overheads are low, long-term planning is unnecessary, or employees are unskilled or easy to train or readily available with the necessary training. There, the costs of turnover will often be an inadequate rationale for inducements to stay and to train others. One leaves the world of the autoworker and enters the world of the farmworker.[27]

Similarly, considerations of attitude and inducement distinguish the situation of professional and managerial employees from blue-collar employees, management from nonmanagement, and higher from lower ranks of management in a capitalist economy. For example, the rewards needed to retain professional and managerial employees are specially high, for a variety of reasons, unrelated to special training costs paid by those employees or special innate talents. It makes for efficiency if professional and managerial employees have room for independent initiative; so initiative in seeking a better job is not an obviously undesirable trait, to be avoided in hiring-decisions. Professionals and managers are often in a position to set up private practices or new, smaller firms. When they move to new firms they take with them useful knowledge of the old firms' workings. Their most important skills are more apt to be general ones, which can be extrapolated to new cases. At the same time, the need for fluent, reliable, knowledgeable cooperation and supervision makes it desirable for a firm to induce staying from these easier leavers. So typical inducements to stay will be higher than in the blue-collar case.

[27] In *Prices and Quantities* (Washington: Brookings Institution, 1982), Arthur Okun presents a detailed general theory of the conditions making it rational for firms to induce reliability through long-term expectations. His account of the implicit contract between the dominant firms and their relatively skilled blue-collar workers is especially powerful because of its integration with a general theory of prices in an advanced industrial economy. Okun shows how, in such an economy, a hierarchy of different job-desirabilities will tend to be self-perpetuating, despite the flux of economic conditions. The violation of expected relationships triggers responses that restore the old sequence of Keynesian "wage floors." Guy Routh, *Occupation and Pay in Great Britain, 1906–79* (London: Macmillan, 1980) offers a wealth of empirical data in support of a similar theory of self-perpetuating inequality.

In addition, the autonomy—and, for that matter, the quiet and clean surroundings—which contribute to the efficiency of managerial and professional work also contribute to the distinctive desirability of such work. Finally, the professional and managerial work force are apt to supervise blue-collar and clerical workers and will do so more efficiently if they have the high incomes that evince respect in nonintimate relations in a capitalist economy.[28]

The latter, emblematic role of higher income seems to be specially important at the top of the work force. Relations of authority among executives are maintained by a system of salary differences constituting the differential success generally deemed to merit appropriate deference. It is a remarkable fact that the salary of the highest-paid executive in a firm is strongly correlated with its size and not with its profitability. Simon, reflecting on the correlation, derived the parameters to a remarkable degree of precision just by assuming that the number of executives is proportional to the size of the firm, that each executive has the number of subordinates that is the average according to corporate lore, and that the relation in salary between superior and subordinate is one that is appropriate according to corporate lore.[29]

These pervasive hierarchies, with their feudal or military air, make us modern individualists uneasy. Before this century, these hierarchies were not all present within capitalist firms to the same degree. But nostalgia would be misplaced. Nineteenth-century firms relied more exclusively and more directly on fears of unemployment among those with no savings, unprotected by social services or social insurance. The consequent special pressures on those whose only resource was their own labor was a special burden on them in wage-bargaining, advantaging owners of substantial wealth. In any case, the modern capitalist world of economic differences is the uncoerced result of the rational pursuit of self-advancement in those earlier times.

In an economy in which organizational needs, as opposed to individuals' talents, are an important determinant of job-desirabilities, one would expect the relation between rewards and marginal contributions to be substantially different in different kinds of jobs. Thurow has argued for just such an assessment of United States data. For example, he reports a study of broad occupational categories by Peter Gottschalk according to which service workers, the lowest-paid, have median earnings that are half of their marginal revenue

[28] Richard Edwards, David Gordon and Michael Reich, in *Segmented Work, Divided Workers* (New York: Cambridge University Press, 1982), describe the association of different and differently rewarded segments of the job market with distinct constellations of rewarded traits, and argue that the association mainly serves to sustain a structure of authority, rather than reflecting individual marginal productivity. Erik Olin Wright, *Class Structure and Income Determination* (New York: Academic Press, 1979) documents the independent impact of location in structures of authority and control on economic prospects.

[29] Herbert Simon, "The Compensation of Executives" (1965) in Atkinson, *Wealth, Income and Inequality*.

products, and managers, the highest-paid, have median earnings twice their marginal revenue products, with similarly oriented differences for virtually all categories in between. In light of the Jencks, Perman and Rainwater study, the overall skewing of job-desirabilities is even greater than the skewing of earnings in relation to individual marginal contributions.[30]

In sum, because of its need for hierarchy, a reasonably efficient modern capitalist economy cannot close the opportunity gap it creates. According to the minimal specification of justice as social freedom, such an economy is only just if it is better for the worst-off than any otherwise acceptable alternative.

Who Is Worst Off?

Who are the worst-off and in what respect should they be better off? In a demand emerging from reflections on equal opportunity, the worst-off cannot simply be identified with those of lowest income, who are then required to have as many goods as the poorest in any otherwise acceptable alternative. Someone might, after all, have less money than another because he chooses to work less, preferring the leisure preserved to the money lost. The lower income, then, is due to his choice, not to an imposed competitive disadvantage. Indeed, the person who has little but does not work might, if he cares for leisure, be better off all told than someone who has a bit more but works in burdensome ways. Egalitarianism is sometimes taken to be a demand that everyone have an equivalent bundle of material goods. But such material equality would be part of an unequal outcome if some were, at the same time, more tired than others.

In some frameworks, for example, utilitarianism, these considerations lead to the moral that money, or material possessions, are not an accurate indicator of well-being. But this is an inadequate summary, in interpreting the dictates of social freedom. Important aspects of well-being may be irrelevant to the minimal specification because they have inappropriate origins. A disease, or even a crazy-making parent, may give rise to much unhappiness without

---

[30] See Thurow, *Generating Inequality*, p. 72. Thurow's empirical investigations, and his "job queue" model of the labor-market, are part of a wide-ranging criticism of orthodox neoclassical theories, which assert a tendency for rewards to equal marginal contributions to output. He also discerns a further departure from this tendency, which I will subsequently trace in part to inequalities of bargaining power unrelated to productive contribution: the return to capital appears to be greater than its marginal product, the return to labor less, on every plausible assumption about the general structure of technology. On some plausible assumptions, the return to labor is half or less than half its marginal product. See ibid., pp. 70–73 and Thurow, "Disequilibrium and the Marginal Productivities of Capital and Labor," *The Review of Economics and Statistics* 45 (1968). In *Occupation and Pay in Great Britain, 1906–79*, Guy Routh attacks marginalism through a different, complementary empirical argument, investigating historical trends in differential earnings and their likely explanation. Later on, I will discuss the unreality of neoclassical models in detail.

constituting a barrier to self-advancement in competition with others as a result of institutions and practices coercively protected by the state.

Whether a ranking is relevant depends on what moral demand is to be fulfilled and on what facts and limits to knowledge confront someone seeking to implement the demand. The demand for social freedom is a response to social barriers to self-advancement. The rankings it singles out as intrinsically relevant are concerned with prospects conditional on willingness to try. In the final analysis, the minimal specification directs concern toward those who are most disadvantaged. The most disadvantaged are those whose prospects for self-advancement given various degrees of willingness to make sacrifices for self-advancement are most reduced by unequal access to competitive resources. Bettering the worst-off means raising those conditional prospects of the most disadvantaged.

Granted, the restrictive and the situational perspectives differ in what they count as the worsening of access. But the difference has turned out to be negligible for purposes of large-scale social choice. Also, social circumstances creating irrational unwillingness to try are to be avoided, and I will assume further adjustment for their presence. But unequal access to competitive resources has turned out to be a much more important source of inequality.

Finally, I will assume that there would be no important, widespread problems of overall comparison if all the objective conditional probabilities of success-given-sacrifice were known. For example, if one person's prospects given willingness to make moderate sacrifices are less than another's, so are her prospects given willingness to sacrifice a lot, and conversely; if someone's prospects of achieving one goal are less than another's, so are his prospects of reaching another goal, if neither goal is eccentric and specially demanding. The relative impersonality of modern capitalist economic activity and the all-purpose quality of the resources employed in such activity make these safe assumptions. In other societies, for example, the sons of the gentry might do better than the sons of merchants with a little trying, but find greater prospects from greater trying blocked by others' responses to the unseemliness of such exertion in one of noble birth. Those living inland might have greater prospects of a balanced diet than those on the shore, but less prospect of travel, in spite of any feasible exertion.

By interpreting the rankings in terms of these prospects of success given willingness to try, one favors those who, unless so favored, would lack non-coercive reasons to accept the social setting into which they were born. The egalitarianism that results (if my previous arguments are right) reconciles freedom with equality because it represents the sort of equality that freedom itself requires. Though the worst-off, in the relevant sense, are to be favored, this demand does not, as Nozick fears, "reduce questions of evaluating social institutions to the issue of how the unhappiest depressive fares." In contrast with Nozick's warnings, its emphasis on differences in prospects due to the impact of institutions and basic policies is not ad hoc, but the result of the underlying justification for bias toward the worst-off.[31]

This description of who the worst-off are and how they should be better off than in other alternatives is the right interpretation of the ultimate demand for maximum betterment, the standard whose satisfaction makes a society just. But a more specific description is needed, to judge the extent to which an actual society meets this standard, on the whole. For we cannot apply the general standard to particular individuals, comparing the actual prospects of each conditional on appropriate degrees of willingness to try with his or her similarly conditional prospects as they would be in the absence of competitive inequalities. What we know in each individual case is the outcome so far. We rarely have means of knowing how much more or less an individual would have achieved if she had had the same willingness to try as another. (Does a real-life analogue of Brando's punk speak truly when he says he coulda been a contender?) Indeed, it is usually impossible to assess the actual willingness that contributed to the actual outcome, or to factor out contributions of mere luck, good or bad. And all of these uncertainties are only the prelude to assessing someone's prospects of success in the course of his or her whole life, given various degrees of willingness to try.

In the face of these uncertainties, we ought to do the best we can, finding the most useful description of the group of primary concern, i.e., the description whose actual employment will provide the most accurate measure available of a society's distance from justice as social freedom. This is feasible in an advanced industrial capitalist society because virtually everyone's prospects are powerfully affected by the competition for a good job, and because the competitive resources for advancing toward one desirable outcome in this process tend to be useful for most others as well. We discover the differences between families that have the greatest impact on outcomes in economic competition. Since these differences do not consist of inferiorities and superiorities in innate productive talent, those worst-off in these respects will, on the whole, be the most disadvantaged, in any defensible specification of social freedom. Then we ask whether their prospects conditional on willingness to try would be higher if their competitive resources were increased or if the importance of competitive disadvantage were reduced.

At this stage in my description of the effort to implement justice, concern is still directed at the most disadvantaged, not those with the lowest income or, more broadly, those least materially well-off. For the objects of concern are defined in terms of initial resources for competitive success, not in terms of different degrees of success on account of actual employment of resources. For example, an unequal pattern in outcomes due to different degrees of willingness to try would be unobjectionable. The ultimate goal is hardly distrib-

---

[31] See *Anarchy, State and Utopia*, p. 190.

utive at all. . . . However, further facts constraining the achievement of the goal require the use of rules of thumb directing concern at the poorest and at large inequalities in economic success. The outcome of rational, informed pursuit of justice as social freedom in a capitalist setting is as much emphasis on equality of outcome as any rational informed pursuer of equal distribution could demand. For purposes of quick summary, it does no harm to simplify in the familiar way and insist that basic social arrangements should be best for those worst-off, and so on up the line.

On the one hand, large inequalities in outcome constitute inequalities of opportunity because they provide unequal competitive resources for the children of the winners and losers. This is the most elementary way in which social freedom conflicts with inequality. Large differences in parental earnings have a significant impact on prospects given willingness to try. The impact is especially great, as we have seen, for the compound of parental earnings and occupation measured by parental socioeconomic status, a compound which represents the economic successes people pursue more accurately than earnings alone.

So far, the connection of the pattern of success with the demands of social freedom has concerned the role of successes and failures as inputs to further strivings. However, their intrinsic status as outcomes is also important, in light of empirical findings that I surveyed. Inferior location in the pattern of outcomes is not the result of lesser willingness or innate productive capacity in the typical case. Inequality of competitive resources is the best explanation of the overall pattern. So improvement from the standpoint of those with much less is apt to be the improvement from the standpoint of the disadvantaged which has ultimate moral relevance. One would put these typical connections to one side, and directly identify those with the least prospects given equal willingness to try, if there were a way of doing so that was accurate and that imposed no morally prohibitive costs in loss of benefits to the actually disadvantaged. But there is usually no such means. In the final analysis, someone's having a lot less than another may not be relevant to justice. But the existence of an overall pattern in which large inequalities of material goods are typical is relevant to the *pursuit* of justice, in industrial capitalist societies.

As one considers smaller and smaller inequalities of outcome within the larger pattern, both kinds of connections with the demand to better the disadvantaged become weaker. The differences in outcome are more apt to reflect different degrees of willingness to sacrifice and the consequences for the next generation are less apt to be unequally effective resources for competition.

There is a similar lack of relevant causes and effects when one considers differences, even large ones, at the high end of modern distributions. This is one good reason to have as little moral concern as everyone does for the fact that some make five hundred thousand dollars a year while some make do with only half as much.

In addition to the general reasons for concern with large, overall inequalities, there are special reasons for adopting a rule of thumb according to which the poorest are to be treated as disadvantaged, in comparison with those less poor. The situation of the poorest would be so undesired an outcome by virtually anyone that it is especially unlikely to reflect unwillingness to try for more if one had the same resources as everyone else. Moreover, parental poverty is a specially dramatic competitive disadvantage. Finally, in the case of the poorest, the rule for responding to uncertainty, viz., that one should avoid risking the most painful nonalleviation, applies with special force.

In saying that "Give priority to the poorest" is a rule of thumb, I mean to concede that the priority should be modified if there is a well-substantiated reason to suppose that a policy excluding some of the poorest from preference would benefit the most disadvantaged. But the burden of proof is significant. It would be wrong, an assumption of avoidable moral risk, to base the exclusionary judgment entirely on one's favorite economic theories. There is no well-confirmed, sufficiently determinate theory of how different policies affect conditional life-prospects, so uncertainty directs attention to the poorest, as most vulnerable. It would also be wrong to postpone the mitigation of poverty until after the gathering and interpretation of data have established that no alternative will more accurately identify the most disadvantaged. Those who complain that inaction is unjust will rightly complain of the decades required for such assessment, assessment which will in any case require some controversial empirical commitments.

Who should pay for the mitigation of poverty? Preferentially, those who have benefited the most from advantages in competitive resources. Moreover, money payments should be governed by other egalitarian rules of thumb. The same amount extracted is a greater sacrifice in general for the less well-off nonpoor than for the better-off. The difference in the sacrifice of competitive resources, both for oneself and for one's children, is especially great when the same amount is extracted from those with different incomes. For wealth tends to increase with income but at a much steeper rate. While the top 5% of households in the United States receive 18% of current annual income, the wealthiest 1% of households own one-third of personal wealth. For them, higher taxes are unlikely to affect the question of whether to send a child to college, to start up a small business, or to quit a job and seek more desirable work. So progressivity in taxation is the right rule of thumb. And, of course, it is supported by the other rule of thumb, that unjust differences are apt to be reduced by reducing large inequalities in outcome.[32]

---

[32] For the income distribution, see *Current Population Reports (U.S. Bureau of Census)*, series P-60, 167 (1990), p. 9. For the wealth distribution, derived from Federal Reserve Board surveys,

Admittedly, arrangements governed by these various egalitarian considerations will sometimes bring it about that someone gains and someone loses through a transfer that does *not* equalize prospects conditional on willingness to try and does not work to the benefit of the one who suffers from imposed competitive burdens in competing with the other. Those who merely exercise a preference for leisure are helped by progressive income taxes—even helped by programs to mitigate poverty if their preference is sufficiently extreme. However, these transfers are not unjust, so long as they reflect the need to base policies on typical cases. For this need must be respected on quite minimal grounds. Fine adjustment to individual circumstances requires crushing burdens in information-gathering or disastrous discretion on the part of officials. Of course, there is the alternative of inaction, but this will be unjust if intervention is apt to remove more serious imposed burdens than it creates.

It might seem that concern for large inequalities in success and special attention to the poorest are only a faint echo of demands that economic goods be equally distributed unless an inequality benefits those with less. But really, in a modern capitalist setting, this coarse-grained concern for equal distribution is as fine as any rational, well-informed egalitarianism permits. So long as resource-allocation is mainly guided by the decisions of firms responding to investors' desires for maximum returns, incomes will differ substantially. Market processes will subvert any fine-grained effort to legislate a pattern of economic success. Given capitalism, any nondisastrous demand for equality will be coarse-grained. It will consist of the rules of thumb for pursuing justice as social freedom.

THE IMPORTANCE OF STARTS

A final general problem of implementation concerns the rule that one should increase the competitive resources of the disadvantaged, starting with the most disadvantaged, or mitigate the impact of lesser resources on prospects of success contingent on willingness to try. Which course should one take, increase in competitive resources or mitigation?

In practice, it is easier to persuade people that there should be more equality in the earlier stages of life, in which the young are prepared for adult competition, than to persuade them that the long-term importance of initial inequalities should be reduced. An absolute bias toward the preparatory and the early would be unreasonable, here. If the reduction of inherited disadvan-

---

see "Rich Got Richer in 80's," *New York Times*, January 11, 1991, p. A20. Much wealth consists of consumer durables, household inventories and net equity in owner-occupied housing, assets that are relatively useless for competitive purposes. When this part of wealth is put to one side, the distribution is much more unequal, with 48% owned by the top 1%, 75% by the top 2% in 1983. See Edward Wolff, "Estimates of Household Wealth Inequality in the U.S., 1962–1983," *The Review of Income and Wealth* 33 (1987), p. 238.

tages justifies taxing rich devotees of prep schools to support public education, it can justify public provision of health services, so that inherited competitive disadvantages are not the cause of anyone's dying of an operable tumor through inability to pay a surgeon's fee. Still, a less-than-absolute bias toward equalizing resources for competition, rather than transferring results of competitive activity, is rational in the implementation of social freedom.

The rationale has to do with special problems of misallocation affecting the direct transfer of benefits. When one mitigates by transferring benefits, there is a danger that benefits will flow to those who only seem to be worst-off. Benefits to those who are worst-off may be less, as a consequence of the misallocation. In any case, transfer to those who suffer from no imposed competitive burden is, as such, a basis for complaint on the part of the advantaged. (This is one of many ways in which redistribution differs from punishment. Criminals are in no position to complain if the fines they pay are misspent.) These consequences are "local injustices" in the following sense: because of further effects and constraints on feasibility these effects of a policy might not make it unjust, but they would certainly make it unjust if they typified the total distributive effect. These local injustices ought to be avoided by any means that does not worsen the life-prospects of the relevantly worst-off.

Unfortunately, as tests become more efficient in eliminating the free-riders, the tests themselves become more burdensome to all who are tested, including the deserving. No doubt, the lazy poor were excluded by the mid-nineteenth-century British policy of confining the unemployed in virtual prisons and setting them to work at such tasks as breaking boulders with sledgehammers, as a condition for receiving food. But this very efficient test worsened the prospects of those who really were prepared to make sacrifices for self-advancement. In sum, transfer creates local injustices which should be kept to a minimum by morally tolerable means, but these local injustices are hard to regulate by such means because of the side-effects of exclusionary interventions.

The equalization of goods that are only useful as competitive resources does not tend to give rise to as much local injustice. The usefulness of the competitive resources depends on exertion in employing them. So their provision is not apt to attract use by those whose lesser holdings reflect less willingness to make sacrifices in order to succeed. Free provision of television sets is more apt to attract the lazy than free classes in repairing television sets. This reduced danger of local injustices is especially characteristic of the earlier stages of education, since most children are willing to learn and, in any case, they are not fully responsible for choices that worsen their ultimate prospects. In addition, familiar economic worries about reduced incentives and efficiencies do not apply at the level of basic education, since it is efficient to allocate basic education to all and children are not mainly motivated by financial incentives. For all of these reasons, the imperative to reduce local injustices by all morally acceptable means supports a preference for enhancing competitive resources as against mitigating lesser resources by providing improved outcomes.

Still, the resulting bias toward the equalization of initial resources will hardly be absolute. As we have seen, in spite of all changes of this kind that they could rationally accept, some will still be worsened by remaining imposed inequalities in competitive resources. Children of farmworkers and children of investment bankers will not have equal prospects. Further mitigation through transfer of benefits will result in local injustices favoring some whose disadvantage is merely apparent. But someone who is relevantly disadvantaged will, rationally, consider the net effect on her of such arrangements. She will balance the losses from free-riding against the costs of more efficient testing. Some form of mitigation may better her, on balance. Then, it should be provided, in a setting of unequal opportunity, if no similarly advantageous arrangement gives rise to less local injustice.

Beyond Inheritance

Evidently, one inequality to which free enterprise gives rise, namely, unequal inheritance of competitive resources, is subject to criticism in the name of freedom. Another sort of defect, to which I have alluded, is the tendency of unregulated private production and exchange to give rise to harmful side-effects and unearned benefits due to facts of nature—pollution being the prime example. Suppose these defects were removed, while people were otherwise protected in all noncoercive, nondeceptive uses of results of noncoercive, nondeceptive production and exchange. In an advanced industrial setting, would such a system be unjust?

As a basis for describing an attainable just social system, the supposition is absurd. Given the protection of private enterprise, there will be winners and losers. Parents will be partial to their children. So unequal inheritance is bound to result. However, as a way of distinguishing different bases for moral criticism, the absurd supposition is revealing. A critic of laissez-faire might assume for the sake of argument that capitalist acts could wholly determine outcomes in a setting in which no one suffers from initial competitive disadvantages and in which naturally mediated side-effects have all been rectified. Everyone, we might suppose, comes of age equally well-prepared to compete for a good job, and, on coming of age, receives the same vouchers granting access to venture capital. Apart from guaranteeing this initial competitive equality, the state does nothing except to protect private control of the results of private acts of noncoercive, nondeceptive production and exchange. With problems of initial endowment and naturally imposed interaction put to one side, can anything be said in criticism of the commercial process itself?

In this quasi-laissez-faire setting (laissez-faire except for the regulation of initial competitive resources and naturally mediated side-effects), unregulated free enterprise still reduces freedom. The objectionable constraint does not involve an imposed process guaranteeing that some will have lesser life-prospects of desirable outcomes than others, despite equal willingness to try and equal innate productive capacity. No one is forced to play the great competitive game with fewer cards than others. Rather, the unfreedom involves the character of the pattern of outcomes within which people have to strive for desired end results, with initially equal prospects of success. People are forced to gamble for high stakes, when they would rationally prefer a different game. If we were all forced to play Russian roulette on reaching twenty-one, with a substantial payoff for those whose skulls survive, we would complain in spite of knowledge that everyone's Twenty-First Birthday Revolver was identical. This will suggest the general form of the following critique of quasi-laissez-faire.

I will develop the details of the critique by noting ways in which economic outcomes of quasi-laissez-faire would depart from a certain model, "the model" as I shall call it, which dominates many discussions of market processes. The proper home of the model is the most austere region of price theory, the General Equilibrium Theory of Arrow and Debreu. There, the model is explicitly presented and used to demonstrate that prices with various desirable characteristics would exist if the model were real. Highly simplified variations of the model are perhaps the most common teaching device in economics textbooks. For these reasons, prestige and familiarity attaches to the uses that are most important for our purposes. In these uses, the question of what economic life would be like if initial endowments were equal but laissez-faire were otherwise the rule is answered by describing consequences of the model. This is a misuse of economic theory, as I will try to show. It obscures the risks we would encounter in a quasi-laissez-faire economy.

No one could complain of confinement to market transactions, given equitable initial endowments, in the imaginary worlds fitting the model. In these worlds, fully rational, perfectly informed economic agents advance their interests solely by buying and selling commodities, at prices that no single individual's offers and purchases affect, through contracts binding them in all future economic actions; the agreements are reached in costless negotiations taking no significant amount of time and accurately conveying all offers, offers which are always entirely reliable; the technology embodied in production decisions affords no economies of scale. It is as if commercial activity were wholly determined by a vast instantaneous auction administered by an omnipotent auctioneer, charging nothing for his services. The effect of the Great Auctioneer is to make it possible for everyone to better himself by exchange. Any grounds for complaining about the auction he administers would have to concern a difference in initial endowments which makes the Auctioneer's availability more beneficial to some than to others. So, assuming the initial endowments are beyond criticism, the economic process cannot be unjust.[33]

However, the fact that no one could complain of confinement to such transactions says nothing, in itself, about justice among us. It might be as uninteresting as some fact about what we would all prefer if we were immortal, in an investigation of justice in military tactics. We need to consider what people would actually do and suffer if all entered economic life with equal competitive resources, all gains from commercial activity were protected (naturally mediated side-effects to one side) and no losses from commercial activity were mitigated at public expense. Apart from these stipulations, people's lives should be taken as governed by the factors affecting commercial self-advancement in the real world, which may be very different from the factors defining the model. Otherwise, the thought-experiment tells us nothing about the moral criticism of actual institutions.

In reality, crucial factors *are* very different from those in the model, in ways that would make the quasi-laissez-faire alternative morally defective. Because of these differences, the protection of market competition would impose risks that most seekers of justice would rationally prefer to avoid, while depriving them of means to reduce those risks.

Unlike cicadas, competing humans do not all come of age together. (In this they also differ from the people in the model, who all at once deploy their initial resources.) So, in the quasi-laissez-faire world, one brings one's preparation and one's vouchers into an arena in which others have acquired certain resources through a prior history of competition. In particular, some of these others will have acquired substantial competitive advantages through success in past competition.

Most of those who have ventured their vouchers will have lost, while a few will have acquired substantial advantages. This is a result of further departures from the model. Since foresight is imperfect (and indefinitely complex futures contracts are not always on offer with no transaction costs), differences in luck are bound to create some inequalities. In the market setting, greater success is an advantage in further competition, providing economies of scale, cushions against future calamity, special resources for research and development, and the greater access to credit of more secure creditors. (None of this

---

[33] This is a rough sketch of the world of General Equilibrium Theory, Arrow's and Debreu's refinement of the models of Walras, Jevons and Menger. My main simplification has been to stipulate perfect foresight where Arrow and Debreu stipulate that the perfectly rational agents have no difficulty whatever in hedging their bets with every conceivable futures contract, no matter how elaborately the conditions for payoff are defined. For pithy summaries by a leading explorer of these worlds, see Frank Hahn, *Equilibrium and Macroeconomics* (Cambridge: M.I.T. Press, 1984), essays 2–6. Hahn makes clear both the artificiality of the postulate about futures contracts and the importance of the postulate for the model. For our purposes, the consequences of imperfect foresight have the same moral significance as the consequences of imperfect hedging.

exists in the model. Indeed, there is no place for money, much less banking, in the model.) Because of this tendency for markets to magnify differences, the initially less lucky are apt to go bankrupt in the end. Thus, the fledgling entrepreneur will probably fail—here, as in the real world—and will, in any case, compete at a disadvantage with past winners.

Still, the newcomer can exploit her equal initial preparation to compete for a desirable job. In doing so she faces a different structure of inequality. Firms will still find it efficient to organize work on the basis of a hierarchy of jobs and careers. (In contrast, in the model prospective employers offer indefinitely complex and long-term specifications of desired work characteristics, in the certainty that the terms will be observed by anyone taking up the offer. There is no need to induce appropriate attitudes. Indeed, in the model, there are no firms, as such.) The newcomer finds the more desirable jobs already occupied by people who are hard to displace because job security is an important part of the more desirable packages and because important aspects of training are best obtained on-the-job.

Still, some hiring of newcomers is usually being done somewhere at the bottom rung of job ladders. But there are normally fewer more desirable bottom rungs than people who are willing and able to assume their responsibilities. For differences in desirability will be dictated by relationships of authority and by differences between different markets and different branches of production. The newcomers cannot all attain the highest ladders by all displaying the highest willingness to deploy their equal initial preparations. In addition, in their searches for desirable bottom rungs on offer, newcomers will have to settle for the best jobs they can find under time-pressures imposed by their need for food and shelter. The decision to settle for less than the best, though rational, will be fateful. It is hard to find a new job while working, harder as one becomes older and able to promise less return for on-the-job training, especially hard in the job-competitions in which job-switching is taken to be a sign of undesirable disloyalty. (These considerations, bearing as they do on the cost of information gathering, time, and screening for attitudes exceeding contractual obligation, would have no impact in the model.)

Whether this setting is inspiring or dispiriting will now depend on the situation of relative losers. Exclusive reliance on the venture capital vouchers is likely to result in failure. So the crucial outcome is the situation of those who do not have the more desirable jobs. Here, job prospects tend to be much grimmer than they are in the real world, which has so far roughly resembled the quasi-laissez-faire alternative.

To begin with, some people will be unemployed, in spite of a willingness to work which is as great as, or somewhat greater than the willingness of those who are employed. Since commercial activity requires cash and credit, while its planning is based on guesswork, there will be layoffs, bankruptcies, and firings of competent employees. There is no Great Auctioneer to achieve the most complete employment of productive resources compatible with people's desires to relax and to consume. In addition to unemployment arising from commercial activity itself, the newcomer will be faced with other competing newcomers resulting from acts of procreation not performed with an eye toward maximum return from eventual employment. (In the model, only acts of rational buying and selling affect eventual outcomes.) Finally, competition among the unemployed will be desperate, in the quasi-laissez-faire world, much more desperate than in ours. For those who have exhausted their venture capital vouchers and spent their savings will soon starve if they do not find employment. By definition, there is no state-administered unemployment insurance and no welfare system.[34]

The desperate situation of the unemployed is both a disadvantage for job-applicants in bargaining with firms and a drag on employed workers for whom firms could substitute desperate applicants. For the desperate encounter inequalities of bargaining power in seeking work from firms, inequalities of kinds that do not exist in the model. They sell their labor under the pressure of urgent needs, seeking to sell to firms which have inventories and cash reserves. (In the model, all bargains are, in effect, instantaneous; there is no special pressure to strike a deal.) In addition to the unequal pressure of time there may be an unequal pressure of space: to sell one's labor elsewhere one must move, and hence abandon personal ties which are fundamental emotional resources. For firms, the task of moving production from higher- to lower-wage locales is apt to be the much less wrenching project of coordinating the physical depreciation of an old productive plant with investment in a new one.[35]

The low wages encouraged by these pressures on prospective employees

---

[34] For an influential demonstration of how as elementary a fact as the role of money in commerce makes persistent unemployment possible, see Robert Clower, "The Keynesian Counter-Revolution: A Theoretical Appraisal" (1963) in D. Walker, ed., *Money and Markets: Essays by Robert W. Clower* (Cambridge: Cambridge University Press, 1984). There can also be extensive involuntary unemployment in equilibrium because of jobseekers' rational assessments of relevant probabilities, for example, the probability of finding a job at a wage that would be acceptable if the job were actually found. See T. Negishi, "Unemployment, Inflation and the Microfoundations of Macroeconomics" in M. J. Artis and A. R. Nobay, eds., *Essays in Economic Analysis* (Cambridge: Cambridge University Press, 1976). In both of these cases and others, as well, markets fail to move in the direction of the model because rational reliance on available signals does not do enough of the work of the Great Auctioneer. These intrinsic limitations of commercial activity in any important market, rather than the impact of externalities, have achieved a large, perhaps a dominant role in discussions of the defects of the model as a tool for investigating actual market processes. (See Hahn, *Equilibrium and Macroeconomics* for perspicuous surveys.) Such considerations ought to be similarly fundamental in investigations of market-based injustice.

[35] In the model, initial competitive resources could be adjusted to compensate for different degrees of remoteness from competitive opportunities. But in reality, these opportunities constantly and unpredictably shift in space, over the course of time, undermining any initial equalization.

would soon be reduced by competitive pressure among employers if, as in the model, the latter pursued self-interest solely through the costless exchange of commodities unconstrained by economies of scale. But in the real world employers can benefit from the pressure on prospective employees, because there are barriers, financial and technological, to market entry, and "a sort of tacit, but constant and uniform, combination [of employers] not to raise the wages of labor above their actual rate."[36]

As a result of these unequal capacities to advance one's interests through bargaining, the wages and working conditions of a significant worst-off fraction of workers will be exceptionally low. In times of high unemployment, the situation of the unemployed will be even worse. Moreover, because of ongoing, rational processes that screen for desired attitudes and sustain them with emblems of authority, those who have spent some time as working poor or desperately unemployed are quite unlikely to compete successfully with newcomers or established winners. Residence in the lower ranks will be taken as an indication that one has acquired the wrong attitudes and habits for the higher ranks.

In short, as observers of nearly laissez-faire societies have always noted, the prospects of success are accompanied by substantial risks of dire lifetime failure. Virtually anyone facing such odds would want there to be a safety-net, mitigating the costs of failure, even if this had to be purchased by lowering the heights of success. More precisely, this would be the preference of the vast majority, apart from a tiny entrepreneurial minority who prefer to gamble for high stakes. And in this case, the attitude of the vast majority is as morally decisive as it would be if it were the attitude of all. For if bargaining were an equally effective resource for all, the vast majority could persuade the entrepreneurial minority to enter into the majority's preferred general insurance scheme. On the basis of prior agreement among themselves (which time-pressures and coordination problems would in fact obstruct), the majority would propose otherwise to exclude the minority from their commercial transactions, transactions on which great payoffs to entrepreneurship depend.

"But wouldn't dire consequences be avoided by a private commitment of each newcomer to finance a safety-net with part of her proceeds, if she should succeed, extending this aid to everyone who enters into the same agreement upon coming of age?" Because of the banal problems of time, coordination and enforcement that were absent from the model, this endeavor would not

---

[36] Adam Smith, *The Wealth of Nations*, p. 169. In general, chapter 8, "The Wages of Labour," is a compelling description of the disadvantages in bargaining of not especially skilled workers in normal times. Smithian collusion arises in the quasi-laissez-faire alternative because a relatively few entrepreneurial winners control established firms with special resources for information-gathering, coordination and commercial retribution. In the model, interests are solely advanced by buying and selling, among agents whose individual resources are supposed to be too minutely and equally distributed to permit any influencing of prices.

work, even if every newcomer would want it to. At any given time at which the scheme might be started, the disposable income needed to sustain a safety-net for the next substantial length of time is in the hands of those who have already succeeded. The latter are protected by diversified portfolios or relatively secure careers. The proposal only generates adequate insurance funds after many years in which people reliably commit themselves to it, contributing if they do succeed. Newcomers are apt to suffer dire consequences before then, and the scheme would, in any case, face overwhelming problems of coordination, assessment and enforcement—overwhelming precisely because of the vulnerabilities that make the success of the scheme so desirable. So newcomers will, rationally, take their chances, instead.

The perils of the quasi-laissez-faire alternative are the source of its moral defects. Because of the limitation on state action, the system does not even include state enforcement of a self-financed insurance system to which each newcomer is to subscribe, committing himself or herself to contributions conditional on success. (Residents of the United States will think of the payroll deduction aspect of Social Security.) The absence of this arrangement puts every newcomer at peril on account of confinement to a system of transactions and control coercively protected by the state. A newcomer pursuing the cooperative goal could certainly reject the system in favor of one with an insurance scheme administered by the state. For the minimal scheme that I have just described would be in the rational interest of every subscriber.

But what about the initiation of a more extensive protection against risk, extracting resources from those who have already won, and protecting those who have already begun to lose? This, too, is required by justice as social freedom. It may be sufficient to base this judgment on a principle concerning justice and time: those who seek free and rational acceptability to all will not reject arrangements that they would have accepted if everyone's life-prospects *had been* regulated in ways freely and rationally acceptable to all. This principle seems implicit in the cooperative goal. A chooser of justice seeks maximum equal inducement to cooperate for everyone. Clearly, this is not a demand for an appropriate pattern of benefits and burdens at every point in time. Otherwise, new commercial events, which do, constantly, change the pattern, would almost instantly render just arrangements unjust. Rather, one seeks maximum equal inducement to cooperate over the course of everyone's whole life as measured by everyone's life-prospects. So, it would seem, an arrangement that would have provided such prospective benefits to all is always to be preferred, in the name of justice.

Still, some might reject the principle about justice and time in situations like the one at hand, where actual winners and actual losers were subjected to the same perils. (They received equal inducement at their respective starts, though not maximum equal inducement, since undesirable avoidable risks were imposed.) It might be said that gains from such arrangements are not subject to just redistribution since the earlier arrangement, though morally defective, was equally undesirable to all.

Even if the principle about justice and time is rejected on these grounds, other considerations will still come into play, leading directly from considerations of unequal opportunity to much the same result. Suppose that the limited insurance scheme was inaugurated in year 1, and that nonsubscribers did not all die or retire until year N. In between, those who had won before year 1 would benefit from unchosen competitive disadvantages of others with whom they interact, i.e., with those who have become the working poor or unemployed by year 1 and with many subscribers in the underfinanced years of the scheme. The benefits are most notable in the case of those who derive their income largely from wealth. They directly receive the benefits of the unequal bargaining pressures on firms interacting with sellers of not-very-skilled labor. In addition, those who have won relatively desirable and secure positions will often benefit, to some degree. The work-life or lack of it of the most vulnerable makes them less threatening as competitors displacing the better-off employees. In sum, from a perspective uncommitted to extensive rectification for the mere past absence of insurance, justice as social freedom would still require contributions from the wealthy and, to some extent, from the better-off employees to protect both newcomers and losers from future perils.

Evidently, in addition to unequal inheritance, the unchosen risks of market competition stand in need of justification. The depth of failure should be raised and the heights of success reduced to finance this raising, to the extent that the vast majority would desire if all competed with equal initial resources. This risk-averse perspective on life-chances is, roughly, the attitude of the participants in the "original position" in *A Theory of Justice*. As often happens in this defense of the minimal specification, a Rawlsian conclusion results from concrete facts about our effects on one another, rather than Rawls' own morally controversial insistence on a Kantian ideal of personality.

No indeterminacy results from the combination of two demands, avoidance of grave imposed risks and maximum improvement of the prospects of those who suffer most from unchosen competitive disadvantages. For in any actual capitalist economy, the most burdened in terms of market vulnerability tend to be the most burdened in terms of unequal inheritance.

GAUTHIER'S MARKETS *

In recent discussions of justice, price-theoretic models have gained special prominence from their presence in Gauthier's *Morals by Agreement*. In developing his basis for assessing justice, Gauthier often refers to model worlds of neoclassical price theory equivalent or identical to those I previously described. He calls the processes governing economic life in such models a "perfectly competitive market" (see pp. 85–90). He is well aware that real market interactions would lack many of these characteristics. Perhaps he insists on nothing more than the following reliance on market processes in the construction of a theory of justice: the idea of a perfectly competitive market helps to describe an imaginable circumstance, the market as a "morally free zone," in which no one has a basis for moral criticism of any interaction yet everyone is out to advance her own interests (see p. 13). More specifically, transactions in a perfectly competitive market would not give rise to valid moral criticism in the absence of rent, i.e., the acquisition of something for less than one would willingly pay because of the scarcity of a factor one controls in one's initial endowment. Those who complain of the effects of a perfectly competitive market, apart from rent, want to benefit from another's participation in interactions by imposing terms that would make him worse off than he would be in the complainers' absence. So (Gauthier concludes) they want to take advantage of someone, and have no just complaint. Complaints would only have standing if directed at the initial endowments that people bring to bear.—I will not criticize this characterization of the perfectly competitive market as an imaginable morally free zone.

Sometimes, however, Gauthier seems to put a conception of market interaction to a much more important use, in constructing baselines from which gains from cooperation in actual societies might be measured in determining whether the gains are distributed as justice requires. This strategy for baseline construction assigns—with certain adjustments—the holdings that each would acquire, in the actual economic setting, through the use in production and exchange of her basic endowment, i.e., her natural capacities. The adjustments concern the various ways in which these commercial outcomes might fail to be fully determined by what each agent is rationally willing to forgo in pursuit of private enjoyments. Thus, benefits from exclusive access to raw materials and territory are excluded, along with advantages from inheritances. Benefits and losses from externalities, i.e., unchosen effects of production and exchange, are also excluded. (Externalities result from the presence of unowned goods, absent from the perfectly competitive market.) Finally, people are not protected in rent derived from the scarcity of factors in their basic endowments.

I am not sure that Gauthier does intend this use of corrected market interactions in the moral assessment of actual social arrangements. It is suggested by parts of his description of how an ideal chooser would deliberate over questions of justice (p. 261) and by his characterization of justice as a response to "externalities in our environment" (p. 116). Gauthier certainly needs some means of constructing baselines. He thinks that baselines may well be unequal. But mere possession of basic endowments such as he describes would generate no inequality—they are used as means, not consumed directly. One has to describe the processes in which the capacities are used, and corrected private-enterprise is the only description he offers that might be applicable in the real world. In any case, this apparent appeal to market processes has gratified, outraged or puzzled many readers, according to their prior dispositions. So it will advance the discussion of social freedom, now deeply influenced by Gauthier's book, to see that this important use of a market ideal is misguided.

The difference, in the last section, between the model and the quasi-laissez-faire alternative reveals the misstep. In effect, the perfectly competitive market is the model, while the corrected transaction process used to construct baselines is the quasi-laissez-faire alternative (further corrected for rent and externalities). Suppose that the process of private transaction, if it were to unfold in an actual society, would not depart from results of a perfectly competitive market except in ways corrected for by the prescribed adjustments. Then people would have no cause to complain of the use of the corrected holdings as baselines—assuming, as I shall, that the basic endowments which Gauthier describes would be equitable initial competitive endowments. But, as we saw in the last section, the corrected process of private transaction would, in fact, depart from the similarly corrected perfectly competitive market, giving rise to justified complaints in spite of the prescribed adjustments. The complaints are not responses to inheritance, exclusive ownership of natural resources, scarcity of factors in basic endowments, or side-effects mediated by nonprivate goods (unless the market itself is regarded as such a good). The losses generating just complaints arise from imposed risks, which do not depend on any of those intrusions on commercial self-advancement.

Note that rent is, quite generally, irrelevant, here. Though the imposed risk is morally unacceptable, it is imposed equally on all. As a result of confronting the equal risk, some win while others lose. But the assumption of risk is itself a sacrifice, and this sacrifice is equated with outcomes as well as can be in an extremely risky process.

Note, too, that it would be inappropriate to identify actual baselines with benefits that would be obtained in a purely hypothetical perfectly competitive setting, while accepting its departure from actuality. In assessing the adequacy of one's baseline for cooperative inducement, it would be unreasonable to insist on benefits that one would enjoy in a situation quite different from the conditions one encounters, when that situation would not result from general conformity to morally valid principles. And many distinctive features of the perfectly competitive market, such as omniscience and costfree, virtually instantaneous bargaining, are both unreal and morally neutral. In any case, the difference between these conditions and actual conditions for self-advancement is so great that it seems impossible to estimate the effectiveness of different people's hypothetical uses of their initial endowments in a perfectly competitive market. In sum, rather than consulting the model of perfect competition, one should admit that market activity itself, quite apart from externalities and natural scarcities, can constitute a barrier to free and rational self-advancement.[37]

A MINIMAL CASE FOR CAPITALISM

The minimal argument for equality has so far been confined to advanced industrial capitalist societies. By "capitalist," I mean a society in which the decisions with the greatest bearing on the allocation of resources are decisions of firms which hire people who must sell their labor, firms seeking to satisfy the expectations of investors only interested in making money. If it is to avoid inefficiencies that everyone would want to avoid, a capitalist society must impose burdens of unequal inheritance and of risk, burdens that are only justifiable if the most disadvantaged are better off than those in any capitalist alternative.

This assessment of capitalist ways of organizing modern economic life might tell us nothing about the features of a modern just society. The alternatives to capitalism have to be considered. After all, though choosers of justice will prefer, among master-slave societies, those that are best for the slaves, this hardly shows that the preferred version of slavery is just. However, when we turn to noncapitalist alternatives, the opening up of the discussion threatens to undermine the project of basing a standard of justice on minimal considerations.

Apart from capitalism, there is a substantially different way in which resource-allocation can be coordinated in an advanced industrial economy, namely, through central planning. In central planning, a single central authority allocates the most important resources, mobilizing the work of people who receive work as a result of a standing government commitment to full employment, and subjecting the allocation decisions to criteria that are not enforced by investors' desires for maximum return.

In principle, central planning could eliminate those inequalities and im-

---

[37] I am not sure whether Gauthier would in fact insist that a corrected market process is a means of constructing actual baselines. But there is one quite explicit argument in *Morals by Agreement* that does require a false equation of corrected perfect competition with quasi-laissez-faire. On pp. 110–12, Gauthier offers a refutation of the claim, attributed to Marx and Marxists in general, that private ownership of means of production is "necessarily exploitive" (p. 110). His argument is a demonstration that the sacrifice involved in providing the last unit of labor-power employed is equal to the wage paid for its use in the perfectly competitive market. But Marx is not talking about the perfectly competitive market, in Gauthier's sense. Indeed, Walras et al. had not presented the first descriptions of that imaginary world, when Marx developed his view. Rather, Marx describes a process of nondeceptive, noncoercive commercial activity, looking at the fate on average of the main kinds of productive agents and (often) ignoring differences in initial endowment. In effect, he explores the quasi-laissez-faire alternative. His inevitabilities are based on inevitable consequences of luck, time and scale. In this he follows Smith and Ricardo.

posed risks that are objectionable on minimal grounds, and then promote even more equality. Perhaps life-prospects are equalized for everyone in spite of innate productive differences, satisfying the situational perspective but violating the restrictive alternative. Or perhaps people with entrepreneurial inclinations are deprived of opportunities for self-advancement even though background institutions protect all from burdens of unequal inheritance or imposed risk. This deprivation would violate the free enterprise principle in a situation in which it is defensible. In these and other ways, a centrally planned economy which achieved justice in some specifications could violate it in others.

In an advanced industrial setting, these deep divisions can be evaded by considering another sort of factual constraint. The situation of those in the worst-off economic positions in the capitalist society which best satisfies the demands of the minimal specification are better off than they would be in any centrally planned alternative. A change to central planning is precluded by the argument that always wins: some would lose and no one could claim relevant benefits.

In the phase of economic development in which improvement is largely improvement in extent—mechanizing more, mobilizing more resources in industry, making more things—centrally planned economies have sometimes performed well. The same cannot be said for central planning in the intensive phase, in which improved quality is the basis for productive improvement and most people are interested in better, not just more. The obstacles are, largely, the absence of certain kinds of fear in production governed by central planning and the presence of other concerns that create distortions.[38]

For example, in central planning managers of state enterprises fear inadequate allocations for reaching quantitative production targets and struggle to hoard inputs, creating a shortage of obtainable goods. Production is relatively unconstrained by the drive to economize inputs, while the goods produced have the characteristic dreariness of goods sold in a sellers' market. Of course, capitalist managers like inputs, too. But if they take on excessive costs in inputs, they will suffer from desertion by investors who only care about their return. In a centrally planned economy, there is a good chance that the supervisory officials can be talked around—in all good faith. The entanglement of central allocations with local actions almost always creates a significant possibility that a local inefficiency is due to a central mistake. Also, in assessing the performance of productive units that meet quantitative goals but fall short of goals in improved efficiency, the central authorities must, in general,

---

[38] In describing the systematic limitations of central planning in an advanced economy, I am especially indebted to Ed Hewett, *Reforming the Soviet Economy* (Washington, D.C.: Brookings Institution, 1988); Janos Kornai, *The Economics of Shortage* (Amsterdam: North-Holland, 1980); Kornai, *Contradictions and Dilemmas* (Cambridge: M.I.T. Press, 1986); and Alec Nove, *The Soviet Economic System* (London: Allen and Unwin, 1977).

emphasize the quantitative targets. For the reliable meeting of these targets is the prerequisite for coordination by a central plan. Finally, the commitment to full employment guarantees that the penalty for inefficiency will not, in general, be the denial of resources to the inefficiently producing unit.

Pressures to innovate are also very different in the two systems. The need to sell in a buyers' market and to satisfy banks, investors and boards of directors with the proceeds creates capitalist pressures to innovate. Under central planning, it is much less apt to be rational to take on the inherent risks of innovation, since discontented consumers, investors, bankers and boards of directors do not threaten to punish the stagnant. Again, the central planners can usually be talked around, when innovation seems to be too sluggish in a state enterprise. Since no one knows what the nature or pace of innovation would be in an enterprise if utmost intelligence and rational daring were applied, innovation targets will be loose guesswork, not fit for strict enforcement.

A final example: in centrally planned economies, trade with other countries has to be conducted by specialists at the center, so that the plan is not unbalanced from outside. So the comparison between domestic and foreign means of production, domestic and foreign sales options is not made by the individual producing enterprise, a prerequisite for any efficient use of international differences.

These are essential defects in a centrally planned economy. Though these defects entail corresponding virtues in capitalism, capitalism has essential defects entailing virtues in central planning. Extensive unemployment makes most of the unemployed unhappy and many of the employed anxious; and it is, as such, a waste. Striving to produce profits is bound to have different consequences from striving to satisfy the most urgent unsatisfied desires of consumers. For example, an advertising campaign, a leveraged buy-out or the destruction of low-rent housing and the construction of luxury housing are efficient means of producing profit. Yet they neglect urgent needs and demand much work. These are sad facts about capitalism, not at all denied in the criticisms of central planning. Still, if one compares alternatives with all their essential defects and virtues—comparing muddle with muddle, not model with model, to adopt a phrase of Alec Nove's, the most acceptable muddles that capitalism allows have turned out to be preferable for all to the most acceptable muddles that central planning allows, in an advanced industrial setting.[39]

[39] The preferability of capitalism in less advanced settings is not so clear, in general. The burdens of unequal inheritance and imposed risks are especially severe, while the political advantages of the best-off make it especially unlikely that burdens will be mitigated. Moreover, in some of these settings, the best-off can, in effect, ally with one another to ward off pressure to innovate or to allocate efficiently. Conversely, when the network of production is relatively simple and only partly industrialized, central planning can take greater advantage of cooperative incentives

Capitalist societies cannot fill the opportunity gaps they create. So a capitalist society is only just if superior for the worst-off. At least in an advanced industrial setting, a capitalist society with this feature will be just. A change to a different mode of resource-allocation will lead to losses to many, and relevant benefits for none.

Short of intense and uncertain empirical controversy, at least one more constraint can be imposed on just economic arrangements in an advanced industrial setting. They will be some ordinary form of capitalism, quite different from either laissez-faire capitalism or "market socialism."

In a laissez-faire capitalist society the state protects, and does nothing but protect, all nonviolent, nonfraudulent uses of the results of nonviolent work, nonfraudulent transactions and voluntary gifts. Such a society will give rise to grave burdens of unequal social inheritance and imposed risk, as successes and failures are perpetuated along family lines. Substantial departures from laissez-faire have usually been accompanied by learned warnings that even the worst-off will be worsened by resulting inefficiencies. Yet the worst-off—indeed, the vast majority—have never come to regret the passing of systems approaching the laissez-faire ideal. Some of the most efficient capitalist economies, the Federal Republic of Germany, for example, are among the furthest from laissez-faire in resource-allocation and in social provision. So we can dismiss this extreme, but without much sense of progress in political deliberation. For no society now approximates the laissez-faire ideal.

At another extreme, my definition of "capitalism" was so broad that it might be taken to encompass the worker-owned enterprises often associated with the phrase, "market socialism." But "market socialism," understood as production for profit by such enterprises, is not the right response to the pains of laissez-faire. What is done when a worker-owned factory fails? If subsidies are provided, or painless unemployment is guaranteed, the system takes on the inefficiencies of central planning, without the capacity of the latter to mobilize vast resources for special large-scale goals. Yet without such provision, the consequences of business failures are especially enduring and severe. For successful enterprises have no incentive to expand and take on more worker-owners, including those left unemployed by failure elsewhere. Since expanded ownership cannot be acquired by financial means, a group of workers does best to find a highly profitable branch of production, maintain it and live off it.

Evidently, the just society will be plain capitalist, neither laissez-faire nor market-socialist. Far from constituting an end to basic moral controversy, this

---

requiring routine personal contact, and can mobilize, albeit often inefficiently, resources that would not otherwise be used at all in the less industrialized sectors. Two broadly sympathetic accounts of the role of central planning in such settings, rich in detail and relevant worries, are Claes Brudenius, *Revolutionary Cuba* (Boulder: Westview, 1984) and Maurice Meissner, *Mao's China and After* (New York: Macmillan, 1986).

outcome requires desperately important choices. Even among current advanced industrial economies, the differences in departure from laissez-faire are vast. To take one crude measure, government expenditures on social services (health, social security and welfare, housing and community amenities) were 13% of the Gross National Product in the United States in 1985, 20% in France, 29% in West Germany.[40] And, of course, current variations in plain capitalism may not reflect the range of options a seeker of justice should consider.

We advanced-industrial folk should support the plain capitalist system that is best for the most disadvantaged. Many of us, committed to a defensible specification of social freedom, have hoped for something better than the best plain capitalism, and receive this conclusion joylessly. Still, it is an occasion for epistemic joy, since every partisan of social freedom has grounds to accept this standard.

HARDER CHOICES

If one turns from questions of justice in social arrangements to the questions of choice among courses of conduct whose answers determine whether justice is achieved, the prospects of a shared moral standard among all partisans of social freedom, indeed, of a standard that is satisfactory in any defensible specification, are much more clouded. Ironically, the difficulties are due to the social facts producing the minimal case for a single way of judging the arrangements themselves.

In a society in which resources are allocated in the capitalist way, substantial inequalities in wealth, disposable income and managerial authority are inevitable. Such advantages are sources of political influence. Timeworn worries about the effects of economic difference on political power imply that nonelectoral actions by the worse-off, of a disruptive and coercive sort, play an essential role in the promotion of justice, even in advanced, industrial parliamentary democracies. In such societies, to this day, those who go on strike sometimes use force in the attempt to keep out strikebreakers. In times of war, enlisted people sometimes use force or threats to slow the pace of combat, or engage in outright mutiny. People in disadvantaged groups sometimes seize control of whole neighborhoods. Even more commonly, the mere possibility of disruption has led people with institutional power to pay closer attention to the demands of the worse-off than they otherwise would. As the winning faction in the first Macmillan cabinet politely put it, in opposing proposals to dismantle the welfare state, "It was no less arguable whether the

[40] When education is included, the figures become 34% for France, 33% for West Germany, 18% for the United States. See *Government Finance Statistics Yearbook* (Washington: International Monetary Fund, 1989); World Bank, *World Tables: 1989–90* (Baltimore: Johns Hopkins Press, 1990).

proposed economies in the social services could be enforced without provoking social and industrial discontent on a damaging scale."[41]

Coercion by nonofficials is a normal part of the capitalist political process. Its utter absence would, almost certainly, worsen the worst-off. Yet, in typical situations in relatively just capitalist societies, there is no broadly acceptable specification of justice as social freedom that settles the questions of individual choice that arise for nonofficials who might coerce. People deciding to keep out strikebreakers by force do not know whether their efforts will succeed and substantially promote justice. They know that people may be hurt who do not deserve punishment. They know that they are in no position to compensate for such injury. In what circumstances would it not be wrong to throw a rock at the windshield of a van about to bring strikebreakers through a factory gate? In a partly analogous circumstance, enlisted men in the Indochina War sometimes used violence and stealth against lieutenants who too eagerly led them into combat. Was it always wrong to do so? Perhaps no specification of justice as social freedom resolves such questions in all cases that are important for the achievement of justice in an advanced industrial society. It is even more difficult to see how such questions could be resolved on minimal grounds.

My minimal case for capitalism was like an argument that education should be promoted by a public lottery. A lottery produces inequalities through state action. No one has a right to such state action. But a lottery might be such an efficient way of raising money that no one could rationally object. Now, because of the connections between economic inequality and power, capitalism has turned out to be like a system for raising funds by lotteries which imposes social injustices unless some people cheat, breaking rules that the system must enforce. When is it all right to cheat? We lack widely shared means to answer this question. The only ground for epistemic hope, here, is ignorance: this democratic version of the problem of dirty hands has not been well explored.

[41] "1958 Cabinet Papers: Battle That Shaped the Future of Conservatism," *The Times* (London), January 2, 1989, p. 4.

Chapter Eight

THE SCOPE OF JUSTICE

FOR ALL their assertiveness concerning economic justice, the previous arguments from the minimal specification have been modest, in several ways, in their guidance for institutional choice in an advanced industrial setting. First, I have not considered two familiar topics in debates over laws and policies: the extent to which civil and political liberty should be protected and the proper role of attention to aggregate welfare, the weight of numbers. Second, I have not considered the capacity of justice as social freedom to justify rules for coping with those who reject this very outlook as inappropriate for social choice. The arguments in the first part of this book suggest that some of these dissenters will not be burdened by ignorance or unreason. The need to coerce them may pose a specially serious challenge to justice as social freedom, an outlook which generally seeks to replace coercion with rational persuasion.

Finally, the judgments defended so far were assessments of societies in light of effects on those living in them. Rules enforced by the coercive power of a state were justified in light of their effects on people living in the territory in which the state exercises a monopoly over permission to use force. This territorial restriction might be myopic. After all, the questions addressed in the domestic setting were largely concerned with the moral significance of economic inequalities, and moral significance often depended on the inescapable effects on some of the conduct of others. Yet the starkest inequalities are international, and the International Monetary Fund is now the prime example of an inescapable institution. So justice as social freedom may also dictate changes on account of effects across national borders. If it does not, the demands of social freedom are apt to be far removed from the concerns of compassion. Perhaps, as utilitarians warn, this distance is morally intolerable.

For these reasons, a defense of the basic adequacy of the minimal specification requires consideration of other topics, other people and other societies, not just the question of economic justice as seen by partisans of social freedom in one's own society. I will begin this broadening of scope with the further topic of civil and political liberties.

Two ROUTES TO LIBERTY

Justice as social freedom in the Hobbesian interpretation has a strong bias toward civil and political liberty for two different but related reasons. The first

concerns an important psychological constraint on the equalization of benefits. In certain realms of conduct, people's preferences often have these two
features.

1. The preference partly determines the sort of person one is and sees oneself as being. One could not willingly accept coercive prevention of the exercise of the preference while respecting oneself.

2. The preference does not include a desire that others be coerced.

The first feature, connecting self-assertion with self-acceptance, is usually—indeed, almost universally—a feature of the desires to express one's
views, to develop intimate relationships of the kinds one prefers, and to exercise one's preferences among spiritual practices (which might consist of the
atheistic rejection of spiritual practices). A preference that is part of oneself
in the deep sense of the first condition might lack the second feature. Thus,
a preference that nonbelievers be taxed to support a state church includes a
desire that others be coerced. On the other hand, a preference for open advocacy of one's views, whatever they might be, does not include a desire to
coerce, even if it happens that one does have the view that there should be a
tax-supported state church.

Because of the second feature, the interest in satisfying the preference is an
interest in benefits relevant to the pursuit of justice as social freedom. One
could insist on such a benefit, which requires no coercion of others, while
pursuing the cooperative goal. Because of the first feature, willing acceptance
of coercive interference in these aspects of one's life would involve such a
grave injury to oneself that the total system including such interference is
almost guaranteed not to provide maximum equal inducement to all.

This is the basis for a strong bias, but not an absolute prohibition. For
interference with some people's exercise of the relevant sort of preference just
might be necessary to maximum raising of the life-prospects of the most disadvantaged. This is most plausible when laws prohibiting public advocacy of
the inferiority of races, religions or ethnic groups are proposed as part of the
best means to remedy the disadvantages of groups with lesser prospects of good
jobs, or lesser prospects of any employment. Perhaps such proposals should
typically be rejected on familiar instrumental grounds, as increasing resentment in the long run, encouraging further unjust prohibitions or reducing
support or resources for more effective measures. Perhaps, in many societies,
such proposals would be excluded by wholesale constitutional protections that
are desirable because of their effectiveness in preventing unjust intrusions.
Still, laws against propagating racist falsehoods, which are part of quite benign west European regimes, might be compatible with justice in some modern circumstances.

Rawls' arguments for the priority of liberty are the most prominent effort to
develop a fundamental understanding of social freedom that excludes absolutely all infringement of basic liberties in pursuit of other goals, at least in

advanced industrial societies. In A *Theory of Justice*, he derived this priority from the role of basic liberties in sustaining self-respect, the kind of psychological connection to which I have appealed. However, unemployment and menial drudgery are also important threats to self-respect in advanced industrial societies. So this psychological argument does not establish an absolute priority, on account of the possibilities described in the last paragraph.

In later writings, Rawls advances considerations that are less directly grounded in the psychology of self-respect. But the more recent argument is overly intellectualist in similar ways. In these writings, Rawls takes the choices determining justice to be governed by a highest-order interest in the rational revision of final ends, and bases the priority of liberty on this interest in autonomy. Insistence on such an ordering of relevant interests may be one defensible specification of social freedom. But even if it were the only one, the priority of political and civil liberties would not follow. For it is overly intellectualist to suppose that the rational revision of final aims requires nothing more than rational deliberation in the context of free discussion, together with other activities guaranteed by civil and political liberties. One cannot rationally assess one's aims if one cannot pursue a variety of relevant options with at least a moderate degree of success, gaining actual experience of reasonably diverse possibilities. In a modern capitalist society, such practice often depends on hiring, admission to educational institutions, financial support or all three. These days, for example, the rational identification and development of one's ultimate interest in theorizing or research, or ultimate concern that they exist, would require, at a minimum, expensive long-term engagement in education and, for full development, employment at a research institution. Even a philosophy Ph.D. of independent means will not know how meaningful to her a career of teaching and research will be if she cannot find a regular job in a college or university; freelance courses taught in her living room provide inadequate data. So economic burdens are threats to autonomy, just as they are threats to self-respect.[1]

---

[1] For the appeal to a highest-order interest in rational self-development see, in particular, Rawls, "The Basic Liberties and Their Priority," *The Tanner Lectures on Human Values*, III (Salt Lake City: University of Utah Press, 1982), pp. 27–29. In this essay, Rawls also seeks to avoid overly formal understandings of the priority of liberty by including in maximum equal basic liberty a requirement that everyone have "a fair opportunity . . . to influence the outcome of political decisions" (p. 42). If this entails an equal prospect of influencing political outcomes should one be willing to try, the requirement would certainly be hostile to large material inequalities. Its problem would be utopianism. In any reasonably efficient capitalist economy, the financial resources, leisure, network of acquaintance, media ownership, information and skills of some will give them substantially greater political influence than others. The situations of chief executive officers and blue-collar workers will be sufficiently different to make it more likely that the former will help to initiate a widely cited policy study or serve as Secretary of the Treasury. Nor would bureaucrats conceivably have no more influence than others in an efficient "liberal socialist regime" (p. 45). Clearly, Rawls would not respond in the spirit of Rousseau, insisting that justice

In sum, an appeal to psychological interests produces a strong bias toward civil and political liberties in many spheres of life, on the basis of the minimal specification—but not an absolute and general priority, even in advanced industrial societies. Short of arbitrary stipulation, it is not clear that any further specification can impose that strict priority. Still, the dictates of the minimal specification are sufficiently civil-libertarian to settle most questions of trade-off in favor of civil and political liberty.

The other source of bias toward civil and political liberties is epistemic and political at once. It affects fewer disputes, but determines the outcome more decisively. Suppose that a policy mobilizing the coercive apparatus of the state has these effects, of very different epistemic kinds:

1. It has effects on some that all regard as harms to them, or would if all reasonably responded to all relevant information and argument.

2. Though some may regard other effects as important benefits, others do not, even though they reasonably respond to all relevant information and argument, and are committed to providing equal inducement to cooperate to all who are similarly committed.

In short, though the harmfulness of the coercion is discernible by all willing cooperators on the basis of reason and evidence, the benefits are not. Then justice as social freedom would rule out this policy.

Consider the establishment of a state church. Everyone, both outside and inside the church, recognizes the costs of its establishment, for example, the taxes imposed on nonbelievers who would never willingly contribute and the difficulties nonbelievers encounter in bringing up children who adequately respect their parents' outlook while showing adequate civic loyalty. On the other hand, reason and evidence permit a nonbeliever to deny the existence of consequent benefits in saved souls and answered prayers, benefits whose sincere avowal depends on revelation or nonrational respect for tradition. Such alleged benefits play no role in inducing the rational, unforced cooperation of nonbelievers. Thus, an extra prospect of salvation is not an inducement for a nonbeliever to accept the state church, even if it should actually exist, to her benefit. For nothing is an inducement to cooperate for someone who would deny that it exists, in fully rational possession of all available evidence and arguments.

Of course, a nonbeliever will recognize that certain believers will experience frustration if a state church is not established. But such acknowledgment

---

can only be achieved when people in a small community are content with extremely sparse material enjoyments. Probably, he would accept that the material equality necessary for equal political influence can be waived when this serves the interests overall of the materially worst-off (cf. p. 41). Could equal basic liberties themselves be restricted in their interests, too, as in the institution of "racial libel" statutes? If not, then the priority of liberty is genuine, but it lacks an adequate rationale if my previous arguments are right. If such restriction is accepted, there is no priority of liberty of the absolute sort that Rawls still proposes (p. 4).

will not lead to acceptance of a state church as part of equal inducement to all. As always, gains and losses are only relevant if appeals to them are compatible with pursuit of the cooperative goal. And frustration by the absence of a state church lacks this status. The frustration of a believer who is frustrated by the lack of a state church depends on his willingness to resort to benefits coercively exacted by a system that all willing cooperators cannot accept on a basis of equal inducement. If he weren't willing to resort to such measures, he would not be frustrated by their absence. In contrast, a nonbeliever, if genuinely tolerant, would rather remove the processes of self-advancement entirely from the realm of coercion, when rational persuasion addressed to willing cooperators will not serve her interests. After all, nonestablishment does not require taxation of the orthodox or celebrations of agnosticism under state auspices.

As a consequence of this difference, everyone's uncoerced and rational participation in arrangements including a state church would require that some be social saints, more willing than others to set their other interests to one side and uphold institutions if others are willing to uphold them. For the nonbeliever is required to accept coercively enforced transfers in a system not providing equal inducement to her, even though she is willing to forgo benefits from coercively enforced arrangements that would not provide equal inducements to all. No such willingness to sacrifice in the interest of general acceptance is required of the believer.

Religious practice, then, must be a private affair. In general, respect for justice as social freedom, even in the minimal specification, requires private pursuit of goals when pursuit by public means would impose costs discernible by all while, at best, promoting benefits not discernible, in principle, by all on the basis of reason and evidence.[2]

---

[2] In some ways, this second route to liberty resembles Thomas Nagel's argument in "Moral Conflict and Political Legitimacy," *Philosophy & Public Affairs* 16 (1987). Nagel takes the coercive aspects of state actions to require that the premises justifying them pass a specially stringent epistemic test. One must be in a position to suppose that evidence and reason would end disagreements over the justifications one advances, and do so on the basis of evidence and arguments whose force one could convey (as opposed, say, to faith or revelation; see p. 232). Applied to the discernment of benefits and burdens on the part of those committed to social freedom, this is the conclusion I have reached, described with rich and useful nuance in Nagel's essay. However, his basis for this conclusion would be different. He would derive it from a requirement that coercion be justifiable in "a highest order framework of moral reasoning . . . which takes us outside ourselves to a standpoint which is independent of who we are" (p. 229). In part because of the arguments of the first part of this book, I think there is no way of explaining this talk of externality and impersonality which permits the derivation of liberal political conclusions. If claims acceptable from the impersonal standpoint must be justifiable solely on the basis of publicly conveyable evidence and nondefective reasoning, then the moral requirement that benefits justifying state coercion be so discernible will itself fail the test. People who reason well on the basis of relevant evidence can reject this constraint. On the other hand, if impersonality only requires of someone advancing a claim that she be justified in advancing it as a claim to truth,

At least in the United States, the exclusion of state religions is an uncontroversial dictate of justice. However, the same underlying epistemic bias also helps to resolve intensely controversial matters, such as the outlawing of abortion. The abortion controversy is similarly resolved in favor of state inaction, on the following assumption: evidence and argument would not make it irrational for some partisans of social freedom to deny that a woman's withdrawal of the use of her body from a fetus is the seriously immoral killing of a person or of a being with similar moral status. On this assumption about the epistemology of the abortion controversy, any sufficiently important benefits of outlawing abortion are in the second epistemic category, indiscernible by some willing cooperators. And there are important harms in the first category. No one, on either side of the abortion controversy, denies that the outlawing of abortion imposes substantial burdens on women who continue unwanted pregnancies only because abortion is a crime. And no one denies that such burdens must be justified by overriding gains. So the minimal specification would rule out the criminal prohibition of abortion. Even if fetuses are persons with a moral right to continued life-support, they lack a right that a just state can enforce. For such coercion would not be rationally acceptable to willing cooperators.

In broad outline, this pro-choice argument is reminiscent of Blackmun's opinion for the majority in *Roe v. Wade*, above all, his most central claim: "In view of all this, we do not agree that, by adopting one theory of life, Texas may override the rights of the pregnant woman that are at stake." I think that justice as social freedom is embodied in the "equal protection" clause of the Fourteenth Amendment and requirements of tolerance in the First Amendment. However, this legal argument would take us far afield. Similarly, though I think that the identification of abortion as wrongful killing of persons is not a dictate of reason and evidence for everyone committed to the cooperative goal, there is no need, for present purposes, to justify this epistemic claim. If such grave harms were discernible by all willing cooperators, then it would not be unjust to outlaw abortion. The dictates of social freedom provide the premises about justice that are needed to resolve the controversy

---

then, while requirements of liberal impartiality are admitted, so too are rival claims concerning benefits and burdens and their political relevance. Finally, one might require that everyone appeal to benefits and burdens that reason and evidence could reveal to all, while one also takes this moral requirement to be a truth that is not itself discernible to all on the basis of reason and evidence. This is the position that I have been advocating (with the further understanding that benefits and burdens are to be assessed from the standpoint of those committed to social freedom). But now liberal impartiality is no longer ultimately based on the priority of detachment and impersonality. Rather, a quite specific kind of impersonality in the assessment of benefits is based on a requirement of commitment to a certain goal of cooperation.—Still, Nagel is surely right to insist that a justified truth-claim must underlie any commitment sustaining a just use of state coercion. The first five chapters of this book help to show how this constraint is compatible with a basis for coercion that reasonable people, possessed of all evidence, could reject.

over abortion statutes. But the epistemic status of anti-abortion arguments, the feature that is crucial according to the premises about justice, will depend on the content of the arguments themselves. Of course, the actual assessment of this epistemic feature will itself be controversial. At the level of constitutional design in pursuit of social freedom, there is good reason to put a burden of proof on legislators who assert appropriate discernibility and to give judges special authority to determine whether the burden has been met.[3]

WHERE THE NUMBERS COUNT

Neither route to liberty depends on instrumental arguments that relevant kinds of interference with minorities reduce the general welfare of the whole community in the long run. Here, as elsewhere, the acceptability sought by justice as social freedom need not correspond to the actual informed preferences of most or even to the creation of the greatest happiness overall. This capacity to subordinate the general welfare to individual claims is unsurprising, given the underlying demand for social freedom. For this demand takes up a "standpoint of unanimity," in Nagel's revealing phrase, requiring that measures be justifiable from the standpoint of everyone, provided that he or she pursues the cooperative goal. The relevant grounds for rejection need not include failure to promote the general welfare, and if relevant grounds for rejection are available to anyone, the number of those who prefer the objectionable arrangement does not matter. Such neglect of numbers is troubling (as Nagel also remarks). After all, numbers do count a great deal in most just assessments of social policies. So there is an urgent need to show how justice as social freedom could give numbers substantial weight in appropriate contexts for choice.[4]

Justice as social freedom requires nearly pervasive attention to the weight of numbers in political deliberations for reasons depending on the piecemeal character of most deliberations. In the overwhelming majority of cases, such deliberations are concerned with particular proposed government initiatives,

[3] The further question of whether my epistemic argument would be politically effective would also take us far afield. But surely, similar considerations influence some of the millions who, according to repeated surveys, assess abortion as comparable to murder but oppose its criminalization. They are certain of the harms that criminal statutes would impose on people of good will, recognize the deep impossibility of showing all people of good will that fetuses are persons with a right to life-support, and take this combination to constrain their approval of coercive measures.

[4] See Thomas Nagel, "Equality" (1977) in Robert Stewart, *Readings in Social and Political Philosophy* (New York: Oxford University Press, 1986), especially pp. 266–68. I think that Nagel is right to deny that a standpoint of unanimity can be a complete basis for valid moral judgment. Some reasons why will be implicit in my discussion of impartial standpoints in chapters 9 and 10. But I do think that justice as social freedom is adequate to resolve questions of political choice in modern industrial societies. To this extent, a standpoint of unanimity can satisfy Nagel's concern for appropriate attention to the weight of numbers.

not with the total system of institutions and policies. Even though the totality of the former determine the latter, it would be a foolish practice typically to assess a political proposal by determining whether its incorporation would give rise to a total system affording appropriate benefits. Questions of long-term differential effects of the totality on life-prospects require lengthy research and speculative theorizing. Effects of individual policies of which some reasonably complain will fall well within the margin of error for assessment of whole systems and will demand quicker resolution than such assessment can provide. For these and other reasons, the piecemeal character of most political deliberation is appropriate to our moral needs and actual resources. For reasons that I will now present, the fundamental and global demand that the totality be freely and rationally acceptable to all justifies the use of standards giving much weight to numbers in our typical, piecemeal assessments.

To begin with, it would not be in the interest of anyone to apply the rule of equal inducement to each individual government initiative taken in isolation. If skewing of net benefits in the case at hand ruled out individual projects, the totality of exclusions would be a great loss for everyone. Overpasses built with Federal highway funds in North Dakota benefit North Dakotan locals more than me, even though the overpasses represent the same proportion of my taxes. People who never fly are not relieved of any of the burden of financing the Federal Aviation Authority. Desert dwellers contribute to flood-control projects. Yet the sum of all individually skewed projects provides a better life for all than their wholesale absence.

One might seek to avoid the skewing of net benefits from a government project without eliminating the benefits entirely, either by appropriate adjustment of the immediate tax burdens or by privatization, withdrawing the project from the realm in which some make tax payments benefiting others. But frequently both options would be undesirable from the standpoint of every partisan of social freedom. Usually, it would be irrational to end individual skewing while keeping initiatives in the publicly financed sector. The assignment of a reliable estimate of individual taxpayers' probable benefit from each project as a basis for individual tax burdens would have nightmarish costs in information gathering. On the other hand, even putting problems of unequal opportunity to one side, laissez-faire solutions often do poorly in these matters. The least controversial problems involve the publicity of certain benefits and the cost of their privatization. If everyone has free access to a good, then it will not be provided in sufficient abundance by private means, since people will count on benefiting as free-riders. There will not be enough roads, streetlights, firefighting, or protection from violence. It is (virtually) always imaginable that access might be limited to dues-payers. But the means of limitation may be extremely burdensome to all. Travel would be something of a chore if every street had a toll-booth, for both drivers and pedestrians. It would be dangerous for private firefighting firms in modern cities not to put

out fires in non-dues-paying houses, or for private protection agencies, unsup-
plemented by public ones, not to catch criminals until they prey on dues-
paying members.

Skewed benefits, publicly created, are unavoidable. Still, there ought to be
some way of answering a person's complaint that a government initiative imposes excessive burdens on her. And, as we saw earlier, the appropriate standard for such a response must usually be piecemeal, addressed to the policy at
hand.

The right procedure for piecemeal assessment is to choose the alternative
that best promotes aggregative well-being without being subject to complaints
that are serious, in the following sense. A serious complaint is a complaint by
someone who points to a kind of loss which she suffers whose incorporation
into piecemeal assessment as a generally recognized basis for veto would not
generate losses at least as great for anyone else. Mere loss on balance is not a
serious complaint, in this sense, since its recognition as a basis for veto would
generate paralysis, and enormous losses for everyone. Even a heavy burden
may not be relevantly serious. The building of any major highway seriously
dislocates some people, in ways that are not remedied by the payment of fair
market value for their bulldozed property. Yet if all important and irreparable
disturbance were a basis for veto power, then the scope of public initiatives
would be reduced in ways that generate losses that are at least as great. As the
Planning Board says to the distraught shop-owner, "We're sorry that things
will never be as good for you, but no road could ever be widened, if that were
a reason not to."

Still, one should not wreck a whole community merely to shorten the average commute between here and there by two minutes. Enormous burdens
should not be imposed on a few just to provide trivial gains to many. The
justification for the grave losses of someone whose community has been
wrecked would have to appeal to losses to individuals which are just as great
stemming from the accumulation of individually trivial forgone benefits in
similar cases. Perhaps, relevant loss from the kind of veto claimed would result from the cumulative difficulty in coast-to-coast transportation if each
road decision is blocked by appeals to enormous burdens of a few.

This is the process of piecemeal assessment most apt to provide each with
the greatest benefit compatible with equal inducement for all. If veto is easier,
the situation of the worst-off is no better, so universal acceptability of the
whole system is not more apt to result. If veto is harder, the situation of those
least-helped by the totality of institutions is apt to be worse than it might
have been. Because greatest total benefit is sought in each case, subject only
to relevant veto, everyone's expected gain from the whole process is as great
as pursuit of equal total inducement allows. So no one with the cooperative
goal can reject such processes of piecemeal assessment. Very often, the proviso for serious complaint does leave room for significant attention to num-

bers. In these cases, atypical people lose because they are atypical—although they can expect to benefit from the whole process of assessment in the course of their whole lives. So numbers do count, because, not in spite of the fact that justice consists of free and rational acceptability to all.

Reassuringly, though, the weight of numbers is not always decisive, for justice as social freedom. Sometimes, a veto is allowed because of the relative size of the loss complained of and the individual gains that the veto would forfeit. No one in the hamlet loses her network of neighborly relations just because so many commuters would get home two minutes earlier. In the sphere of civil and political liberty, noncoercive choices fundamental to a person's sense of self are almost always protected; for a generally recognized veto against injuries of this kind would almost never give rise to injuries as serious in someone else. Finally, the benefits counted as contributing to the general welfare must be discernible, in principle, by all willing cooperators, an epistemic requirement that has turned out to be a substantial protection.

In this section, I have been using such phrases as "aggregative well-being" and "the general welfare" as if their meanings were clear. Of course, they aren't. Still, it is clear enough that a policy benefiting some more than others, even benefiting some and burdening others is sometimes justifiable in ways that depend on how many people receive the greater benefits. Well short of providing an adequate analysis of "the general welfare," my intention has been to supply an underlying rationale for this attention to numbers, on the basis of social freedom.

Going further, I think one could identify the kind of aggregation called for by asking what procedure of piecemeal assessment would be relevantly acceptable to all, given appropriate allowance for veto. Rather than seeking some fundamental procedure for measuring the general welfare and then describing how the promotion of this quantity is overridden, one begins with the nonaggregative standard of maximum equal inducement for all, which applies to the totality of institutions. This fundamental standard, we have seen, justifies practices of piecemeal assessment in which a local standard sensitive to the number of those most benefited is hedged with a veto sensitive to those most burdened. So one can take the general welfare to be specified, from case to case, by the various local number-sensitive procedures to which a veto-provision is attached, in a justified practice of piecemeal assessment.

Depending on the kind of choice in question and the circumstances in which it is made, the procedure could be one of these, among many others: a legislature's effort to simulate a referendum of self-interested, fully informed voters; the reaching of an equilibrium through a market process; the determination of what the market equilibrium would be if all had equal purchasing power; a legislative process sensitive to various pressures from the electorate and from interest groups; the pursuit of maximum stable growth in gross national product. These procedures are diverse. Some are superficial, lacking great intrinsic power to justify imposing a policy that some may find burdensome. The appropriateness of each may depend on the actual distribution of means of influence, or the nature and scope of other number-sensitive procedures already in place. So this way of specifying the general welfare is unavailable to anyone who takes its promotion to be an independent, fundamental, important consideration in all political choices. In other words, this strategy is incompatible with utilitarianism, or even the more modest appeal to utilitarian considerations that I described in the final section of chapter six. However, if the arguments of that section are right, the conflict is nothing to worry about. We can take the specification of what the general welfare is to be a continuous by-product of piecemeal just political practice.

PERSUASION, COERCION AND COMMUNITY

After this broadening of the topics to which justice as social freedom is applied, it is time to consider the actual diversity of those on whom the justified institutions and policies are imposed. Even in the minimal specification, justice as social freedom has shown a strong bias toward tolerance. Yet partisans of justice as social freedom share common institutions with partisans of other, relatively intolerant outlooks. So some of their neighbors will be thwarted if social freedom is achieved. The arguments of chapter one entail that those who dissent from justice as social freedom need not be unreasonable or uninformed. So the thwarting cannot be justified as subject to no rational complaint. In this it will differ from just paternalistic interventions.

The imposition of barriers that are a source of rational complaint might seem a defect in a standpoint naturally summarized in the slogan that institutions should be freely and rationally acceptable to all. Perhaps justice as social freedom is not coherent, or commitment to it lacks rational motivation, or the rational motivation to uphold it is too weak to sustain it in practice. Though none of these charges will turn out to be valid, it is useful not to answer them too quickly. Studied answers produce significant complications in the description of the minimal specification and of the motivation to uphold it.

Here are two types of people, rational, informed and opposed to social freedom, types with real instances in advanced industrial societies. I will call the first type "the Bigot" for short, though he is more epistemically diffident than most bigots in the real world. Without thinking that others are irrational or uninformed in their contrary projects and convictions, the Bigot has a life-project of supporting institutions that force others to conform to a certain way of life; he acknowledges that some would only have reasons of force for conforming. Perhaps he has a deep concern that others live in nuclear families, of a churchgoing Protestant persuasion, headed by heterosexual couples, with homemaking the task of the mother. In pursuit of this goal, he would coercively disrupt activities departing from this norm, i.e., he would if he dared and if he thought the disruption would contribute to his goal. In speaking of support for this norm as a life-project, I mean that he would be a different person, whom he would not become as a result of his unforced choices, if he should abandon the desire for this outcome, the anger and disgust to which deviations give rise and the approval of state action as a means to reduce deviations. His deep concern determines the emotional meaning of much else, even though he is aware that other people, rational and well-informed, do not share it.

I will call the other type "the Aesthete," though she is, perhaps, more concerned with political affairs than most aesthetes. The Aesthete seeks whatever provision of public resources best promotes the creative development and expert enjoyment of high culture among those most talented in these matters. She is aware that others, rational and informed, think her emphasis quite exaggerated. She is prepared to use guile and stealth to mobilize resources, coercively extracted by the state, to advance her ends. For example, she would be glad to lie to a Congressional committee about the contribution of the arts to satisfying most people's rational preferences.

If prior semantic investigations are well-directed, the Aesthete might, without confusion, regard her outlook as moral. The status of the Bigot's outlook is much less clear, though further communitarian sophistications might make it a moral outlook. In any case, the Aesthete and the Bigot both present a common problem: why shouldn't their rejection of a social system render it unjust? Their rejections must somehow be discounted, or else such vetos would make justice as social freedom unavailable. But the basis for discounting cannot be irrationality or ignorance.

Clearly, an adequate basis for discounting will specify what is wrong with their desires and the extent to which choices of such people are to be discounted. But it is surprisingly difficult to characterize the defect in their desires on the basis of a minimal specification of social freedom. For a number of otherwise attractive condemnations would be hypocritical, denying them grounds for political choice that are permitted among partisans of social freedom. Thus, though the Aesthete and the Bigot do not regard it as equally urgent to induce everyone's cooperation, this egalitarianism cannot be required in a world including the Aesthete and the Bigot. For partisans of social freedom do not seek to give the Bigot the same inducement to cooperate as others, compensating him, say, for coexistence with active homosexuals. My prior requirement of equal inducement was made under the simplifying assumption of a world of partisans of social freedom, people committed to the cooperative goal. The task, now, is, to define the requirements of the cooperative goal in a world including nonpartisans.

Similarly, though the Bigot and the Aesthete do not put desires to one side when they entail the coercive deprivation of others, it would be too much to require this of them, since such neglect of coercive desires is not required of partisans of social freedom. Someone who is unable to buy a pleasant house on account of racist choices of others could simply adjust to circumstances. She could put the thwarted desire to one side, because its satisfaction would require coercively thwarting others—through anti-discrimination laws, for example. However, such neglect of a desire in the interest of noncoercion isn't a requirement of justice, but the pathology epitomized by Uncle Tom.

Still, the system of desires of the Bigot surely does have a different relation to coercion and deception from the system of a person who refuses to be an Uncle Tom. The Bigot's acceptances and rejections are governed by a desire that he would not have if he wanted others to be governed by their own free and rational choices when this had no adverse effect on him. Of course, if he had the latter desire, he might still want others freely to choose to be Protestant, churchgoing, heterosexual, and so on down his line. But this would not motivate rejection of tolerant institutions. On the other hand, the black who wants a pleasant affordable house would want that house even if he wanted others to be governed by their own free and rational choices when this had no adverse effect on him. So one test of whether a system of desires is relevant would be, "Would it survive a desire for free and rational choice in others when this has no adverse effect on oneself?"[5]

Still, the Aesthete is not necessarily excluded, so far. Even if she wanted others to make their own choices of activities when this had no adverse effect on her, she would want to attend great performances, as the black house-seeker wants the house. So, once the first test has been imposed, a second is required. Bases for rejection are irrelevant if they conflict with the desire for equal inducement of everyone's cooperation.

The systems of desires relevant to justice as social freedom must, to begin with, be noncoercive in the way established by the first test. If so, they must also be cooperative, in the way established by the second test. Consider how the two tests work, in sequence, in the case of the Aesthete. If her system of desires passes the first test, then she wants high culture to be encouraged because she has an interest in enjoying high culture. If, instead, she had regarded the promotion of high culture as a reason to coerce apart from her interest, she would not rationally desire that others pursue their own choices in these matters if there were no adverse effect on her; "Promote high culture no matter what its effects on me" would be her motto, not "Satisfy my interest in high culture." Still, despite her passing the first test, the Aesthete's concerns lead her to pursue policies which make it impossible to provide equal rational inducement to cooperate to all (i.e., all who are motivated by non-

---

[5] This test resembles Ronald Dworkin's distinction between "external" and "personal" preferences, though my emphasis on free choice reflects certain differences in our underlying moral standards. See, for example, "Reverse Discrimination" (1976) in *Taking Rights Seriously* (Cambridge: Harvard University Press, 1977).

coercive systems of desires. As already noted, one need not provide equal inducement to the Bigot. The tests work in sequence). So her system fails the second test, and is not sufficiently cooperative. Someone who passed both tests would not embody the Aesthete, but would simply have specially aesthetic interests and insist that others treat inducing her cooperation as no less urgent than inducing that of any other noncoercive participant.

Should we, then, neglect all claims made by those whose systems of desires do not meet the tests imposed by justice as social freedom? That would be to turn the goal of social freedom into the formation of a self-centered Club of the Just. Like most other nonpartisans of social freedom, the Bigot and the Aesthete do not dedicate their whole lives to pursuing interests excluded by the two tests. So it would not fit anyone's conception of social freedom simply to ignore their interests, many of which are benign. For example, the Bigot and the Aesthete are not and should not be forced to pay higher taxes or to work for the state under conditions of bare subsistence, just because they are profoundly disgruntled at the enforcement of justice as social freedom.

They are not to be discounted. Rather, some, though not all or even most of their rationales are to be discounted. The right rule is: no one living under a system of institutions is to have a well-informed rationale for rejecting them on the basis of whatever goals and interests he actually has whose employment in the rationale would not conflict with the tests for concern for others' freedom and concern for equality. In this sense, justice as social freedom requires that everyone be treated as if she were a partisan of social freedom, in the assessment of institutions.

If systems of desires which fail one or the other test are still rationally available today, it is worth asking why someone would want to be guided by justice as social freedom in her political choices. No doubt, some of the motivations solely depend on individualist benefits, i.e., benefits that are themselves enjoyable whatever one's preferences among different kinds of interactions with others. For example, in a democratic political system in which almost everyone else is a partisan of social freedom, one might as well discuss proposed policies on the basis of the consensus, since no other deliberations will be politically effective. Also, as Hobbes and Gauthier have noted, if one has much to gain from the cooperation of everyone else, if most potentially beneficial cooperators would insist on equal inducement, and if they are reasonably good at detecting an inclination to deviate from such terms, then one will have reason to be the sort of person who prefers cooperation on such terms.

Still, someone will not be genuinely committed to justice as social freedom if he would prefer to deviate should the political system and others' capacities be of kinds that make deviation advantageous. This preference need not respond to an empty fantasy of superhuman power. Plenty of well-entrenched minorities have persisted in advantageous dominance for generations. Someone who takes the road to advantageous domination—say, a white person in Johannesburg in 1950 who votes for the Nationalist Party in clear-eyed pursuit of cheap servants, cheap land and uncrowded beaches—is not a partisan of social freedom. Neither is someone who would take this road if it were open. More precisely, one is not committed to social freedom if one would actively support relevantly unequal arrangements in all situations of substantial advantage. If there is a rational motivation for the commitment, then basing one's political choices on social freedom must have a motivation in addition to individualist benefits that accrue in settings specially favorable to just choice.

The motivation would be a desire for a certain kind of social life, a life governed, so far as possible, by reciprocal noncoercion. In dealing with others, a partisan of social freedom prefers not to benefit from disadvantages of theirs sustained by coercion or misinformation unless this is a means of defense against their effort to rely on such disadvantages in her.

These motivational requirements make it clear that commitment to social freedom is communitarian, even though it is individualist, as well. The individualism is important. Justice as social freedom requires acceptability to every individual on the basis of appropriate interests. So long as they are noncoercive and are regulated by a desire for equal inducement of all, the appropriate interests of each need not include a concern to benefit others. They can include any concern a person happens to have that is compatible with the two tests. Yet despite these elements of individualism, a rational commitment to justice as social freedom has turned out to require a positive preference for a certain kind of social life. More specifically, one must prefer to participate in a certain kind of social life and a desire for individualist benefits that happen to be payoffs of such willing participation must not be one's sole reason for this preference. One might say that justice requires individualist respect and communitarian commitment.

A WORLD OF INJUSTICE

Traditionally, political philosophy has been concerned with interactions within polities, social systems whose borders are the limits of a monopoly over permission to use force exercised, with reasonable effectiveness, by a supreme political authority. So long as the central questions are concerned with political obligation, there is nothing arbitrary about this limit. However, in the last two chapters, as in most political philosophy now, the central question has been the nature of justice. Questions of obligations to obey a political authority have mainly arisen as means of answering this question.

In the account of justice developed so far, a case for social change in the interest of justice typically rested, in part, on some inequality in life-prospects due to disadvantaged opportunities for self-advancement. The inequalities separating typical people in rich countries from typical people in poor ones are a prime, probably the prime example of such differences. So it would be arbitrary to stop at the borders, without considering whether international processes and the differences they create could provide grounds for condemning institutions as unjust.

Certainly, the international pattern of outcomes is unequal enough to be part of a case for serious global injustice. The inequality of per capita purchasing power among countries is of the same order as the inequality among individuals in typical advanced economies. Per capita income in India is about one-fifteenth of per capita income in the United States (when foreign exchange rates are adjusted for differences in domestic purchasing power. Otherwise the ratio is about one-fiftieth).[6] When international inequalities and domestic ones are compounded, the ratios are even more striking, i.e., as striking as the visible difference between the nicest suburbs of Westchester County and the worst slums of Calcutta. The top tenth in the United States have, on the average, a hundred times greater income than the poorest fifth in India (almost four hundred times, prior to adjustment for domestic purchasing power). India is one of the worst-off countries, but several other populous countries do worse. Since the end of the eighteenth century, and especially in the last hundred years, there has been a continuing, dramatic increase in the gap between the worst-off countries and the rest.[7]

The relation of these differences in outcome to differences in starts is also familiar from discussions of social injustice. No one earns the right to be born to a family living in a spacious house in Armonk, New York, rather than a family living on a straw mat in the slums of Calcutta. Yet the enormous differences at these starts include enormous differences in life-prospects, given the same innate capacities and the same willingness to try. (Fortunately, no serious theorist still tries to explain those inequalities as a product of unequal innate intelligence or unequal effort.) Indeed, the chance of someone moving from Indian poverty to a moderate income in North American terms is laugh-

[6] Here and in the following paragraphs, the United States–India income ratios are taken from Atkinson, The Economics of Inequality, pp. 30–32.

[7] See, for example, Paul Bairoch, "The Main Trends in National Economic Disparities since the Industrial Revolution" in P. Bairoch and M. Levy-Leboyer, eds., Disparities in Economic Development since the Industrial Revolution (New York: St. Martin's Press, 1981). Bairoch estimates that the ratio of per capita GNP in the most developed countries to that in the least developed has increased from 1.8 in 1800 to 4.5 in 1860 to 10.4 in 1913 to 29.1 in 1977 (p. 8). Aficionados of colonial development might note that per capita GNP in countries now least developed, almost all of them former colonies de jure or de facto, was, in his widely respected estimates, essentially static from 1750 to 1950, i.e., in the colonial era (ibid.). In Asia, Africa and Latin America, taken together, the increase from 1800 to 1950 was 9%, while the figure for the most developed countries multiplied tenfold (pp. 9, 15). In the same volume, Robert Summers, Irving Kravis and Alan Heston, "Inequality among Nations," report 1950–1975 growth in per capita GNP of 1.76% per year in the poorest 27 non-socialist economies, 2.48% in the richest 18.

ably small, if he stays within India. (If she stays, it is even less.) The per capita income of the richest tenth in India is far less than that of the poorest fifth in the United States. Quite as much as beta-assignment, the initial differences characteristic of the great international disparities are disadvantages in opportunity, unchosen and evaded, if at all, by costly emigration.

Life-prospects throughout the world are now substantially affected by transactions across national borders, in world trade, multinational production and banking. A controversial specification of justice as social freedom might insist that the institutions and rules involved in the international economy are unjust unless the least prospects of success are as great as possible. From this standpoint, the bare facts of international inequality just rehearsed would condemn the rules and institutions of international economic activity as unjust, unless no alternative would be better for the worst-off. But it is a much harder task, the task of this section, to assess international inequalities and the processes sustaining them on minimal grounds.

In the minimal specification, the charge of injustice points not to mere unchosen or undeserved disadvantages, but to imposed ones. What this typically involves is an inequality of resources in a competitive process, in which gains for others may be losses for oneself, an inequality due to choices of others protected coercively. Perhaps the international disparities are not due to disadvantages in competitive interactions, in a system of unequal opportunity which is coercively protected. Perhaps they are just the outcome of the inefficiency of locally available means of production combined with the geographic remoteness of more efficient ones—as the very phrase "less developed country" suggests. Then, there would seem to be no minimal grounds for a charge of international injustice. Different specifications of social freedom will probably lead to very different assessments.

In fact, in the international economy, as in the domestic one, processes of interaction in which we get in one another's way reconcile differences among rival versions of social freedom. Consider the burdens imposed on people in the poorer countries in three kinds of competition, competition for situations favorable to self-advancement, competition for land and raw materials and the competition between firms and prospective employees over the terms of employment.

The self-advancement of someone who is born in a poor country and stays is not just limited by what his or her family provides. It is limited, independently, by aspects of the country's poverty. If he seeks to advance his interests by farming, he may, for example, confront a domestic shortage of arable land and low domestic effective demand owing to the poverty of the country's consumers. If he seeks employment he is apt to confront a labor-market dominated by unemployed people desperate for work, some of them quite skilled. If he embarks on entrepreneurship, he may confront limitations in domestic demand combined with the instability and limited economic niches of an economy dependent on sales of a few primary or semi-processed commodities on world markets. A woman born in this setting is apt to face additional local traditional impediments. In short, quite apart from differences in the talents, personal assets and willingness to try of individuals, richer countries provide more advantageous situations for advancement than poorer ones.

As a result, many people in poor countries would like to "venture their luck abroad" as Irish newspapers sometimes put it. The worldwide competition for favorable situations which would otherwise ensue is largely blocked coercively, in the interest of those in richer countries. An inhabitant of the Ganges delta who chooses, without prior permission, to make his way to California, will, if he gets as far as the border, be met by people with guns who will forcibly turn him back.

Indeed, nothing could be more suspect, from the standpoint of justice as social freedom, than disadvantages maintained by coercively regulated borders. Here, the governments that praise competition the loudest shamelessly commit themselves to reduce competition for desirable jobs and other resources. Corporations proudly supporting the free worldwide pursuit of corporate advantage gladly benefit from people's confinement to grim prospects in the pursuit of personal advantage. Yet "barrier" is the aptest metaphor for what justice as social freedom forbids.

As with domestic barriers to advancement, these international ones most disadvantage those who are otherwise worst-off. People in the United States do not suffer, on the whole, from whatever difficulties there are in emigrating to Bangladesh. So we can take benefits enjoyed in rich countries which depend on these barriers as a fund to be distributed in the interests of people in poor countries, unless every means of reducing inequality would hurt them.

In addition, the justification of further sources of inequality, apart from coercively regulated borders, must not presuppose the legitimacy of such borders. As it happens, this requirement has considerable impact on a further source of advantage, exclusive control of land or raw materials.

Thoughtful fervent partisans of private enterprise have always conceded that it is hard to justify enjoyment of exclusive control over unimproved land or raw materials, even if benefits exclusively depending on one's use of one's own mental or physical capacities have been justified. The Hobbesian interpretation of justice as social freedom makes the special difficulty clearer. Suppose that John uses some land, while as much land which lends itself as well to Robert's uses is not readily available to Robert. Robert would not do wrong to try to use the same land, even though he *would* do wrong to force John to work for him. So, in the absence of other considerations appealing to Robert's interests, his only reason to leave the land alone is John's superior coercive power. If this is indeed the only reason for Robert's acceptance of an arrangement assigning exclusive ownership to John, then the arrangement violates the minimal specification.

If an unchosen arrangement assigns some exclusive rights over land or raw materials and an unequal distribution of benefits results, the only way to justify the arrangement is by showing that those excluded would be worse off in any alternative. It is very unlikely that this demand will support either of the two extreme arrangements concerning exclusive rights, namely, the total absence of any right ever to exclude anyone from access for any purpose, and the absolute right of anyone who has some favored initial relationship to the natural resource to benefit from all noncoercive, nondeceptive uses of total exclusive control, conveying that control, as he wishes, to others. The first alternative, of free-for-all, will be worse for all on account of inefficiency and absence of incentive to improve. But the alternative of total enjoyment of total exclusivity will, presumably, be worse for the excluded than some arrangement in which exclusivity is conditional on some transfers to the excluded. These transfers might take the form of a tax on property. But they might occur more indirectly as part of a total system in which those generally worst-off are bettered. For those worst-affected by exclusive rights over land and raw materials are apt to be worst-off in other ways as well. So the justification of exclusive control might depend on a specially progressive income tax or a particularly substantial welfare program. Finally, the kinds of control to be compared are not just exclusive, comprehensive acquisition by individuals, on the one hand, utter nonexclusivity on the other. There is the option of letting appropriate transactions generate exclusive individual rights to some uses but not others, and the option of control by a public authority, distributing the benefits in such a way that everyone has noncoercive reasons to acquiesce in the authority's exclusive control.

If national borders were naturally impenetrable, the choice of a just mixture of private control, private enjoyment, publicly mediated transfer and public control would only concern the interests of people within the borders enclosing the natural stuff at issue. More precisely, the minimal specification would dictate no more extensive consideration, since inaccessibility from outside would not depend on coercion. But these days, more than ever, borders are largely social, not natural impediments. So the assessment of exclusive control requires much more extensive consideration of interests. For those who would be most disadvantaged by exclusion from use of land or raw materials are apt now to live abroad. If the United States were naturally isolated, the justification of exclusive individual control of vast tracts of farmland in California would only have to appeal to the interests of the land-hungriest of the United States. But in fact, those who would be most disadvantaged by such exclusivity if they were not coercively excluded at the borders live in such locales as Bangladesh and Ethiopia.

In general, transfers needed to justify benefits from exclusive control should take special account of the interests of those most affected by confinement to other natural resources. They should do so to satisfy demands of freedom, quite apart from demands of compassion. On the whole, people in the poorest countries are specially burdened by confinement to local resources. So there is an additional basis for requiring betterment of those in the poorest countries at cost to people in richer countries.

Finally, a third barrier to self-advancement is strengthened by the restrictions on borders and resources, but is not reducible to them. These days, it is probably the most important source of international inequalities that is subject to criticism on minimal grounds. It derives from the vulnerability of people in poorer countries when they look for jobs.

In poor countries, even someone with substantial skills and willingness to work hard will find it hard to earn much because of competition with others, some of them desperate for work at virtually any wage and some of them quite skilled. Even a tourist can sometimes see this. In the capital of Mexico, a rich country as poor countries go, a crowd of skilled workers assembles at dawn in front of the National Cathedral, carrying tools and hoping for work. Many remain at nightfall.

Specially desperate competition is one aspect of the local poverty that limits purely local markets. However, it is, as such, an advantage, for firms that can sell throughout the world while locating labor-intensive parts of production in poor countries. This advantage helps to explain a variety of lucrative differences between manufacturing in rich countries and in poor ones. Perennially, the rate of return on U.S. investments in manufacturing in less developed countries has been half again as much as the domestic rate of return. Workers' earnings as a percentage of value added in manufacturing were 39.7% in the United States in 1986, 40.3% in West Germany, 36.7% in Japan, but 23.6% in Thailand, 26.3% in Mexico, and 19.0% in Indonesia (despite the trivial costs of subsequent transportation to lucrative markets).[8]

In part because of the special vulnerabilities, the return from investment in a typical poor country of a typical multinational firm includes a surplus over the least return that would induce investment in those costs of production if there were no more attractive investment opportunity elsewhere. Note that there need be no surplus over what the firm would rationally require given the actual opportunities elsewhere. Perhaps a bit less return in Thailand would make it irrational not to produce instead in Indonesia. Indeed, there may be nothing left from the surplus-generating production when investors and creditors have been paid what they require for the use of their funds. The demands

---

[8] See the tables for the respective countries in World Bank, *World Tables, 1989–90*. It is sometimes said that specially high returns from manufacturing in poor countries are due to special risks and specially high start-up costs. Though this may often be part of the explanation, it does not seem to be the largest part. The countries affording the highest returns are often politically stable and often reward start-up with tax moratoriums and infrastructure provided at local public expense. Indonesia, post-Sukarno, is one example. So is Puerto Rico in the 1960's, when Puerto Rican textile manufacturing provided a return four times the norm in mainland manufacturing.

of investors and creditors depend on the alternatives actually available else-where. The surplus is a surplus over and above input costs that are independent of anyone's special bargaining advantages. In effect, the relevant surplus is the firm's portion of a collective one: the advantages derived by investors, creditors and others in the home countries of international firms from the vulnerability of those selling their labor-power in poor countries.

In the purer neoclassical models of production on a worldwide scale, these surpluses are evanescent. Aware of the opportunity for a surplus, other firms enter the fray, bidding labor up and forcing output prices down so that the surplus is eliminated. In the purest models, a worldwide Great Auctioneer would guarantee that no such surplus ever arises. However, in the real world, such internationally organized production and sale is a prime example of protection from entry by outsiders which is generated by the commercial process itself. Benefit from the local vulnerabilities is, on the whole, the province of firms that can allocate segments of production on a worldwide scale, reduce unit transportation costs to virtually nothing on account of economies of scale, and gain ready access to lucrative markets through brand names. Access requires a structure of production, interpersonal contact, finance and distribution on the order of that possessed by the two hundred largest transnational corporations, whose total annual turnover is equivalent to about 30% of the gross product of the world.[9]

Those who benefit from the returns of these corporations benefit from a social monopoly analogous to the natural monopolies that trouble neoclassical economic arguments. There is a worldwide shortage of such large-scale structures for production and sale, a monopoly maintained by the daunting risks to upstarts—for example, the problems of establishing a new worldwide brand name or of simultaneously attracting sufficient numbers of investors and creditors and placating them for a long gestation period.

If this is the causal basis for a process tending to benefit people in richer countries, the process is based on worldwide practices and institutions that should be changed, as unjust, if the worst-off could be bettered. For the social monopoly, on the one hand, and the vulnerability, on the other, are unchosen burdens for the worst-off in worldwide competitive bargaining among buyers and sellers of labor.

Granted, some exploitation may be better than none in present worldwide circumstances. Perhaps if the poor of Thailand were to become less willing to accept low wages, so many firms would set up shop in Malaysia, instead, that less Thai desperation would be self-defeating. But suppose, instead, that workers in Thailand, Malaysia and all poor countries were to coordinate their

---

[9] See Frederick Clairmonte and John Cavanaugh, "Transnational Corporations and Services: The Final Frontier," *Trade and Development* (1984). The surplus is also shared, to some degree, by local contractors dependent on transnational corporations. The morally urgent question concerns the disadvantages of the many specially vulnerable locals, not all locals.

demands so as to eliminate the surplus. To do this, they would have to be well-informed, well-coordinated, free of urgent pressures to make independent deals and capable of overcoming the problems of free-ridership that plague large groups. In short, they would have to have coordinative resources as powerful as those created by the social monopoly in big commercial structures, which includes an international version of Smith's tacit combination of masters to keep wages low. If the vulnerable of poor countries had this coordinative resource, they would do better—in the OPEC way, as it were. But they will not achieve this parity. (Even OPEC has not, really.) In this way, as in others, the institutions and practices governing commercial dealing worldwide invest some people with unchosen burdens in advancing their resources in commercial dealing.

The rules and institutions of worldwide commerce are coercively protected. Admittedly, the protection is the work of many governments, not one. But this hardly frees a system from a charge of injustice. One might as well say that no injustice can arise if effective joint projects must pass the scrutiny of many warlords, not just one. In any case, quite apart from the role of governmental coercion, inequalities based on the disadvantages in coordination that I have just described might be seen as needing justification from the standpoint of the worst-off. In previous explorations of the state of nature, it turned out not to be wrong to resist inequalities wholly due to the preferential channeling of information or skills to others. Thus, there was no wrong in the outsiders' refusing to pay the full price of services made scarce by the cobblers' guild. Similarly, it might be said, victims of past actions giving others superior coordinative capacities in a competitive process are not wrong to rebel. But once this is granted, benefits actually derived from the coordinative advantages depend on the incapacity of the worse-off to engage in effective non-wrongful coercion. So those benefits must be justified on the basis of equal inducement.

The three interlocking competitive inequalities, concerned with migration, natural resources and bargaining power, are surely important contributors to international differences in typical individual life-prospects. Justice requires international measures, financed from the benefits of the inequalities, which improve, so far as possible, the life-prospects of the disadvantaged. The beneficiaries of these inequalities are, above all, the best-off in the best-off nations, while the disadvantaged are, above all, the worst-off in the worst-off nations. So justice as social freedom is egalitarian on an international, as well as a national scale.

To what extent should the institutions and practices of better-off nations be revised, to benefit the worst-off internationally? The arguments for international demands of social freedom do not establish any specific way of satisfying these demands. Grants and cheap loans encourage waste, while loans on commercial terms either exclude the worst-off or produce crises in international liquidity when the loans come due. Outside experts do not know local conditions, local experts are often tied to local elites, while local nonelite producers lack experience in large-scale planning. So the task of lessening international inequalities without making the worst-off worse is not simple. As in the domestic scene, certain facts have pointed to standards emphasizing the interests of the worst-off as ones that just arrangements must satisfy. More, and more controversial, facts are needed to discover what arrangements satisfy these standards. Still, it is extremely unlikely that justice requires no more transfer than now occurs. After all, the advantages of the best-off in the richest countries include abundant resources which should, in all justice, be available to remedy failed experiments in improving the worst-off.

Still, there may well be depths of poverty whose relief would not be a minimal demand of local and world justice combined. Perhaps in a world satisfying the minimal specification the poor of India would remain poor because too many people there live on too few resources, but are rationally unwilling to leave because of local ties, interpersonal, cultural and linguistic. Then, only a more than minimal specification would require further outside contributions—say, on the grounds that one would want a certain world minimum to be guaranteed if one could not rely on knowledge of whether one was born in the Indian countryside. It is much less likely here than in the domestic modern industrial case that identical demands will result from all specifications. Advanced as the world economy is, it does not go as far as an advanced industrial domestic economy toward reducing all barriers to self-advancement to institutionally determined barriers.

Still, for sad reasons, the minimal case establishes all feasible demands of justice. More strenuous requirements of international change in the special interest of the internationally worst-off will not be satisfied. Indeed, the minimal demands themselves will not be satisfied if a large-scale transfer of the benefits they identify would benefit the internationally worst-off. For the attractiveness of social freedom to those who are not themselves burdened by unfreedom would be too weak, on a world scale.

There is no world government, much less a democratic one, so people in rich countries are under no significant pressure to find common terms of political deliberation with people in poor countries. People in rich countries would not gain, on balance, in individualistic goods from cooperation with others in poor countries on a basis of international justice. What their relative invulnerability yields in individualistic benefits is more than what cooperation on a just basis would yield in such benefits. People in rich countries do not have much to fear from aggression launched at them from poor countries, and in any case, quiet is usually bought most cheaply by placating local elites. In short, even if those advantages of injustice of the white man in Johannesburg in 1950 were to become atypical of domestic settings, they would be typical of many relationships in the world setting.

The remaining motivation for just choice was a preference for reciprocally noncoercive relationships as such. For most people, the unavailability of such relationships with extremely distant strangers does not seem to be a cause of frustration adequate to motivate a full commitment to worldwide justice. They would not be led by frustration of the desire for such long-distance relationships to abandon individualistic benefits from remote injustice. Because remoteness matters psychologically, the preference for a just social life seems to be weakest where it has the most work to do.

Still, arguments about international justice are not pointless. Recognition of injustice usually has some tendency to contribute to its remedy. This helps to explain a common defect in moral insight: rather than recognize that benefits of ours depend on injustice, we often prefer to avert our gaze. In rich countries, arguments about international injustice interfere with this maneuver. Arguments from the minimal conception interfere the best, or, in any case, the most pervasively. For they appeal to the most widespread capacity for detecting injustice and extract the greatest concessions to justice that are in the offing.

In these last three chapters, I have been considering resources of morality for assessing conflicts of interest between people, even on a worldwide scale. Before, I considered the limits of our resources for resolving conflicts between the moral outlooks of different people. Despite (or perhaps, because of) their vast extent, neither investigation touches on one kind of conflict involving morality, namely, a person's own conflicts with the demands of her own morality. Even if one is untroubled in accepting an outlook as morally right, and even if one takes that outlook to produce morally valid resolution of all conflicts of one's interests with others', one may be profoundly troubled by the demands that one's morality places on oneself. In the next, and last, three chapters, I will consider the terms on which such internal conflicts should be assessed. Here, the attempt to ground reason in general rules, which so distorted accounts of justified moral belief (according to the first part of this book), will have to be combated in other forms, to gain a clear view of the role and nature of the dictates of conscience.

Chapter Nine

MORAL BURDENS

"I wish I could do something else in good conscience." Someone who can tell the difference between right and wrong might, conceivably, never need to say this. But probably, no one has ever been so lucky. Morality is sometimes a burden.

Should the burden be lifted, at least at some significant points, so that people who are now inhibited by their knowledge that a choice is morally wrong would sometimes be unconstrained? In one way, the answer is obviously "yes." A world in which morality never requires self-sacrifice, in which everyone could painlessly live up to everyone's justified moral expectations would be much better than ours. It would be so much better that anyone who could help bring it about should . . . unless the helping requires too much self-sacrifice. However, because our world is so much worse, there are circumstances in which the only judgments that could lift the burden of morality permit or even recommend doing what is morally wrong. A burden lifter who likes to flirt with paradox might say, "It's not always the case that you ought not to do what is morally wrong."

The burdensomeness of morality gives rise to a third kind of conflict within the subjectmatter of moral philosophy, conflicts within oneself between one's own conscience and one's nonconscientious interests. In these last three chapters, I will investigate the terms on which these conflicts might be resolved, by assessing claims that might be intended by the troubling denial that one ought never to do what is morally wrong.

Like my earlier conclusions about the role of morality in belief, my assessments of the role of morality in choice will be a mixed verdict, combining options that are often part of opposed positions. And, as in the first part of this book, I will argue that this many-sided truth is masked by a worship of generality, in which rationality is based on responses wholly governed by abstract, a priori rules.

The two main mixtures will overflow boundaries that are suggested by the phrases "internal as against external reasons," in the one case, "impartial morality as against partiality toward one's intimates and projects," in the other. Boundaries between the internal and the external will be transgressed in my discussions of whether people can knowingly do what is morally wrong without displaying a defect in rationality. I will argue that they can, even if they have a deep concern for acting morally. This argument will have the internalist outcome that choices are reasonable just in case the chooser could reach them in her rational deliberations, starting with motives she actually has. On the other hand, I will argue that it is always a reasonable choice not to do what one knows to be morally wrong. And this argument will appeal to the special power of moral considerations to make choices and deliberations rational, a power that is not based on any special psychological influence. Something external to psychological processings determines which are rational, and favors those that are morally based.

The standard association of morality with impartiality will be violated when I assess the possibility that what is morally wrong might not be wrong all told. These days, such radical rejection of the demands of morality usually reflects a fear that morality might require intolerable detachment, and defenses of morality involve a defense of the overriding claims of some impartial perspective. I will be defending the supreme authority of morality in questions of what is wrong all told. But this defense will involve the discovery of considerable room for ultimate partiality within morality itself. Once this room has been established, moral norms will turn out to provide what objective guidance there is in answering further questions of what one should do and what sort of person one should try to be.

Like the mixed verdicts concerning moral belief, these mixed verdicts concerning moral choice depend on the rejection of overly abstract images of rationality. Suppose that the rationality of a choice was wholly determined by given psychological inputs and topic-neutral a priori rules singling out an alternative as rational given those inputs (for example, those beliefs and desires). Then, as we shall see, there would be no room for the fact that a premise for choice was a moral consideration to play a special role in making choices rational. Suppose that what is morally wrong is determined by fully informed deliberations applying some general standard that connects properties of a choice that are not individually intrinsically moral with conclusions as to moral wrongness. If the standard is to be nonarbitrary yet sufficiently different from what might govern the rational deliberations of a morally irresponsible person, it will have to prescribe some impartial weighing of relevant interests, detached from the chooser's particular attachments.

In these and other ways, the philosophical worship of generality creates an exaggerated appearance of conflict between respect for morality and respect for oneself. This appearance has motivated important efforts to lift the burdens of morality. These efforts should be abandoned, but with deepened appreciation of the concreteness of the life of reason and of late-twentieth-century moral norms.

THE NEW MIXED VERDICT

In assessing the burdens of conscience, it is best to begin by disentangling some of the many possible meanings of a burden lifter's denial that one ought never to do what is morally wrong. The denial is offered as a bit of advice to the burdened. Unless she is ridiculously glib, an adviser will usually intend her advice to be applied by people of certain kinds, and only claim certain kinds of advantages for the recommended practices. This is true of any sane recommendation to concentrate on growth stocks or to pursue a graduate degree in philosophy. The proposal that one ought not always to avoid what morality forbids has usually been limited in these ways.

In earlier centuries, anti-moral recommendations were usually addressed to people with remarkable capacities and goals. Thus, Nietzsche often seems to recommend that the constraints of morality be ignored, but it would be a misreading of his intentions to infer that morality ought to be ignored by someone with middling abilities or a primary interest in family life, or by someone whose characteristic striving is a successful leveraged buy-out. In contrast, the troubling recommendations at the center of current disputes are very broadly addressed. In particular, Bernard Williams' influential warnings about morality are addressed, primarily, to people with normal attachments to others and to their own projects, projects which may be of ordinary sorts.[1] I will follow him in this emphasis. As it happens, the implications for an elite will be obvious enough. I will also concentrate (though not exclusively) on those who are morally insightful and who care about violations of morality. After all, these are the people who have most cause to worry about the actual burdens of morality.

Another ambiguity in advice to reduce the impact of morality on choice is extremely important for assessing it, but often hard to clarify when such advice is given. What advantage is claimed for lifting the burden of morality, or what disadvantage is claimed for leaving it in place? I will concentrate on four different claims that might be directed at a choice faced by someone who knows that the conduct in question would be morally wrong.

"Your doing it would be reasonable, though it is morally wrong."

"Your not doing it would be unreasonable, though it is morally wrong."

"It would not be wrong of you to do it, though it is morally wrong."

"It would be wrong of you not to do it, though it is morally wrong."

I have arranged these comments in ascending order of shock. As usual, I will argue for a mixed verdict. The first claim is sometimes valid, even for a normal morally serious person. But the second is always invalid for a morally serious person—indeed, for anyone aware of the moral wrongness of the act in question. The third and fourth claims are always invalid.

In speaking of choices as "unreasonable" (or "reasonable"), I do not mean,

---

[1] I have in mind, for example, the disconnection of questions of rationality from questions of moral obligation in "Internal and External Reasons" (1980) and "*Ought* and Moral Obligation" and the denials of the general priority of morality over personal attachments in "Persons, Character and Morality" (1976) and *Ethics and the Limits of Philosophy* (Cambridge: Harvard University Press, 1985), especially the last chapter. (The essays are included in *Moral Luck* [Cambridge: Cambridge University Press, 1981].)

of course, to assert (or to deny) that they impose morally excessive demands. The question is whether someone's embarking on the course of action which is morally wrong would be a basis for criticizing her rationality in making choices. So one might speak, alternatively, of whether doing something would be rational or irrational on her part, so long as irrationality is not confined to thoughtlessness or to large-scale cognitive disorder.—Now that certain implications have been canceled, I will use "reasonable" and "rational" interchangeably, without, I hope, obscuring disagreements with perspectives in which more regimented usage would be preferred.

An example will help to clarify the distinctive content of each of the four kinds of claims. Consider the different ways in which a preference for protecting the interests of a friend might be endorsed, in a case in which someone wishes that such protection did not require doing what is morally wrong. E. M. Forster is famous for having said that if he had to choose between betraying a close friend and betraying his country he hoped he would betray his country. He may have been proposing that friendship has greater moral weight than loyalty to a basically just regime (one that merits the "two cheers for democracy" in the title of the book in which he proclaimed his preference). However, it will be helpful to us to suppose that Forster had in mind the moral perils of friendship, the possibility that close friendship will incline one to keep trust with the friend at the cost of moral wrong to others.

Suppose that George has a long, ongoing friendship with Jim. They have deep affection for one another, share common interests at the center of their interests in life, and have helped one another in many troubles. It is 1950. George stumbles upon definitive evidence that Jim, acting from conscientious, reasonably well-informed, but ultimately misguided political commitments, spied for the Soviet Union in the not-too-distant past. If George reveals the secret, which Jim begs him not to do, his friend's life will be ruined. If he does not, let us suppose, there is a chance that thousands of people will be worsened, some of them in ruinous ways. George is morally insightful. He is also morally serious, i.e., he cares about doing what is morally right and thinks it important to take moral reasons into account. Were it certain that people would die on account of his silence, George would tell. If it were certain that telling would help no one, perhaps he would not. But, as usual, no such certainties are available. George's actual assessment of risks and moral responsibilities leads him to think it morally wrong not to report what he has found. In not telling the authorities he will wrong others besides himself and Jim, imperiling them more than morality permits. Still, he will almost certainly wonder whether he ought to keep his friend's secret, nonetheless.

It is highly ambiguous what someone is proposing in denying that George ought to report Jim to the police while conceding that silence would be morally wrong. The intended disconnection of morality from choice might be that it would not be unreasonable for George to keep the secret. This claim, that someone could choose to do wrong without irrationality, would be especially interesting in a case such as this, where the chooser sees that the choice is morally wrong and cares about acting morally. I will argue that someone with such insight and interest might, nonetheless, reasonably do what is morally wrong, because of other concerns such as a sufficiently deep bond of friendship.

Alternatively, in light of further information about George the claim about reasonableness might be strengthened into the emphatic judgment that it would be unreasonable of George not to keep his friend's secret. For someone who takes aesthetic reasons seriously, it might, nonetheless, be unreasonable to buy the only aesthetically appealing house on the market, because it costs too much. Similarly, it might be said that George, who takes moral reasons seriously, would be unreasonable to choose one of the available alternatives to wrongdoing, because they do too much damage to his friend. Whether this is true will, presumably, depend in part on the depth of George's attachment and caring. An interesting question is whether any degree of attachment and caring would make it unreasonable for George to report Jim, despite George's belief that silence is morally wrong. I will deny this. A decision on George's part to turn his friend in, on the basis of the moral considerations that he recognizes as making silence morally wrong, would always be reasonable. A related question is whether given his attachment to Jim as it happens to be, George could be reasonable to report Jim, but, also, reasonable not to. I will argue that such indeterminacy could exist, and represents a normal psychological situation among rational choosers.

Another pair of judgments concern wrongness rather than unreasonableness. It might be said that George would not be wrong to keep the secret, even though it would be morally wrong for him to do so. Alternatively, the warning about morality might be strengthened to require what is morally wrong: it would be wrong for George to tell, even though not telling would be morally wrong.

Of course, these sayings would be not just radical but incoherent on certain construals of "morally wrong." For example, "morally wrong" might be taken simply to mean wrong, i.e., strictly and literally wrong in light of all relevant considerations. The adverb would just serve to emphasize the strict and synoptic character of the judgment. Alternatively, the phrase might be taken to entail strict and literal wrongness on balance together with some further feature such as the desirability of certain sanctions discouraging wrong choices of the kind in question. In either case, "morally wrong but not wrong" would, strictly speaking, be nonsense.

These readings would cut off discussion too soon. Morally insightful people distinguish between moral reasons and reasons of other kinds, and do so, from case to case, without asking whether the reasons under scrutiny would conclusively establish wrongness if all considerations were brought into play.

Prior to extensive argument, it is not clear whether an action is always wrong when it is ruled out by the totality of moral reasons, assessed as a morally insightful person would. So one should leave important questions open, at the start, by taking the anti-moral judgments to concern the possibility that a choice is not wrong even though it conflicts with the totality of moral reasons, as any morally insightful person would assess them. "Not wrong, though aesthetically wrong" may apply to a choice, as when I give up pursuit of the authentic country-Sheraton sofa that is aesthetically right for the living room so as not to bankrupt my family. Perhaps "not wrong, though morally wrong" sometimes applies, as well.

Without tying wrongness to moral assessment at the outset, we can give some further substance to judgments as to what is or isn't wrong. To begin with, these judgments must be universalizable. If an act is not wrong, it would not be wrong for anyone with the same relevant characteristics, in a relevantly similar kind of situation. This is true, not just for moral wrongness, but for any judgment of wrongness, including, for example, judgments of aesthetic wrongness or gastronomic wrongness.

Another constraint describes a burden of proof that any "not wrong, though morally wrong" judgment must bear. The universalized judgment must be justified in light of relevant considerations, as a morally insightful person could assess them. Such a person will, of course, regard moral wrongness as having a positive bearing on wrongness. So, if a choice is morally wrong, there must be overriding reasons for doing it, nonetheless, in this and in all relevantly similar cases. "It is morally wrong for George not to tell, there is no overriding reason why someone in his situation should keep such a secret, but it is not wrong for him to keep the secret" is absurd.

One further test that the anti-moral permission must pass concerns the relation between one's actions, one's assessment of them, and one's assessment of oneself. When a choice would not be wrong and the chooser knows this, self-reproach, having made the choice, would not be rational—though it might be unavoidable.

In sum, the proposal that George would not be wrong to do what is morally wrong is, at a minimum, a proposal that features of his situation justify a choice ruled out by moral reasons, so that George and any similarly insightful, similarly situated chooser can rationally avoid self-reproach. Is such a defense of moral wrong available, in George's case or others? I shall argue that it isn't. If George's choice would be morally wrong, then, there are no overriding reasons in light of which his choice would not be wrong; if he is morally insightful and otherwise well-informed, self-reproach would not be irrational for him. Morality takes adequate account of the considerations that might otherwise make it rational to avoid self-reproach while doing what is morally wrong. However, this absorption does not result from the capacity of impartial principles to assign appropriate value to the satisfaction of partial concerns. Moral choice is not impartial, in any sense exceeding the demand for universalizability; partial concerns do not have moral weight just because their satisfaction helps to attain a further goal; and the moral point of view is not adequately expressed in general principles.

Does any influential writer these days actually mean to deny that what is morally wrong is always wrong? Perhaps. Toward the end of "Persons, Character and Morality," Williams speaks, quite generally, of conflict between morality and personal relations, and denies the universal claim to priority of the former in assessments of what ought to be done that are not just judgments of what choice is reasonable for the chooser (see p. 17). In *Ethics and the Limits of Philosophy*, he criticizes the abstraction and detachment demanded by morality, emphasizing that "morality is not the invention of philosophers. It is the outlook, or, incoherently, part of the outlook, of almost all of us" (p. 174). Perhaps, though, the former restrictions concern impartial morality, not morality as such, while the latter criticisms are narrower than they seem because of Williams' distinction between "morality" and "ethics." Similarly, Michael Stocker thinks that someone accepting the guidance of any contemporary ethical theory would either lead a stunted moral life or suffer from deep divisions between values and motives.[2] But perhaps he would not go so far as to direct these criticisms at an overriding commitment to morality as such. What is more important than definitive exegesis, here, is the fact that thoughts about impartiality and the self which these writings stimulate are an impressive and revealing challenge to the claim that what is morally wrong is always wrong. Williams and Stocker create space for the challenge, regardless of whether they take a stand in that space.—On the other hand, they are explicitly committed to the claim that an excessively demanding perspective on choice of a moralistic sort is pervasive in modern times. I will be disagreeing with them when I finally reject such criticisms of modern life.

I will mostly be concerned with these questions about the bearing of moral wrongness on reasonableness and on wrongness all told. However, I will also discuss a further topic for burden lifting, the assessment of what one should do and the kind of person one should try to be. When questions of reasonableness and wrongness are settled, these questions may remain. For example, one's failure to be as sensitive as one should to the feelings of another need not be so gross as to involve wrongdoing. Obviously, morality has something to say about what one should do and the sort of person one should try to be. The burden lifting claims, here, deny that what morality says is always valid, if taken as the last word. Perhaps, it is not always the case that what one should not do, morally speaking, is what one should not do. Perhaps, more radically, one sometimes should do what one should not, morally speaking.

[2] See "The Schizophrenia of Modern Ethical Theory," *Journal of Philosophy* 14 (1976), pp. 453–66.

Analogous prospects of burden lifting arise in life-choice, the determination of the sort of person one should or should not try to be.—Since what counts as a judgment made "morally speaking" may depend on relevant resemblance to the bases for judgments of moral wrongness, I will postpone these questions of what one should do or who one should be until the end. My argument will be that all objective questions of what one should do or who one should be that are not matters of self-interest are accurately settled through moral assessment entirely. But, as we shall see, this is hardly obvious. Most descriptions of morality provide a distorting basis for such judgments. And most fundamental ideals by which rational, responsible people regulate their lives are not moral norms.

Reasonable Wrongdoing

It is reasonable of someone to do what is morally wrong if three conditions are met. The choice would be to his own advantage. He does not care about its harmful effects on others, although those effects make it wrong. And his not caring is not unreasonable.[3] The first two conditions are certainly sometimes met. Strong people roaming at night sometimes find it to their advantage to beat up and rob defenseless strangers, and do not care about harming strangers.

It is a further question whether the not caring could be part of a reasonable choice of conduct that is wrong. In the first part of this book, I argued that someone could, conceivably, not care at all about others while rationally responding to all relevant evidence. For such a person, doing wrong would not be unreasonable. Still, this person, the nihilist, differs from the targets of the anti-moral advice that is our main concern, advice that is directed at people who can tell the difference between right and wrong and who have the normal degree of caring about avoiding wrong. Indeed, the nihilist's total absence of caring turned out to be incompatible with his making any positive moral judgment, much less telling the difference between right and wrong. In a less splendid way, the repugnant characters in the last paragraph lack the normal degree of caring. Perhaps they also care so little that the beliefs of a morally insightful person should not be attributed to them.

Since most of us care somewhat about all wrongful harm to others, the three blatant conditions for reasonable wrongdoing do not apply to most of us. Still, a more moderate version of the three conditions is also sufficient for reasonable wrongdoing. I will argue that this version does apply to some of us morally insightful, normally caring people at some times. So the first bit of anti-moral advice is valid, as intended.

[3] In this section, the next, and some other places where no harm is apt to result and much awkwardness is avoided, I use "wrong" and "morally wrong" interchangeably.

Someone is reasonable to do what is wrong if this course of action is the only way of attaining a goal for which he cares a great deal, he cares more about the goal than about the avoidance of the wrongful harms to others that he will bring about, and his caring more is reasonable. If someone knows the act would be wrong and cares about avoiding wrong as people normally do, could he, reasonably, care more about the goal that intrudes upon morality? The best way of assessing this possibility is by explaining why substantial caring to avoid wronging others is normal and a normal accompaniment of knowing the difference between right and wrong. If the explanation of the normal degree of caring also explains why some normal, morally insightful choosers would sometimes care even more about a goal intruding on morality, then, presumably, their caring is not unreasonable.

In chapter three, doubts as to whether an absolute noncarer about others could have moral beliefs were doubts as to whether such belief attribution could play an appropriate role in explaining his choices. On these grounds, the mere fact that someone is morally insightful seems to entail some minimal degree of caring. But all that is required so far is the bare minimum. Moral reasons must sometimes be his reasons for making costfree choices. There is no need for them always to override. Indeed, there is no need, on these purely semantic grounds, for moral reasons to override any contrary considerations whatever, as opposed to motivating costfree choices.

Putting aside purely semantic considerations as inadequate to rule out reasonable wrongdoing, what other, psychological considerations explain our caring about avoiding harm to others? Of course, if we like or love someone, the caring leads us to care about avoiding harm to that person. But morality reaches beyond such relatively intimate connections. The puzzle is why we specially care about harm to others when we do not specially care about them.

A start toward solving the puzzle is our routine need to rely on others, including nonintimates. We need to rely on others, mostly strangers, to transact with us, and they will not do so if they cannot rely on us not to wrong them. Living in a world in which cooperation with strangers is important, one will not want to be seen as a doer of unacceptable harm.

The motivation supplied so far is only a reason to avoid being seen as doing unacceptable harm. If undetected, such doing may be much to one's advantage. However, such covert doing, if intentional, will almost certainly have a great cost to a rational product of this social world. She will rely on others to see her as very different from the person she is and the sort of person she hopes and expects others to be. This failure to be reflected in the valued gaze of others would be a great loss to most people. The cost is suggested by such idioms as "I could not look other people in the eye" and "I could not live with myself." It is also reflected in the bizarre rationalizations of people struggling to avoid the thought that if others really knew them they would have cause for complaint. The normal, morally insightful, morally serious person will

care about doing wrong, even to strangers, because her comfortable acceptance of herself is damaged by knowledge that she is doing wrong. Thus, for
most of us, undetectable stealing from strangers would not be a reasonable
choice. Possessions gained by the wrongdoing would not be worth the reduction of the security in one's self on which one's enjoyment of possessions depends.

In short, the motive that makes wrongdoing typically unreasonable is the
protection of one's self. But such a case for the normal unreasonableness of
wrongdoing cannot extend to all the choices of morally insightful, morally
serious people relying on others in a diverse and open social world. For one's
self has other supports, and corresponding perils. Comfort in one's existence,
interest in what befalls one, and the capacity to enjoy what one has may also
depend on not ruining the life of a close friend. That is the danger posed by
the avoidance of wrongdoing, in the case of George and Jim. Though George
will care about not harming strangers, he will care about not harming Jim,
from the same sort of motive. Even if moral reasons favor not harming the
strangers, the protection of his self, together with his love for Jim, may make
it not unreasonable of George to keep Jim's secret.

In addition to the considerations on account of which undetected wrongdoing normally would not pay enough, there are also, as Gauthier has emphasized, reasons to become the sort of person who does not calculate the chance
of gains from deception, but instead spontaneously lives up to others' expectations of nonwrongdoing. Because such calculation is itself a burden, sometimes goes awry, and requires its own concealment, the policy of spontaneous
noncovertness is prudent in circumstances in which the risks of detection are
sufficiently weighty. But this reason to become or remain a nondeceiver, like
the reasons for nondeceit that are part of a normal personality, is not sufficiently all-embracing to make all wrongdoing unreasonable. For risks of detection are not pervasively overriding and available personalities lie on a
broad spectrum in between extreme furtiveness and total candor. George may
have a personality leading to candor in situations in which deep personal
attachments are not at risk, and still be willing to pursue the surprising gain
from non-self-revelation that has become available. In any case, sufficient
special gains can make it reasonable to suppress, in part, traits of personality
that one has reasonably developed. On account of their long-term consequences, deep personal attachments to people or projects are one basis for
prudently overriding general traits that one has prudently developed, when
unforeseen circumstances arise.

George is a victim of bad luck. Morally insightful, morally serious people
try to avoid attachment leading to such dramatic quandaries, and usually succeed. But many such people expect to encounter possibilities of less dramatic
and extreme reasonable wrongdoing in pursuing chosen policies of engagement. There are people whose secure sense of self depends on creative proj-

ects, pursued alone, over long periods and in quiet. Suppose such a person also deeply desires a wife and a child, has his wish fulfilled, but finds he cannot give the child all the attention that is rightfully hers without threatening the aspect of his security that depends on writing. He will sometimes do wrong, when it is not unreasonable for him to do so. Is his sort so uncommon?

REASONABLE RIGHTNESS

Is it ever unreasonable to avoid doing what is morally wrong? Someone who is unaware that a course of action is wrong but aware of its great advantages might be unreasonable not to choose it if his lack of awareness is rational. But, to begin with the case that has most concerned us, what about people who are aware of the wrongness of a course of conduct and who care about avoiding wrongdoing as morally insightful people normally do? Is such a person ever unreasonable to choose to avoid wrongdoing?

It might seem that the answer to this question about unreasonable rightness is already contained in the conclusion about reasonable wrongdoing. It turned out to be reasonable, on certain occasions, for people to do what is wrong, even if they are morally serious, i.e., morally insightful choosers who care, in the normal degree, to avoid wrongdoing. It might seem that on these occasions—with marginal exceptions—the morally serious choosers would be unreasonable not to choose to do wrong. The greater caring about what intrudes on morality that makes wrongdoing reasonable might seem to make the avoidance of wrongdoing unreasonable. Perhaps there are also cases in which the caring that intrudes on morality is precisely equal to the caring to avoid wrongdoing. These ties will be the marginal exceptions to the rule that when wrongdoing is reasonable its avoidance is not. But such precise equality ought to be rare. And it could not affect the finding that morally serious people sometimes are unreasonable not to do wrong. For if the rational indeterminacy depends on perfect ties, one can be sure that some other morally serious person for whom the choice to do wrong is reasonable will care a bit more about the commitment intruding on morality, so that (according to this line of thinking) the choice to avoid wrongdoing would be unreasonable for her.

Though the argument is tempting, the conclusion is quite incorrect. It would never be unreasonable for a morally serious person to choose to avoid wrongdoing. Indeed, mere moral insight is enough: someone aware that a course of action is wrong is never unreasonable to choose to avoid it. The temptation to deny this is due to a certain conception of how belief and desire inputs determine rationality in choice, the analogue to the positivist conception of how observational inputs determine rationality in empirical belief.

When one reflects on particular internal struggles of morally serious people, the pervasive reasonableness of avoiding wrongdoing is clear enough. George loves his friend, but he also thinks it wrong to expose so many others to such danger and he cares about avoiding wrongdoing. He struggles over what to do. If he could easily decide to keep the secret, he would not be a morally serious person. If he were to conclude the struggle to decide with a decision (which would have to be agonized, given his love) to turn his friend in, surely this could not be an unreasonable choice. By hypothesis, George takes the danger to thousands of others posed by keeping Jim's secret to make keeping the secret wrong. If George is morally serious, this consideration of danger could be decisive in George's rational deliberations over what to do. And the conclusion of someone's rational deliberations identifies something that it is reasonable for him to do.

Granted, the wrongness here involves grave risks of harming others. Elsewhere, wrongness involves much less important risks of harm, as when a minor promise is broken. However, when the risk of harm is less important, the motives for the wrongdoing must be correspondingly unimportant, or the choice would not be wrong in the first place. My breaking a promise to wash the dishes is not wrong if, instead of washing, I devote myself to a phone call from a close friend far away in the grips of the greatest crisis of his life. In general, infractions are not moral wrongs if they are necessary to protect projects or relationships important to the self. Since minor wrongdoing has, at most, less than fundamental advantages, it is reasonable for a morally serious person to choose to forgo the advantages.—Thus, George's drama simply magnifies more routine quandaries, with larger moral costs and larger costs to the self than usual.

Still, it might appear that if rational deliberation on George's part could end with either one of the opposed conclusions then one of these conclusions must depend, for its rationality, on some change in the course of the deliberations which makes the choice at the end something other than a successful conclusion to rational deliberations of the sort of person George was at the start. If his caring for his friend could have made a choice of wrongdoing reasonable, then the reasonableness of any contrary choice must reflect a change in George that is not a product of rational deliberation. (As usual, I will put to one side the exceptional case in which rational deliberation would assign precisely equal desirability to the two alternatives.) Certain real aspects of deliberation give rise to this appearance, but only as a result of confusion.

When one embarks on deliberation, there are two different aspects, among others, of the success one seeks. One aspect might be called "expressive," since it requires an outcome expressing who one is at the start. One wants to find an alternative that is reasonable for oneself, i.e., oneself as one begins the project of deliberation. Of course, one may have to abandon beliefs and, perhaps, abandon desires as a consequence. But the motivation for one's abandoning desires in the course of deliberation will have to come from one's psychology at the start, if the deliberation is to serve its purpose. Otherwise, one does not find the answer to the question, "What is reasonable for me?"

but instead, "What will be reasonable for me?" Because of its expressive aspect, a rational deliberation, successfully concluded, enriches the characterization of the deliberator's psychology as it was at the start. She was someone for whom this was a reasonable choice—a fact revealed by the outcome of her deliberation.

The other aspect of deliberative success is conclusiveness. One seeks an ultimate resolution, a commitment to act in one way or other. (In the marginal cases of dead heat, the resolution is to let whim, chance or laziness decide because the outcomes are indifferent.) The final commitment that one seeks from the start is sufficiently decisive that a subsequent failure to implement it would constitute weakness of will, oversight, confusion or some other lack of full rationality. After all, if failure to carry through does not constitute irrationality, it involves having second thoughts. If the rational nonperformance were to involve second thoughts, the deliberation was not successfully concluded. So at the end of successful deliberation, only one alternative is reasonable (dead heats among opposed desires to one side).

It is tempting to combine the expressive and the conclusive aspects, making the unique rationality of the alternative at the end of deliberation a feature of the psychology at the start. But there is no need to do so. That the resolution ended a successful project of deliberation shows that one started out as someone for whom the chosen action was rational, not that one started out as someone for whom it was uniquely rational. The ultimate resolution sometimes changes the deliberator, making his rational options more determinate than they were, even though it results from successful deliberations, with the initially desired connection to who he was at the start. Perhaps a certain background insecurity about the stability of our selves encourages us to forget this risk of change.

When contrary resolutions could have been deliberative successes, one might speak of the initial outlook as motivationally vague. The actual deliberation clarifies one's motivations, without producing the sort of rejection of one's initial psychology that would thwart one's initial goal of finding what was reasonable for oneself as one was. This process of clarification is familiar in nonmoral deliberations, for example, in agonizing over what car to buy. Handling, acceleration, fuel economy, looks and comfort are all relevant. Prior to reflection on particular models, a prospective buyer can often roughly sketch her priorities among these dimensions. Still, in the actual shopping, some choices are usually hard in spite of this preparation and even in the face of complete automotive information. In deciding which to buy, the customer will determine whether, say, she cares about fuel economy enough to justify the choice of the slightly less speedy car. Perhaps her preferences were vague and were clarified in the process of shopping around. It is psychological myth-making, then, to insist that if she chose reasonably, her previous, vague desires could not have been clarified in favor of the other car, in equally rational deliberations. She has become one car buyer, sufficiently anchored in who she was, but she could have become another without loss of the anchorage required for the success of her deliberative project.

Perhaps the car buyer's initial total electrochemical state makes just one outcome inevitable, and similarly for George's initial electrochemical state in his deeper agony. Still, a different electrochemical state would have been compatible with the same motivational system. Belief-ascriptions, desire-ascriptions and psychological ascriptions in general are among the prime examples of causal ascriptions that can be made true in many electrochemical ways. More than one outcome is qualified to express one's motivational state at the start even if only one outcome is compatible with one's electrochemical state at the start. And the former continuity is what is required for an outcome to reveal what was reasonable all along.

The psychology of a morally serious person for whom wrongdoing is not unreasonable, who has not yet actually resolved to do wrong, is always sufficiently vague that avoiding wrongdoing would be reasonable. And of course if her psychology is, on the other hand, determinate in a way that makes wrongdoing unreasonable, then avoiding wrongdoing is reasonable for her. So, for a morally serious person who has not resolved to do wrong, avoiding wrongdoing is always a reasonable choice. What of the morally serious person who has resolved, after appropriate agony, to do what is morally wrong? If she has second thoughts, this will not be unreasonable, and could start a new phase in rational deliberations sufficiently anchored in her initial psychology that leads to a reasonable, implemented choice to avoid wrongdoing. What must be conceded is that a morally serious person could, on certain occasions, reasonably resolve to do what he knows to be wrong, so that avoidance of wrongdoing without second thoughts would entail weakness of will or some other defect. But this concession does not entail that reason dictates wrongdoing for a morally serious person once a certain point has been reached. "Unless there are second thoughts, nonperformance will involve some defect in rationality" is a comment that is true of any resolution, even a quite unreasonable one. Even if I have resolved to take a route to Syracuse that is utterly foolish, and I should have known better, I will display some such defect as weakness of will unless my departure from the foolish route reflects second thoughts. In sum (and taking the possible need for second thoughts as understood): it is never unreasonable for a morally serious person to avoid wrongdoing.

Reflection on the facts of agonized deliberation leads to this conclusion. Its acceptance requires the rejection of a model of rational action that parallels the positivist model of rational belief. According to that model, an action is reasonable just in case certain general rules connect it with beliefs and desires at the time of action. The rational agent is assumed to have preferences among all possible states of the world, simultaneous preferences at any time, preferences that constitute his basic desires. The beliefs are concerned with the probable occurrence of states of affairs, should a given choice be made. The totality of relevant desires and beliefs must satisfy certain highly general requirements of coherence, or else no action based on them is reasonable. The rational choices are the ones than which none ranks higher when rankings are adjusted to account for probable outcomes according to the general rules for rational decision making, rules made precise in the theory of expected utility. Two contrary choices are only both reasonable, in this way of thinking, if the strength of the desires and the degrees of confidence in states of affairs are precisely calibrated to make for a tie. Putting this marginal, unstable phenomenon to one side, there will be just one reasonable choice on any occasion. So if George was reasonable to choose wrongdoing, he would have been unreasonable not to. If another person with the same beliefs could reasonably choose to do the right thing, he must have different desires from George.

This input-output model does not fit the internal struggles of morally serious people and other complex deliberations, as well. It should be rejected. The crucial mistake for present purposes is the assumption that a rational person always has preferences among all alternative possibilities with a bearing on actions available to her. Morally serious people for whom wrongdoing would be reasonable violate this assumption until they have actually resolved on wrongdoing.

The discussion so far has largely concerned moral seriousness, an attribute that had a double definition in terms both of knowing and of caring. The requirement of the degree of caring that is normal among morally insightful people added something to the mere requirement of moral insight. Most of us care more about avoiding wrongdoing than bare knowledge of the difference between right and wrong requires. Indeed, even if we did not think that harms to others were wrong we would be inclined to avoid them, on account of spontaneous sympathy and other tendencies that do not require moral awareness. We could take up a perspective analogous to Huck Finn's at the moments in which Clemens has him yield to what he thinks an immoral temptation, to treat a black person as an equal.

Suppose that the independent requirement of caring is dropped. Someone knows that an option is wrong, but we add no further assumption about his caring to avoid wrongdoing. Of course, such a person might sometimes reasonably do what he knows to be wrong. Even full-fledged moral seriousness permits this. But could it ever be unreasonable for a bare knower to avoid doing what is morally wrong? This is never the case for a bare knower, as well as for a morally serious person who cares to the normal extent. The impossibility is important, since it reveals another way in which simplified accounts of rational choice muddle the assessment of burdens of conscience.

Consider Bob, the callous hamburger maker. Setting up a temporary, anonymous stand in a remote one-night carnival that he will never visit again, he is tempted by an offer of cheap but tainted meat. The attitudes toward wrongdoing on which Bob bases his deliberations involve no more initial caring to avoid wrongdoing than bare moral knowledge requires. The sources of his attitudes toward harm are the minimum for moral insight, and unlike Huck Finn he would never give up something for someone else unless he thought withholding was morally wrong. He likes to make money, and would be reasonable to buy the meat, though he realizes that his use of it would be morally wrong. Still, he might reason, "I would hate to suffer from such stomachaches as I will inflict. If the customers only knew whence the pain came, they would furiously complain, and with every justification. So my use of tainted meat would be wrong." Bob, as I have described him, might, further, decide not to buy and use the meat, on these grounds. He might choose, on this occasion, to avoid advantageous wrongdoing, choosing not to advance his own interests where this would justify others in complaining of what he does.

Bob's choice would be reasonable. Yet it is the outcome of deliberations proceeding from a standpoint of bare moral knowledge. His persistent callousness is reflected in the fact that selling tainted hamburgers would also have been a reasonable choice for him. Gains that could not be a rational basis for such serious wrongdoing on our part could be for him.

It might seem that Bob's basis for avoiding wrongdoing is too bare a commitment to make his choice reasonable. At any rate, it might seem too bare to withstand the intrusions of immorality in other similar cases, as when the gains from wrongdoing are great wealth, or Bob is imagined not just to like making money but to love it. Of course, it is conceivable, in all of these cases, that someone such as Bob might choose to avoid wrongdoing, committing himself to acting on moral principles. But, it might be thought, if the commitment so utterly lacks the usual support in caring about others, the action, though consciously and deliberately chosen, is not reasonable because of the lack of support. Bob acting morally might be seen as the analogue of a person who waves his left arm in little half circles for fifteen minutes at a time, telling us that he has chosen to act in this way and denying that he does so because he enjoys it or because he expects any consequent benefit to accrue to anyone.

The case of the armwaver poses an important challenge. An action done at some cost stands in need of justification, on pain of irrationality, and the case of the armwaver shows that it is not enough to point to a principle on the basis of which one acted. The armwaver, after all, is also committed to his principle of periodically waving his left arm in little half circles. If Bob is rational, he must have a reason for choosing to act on his moral principle, one which makes his choice reasonable for him in spite of its cost as armwaving isn't for the armwaver.

If and when Bob decides not to buy the meat, he decides that his self-respect is more important than the gains of immorality. Bob, after all, has moral knowledge. So he knows that buying and using the meat would be blameworthy. If he chooses to avoid the wrongdoing because he sees that it is wrong, then he cares enough about not being blameworthy to make the choice a means of protecting his self-respect. Avoiding the lowering of self-respect is a rationalizing motive, a sufficiently overriding reason given the cost of his decision. The armwaver, by contrast, has no rationalizing motive. Of course, if the armwaver thought he would experience anxiety or some other feeling to a sufficiently uncomfortable extent, if he did not wave his arm, then this might be his rationalizing motive. The stipulation that he takes no further benefit to accrue to anyone was meant to rule this out. Bob's situation may be taken as analogous so far as uncomfortable or comfortable feelings are concerned. He need not expect any overriding discomfort in the way of feelings of blameworthiness should he save the money and buy the meat. His rationalizing motive is the thought that by refusing the meat he avoids blameworthiness. It is not unreasonable for him to turn down the offer on the basis of this thought, which is part of his awareness of what he is doing.

In rough sum: it is reasonable to say, "I have decided, at some cost, to avoid this harm to others because that is the only way to avoid wrongdoing—even though I don't care about those others apart from the moral principles involved," but it is nonsense to say, "I have decided, at some cost, to wave my left arm in little half circles because this is the only way to wave it in little half circles for fifteen minutes every waking hour—even though I don't care about the activity apart from the armwaving principle involved."

There is, however, a simplification of rational choice that would make Bob analogous to the armwaver. In this view, choices are only reasonable in light of rationally foreseen payoffs, and the payoffs are of a psychologically homogeneous kind, in the final analysis. A choice is reasonable if it is rationally believed to be the available means most effectively promoting payoffs of this kind. Otherwise, it is inadequately supported armwaving. This requirement for rational choice is analogous to positivist demands that rational belief be inferable from inputs of a homogeneous, observational kind.

For present purposes, the crucial mistake here is the requirement that payoffs be of a single psychological kind in the final analysis. Enjoyments are obviously relevant to the rationalization of goals. The most promising way to make the armwaver's commitment reasonable was to base it on his enjoyment of the armwaving. So the accurate perception that mere acting on principle needs to be justified quickly leads to hedonism, if one looks for a homogeneous sort of rationalization. Yet there is no basis for supposing that Bob's choice is a rational means of promoting enjoyment (or any other plausible candidate for the crucial kind of payoff). It could be a means, as when someone is sufficiently certain that he won't be able to sleep at night or will otherwise be unable to enjoy his ill-gotten gains. But bare moral knowledge hardly guarantees such wages of wrongdoing. Bob, though aware that what he does is wrong, may be sure he will quickly forget the wrongdoing. Moreover, Bob's present experience of blameworthiness may not be especially painful. In both ways, he is less than he should be, even less than most of us are. But he was unattractive *ex hypothesi*. So, it might seem, the bare moral knower might be unreasonable to avoid wrongdoing given the likely enjoyments of which he is aware.

However, there is no need to go from the truth that appeals to bare principle are not enough to the further conclusion that rational action on principle pursues one kind of psychological payoff. The rationality of aiming at a goal can depend on a variety of psychological effects—though not just any psychological effect. (The mere kinesthetic sensations of the armwaver were not enough.) Some of these relevant effects, but not all, consist of the satisfaction of knowing that one is a person of a certain kind. The weight of the satisfaction need not consist of how much one enjoys basking in it. Some such satisfactions are always weighty enough to rationalize if one makes the choice in question in order to avoid the corresponding frustration. Bob's satisfaction of knowing that he was not blameworthy was a satisfaction of that kind. Satisfaction that one is not blameworthy is rational, i.e., an appropriate motivating goal for a rational person, even if it serves no further purpose. Satisfaction that one is waving one's left hand in little half circles, apart from enjoyment of the process or any other further purpose, is not rational.

Moral principles, then, have a special relation to rationality. If someone is committed to moral principles her choice not to depart from them in her conduct is not unreasonable (at any rate it is not, if her commitment does not depend on some unreasonable belief). The same cannot be said of commitment to just any principle.

Such a special role for morality would be entailed by the externalist doctrine that valid moral reasons make a choice reasonable for someone regardless of whether the choice is appropriately related to her own aims. In fact, however, the special role for moral reasons did not require any such implausible intrusion from outside the chooser's psychology.

If Bob hadn't aimed for self-respect (as he might, reasonably, have chosen not to), then his avoidance of wrongdoing would have been unreasonable. As internalists insist, the reasonableness of moral choice is dependent on the chooser's motives. What is reasonable for someone must always be anchored in his actual psychology. However, any topic-neutral description of a process of anchorage, according no special place to moral reasons and reasons of other specific kinds, will be insufficient to characterize the requirements of rational choice. The choice of the armwaver, though based on motives and deliberations that have the same form as Bob's, is not rational. Some total internally coherent systems of motives are rational, some not. Some processes of deliberation are rational, while others of the same structure are not. The fact that the ultimate reason on which the chooser relies is a valid (or at least approximately valid) moral reason may be essential in making the choice reasonable. This is quite compatible with saying that it was also essential that the motivating reason was one on which the chooser relied. Rationality is based on internal reasons, but the fact that an internal consideration is an adequate reason may depend on a rationalizing capacity of that consideration which is quite separate from matters of psychological influence within the chooser's mental constitution. Morality is an external authority investing internal considerations with this rationalizing power. The labels "internal" and "external" provide bad guidance among philosophical options, as "realist" and "antirealist" did before.

Chapter Ten

NORMAL MORALITY

NONE OF OUR findings about reasonableness settles the questions about wrongness, above all, the question, "Is it ever not wrong to do what is morally wrong?" This question will turn out to shed much light on the nature of rational deliberations about what morality demands, as the others shed light on the relation between the demands of morality and rational deliberations about what to do. In the final analysis, the difficulties in affirming that what is morally wrong is always wrong will turn out to be a symptom of standard false connections between morality, personhood and deliberation. In standard moral theories, the reasons why an act is morally wrong are supposed to be validated by assessment from some detached and impartial point of view. Some such conclusion is unavoidable if one takes some general rule for connecting moral wrongness with properties that are not individually intrinsically moral to be all the equipment that is essential in discerning moral wrongness. Ultimately, I will trace the false appearance that morality misdescribes the limits of wrongness to these false conceptions of morality and moral judgment. In the conception that I will ultimately defend, after much discussion of standard alternatives, moral wrongness is determined by choices in which morally responsible people respond to the totality of their concerns without insisting on the ultimate authority of an impartial standard. The bases for self-regulation on which morally responsible people do insist involve a variety of concrete norms of character. In the next and final chapter, I will use this aspect of moral responsibility in rejecting a final attempt to limit morality, the denial that one should always try to be the sort of person that one should try to be, morally speaking.

Embedded in normal late twentieth-century advanced-industrial morality are norms of character with much room for partiality, norms as specific and rule-independent as the ancient Greek ideals to which modern burden lifters sometimes direct us. The authority of morality's demands depends on this rejection of the insistence on a comprehensive impartial standard in most moral philosophy and of the worship of abstract rules in philosophy as a whole.

If my arguments are right, challenges to the authority of morality have the same, great value as philosophical skepticism concerning claims to knowledge. The authority of what morality says is not undermined, but the nature of what is said is illuminated. Claims that were inhumanly demanding on common, tempting philosophical construals turn out, really, to be livable.

"Impartial Morality"

Earlier, I argued that the question about the availability of morally wrong choices that are not wrong is worth asking, despite its paradoxical sound. There seem to be many different kinds of considerations determining whether an act is wrong, corresponding to different universalizable rationales for self-reproach or its absence. The considerations that are moral might not always be overriding. Nonetheless, there is a burden of proof on someone who seeks to lift burdens of conscience, claiming that what is morally wrong is not always wrong. Moral reasons do have weight, and must, at least, be overridden. That morality is generally important in assessing wrongness would not, by itself, cast doubt on the possibility of such overriding, since nonmoral considerations may also be important and violations of morality are sometimes trivial. What casts doubt on the possibility of overriding is, rather, the absorptive capacity of morality, its tendency to take significant account of nonmoral considerations. For example, if the violation of a trivial duty is necessary to advance an important but nonmoral interest of the violator, accurate moral reasoning takes this into account; the violation is not morally wrong because the interest at stake, itself nonmoral, was so important to the transgressor. It is not morally wrong of me to arrive three minutes late for an appointment because I wanted to write down the most brilliant argument I ever thought up. Conversely, if a choice would be morally wrong even though its avoidance would thwart the pursuit of an important nonmoral consideration, then the seriousness of that thwarting must have been taken into account in the moral assessment. Given its capacity to take into account considerations that would otherwise compete, it is not clear that morality can be overridden by considerations that it does not absorb.

This challenge would be met by singling out some feature of morality and showing that the feature makes it impossible to give enough credit to considerations on account of which a choice might not be wrong. Of course, it would not do just to single out a distinctive characteristic of one moral theory and then to show that this feature is too constraining. For the inadequacy might well be a sign that this theory does not accurately describe the demands of morality. Rather, one should point to some common feature of many otherwise contrasting moral theories. The claim will be that this feature, which excludes considerations that can have a crucial bearing on wrongness, is a feature of any morality that could be valid.

The leading candidate is impartiality. It figures in an important argument, suggested, at least, by Williams' and Stocker's writings, for the existence of moral wrongness that is not wrong. Moral considerations (it might be said) are a means of assessing a choice from an impartial standpoint. Yet (the argument continues), other important reasons for choice are not means of impartial assessment, as when one is inclined to keep someone's dangerous secret for the reason that he is one's friend. The partial reasons are sometimes available as reasons why an action—say, keeping the dangerous secret—would not be wrong. Their power to show that a choice is not wrong does not depend on derivability from means of impartial assessment. Yet they can have considerable power. So it would be a fluke, enormously unlikely, if every action excluded as wrong by moral considerations were also excluded by the totality of considerations, partial as well as moral.

The first need, in filling in this argument, is for a more detailed description of impartiality. For the argument to get started, impartiality has to be at least a troubling constraint in the assessment of wrongness and at least a plausible characterization of moral assessment. It is not easy to meet both demands at once.

To begin with, it would be a wild distortion to require that a moral deliberation never give special weight to the chooser's special caring for certain people, relations or projects. That would mean that the moral assessment of my response to a little girl's demand for a chocolate birthday cake could not depend on whether she is my daughter. Rather, the justification is relevantly impartial if the fact that I have various partialities is given whatever importance it has by general principles of the appropriate impartial sort. Perhaps the fact that the chocolate cake requester is my daughter is only given special weight because one ought not seriously to worsen people's lives to avoid trivial costs. Deprivation by me would weaken structures of trust and hope contributing to this girl's future happiness, and a similar nonsatisfaction of the same request from the little girl down the street would have no such effect since she is not my child. In general, impartiality applies directly only to the general evaluative principles in a more or less completely analyzed deliberation.

What is this characteristic of impartiality that must apply to ultimate principles in a distinctively moral justification? To insist that the ultimate principle apply equally to everyone would be to require too little. For this requirement could involve nothing more than the universalizability that is a feature of every valid judgment about wrongness, whether moral, aesthetic or culinary wrongness or wrongness all told. Perhaps in deciding to keep the secret, George relies on an ultimate principle according to which someone's keeping a dangerous secret is never wrong when only strangers are imperiled by silence and his or her close friend would be hurt by disclosure. Then his judgment that keeping Jim's secret would not be wrong lacks the impartiality which the burden lifter's challenge ascribes to moral judgments. But his ultimate principle is completely general, applying equally to everyone.

On the other hand, to insist that ultimate evaluative principles must not, by themselves, ascribe special importance to special attachments such as friendship would be to require too much. Perhaps George's deliberations are guided by his enthusiasm for G. E. Moore's *Principia Ethica*. He determines what is wrong by asking what would give rise to the best states of affairs, and thinks, with Moore, that certain pleasures specific to friendship are among the few phenomena of ultimate value. Such deliberations would be impartial.

Often, the distinction between impartiality and partiality is used to characterize motivations and their expression, as in warnings against showing partiality among one's children. This might seem a clue to a more satisfactory alternative, basing impartiality on motivations for relying on the principles to which one appeals, rather than on the content of these principles. However, such specifications are also overly restrictive.

In characterizing impartiality, it would be too much to require that someone's use of a principle not depend on her caring about specific people, relationships or projects. For then, one would have to deny the impartiality of deliberations that seem typical of morality, including impartial morality. Moral responsibility almost always depends on specific past attachments to others. Indeed, a childhood without such attachments is a characteristic mark of a psychopath. Few of us have reason to be confident that we would remain committed to moral principles if we ceased to care about specific people. Yet such doubt does not put in doubt the morality of our actual commitment. The demand that genuine respect for moral principles be causally independent of specific, nonmoral attachments has always seemed the least plausible aspect of Kant's purism, rejected even by those present-day theorists otherwise most respectful of Kant's ideas. The proposed restriction on causes of commitment would exclude from impartial morality anyone's moral commitment to utilitarianism or to a demand that all be treated as ends, not means—so long as the general commitment depended on that person's caring about particular people. This would be quite artificial and unhelpful.

Still, there does seem to be an important difference between justifying George's keeping the secret merely on the grounds that Jim is such a close friend, and any of the justifications produced by standard philosophical moral theories. The friend-centered justification is even different from reliance on Moore's theory, in which friendship is a specially valuable phenomenon. In deliberations over wrongness guided by any of these moral theories, a chooser does not ultimately rely on a principle allowing preference for one's own attachments as against interests of strangers; that is, she relies on no such self-serving principle unless it is justifiable in turn on the basis of a further principle about wrongness, which by itself gives no such permission for discrimination, combined with a characterization of her attachments and situation. Even Moore's evaluation of friendship by itself licenses no preference for one's attachments to one's friends over strangers' interests. It is supposed to lead one, all else being equal, to avoid conduct that would reduce the scope of friendship among all, a requirement that gives friendship among those whom one will never encounter the same weight as relations between oneself and one's own friends. On the other hand, George would show a contrasting partiality if he justified the decision not to disclose Jim's secret by a principle according to which it is not wrong to protect one's own close friends in ways that gravely imperil strangers. In any case, this is so if he employs such a principle without further justification.

The appropriate understanding of impartiality is this. A type of deliberation is relevantly impartial if one is fully equipped for it when the evaluative principles in one's equipment do not, by themselves, entail that any preference for one's own relationships and projects over the interests of strangers is not wrong; they are not intrinsically permissive of such discrimination. In contrast, universalizability only entails that what is good equipment for one in deliberations over wrongness, is good equipment for everyone, including strangers. Judgments of moral wrongness might, plausibly, be required to be sustainable by deliberations of the former, impartial kind, while generic judgments of wrongness only require universalizability.

(Of course, it is obvious that all current moral theories that are impartial in this sense will, in fact, allow, as not wrong, many acts that are motivated by attachments to particular people. Which acts depends entirely on further facts of the cases in question, but one is sure in advance that there will be some facts admitting some such conduct. So it might seem overly dramatic to speak of the rejection of these theories as the rejection of impartial morality, unless they are rejected in favor of ultimate standards providing substantial intrinsic permission for favoritism, in a shift removing moral pressure to reconcile certain choices based on attachment with non-intrinsically-permissive standards. In fact, the "person-centered approach" to morality that I will ultimately defend contrasts in just this way. So there will be no need to worry about overly dramatic labeling.)

If the sort of impartiality that I have described is a necessary condition for an assessment's being moral, the burden of proof is shifted to those who claim that what is morally wrong is always wrong. When an act harms, deprives or imperils utter strangers, it is sometimes justified by partial reasons, reasons appealing to the agent's special relation to certain people or projects—for example, "but this would ruin my closest friend." The force of these reasons as showing that the action is not wrong does not seem to derive from facts combined with further evaluative principles of the impartial sort, i.e., principles that do not, by themselves, permit favoritism toward one's own attachments. Short of a successfully ambitious argument that such appearances are always deceiving and all force of partial reasons is derivative, we should take the partial reasons to have independent force. But then, this independent force will sometimes be enough to justify, as not wrong, an action that is wrong from the impartial standpoint of morality.

A defender of the burdens of morality could counter this argument in two different ways. On the one hand, she could take on the burden of proof, and try to show that the force (or, at least, the potentially decisive force) of appeals to special attachments is entirely due to standards for choice that do not by themselves permit such favoritism, applied to the facts of the case. On the other hand, she could reject the underlying characterization of morality, and assert that the totality of moral considerations appropriate to judgments of wrongness includes nonderivative permission to discriminate. I think the second tactic, lightening the burden of morality, succeeds, and that the first does not. Impartial moralities exclude acts that are not wrong because such impartial standpoints misrepresent morality, which is not impartial.

As a basis for developing my own account of morality, in which morality is nonimpartial and is decisive in matters of wrongness, I will criticize three major kinds of alternatives to it. First, I will consider the dictates of consequentialist impartiality, arguing for the familiar verdict that such impartiality is excessive because a sacrifice of some benefits for the world as a whole to the benefit of one's personal attachments or projects is not always wrong or morally wrong. Then, I will consider the simplest correction of consequentialist detachment, an "agent-centered prerogative" describing the permissible ratio of sacrificed general benefit to individual gain. Natural extensions of the arguments against consequentialism will also exclude such an agent-centered prerogative, as failing to take account of the relation of personal histories to moral responsibilities. Then, turning away from moralities that determine wrongness by weighing impacts on the basis of quantitative principles, I will consider the main current systematic alternative, contractualist moral theories. Here, moral wrongness is determined by rules general agreement to which would be acceptable to all reasonable choosers governed by an appropriate interest in a social life regulated by general agreement. I will try to show that such an outlook imposes excessive demands in its pure, formalist version, and that it cannot be made sufficiently flexible to describe the nature of moral wrongness, because of its pervasive emphasis on social coordination. (Although they are usually concerned with partial attachments, as in Williams' and Stocker's critiques, my arguments that these versions of morality fail to determine wrongness accurately are also meant as arguments that they fail to determine moral wrongness accurately. So, while I will often use the unmodified adjective, "wrong," in the interest of verbal simplicity, my criticisms should be read—and would be read most naturally—as directed at both targets.)

In light of these criticisms, I will present my own account, which bases moral wrongness on the distinctive concerns of responsible people, in their self-regulation. The norms of character governing such self-regulation intrinsically permit favoritism toward personal attachments and projects. So morality is not impartial. That what is morally wrong is always wrong is a further consequence. A remaining task is to account for the productiveness of principled moral reflection, if morality rests on concrete norms of character.

In one way, this long journey will lead away from modern inclinations. At least in the most technologically advanced countries, modern economic life is dominated by assessments of impacts according to abstract standards that place no value on personal attachments, while modern political argument is supposed to put to one side favoritism toward people or projects whom one specially values (with a standard, troubling exception for favoritism toward one's fellow-citizens as against foreigners). No doubt, this milieu encourages similar abstractness in specifications of the moral point of view, an abstractness which I will be attacking. Yet in another way, my defense of the concrete will defend modernity, since the standpoint that I will ultimately describe will be recognizable as the standard outlook of modern folk.

I hope that these arguments will also contribute to the defense of morally appropriate abstractness in the political sphere—i.e., the forms of neutrality and universality required by justice as social freedom. For nothing can do more to discredit political liberalism, in this or any other form, than its extrapolation into a general basis for self-regulation. The abstractness that justice as social freedom dictates in modern institutions does not fit the whole gamut of moral choices. More to the point, people will refuse to bear the burden of such comprehensive abstractness. So the political feasibility of the outlook on institutions defended in the middle chapters of this book depends on its limitation here.

THE DETACHMENT OF CONSEQUENTIALISM

One kind of moral theory which claims to provide a comprehensive impartial basis for ascribing wrongness asserts that an act is not wrong just in case the total consequences of engaging in it, assessed in an impartial manner prescribed by the theory, are as good as those of engaging in any alternative to it. Williams first developed his challenge to impartial morality in response to this consequentialism, and understandably so. Consequentialist impartial morality rules out, as wrong, the least sacrifice of total goodness of consequences for the sake of personal attachments. It certainly seems that acts which consequentialism forbids could be all right because, with minute loss in total goodness, they express the agent's deep attachment to particular people or projects.

Consequentialism is most familiar in utilitarian versions, which also constitute the most enduring and articulate project of responding to this challenge. In the writings of Mill, Sidgwick, Harrod and Smart—indeed, of all the major utilitarians starting with Mill, there is a characteristic moment in which these humane people eloquently acknowledge the appearance that utilitarianism imposes inhuman demands by excluding any choice as wrong if some alternative would make the world even slightly better. In broadly similar ways, all of them try to eliminate the appearance of inhumanity toward choosers by showing that utilitarianism would endorse familiar motives, character traits or normal reasons for choice as serving to make the world best, among the humanly available alternatives. Utilitarianism is not excessively demanding, they say, in its assessments of agents, motives, dispositions and the like—and once this is appreciated, its demand on acts themselves will be seen as non-excessive, too. Thus, Mill acknowledges the need to respond to objectors to utilitarianism who "find fault with its standards as being too high for humanity. They say it is exacting too much to require that people shall always act from the inducement of promoting the general interests of society. But this is . . . to confound the rule of action with the motive of it. . . . It is the business of ethics to tell us what are our duties . . . but no system of ethics requires that the sole motive of all we do shall be a feeling of duty . . ." In a note to the same paragraph, he remarks, ". . . [T]he motive . . . makes no difference in the act . . . though it makes a great difference in our moral estimate of the agent, especially if it indicates a good or a bad habitual *disposition*—a bent of character from which useful, or from which hurtful actions are likely to arise."[1]

In "Alienation, Consequentialism and the Demands of Morality," Peter Railton has done much to clarify the long debate over the demands of consequentialist impartiality through an exceptionally clear, psychologically subtle argument that consequentialism gives the agent's attachments their due. Railton notes that the validity of the consequentialist criterion of wrongness in acts does not entail that the consequentialist criterion should be the reason on which one normally relies in deciding what to do. He does think that one ought on occasion to engage in assessment of the relationships and projects that supply one's normal reasons for choice. (Adapting an occasional phrase of Railton's, I will sometimes call the considerations supplying one's reasons for choice as particular options become salient one's "motivational structure.") In such assessments, one ought to consider whether one's normal en-

---

[1] *Utilitarianism*, chapter 2 in S. Gorovitz, ed. *"Utilitarianism" with Critical Essays*, p. 25. In the same context, Sidgwick notes that "the Utilitarian . . . may without inconsistency admire the Disposition or Motive if it is of a kind which is generally desirable to encourage, even if he disapproves of the conduct to which it has led in any particular case" (*The Methods of Ethics*, seventh edition [Chicago: University of Chicago Press, 1962], iv, v, 4, p. 493). Elsewhere, Sidgwick is characteristically thorough in making a utilitarian case for "the special claims and duties belonging to special relations, by which each man is connected with a few of the whole number of human beings," and appropriately nuanced in his discussion of the ways in which a utilitarian code of conduct must take into account "the state of men's knowledge and intellectual faculties, and the range of their sympathies, and the direction and strength of their prevailing impulses, and their relations to the external world and to each other" (iv, iii, 3, p. 432; iv, iv, 2, p. 469). R. F. Harrod, "Utilitarianism Revised" (1936) responds to the worry about the "cold" and "wide" character of the utilitarian standard with utilitarian justifications of "the more homely virtues," especially those involving affection and love toward particular people; see Gorovitz, op. cit., p. 78. J.J.C. Smart responds, similarly, with an argument that the utilitarian "should consciously encourage in himself the tendency to certain types of spontaneous feeling," An *Outline of a System of Utilitarian Ethics* (1961) in Smart and B. Williams, *Utilitarianism: For and Against* (Cambridge: Cambridge University Press, 1973), p. 45.

gagement in choices guided by those attachments is as effective a basis as any for making one a producer of good consequences. If not, one should seek to weaken or replace one's attachments in favor of others that increase one's "over-all contribution to human well-being" (p. 159). Thus, someone's reasons for action are as they ought to be just in case no alternative motivational structure would lead him to live in a way more effectively producing well-being (pp. 151–53). This consequentialist defense of a motivational structure must take into account all relevant facts about the agent. These will, no doubt, include the fact that he will lose energy, interest in life, and active concern for strangers if he has no attachment to particular people or projects. So, on consequentialist grounds, special attachments ought normally to play an important role in one's life as a source of reasons for choice. Nonetheless, it is always true that an act is wrong just in case "it would produce worse consequences than other acts available to the agent in the circumstances" (p. 158). Total goodness, here, is determined, impartially, by the "weighted sum" of eventual consequences, weighted according to the intrinsic goodness of a plurality of phenomena (p. 150).[2]

I will sometimes use the label "the counterfactual test" for the requirement that no alternative to one's actual normal motivational structure would make one a better producer of good consequences. For our present purposes (cf. footnote 3, below), the counterfactual test is important as part of the most promising consequentialist strategy for coping with worries about excessive condemnation of acts sacrificing some overall benefit to personal attachments. It sometimes appears that consequentialism is excessive in condemning such an act as wrong (the consequentialist concedes); but (she continues) the appearance depends on the failure to appreciate the difference between the consequentialist criterion of wrongness in acts and the consequentialist standard for assessing normal reasons for action, namely, the counterfactual test; once one sees the extent to which acts that are wrong by the consequentialist standard are due to reasons whose role in choice consequentialism would endorse, one will see that consequentialism gives partial attachments their due, in moral assessment. Or, in any case, arguments about attachment and consequentialist impartiality will no longer provide special, powerful grounds for doubting the consequentialist standard for wrongness in acts.

Railton defends his view that attachments are properly appraised through the counterfactual test by means of a detailed and vivid example, the case of Juan, who seeks to meet the counterfactual test yet also loves his wife.

---

[2] "Alienation, Consequentialism and the Demands of Morality," *Philosophy & Public Affairs* 13 (1984), pp. 134–71. More precisely, Railton intends to show that considerations of detachment and excessive impartiality are not good reasons for rejecting this aggregative consequentialism. Beyond this, he does not propose to justify it, though he takes it to be the most plausible sort of morality. See pp. 148, 150.

When a friend remarks on the extraordinary concern he shows for his wife, Juan characteristically responds, "I love Linda. I even *like* her. So it means a lot to me to do things for her. . . ." But his friend asks . . . what about all the other, needier people Juan could help if he broadened his horizon still further? Juan replies, "Look, it's a better world when people can have a relationship like ours—and nobody could if everyone were always asking themselves who's got the most need. . . . I know that you can't always put family first. . . . But still you need that little circle. People get burned out, or lose touch, if they try to save the world by themselves. The ones who can stick with it and do a good job of making things better are usually the ones who can make that fit into a life that does not make them miserable. . . ." . . . [W]hile Juan does not do what he does simply for the sake of doing what is right, he would seek to lead a different sort of life if he did not think his was morally defensible. (Pp. 150f.)

Juan's outlook on personal attachments certainly makes a difference that Linda would appreciate. Railton imagines that Juan and Linda are a commuting couple, normally getting together every other week. One "off" week Linda seems depressed, and Juan makes an extra trip when he could instead have given the price of the ticket to OXFAM to dig a well in a drought-stricken village. Even though the donation would contribute more to human well-being, the deliberation that leads him to fly to Linda is based on reasons that Juan, as consequentialist, can endorse, on the basis he sets forth in the monologue from which I quoted.

Through these psychological narratives and logical resources, Railton makes it clear that many motivational structures supplying partial (i.e., nonimpartial) reasons for action will pass the counterfactual test. How effective is this consequentialist basis for endorsing departures from impartial deliberations in defending consequentialism against the charge of excessive condemnation of acts expressing personal attachments? No doubt, there are cases in which the initial appearance that consequentialism demands too much disappears once one fully appreciates the fact that the motive leading the chooser to do less than the best for the world is a reason for choice that consequentialism would endorse: the consequentialist judgment of the act only seemed to neglect the moral force of personal detachments because one confused the judgment of acts with the judgment of motives. Nonetheless, the counterfactual test combined with psychological facts will not produce an effective defense against charges of excessive impartiality if there are cases of the following kind. There is the usual inclination to reject the condemnation, as wrong, of an act in which the agent favors a personal attachment at some cost to total good consequences, while the agent's reasons involved in its justification depend on attachments in a motivational structure that *fails* the counterfactual test. A consequentialist cannot explain away the appearance of nonwrongfulness in such a case on the grounds that the genuine acceptability of the motivating reason has been transferred, through confusion, to the act. For here, consequentialism does not justify the motivating reason, either.

Note that the anti-consequentialist finding that a nonoptimific act based on a structure failing the counterfactual test is not wrong is different from other conclusions, namely, claims that applying or conforming to the counterfactual test is sometimes the wrong thing to do or sometimes leads to actions that are wrong, even if optimific. Since these are much more controversial claims, we should begin with the milder one.[3]

When we look at certain nonoptimific acts expressing motivational structures that fail the counterfactual test, the appearance of nonwrongness is at least as vivid as in the other cases in which a consequentialist may be able to explain the appearance away as due to a confusion between act-appraisal and character-appraisal. Both our attachments and our potential for adding to human well-being partly depend on circumstances beyond our control. Life sometimes gives people deep attachments to particular others while giving them an unusual potential for affecting overall human well-being. For them, the rule that attachments are too strong whenever their weakening would help to make one a slightly more effective contributor to overall well-being is specially demanding. The counterfactual test could require shallow attachments, here. But this shallowness would not be a requirement of moral responsibility. Someone who does not weaken his attachments when this would most fully exploit the special potential to produce good need do no wrong in consequent nonoptimific acts.

Phil is a pharmacist, with a drugstore in a remote town serving a large rural area. He is a competent and morally responsible pharmacist, but not a zealous one. The particular project of providing as much pharmaceutical help as possible is not fundamental to his having a secure sense of self. He is deeply

---

[3] Sometimes, Railton is concerned to defend consequentialism from bold condemnations of it as reducing human flourishing (see, for example, p. 140). Sometimes, he is concerned, more broadly, to show that it can cope with apparent conflicts between personal commitments and the demands of impartial morality (see, for example, p. 150; both concerns are expressed in the "Introduction"). I will be interested, primarily, in the broader claim. Even if consequentialism is not to be condemned as yielding a stultified way of life, its all-embracing standard of wrongness in acts might not be sufficiently permissive toward acts affecting special attachments. However, in the course of arguing that the standard for acts is not sufficiently permissive, I will sometimes be concerned directly with consequentialist judgments of motives as well as consequentialist judgments of acts. For I will try to show that it is not wrong to reject the consequentialist strategy for self-appraisal, the counterfactual test. Since such rejection would be the choice (and the reasonable choice) of almost everyone, my arguments that it is not wrong to reject the consequentialist strategy come close to sustaining the bolder claim that the consequentialist strategy is stultifying. I should add that my acceptance of motivational structures failing the counterfactual test is the only part of my argument contradicting detailed and explicit commitments in Railton's article. His discussion is offered as a preliminary assessment of complex problems, and is mainly concerned with the proper structure of people's motivations.

attached to his wife and children. The other pharmacists in town die, retire or move away until Phil is the only one available in emergencies to thousands of people. Whether he makes himself available after hours and on weekends, and whether he takes vacations when no substitute can be found now have a large impact on overall well-being.

Above what threshold should Phil be prepared to drop whatever else he is doing and provide medication? His attachment to Lucy and the kids is at issue, here, since these attachments provide important reasons for limiting intrusions. No doubt, Phil, if morally responsible, will at least make a pact with the local general practitioner to provide medication needed to cope with emergencies that threaten life or threaten to create significant lifelong impairment. But what about the interests of people who do not want to spend the night in acute but transient pain? Below this threshold, what about the needs of those troubled by the after-hours or Sunday onset of real, but not excruciating discomfort, heat rash, for example?

Such questions really are faced by pharmacists, nurses and doctors when, through no fault of their own, they become specially important in the provision of scarce medical resources. In justifying the limits they do set, such people often say, "I have a right to a normal personal life." If Phil were committed to Railton's consequentialism he could say something like this. He could note that if the threshold of permitted intrusion is too low, he will become so burned-out, miserable or apathetic that the gains from aiding intrusive strangers will not more than balance the losses in his family circle. But this is the only protection to which he could appeal in assessing his motivational structure. And the protection is fairly weak. A high level of loneliness, fatigue and listlessness is compatible with the useful provision of medication. If it were not, the municipal hospitals of the United States would be vast morgues.

Suppose that the issue is whether the threshold should be so low that Phil is constantly on call to provide relief for moderate discomfort—rashes and the like. Acceptance of the consequent intrusion might be incompatible with Phil's attachment to Lucy and the kids. Yet, if the gains in well-being due to relief from discomfort were to more than balance the loss from the disruption of Phil's family life, then Phil, to pass the counterfactual test, would have to weaken his special caring for his wife and children. Such necessity could arise in realistic circumstances, given Railton's aggregative consequentialism. Just suppose that, through no fault of his own, a sufficient number of people become dependent on Phil for relief of mere transient discomfort at night and on Sundays and holidays. Still, recognition that his motivational structure fails the counterfactual test leads to no revision of the judgment that he is not wrong to reserve the time and post the signs that protect his relations with Lucy and the kids. (For example, if he posts a sign on the door giving his home phone number, he may add the somewhat forbidding words, "For Medical Emergencies.")

Such combinations of normal attachments with an abnormal influence on overall well-being are by no means limited to health care. Someone I know, an eminent professor in the physical sciences, found, on taking up a new position, that no colleague in his new department was concerned to deal with the needs of graduate students—more precisely, no colleague except for nontenured ones who lacked the time and power to help. He thought it likely that his replacement if he left would be an irresponsible academic seigneur, on the model of his tenured colleagues. So his attachment to his own research, his wife and his young child had a quite unchosen effect on his capacity to produce good consequences, because of the quite unchosen distinctiveness of his influence over the careers of graduate students. On a consequentialist assessment, he should have taken on every graduate student who applied for his supervision, even if this meant the end of active research and family life, provided that he would still have functioned well enough to add more to total well-being through supervision than he subtracted through detachment. As it happens, he left for another, more humane department, instead. If he thought (as he may have) that detached benefaction to many struggling graduate students would have added slightly more to total well-being over the long run than consequent detachment from research and family would have subtracted, do you think his leaving was morally irresponsible?

So far, I have described nonoptimific acts in which someone might engage on account of certain reasons in her normal motivational structure, arguing that consequentialism lacks resources to explain away the appearance that these acts are not wrong. In addition, we need to consider in detail the exceptional moments in which people scrutinize their motivational structures. This unusual but vitally important phase of self-assessment is an opportunity for consequentialism. Perhaps when we reflect on the special tasks of this phase, the counterfactual test will seem, not just the standard that consequentialism produces, but the right standard to employ. And perhaps proper appreciation of the force of consequentialist reasoning in this phase will lead us to revise our judgment that the nonoptimific acts proceeding from nonoptimific structures were not wrong.

At the same time, the phase of self-assessment can pose a threat to consequentialism. If consequentialism rules out as wrong processes of self-assessment and self-regulation (i.e., self-transformation or its absence) which are not wrong, then this is a serious defect in the theory. And in fact, the theory is defective in this way. In the unusual, but vitally important phase of self-assessment, it requires one to take up an attitude toward oneself that one would not be wrong to refuse.

In his moments of self-assessment, someone who is guided by consequentialist reasoning, Juan, for example, has distinctive wishes and regrets. (In these moments, as opposed to the normal drift, he was supposed to be guided by consequentialist reasoning.) At times of self-assessment, Juan would prefer, if it were feasible, to have a personality that freely floats from one person or project to another, always thriving in the choice which, at the moment, creates the best consequences. If he could acquire this maximally productive motivational flow, he would resolve to do so, at the times when he assesses his normal motivations. His choice of a different source of motivation partly depends on his knowledge of the difficulties of calculating what is for the best. Importantly and independently, his choice also depends on awareness of unavoidable rigidity in his own psychology. Even if the choice of visiting Linda over contributing to OXFAM was not the more productive of good, Juan accepts the motivational structure that produced it because, were his attachment to Linda temporarily weakened enough to allow for the more productive choice, it would not spontaneously revive to the level which would sustain maximal good works in his life as a whole. Juan is, sensibly, aware that one cannot tailor one's motivational set to each occasion, even if one knew which stance of the moment would produce the most good at the moment.

In his moments of self-assessment, Juan ought to regret this rigidity in himself, if consequentialism is valid. He should regard it as an inevitable but unfortunate limitation, as an engineer might regret that an otherwise ideal alloy is brittle. In general, in the phase of self-assessment, Juan regards his own psychology as a machine for producing good consequences, taking any difficulty in freely detaching and attaching to be a defect if it reduces efficiency. This is the attitude entailed by the commitment to directly consequentialist reasoning that the consequentialist argument requires as specially appropriate to self-assessment. But surely it would not be wrong to refuse to take this attitude toward oneself, to refuse to regard one's given attachments to other people and to projects of special concern as just so much rigidity, which must, alas, be used as productively as possible in the service of good effects.

No doubt, one should sometimes be willing to change one's bent for certain impersonal reasons. But one is not wrong not to regret the mere fact of having a bent, and one is not wrong to regard minor possibilities of world improvement as insufficient reasons to change one's bent. In their times of self-assessment, Phil and my friend the scientist are not wrong not to regret that their love for wife and children interferes with fluid engagement with the most good-producing project of any given moment. By the same token, in these times of self-assessment, they are not wrong to regard the creation of a bit more psychic efficiency in producing good as an inadequate basis for setting events in motion that will reduce their attachment to wife and children. Perhaps Phil has reason to believe that if he never takes even one day off, tends shop until after the children have gone to bed and makes himself easily available to those in pharmaceutical need at all hours, his attachment to Lucy and the kids will become bland, while a zealous professional commitment will become central to his personality. Even if he thinks that this self-transformation would make him a more efficient producer of good, he is not wrong to choose not to embark on the project, in the phase of self-assessment.

Of course, consequentialism only prescribes the engineering attitude for a special, occasional phase of one's life, the assessment of how one lives. However, Railton is clearly right to attribute great importance to this phase. Consequentialist or not, a morally responsible person should occasionally stop to consider whether she is living as she ought. And, if rational, she will want to reason directly from valid moral standards, here, to consider whether her life as a whole, including her typical deliberations, is morally well-ordered. So consequentialism's inappropriateness in such deliberations is a serious lack in a moral theory. (In chapter eleven, I will offer my own view of the terms for self-transformation that morality does impose.)

The special phase of self-assessment is important in other ways as well. For one thing, the standing commitment to engage in such self-assessment on appropriate occasions (a commitment that really is part of moral responsibility) has distinctive consequences for one's routine attachments, when it is a commitment to put one's normal motivational structure to the counterfactual test. Juan is not as frighteningly detached as the husband who says to his wife, "I love to do things for you because these acts are the best ways I can add to the happiness of humanity." But Juan, like any husband committed to the counterfactual test, is somewhat detached. He would extinguish his love for Linda and cultivate love for another if that self-transformation were part of a whole process that would make the world as a whole a bit better than he could otherwise make it. Of course, such thoughts do not usually occur to Juan. But they do on the occasions when he assesses his motivational structure to see whether it most effectively promotes his production of good consequences. He has attachments that lead him to do things for Linda's sake only because his structure passes the counterfactual test. It is perfectly standard practice to measure the depth of attachments by the conditions on which they are preserved. For example, a husband who could truly say, in an honest and reflective moment, "I love my wife, but of course, I would tear myself away, divorce her and marry someone else if I ever knew that this would make me a bit happier over the long run" lacks something in the way of marital attachment. The goals that would lead Juan to break his attachment to Linda may excite more admiration, but that does not make his attachment deeper. Perhaps Juan's psychology is not defective. But a moral theory goes wrong when it condemns as defective everyone whose attachments are not as shallow as Juan's.

In addition, the phase of self-assessment is important in showing that a certain tactic of retreat is hopeless for consequentialism. So far, the argument against the consequentialist account of wrongness has been: a consequentialist cannot always deploy her tactic for explaining away the appearance of nonwrongness (namely, "You've confused the act with the motive") because in some cases the motive of the act that seems not to be wrong fails the test that she imposes. It might seem that consequentialism could evade this argument by becoming more modest and imposing no distinctive standard for judging motivating reasons. This modest consequentialism would accept nonconsequentialists' judgments that Phil's motivational structure is all right, but claim that nonconsequentialists are confused in transferring this judgment to Phil's consequent acts.

However, conduct in self-assessment, such as one's embarking on a process of changing oneself, or failing to do so, is also action or inaction, right or wrong. Even if consequentialism is solely concerned with conduct, not character, it imposes judgments here. And it will, in fact, judge as wrong conduct in self-assessment that is not wrong—just as clearly as it is excessive in condemning more routine conduct, and for related reasons. Here, there is no hope of a further appeal to the acceptability of the character, allegedly transferred through confusion to the act. If someone does wrong not to change who he is then the character motivating the decision not to change cannot be morally acceptable.

I have argued that consequentialism is excessive in condemning partialities and the acts to which they lead. Should one go further and condemn consequentialism as recommending psychological self-mutilation? It might seem that the self-detachment of the engineering attitude is just a step removed from self-hatred. But this judgment, I think, would ignore limitations on self-assessment that consequentialism permits, indeed, requires. Like any defensible morality, consequentialism does not require routine probing of one's normal motivations. Self-assessment will be a matter for infrequent quiet moments, life-crises, the spontaneous onset of diffuse moral anxiety, and the onslaught of criticism of the sort of person one is from others whom one respects. This exclusion from the general drift of one's life is the policy with the best consequences, hence, the policy consequentialism will require. In the phase of self-assessment, one does painfully detach from attachments and projects that normally invest one's life with interest. However, in every morally responsible outlook, self-assessment is wrenching, and involves a kind of psychic violence to oneself. Continual engagement in self-assessment, as any responsible outlook describes it, would be moral masochism. Since consequentialism does not require this, the occasional wrenching it requires would not constitute an attitude it would be wrong to take, or one unreasonable for any self-respecting person to take.

The particular version of consequentialism that Railton favors, aggregative act-consequentialist morality, has turned out not to give special attachments their due in the assessment of acts or in deliberations over how to live. However, there are other versions of consequentialism. So we need to consider whether analogous arguments would reveal similar excess there. Among consequentialisms, three kinds of variations are important, in general. However, for present purposes, two make no difference.

First, the criterion of maximum production of good is sometimes applied at the level of rules, not acts, so that the most beneficent set of rules determines wrongness. Though liable to charges of ultimate incoherence, this is, at least, an initially attractive tactic for avoiding troubling conflicts between consequentialism and respect for certain rights, rights whose institution produces the best consequences even though violation might produce the most good in a particular, atypical case. However, when the question is whether consequentialism requires too much suppression of the chooser's personal attachments, both variants are on a par. Before, I argued that Phil need not, on pain of doing what is wrong, do what has the best consequences or set in motion self-transformations having the best consequences, on every relevant particular occasion. If so, then the analogous suppression of personal attachments is also excessive on occasions in which it would be required by conformity to the most beneficent rule for pharmacists in the relevant type of situation. Admittedly, constraints that are beneficently required in a tightly defined type of situation, capturing Phil's predicament, may not be part of the most beneficent rules which make a single prescription for all pharmacists' situations. Still, a rule-consequentialism that yields acceptable judgments of wrongness will have to be quite discriminating, deploying relatively narrow specifications of situations in order to capture the many characteristics that can make a moral difference.

Moreover, when the agent reflects on his or her motives, both consequentialisms will require the engineering attitude, either directed toward the goal of producing the most beneficent motivational system or (perhaps) directed toward the goal of producing the motivational system that leads to the most action in conformity with beneficent rules. It would be incoherent for a rule-consequentialist to be less instrumental than this about her motivational structure, since a motivational structure is itself a kind of canon of rules for deciding. If one is not wrong in choosing to be guided by a system of motives that does not have the best consequences, why is one wrong in choosing to be guided by a system of rules that does not have the best consequences? In the special phase of self-assessment, one is, at it were, legislator, not judge, so that a criterion of producing the best should be applied directly. (The system of motives having the best consequences, here, must be the one having the best consequences in one's own case, for no sane rule-consequentialism would require each individual to fit himself into the single mold of the typical optimific personality.)

In the second place, there are consequentialisms that are not offered as moralities, but rather as standpoints for assessing what ought to be done all told. In such consequentialisms, what ought to be done, morally speaking, and what is morally wrong depend on the further question of what guilt feelings, sanctions or other distinctive phenomena of conscience or enforcement would have the best consequences. Such a consequentialism, though impartial, might force a substantial gap between moral wrongness and wrongness all told. However, the arguments of this section were, at once, objections to consequentialist criteria of wrongness, of moral wrongness, and of what ought not to be done. In assessing the demands of consequentialism on the self, the verdict will be the same, regardless of whether consequentialism is taken to be a moral point of view.

There is, however, one variation in consequentialism that does require further discussion of certain variant consequentialist standards, a discussion that I will postpone until the next section. Not every consequentialism bases choice on a weighted sum of individual impacts. There is a nonaggregative option, at least as old as Moore's *Principia Ethica*, according to which the overall pattern of the total consequences can play an independent role in their goodness, as a whole. Such patterned consequentialisms are liable to the charge that they import standards of assessment only justifiable on grounds that would also permit producing less than the best. Still, certain patterned consequentialisms are less vulnerable than aggregative variants to charges of excessive demands on the self, since a grave self-sacrifice to avoid many small losses in others would not fit the preferred pattern. As it happens, Scheffler's "hybrid" moral theory, the subject of the next section, employs such patterning in its consequentialist part. My argument that his theory does not take account of variations in responsibility will apply, a fortiori, to pure consequentialist demands for creation of maximum good of the patterned kind.

THE AGENT-CENTERED PREROGATIVE

Suppose that whenever morality requires choices that intrude on one's nonmoral concerns, the self-denial is morally required because not enough would otherwise be done to promote overall good, impartially assessed. On this assumption, successful arguments that consequentialism demands too much might lead to either of two conclusions. They might lead to the radical burden lifter's claim that what is morally wrong sometimes is not wrong. But they might be taken to show that morality is not wholly impartial despite its impartial aspect, that it includes an ultimate principle which, by itself, permits one to discriminate in favor of one's special attachments and projects. The principle sets limits to moral condemnation for not having produced enough good overall. This approach is extremely attractive, so far. Admittedly, if the permissive principle is fundamental, it requires abandonment of the claim that morality is impartial. But the idea that morality is impartial, in the sense in question, is, after all, a philosophers' speculation, much less deeply rooted than the conception of morality as the single most important standpoint for assessing wrongness.

In *The Rejection of Consequentialism*, Samuel Scheffler has developed this strategy of permissive amendment of consequentialism in rich and revealing detail. He proposes that the right moral outlook limits the claims of a form of consequentialism through some "agent-centered prerogative." The agent-centered prerogative permits one to choose a course of conduct less productive of overall good than another provided that the shortfall in general beneficence is in less than a specified ratio to the loss of benefits to oneself that would be involved in the more generally beneficent choice.[4] Scheffler does not specify the right ratio, but takes such specification to be an outstanding problem for virtually all nonconsequentialist moral outlooks. He offers "a hybrid view that depart[s] from consequentialism only to the extent of incorporating an agent-centered prerogative of this general type" (p. 21).

Though extremely important, Scheffler's departure from consequentialism is moderate in two ways. First, like the criticisms of consequentialism that I have offered so far, his hybrid theory permits but does not require departures from choices that consequentialism would dictate.

Second, Scheffler's proposal relies entirely on the descriptive apparatus of consequentialism to state the ultimate principles of morality. In his view, consequentialism accurately describes what one should aim at if one's self-interest does not get in the way; true morality only adds a description of the extent to which one may fall short of this target, a description stated in terms of quantities of benefit, just as consequentialism describes the target in terms of a maximization of benefit. (There is one apparent departure from this structure. In a brief remark at the end of a footnote, on p. 23, Scheffler says that a hybrid theory might also take choices incurring special obligations, such as the choice to make a promise, to forfeit the prerogative to give one's interests special weight. This possibility of forfeiture is not mentioned elsewhere, and does not fit the detailed description of hybrid theories that precedes the footnote. Moreover, as we shall see, giving independent moral force to particular responsibilities supports the "agent-centered restrictions" against which Scheffler argues at length. Indeed, some of these arguments would work just as well against the concession about forfeiture. So I will neglect this apparent departure, preparing for my eventual account of moral wrongness by emphasizing the rigidity of the usual amendment to consequentialism. In any case, the kind of forfeiture that Scheffler describes is rigid in ways I will, implicitly, criticize. Either one is entirely protected by the prerogative, or one forfeits it entirely.)

---

[4] See *The Rejection of Consequentialism* (New York: Oxford University Press, 1982), p. 20. Scheffler briefly notes a more demanding variant, here. But he regards it as less plausible and the difference would not affect my subsequent criticisms.

Relying as it does on the same descriptive apparatus as consequentialism, the hybrid theory is a minimal departure from consequentialism. This is one reason why it is a good first example of a nonimpartial morality.[5]

The adequacy of the agent-centered prerogative in a hybrid theory will depend on the nature of the consequentialism with which it is combined. Combined with an aggregative consequentialism of Railton's sort, any otherwise acceptable agent-centered prerogative will be too demanding. On any acceptable view of the limits of self-concern, it would be irresponsible of Phil the pharmacist not to tolerate occasional disruption of his personal life to provide for strangers in the throes of an emergency such as angina pectoris suffered without medical relief. But if only the ratio of general sacrifice to self-sacrifice counts and if the general benefit forgone is just an aggregate of appropriately weighted goods, then the same ratio might be exceeded because Phil insists on taking an occasional weekend off, an important basis for enjoyment of family in his circumstances, while many people would suffer from unrelieved mild heat rash as a consequence. The individually mild heat rashes would add up to the intolerable sacrifice of well-being.

However, Scheffler rejects aggregative consequentialism as misidentifying the appropriate ranking of overall consequences. He is receptive to an alternative according to which the better of two states of affairs is always the one in which the worst-off are better-off. But he eventually suggests that numbers should be given somewhat more importance than such a theory allows. In determining which state of affairs is better, one should (he thinks) give more weight to the well-being of the worst-off than a purely aggregative comparison would, while according them less than absolute priority. (See pp. 26f., 31.) In the previous example, the stress on Phil's family life would make him a more afflicted person than someone who occasionally suffers mild heat rash without pharmaceutical relief. So, given Scheffler's preferred version of consequentialism, an otherwise defensible prerogative could, it seems, permit Phil his vacation, unless an enormous number of people depend on Phil for relief of mild afflictions. How many is quite unclear since the degree of favoritism toward the worst-off is unspecified, as is the permitted ratio of overall loss to agent's loss. Still, it is plausible, in this and every other particular case, that both the positions of individuals and the numbers of those in each position should be taken into account, with considerable but nonabsolute favoritism toward the worst-off. After all, it is, at least, debatable whether Phil could, responsibly, go on vacation if he knew that, by some fluke, a million people would suffer mild heat rash that his shopkeeping would avoid.

[5] More precisely, the hybrid theory is a nonimpartial morality if the agent-centered prerogative is an ultimate principle, or in any case does not rest on some deeper, impartial principle applied to relevant facts about choice. I won't make this assumption when I criticize the hybrid view in this section. But it is useful to entertain this possibility, as one way in which morality could prove to be nonimpartial.

Still, something has been left out. The impacts measured against self-sacrifice are now (primarily) impacts on representative worst-affected individuals. These are not individual impacts summed up without reference to distribution among persons—but still, only impact counts, not the chooser's
relationships to those affected by her choice or the chooser's role in producing
the impact in the particular case at hand. This is why the prerogative is conceptually homogeneous with the consequentialism it amends, and why it
gives a false account of wrongness.

The extent of someone's options to produce less than the best without doing wrong depends on her relationships to others and on her past choices, not
just on ratios of impacts. If Phil occasionally goes on a brief vacation although
he cannot find a substitute, and posts a sign that he is available after hours
just "for medical emergencies," someone will eventually die who would not if
Phil were a beneficent workaholic. Some meek person who really should get
a refill at midnight will disastrously postpone the request until morning, hoping that the pains are a false alarm. During one of Phil's brief vacations, someone won't be able to locate the distant drugstore that is open, or won't get the
distant delivery in time. Still, Phil does no wrong in protecting his family life
in these ways if his situation is of the sort I have assumed: he did not know he
would become so uniquely important, he tried and failed to hire a competent
assistant, and he keeps generous, though not unlimited hours.

Suppose, however, that a pharmacist's history though much the same as
Phil's were different in certain ways. This pharmacist, Frank, set up shop
knowing that the only other drugstore in the county would soon close. When
he became unique, he chose not to place a help-wanted ad for a competent
assistant because he just wouldn't be comfortable running that kind of drugstore. He keeps mere nine-to-five hours, just as he did when he was not
unique. A decision to go on vacation that was not wrong in light of the history sketched in the last paragraph could now be wrongful self-indulgence
even if the ratio of general sacrifice to self-sacrifice involved in the decision
were no greater. Unlike Phil, Frank knowingly entered into a situation in
which people would become specially dependent on him and took no special
measures to provide for their special needs for his help. So, when he considers
whether to take a vacation, he owes his customers more consideration than
he otherwise would. But this is not to say that impact ratios govern a kind of
lifelong moral bank account in which one may store up self-sacrifice for others
to maintain the permissible ratio of sacrificed general benefit to self-sacrifice.
Phil wouldn't make the occasional burglary all right by being a sufficiently
self-sacrificing pharmacist. Rather, the wrongness of a particular choice depends in part on the chooser's relationships to those affected and so depends
in part on whether the chooser has done enough to create sufficient credit
within those relationships (a medicine-provider's relationship to specially dependent customers, for example).

Note that the hybrid theory is too close to consequentialism to excuse the decision to go on vacation on the grounds that Frank's total absence from the scene would be even worse than his interrupted presence. Contributing to overall goodness is supposed to be morally obligatory when the impact ratio is exceeded, regardless of whether in doing less one would still make a contribution.

Similarly, it can make a difference in the judgment of Phil's present acts what he has announced to others in the past—for example, whether he has or has not posted a sign on the pharmacy door saying "for prescriptions outside of store hours" and giving his home number. If he has, he might still do no wrong in putting off callers with certain trivial requests. But whatever the impact ratio is above which he is wrong not to comply with a request once he has posted the sign, it is lower than the ratio which is the moral threshold if he has not posted the sign. Posting the sign makes it harder not to do wrong by answering the same telephoned request with the same, "For something like that, you'd better just stop by Monday morning."—Note that it need not be true that the person responding to the posted sign has lost something extra, a valuable opportunity to seek help elsewhere if Phil tells him to wait until Monday morning. Perhaps there was no chance of getting a prescription filled elsewhere. Still, the presence or absence of an announced undertaking makes a moral difference.

In these criticisms of the hybrid theory, I have assumed that the theory describes what someone should aim at, in choosing, and judges actions in light of the chooser's aim. But really, this much concern for intentions is arbitrary in such a theory. If someone need only consider impact-ratios in monitoring his moral responsibilities, then only facts about actual impacts should determine when someone has avoided wrongdoing. Even if Phil made up a prescription while drunk, substituting a high dosage of barbiturates by mistake, he will have done no wrong if, through a further accident, the pills were put out in the garbage before any were taken. This is the sort of blindness to everything other than consequences that gives pure, aggregative consequentialism a bad name.

In general, the wrongness of not taking the interests of others into account depends on one's responsibility to be concerned with their well-being, a responsibility that depends in turn on one's relationships to those people, how they were acquired and how they have evolved. (Of course, such relationships do not always involve personal acquaintance, and one can have responsibilities to others just as fellow persons, responsibilities that are not so much acquired as entailed by one's being a person.) In the fulfillment of these responsibilities, there is a typical, rough relationship between potential drain on the agent and potential threat to those she might let down which can obscure the role of choice and history, rather as other typical relationships between self-interest and the general welfare encouraged overemphasis on Railton's counterfactual test. Roughly, typically and all else being equal, the greater the losses that others would suffer if one did not live up to a responsibility, the greater the minimal loss to oneself on account of which the obligations involved would cease to be binding. Less is at stake for others in Phil's obligation to be available late at night than in his obligation to put the right pills in the right vials. Relatively moderate losses for Phil might be the reason why the first obligation does not bind. But it is hard to imagine the personal stakes that would justify letting customers down in the second way. This rough and typical correlation of the two kinds of seriousness might suggest that moral wrongness is governed by a single impact ratio. However, moral responsibility is also governed, sometimes importantly so, by past choices and particular relationships.

Scheffler does not argue against this view of responsibility. (Indeed, there is the passing remark about forfeiting the prerogative by taking on obligations.) But an argument to the contrary is implied by his extensive criticism of agent-centered restrictions, rules that would, at least on some occasions, prohibit acts with the best overall consequences. It is virtually certain that some agent-centered restrictions will be valid if responsibilities depend, from case to case, on particular relationships and histories, apart from impact-ratios. The responsibilities one acquires are often responsibilities to particular people or groups of people, not responsibilities to all humankind. If those responsibilities can make it wrong to act in one's self-interest, they might make it wrong to do what has the best consequences all told, because of what one would do to those for whose welfare one is specially responsible. Conversely, arguments against agent-centered restrictions cast doubt on the existence of responsibilities which are not the product of a goal of overall benevolence and a general loss-ratio describing permissible shortfall.

Much of Scheffler's criticism of agent-centered restrictions is an illuminating argument against any effort to base such a restriction on the badness of what happens when it is violated. Scheffler points out that an agent-centered restriction must require nonviolation of the boundary it describes in some cases in which what happens through nonviolation would be worse than what happens in violation. Otherwise there would be no restriction of consequentialism. Such a restriction can hardly be justified by appealing to the badness of violating it.—However, this argument establishes, at most, that one justification for an agent-centered restriction is closer to consequentialism than consistency permits. A partisan of an agent-centered restriction says that it is wrong to violate certain rules, but should not say that every violation brings so much badness into the world that it is wrong for that reason.

Scheffler's further criticism seems to be that, once it is detached from rationales based on disvalue, an agent-centered restriction, in contrast to an agent-centered prerogative, would be too superficial to have moral authority.[6]

---

[6] See, for example, p. 128, where he speaks of the restrictions as inevitably appearing "arbitrary and unmotivated" because of the absence of a rationale.

But both the contrast between prerogative and restriction and the underlying moral epistemology are invalid.

Scheffler says, of the agent-centered *prerogative*, that it is justifiable as one rational response to the difference between concern for one's own interests and the detached standpoint in which one impartially assesses the goodness of what one does: "the prerogative . . . embodies a rational strategy for taking account of personal independence, given one construal of that aspect of persons" (p. 67). It is not, he thinks, the only rational response, since consequentialists can, alternatively, accept the actual psychological difference, insist that the personal standpoint only has moral relevance in proportion to its contribution to overall good, and explore the reasons why special attention to one's own interests does, often, contribute to the production of good.

At least as much can be said in support of agent-centered restrictions. The belief that there are some such restrictions (recall that Scheffler only claims, without specification, that there is some prerogative) is one rational response to the contrast between respect for another person and willingness to interfere with her life to promote goals that are not hers. According to an agent-centered restriction, one sometimes fails to express adequate respect for another in interfering with her life in a way that creates the most overall good; adequate respect for a person is fundamentally different from a commitment to an impartial comparison of impacts on her with impacts on others in the production of overall benefit. Consequentialism, of course, requires another construal of respect for persons, according to which morally adequate respect for a person simply consists of counting benefits to her on a par with benefits to others in impartially creating overall good. So far, prerogative and restriction are equally grounded.

If previous arguments are right, we can say something more of permission not to create the best consequences overall. The vast majority of those who rationally reflect on relevant examples will respond in this anti-consequentialist way. The same can be said of the considerations about responsibility and its absence that I offered in opposition to Scheffler's way of specifying such permission. And the same can be said of certain agent-centered restrictions. Scheffler's arguments certainly leave this possibility intact.

Admittedly, nothing would make it unreasonable for a fully informed consequentialist to respond to examples involving interference, or differences in acquired responsibility, in a consequentialist way. So the underlying issue of moral authority may be the one confronted in the first part of this book. One can be in a position to make moral truth-claims in the absence of a rationale that would persuade all others if they were sufficiently rational and well-informed. One is in such a position if one's judgments express capacities to tell the difference between right and wrong—capacities whose status as means of detection may rationally be denied by others responding to one's own data.

Common, stable and well-entrenched judgments entail the existence of agent-centered restrictions (as Scheffler readily acknowledges). To take some well-worn examples, if the framing and flamboyant punishment of an innocent person would improve the world a little on balance, by intimidating violent criminals, most would think it wrong to do so. Most would think it wrong to improve the world a little on balance by lying to someone to prevent the occurrence of two other lies of no greater seriousness. These judgments express a kind of respect for others in their autonomy which is not the same as a high valuation of the goodness of their autonomy. The judgments are true because they are expressions of that attitude (by people who are relevantly reflective and informed). The attitude is a source of insight.

Of course, it is also a result of the subject's upbringing. But the upbringing is, or could be, of a truth-producing kind. For example, such respect arises from cooperation with others in which all seek to advance their self-interest through interactions in which others voluntarily participate, without acquiescence based on others' superior coercive power. To be the person whom one wants to seem to be in such interactions, one becomes disinclined to coerce or deceive similarly disinclined cooperators. And one's basic comfort with one's self comes to depend, to a significant extent, on being the person whom one wants to seem to be. The respect for others to which this process gives rise need not be measured by the badness one attributes to the phenomena of coercion or interference. For that total disvalue might be reduced, among all affected directly and indirectly, when one coerces or deceives a cooperator to create a link in a causal chain reducing such coercion and deception overall. A cooperative process in which each seeks to live up to others' expectations of nonmanipulation is different from one in which each seeks to create the best effects among all affected. The imposition of agent-centered restrictions depends on the characterization of the former process as more apt to give rise to moral insight than the latter.

The connections between responsibility and wrongness that led to the rejection of the hybrid theory imply a similar characterization of certain origins as insight-enhancing. For someone who makes those connections, commitments and attachments previously acquired partly determine whether a loss is an object of guilt or, alternatively, an object of mere regret. Past choices determine the bases for self-reproach, so that one's responsibilities do not reduce in the final analysis to one responsibility concerned with the production of overall good. Such an outlook is apt to result from cooperation in which people rely on expectations created by others. Either being let down or being subjected to unpredictable demands is a burden in such interactions. To reduce both excesses, people cooperating in this way will give a special role to expectations on the part of others which are based on one's particular actions toward them. Such initiatives are means by which people can be held to account, but means that are subject to their voluntary control as general responsibilities to everyone are not. The truth of the more particularistic view of responsibility that conflicts with the hybrid theory is based on the fact that the molding of judgment through cooperation involving individually created expectations is more insight-enhancing than engagement in interactions in which the only reliable expectation is that everyone will work for the overall good.

Perhaps, however, Scheffler's dismissal of agent-centered restrictions does not depend on universalism concerning moral justification, but on a certain view of the balance of epistemic virtues that should be pursued in the assessment of moral theories. A theory describing a target of overall production of the best and specifying an agent-centered prerogative to fall short will provide a simpler definite account of wrongness than one which insists on agent-centered restrictions, restrictions which will have to be tailored to various specific properties of actions. In the absence of a further, general rationale for preferring the restrictions, it might seem that the preservation of convictions about individual cases will not be a strong enough reason for maintaining the less simple or vaguer account.

Presumably, this assessment would be based on an alleged parallel with good judgment in scientific theorizing. For it cannot be a general, fundamental rule that the simple, definite and well-rationalized ought to triumph no matter what the consequences for particular cases. But the actual practice of good judgment in science does not impose a corresponding balance of epistemic virtues. Often, the better theory complicates the explanatory apparatus and has no underlying rationale independent of the need to explain given particular facts in need of explanation. For almost a century, Darwinian evolutionary theory, though better than creative force theory, was more complex and lacked a foundation because of the relative underdevelopment of genetics. In relativity theory, spatiotemporal description is complicated and regulated by electrodynamic principles that are taken as fundamental, where prerelativistic physics had sought to explain them in turn. In quantum mechanics, all explanation of spatiotemporal phenomena is based on complications of principles of analytic mechanics which, before the quantum revolution, were taken to be useful theorems explained by yet simpler classical axioms.[7]

The standards of epistemic judgment required for the rejection of agent-centered restrictions and particular responsibilities correspond to common philosophical stereotypes of rational scientific practice, not to the real thing. Yet once these restrictions and particularities are admitted, we can no longer use the conceptual repertoire of consequentialism to describe the way in which consequentialism demands too much of the self. It is time, then, to

---

[7] Indeed, the formal simplicity which would be reduced by agent-centered restrictions and particularist responsibilities has no importance, as such, in the confirmation of scientific theories. The arguments for this drastic devaluing of formal simplicity, which I sketched in chapter 2, are developed in much more detail in *Fact and Method*, chapter 5.

consider the main current project of deriving all moral requirements from a
basic principle whose concepts and structures lie outside the consequentialist
repertoire. This alternative is contractualism.

Don't Be Unreasonable

A moral theory might be called "contractualist" if it bases considerations on
an ultimate demand that interactions be governed by terms that no participant would have reason to reject if she were appropriately situated and had
an appropriate interest in cooperation. Perhaps there are contractualisms that
are consequentialist, even utilitarian, because their specification of the interest in cooperation is so collective or because the preferred interest in cooperation so quickly and obviously yields an all-embracing consequentialist standard. Rather than insisting on an understanding of "cooperation" that
excludes these possibilities, I will simply note that consequentialism has already been criticized and that other versions of contractualism certainly exist.
Some of those versions, including Rawls', are offered as an account of justice
in institutions, not as general accounts of moral wrongness. But moral wrongness in general is our present topic, and contractualism may be inadequate
here, even if it provides an adequate account of justice. (Indeed, this chapter,
combined with the middle chapters, will argue for this ambivalent judgment,
at least so far as major political choices in advanced industrial societies are
concerned.) Finally, I have argued against contractualisms based on bargaining that fully reflects the bargainers' actual resources. Adequate terms of moral
assessment need not be the terms to which all would agree in fully prudent
and fully informed deliberations reflecting the actual resources of all, for such
deliberation would sometimes be tainted by prudent reliance on inequalities
of coercive power and other irrelevant advantages.

Scanlon's account of moral wrongness is representative of the most powerful work in the contractualist territory that remains. In addition, Scanlon
intentionally chooses an abstract formulation, subject to further controversial
specifications. So I will devote further discussion of the contractualist alternative almost entirely to his account. After some preliminary distinctions, I
will argue that a formalist construal that his discussion invites would be an
impartial morality of a nonconsequentialist kind, and would sometimes be
unresponsive to the moral force of personal attachments. Then, I will argue
that his emphasis on social coordination is bound to create inaccuracies in
the overall account of moral wrongness, even in a kind of hybrid variant,
which adds constraints of character to the formal constraints. Then, in the
rest of this chapter, I will develop an alternative to the quasi-legislative model
of the discernment of moral wrongness characterizing both contractualism
and consequentialism. Morality, on this view, is not impartial, and it is always
wrong to violate its demands.

Scanlon sets out this "account of the nature of moral wrongness": "An act is wrong if its performance under the circumstances would be disallowed by any system of rules for the general regulation of behavior which no one could reasonably reject as a basis for informed, unforced general agreement."[8] This proposal is especially attractive because it seems implicit in the deliberations of morally responsible people, with no prior philosophical commitment, who are concerned to avoid wrongdoing. It seems to capture these concerns without grounding them in a requirement to promote the most good or reducing the limits of responsibility to an agent-centered prerogative in Scheffler's sense.

Someone concerned to avoid doing wrong is concerned with complaints that might be made by someone else who is adversely affected. If one's choice makes someone else worse-off than she would have been if one had chosen another alternative, one wants there to be features of the choice to which the other would want to appeal in justifying similar choices of hers in the face of potential complaints of others. One wants to be able to say, "I know that you have reason to wish that I had done otherwise in this particular case. But you also have reason to take these features of what I did as generally justifying an action in the face of complaints."

Of course, each of us has a rich repertoire of justifying features to which we appeal, usually without giving thought to any general account of moral wrongness. However, in unfamiliar, specially problematic choices, the deliberations of a morally responsible person might conform more explicitly to Scanlon's statement of the basic requirement. Thus, in agonizing over our initial deep problem about friendship and spying, George might find it important that the imperiled strangers also have interests in friendship which would make them want to be free of a requirement always to divulge evidence of a friend's wrongdoing. A policy of reporting every clue to a friend's having committed a traffic violation or evaded taxes would lose friends. Also, general participation in ratting on friends would make it hard to find and sustain relations with the openness of friendship. Still, the potential victims of the secrecy at hand have other interests as potential victims of major crimes. George's moral task seems to be the identification of a rationale for imposing a certain threshold for disclosure which satisfies a certain combination of interests: the interest as potential loser of friendship and the interest as potential crime victim of everyone with the desire for free self-regulation on the basis of general rules. George's moral responsibility might lead him to rehearse, in his mind, arguments that might be offered to those whom he might hurt, thought of as a kind of moral jury, appealing to their interests both as victims and as friends. In trying to construct an adequate case, he might seem to be guided by Scanlon's standard, in which an act is wrong if and only if it is

---

[8] "Contractualism and Utilitarianism," p. 110.

excluded by every system of rules that no one could reasonably reject as a basis for informed, unforced general agreement.

The most pressing choices in interpreting Scanlon's proposal might be stimulated by the worry that this requirement is ridiculously lax, since a sufficiently selfish person, rationally responding to full information, would reject any morally plausible principle out of preference for informed, unforced general agreement to rules grossly biased in his favor. If I am sufficiently selfish, a rational response to full information might lead me to reject any normal system of rules in favor of one requiring preferential treatment for those whose last name starts with the letter "M."—Different construals of Scanlon's proposal might be classified as responding to this concern in different ways. The most important differences for present purposes will roughly correspond to different senses that sometimes attach to "reasonable" and "unreasonable" in ordinary usage.

One response, which sometimes seems to be Scanlon's, identifies the relevant reasonable rejections with a rational, fully informed preference for means to the end of informed, unforced agreement on rules for the regulation of behavior among people assumed all to desire that end and to desire it to the same degree. In the crucial choices, one addresses oneself solely to the goal of finding terms to regulate behavior on which all could agree, if all were free from coercion, ignorance and irrationality and each had a motivational set meeting a certain constraint. The motivational constraint imposed is simply the equally intense desire, on the part of all, to achieve that very goal of regulation by agreement. So long as terms of cooperation are a means of achieving that cooperative goal whose effectiveness does not depend on anyone's specially intense desire to achieve it, rejection of those terms could not be based on any morally legitimate interest.

I will speak of this construal of Scanlon's proposal as "formal," because it prescribes general epistemic virtue in pursuit of a goal fully specified in general terms that are not, individually, intrinsically moral. Given the goal, the reasonableness in reasonable rejections consists of rationality and adequate information. It is the property one ascribes to reasonable beliefs and reasonable strategies. In some passages, Scanlon appears to endorse the formal interpretation (see especially p. 111). Certainly, he does not transgress it. And his most specific finding about reasonable rejection would be supported by it. He says it would be reasonable to reject terms under which one would suffer great hardships if an available alternative would remove this burden without imposing a comparable burden on anyone else. This finding could be derived from the consideration that the goal is unforced general agreement based on everyone's equally intense desire for such agreement. In the circumstance that Scanlon describes, the potential victim's rejection of the proposed rules reflects unwillingness to accept greater sacrifices than others in order to bring about general unforced agreement. Such unwillingness would not be incompatible with a desire for such agreement as great as the others', but no greater. The potential victim just lacks special zeal to sacrifice in the interests of cooperation. So she can rationally reject the unbalanced arrangement in favor of alternatives that would be bases for unforced general agreement if the constraint of equal cooperative desire were satisfied. (Even more obviously, Ms. Smith could reasonably reject my Rule of "M," since the different strains of commitment of Smiths and Millers make it an inferior basis for regulation by unforced, informed general agreement based on equally intense cooperative desire.)

Formal contractualism is impartial. Its impartiality is not so obvious as consequentialism's, because strains of commitment are fundamentally important and such strains, in actuality, reflect special attachments and projects unconcerned with general cooperation or the common good. Still, in formal contractualism, the ultimately decisive rejections and acceptances are made from a standpoint detached from anyone's particular motivational set, even as corrected by the constraint of equal cooperative desire. And this detached standpoint for acceptance and rejection is impartial.

This detachment and impartiality are necessary because the decisive choices are solely directed at a goal of cooperation among people who are not themselves solely concerned with this goal. In formal contractualism, preferences are important at two levels, an upper level at which one considers whether rules could rationally be rejected by any informed person whose desires meet the motivational constraint, and a ground level, providing inputs for the upper-level decisions, consisting of the given desires of individuals. Both levels are essential to determining what is morally wrong, but the lower level only provides data for the upper, data which is assessed at the upper level in an impartial way.

The ground-level fact that one is actually concerned with this or that goal different from general unforced agreement helps to determine what actions are wrong. This is how formal contractualism avoids extreme conservatism in spite of the emphasis on agreement. For if all goals besides general unforced agreement were entirely discounted, any ongoing, effective system of rules for the regulation of behavior, however vicious, would be endorsed, on the grounds that the desires that would otherwise sustain rational rejection are illegitimately disruptive: if every dissenter would suppress the desires leading to dissent, regulation by general unforced agreement would be achieved. Noncooperative desires at the ground level must have some force, or else formal contractualism tells victims to be Uncle Tom on pain of immorality.

On the other hand, one's ultimate judgment of a system of rules must not balance its value as promoting one's desire for general unforced agreement against noncooperative ends. If I accept that a system of rules is as good a way as any under the circumstances equally to induce cooperation by all, it won't do for me to reject it, nonetheless, because I care for fine wines as well as

cooperation. So there must be another level at which the authoritative rejecting and accepting is done, a level of social design at which I solely pursue
the goal of unforced general agreement, looking down on a population including myself who are all assumed to have an equal desire to achieve this
goal, but as one goal among others. This is the morally authoritative upper
level.

Choice at the authoritative level, where arrangements are relevantly rejected as a basis for general agreement, is the same for all, and this standpoint
is detached from anyone's particular attachments and projects. At this level,
my interests are relevant to my deliberations in the same way as anyone else's,
as potential sources of strain which must not lead to violations of the requirement that equally intense cooperative desire be a sufficient basis for general
agreement. Since deliberations at the upper level are decisive, formal contractualism is impartial.

Admittedly, formal contractualism readily contributes to the justification
of derived principles according to which people may favor intimates over
strangers. When special attachments would create strains of commitment to
rules under consideration, this fact is given weight. So partial attachments are
not dismissed. But neither were they dismissed from the standpoint of consequentialist impartiality, which gives weight to any special causal role of partial
attachments in the production of good. Also, because they generate strains of
commitment that ought to be taken into account, the existence, at ground
level, of partial attachments will almost certainly result in the exclusion of
some rules which would otherwise disallow courses of conduct. But just by
itself the formal demand does not guarantee permissiveness toward favoritism.
So, formal contractualism is impartial. What one can say is that formal contractualism is an impartial standard on the basis of which it is relatively easy
to permit acts that sacrifice some overall good to special attachments. If the
latter consideration were used to distinguish the nonimpartial from the impartial, formal contractualism would not be an impartial standpoint. Yet the
criterion that I have been using, the absence of intrinsic permission to play
favorites in the basic moral premise, is not arbitrary in our larger project of
assessing the burdens of conscience. For only this broader impartiality might
plausibly be taken as characterizing all morality (not just consequentialist morality), and then used in a plausible argument that what is morally wrong is
not always wrong.

So much for formal readings of Scanlon's contractualism (i.e., of his initial
statement connecting moral wrongness with general unforced agreement).
The nonformal construals that I will mainly consider make the relevant reasonable rejections partly depend on motivational constraints that are not derivable from the requirement of a desire for unforced, informed agreement on
terms of cooperation among all who share this desire and have it with equal
intensity. I will call these versions of contractualism "character-based."

It might seem that a character-based account is not so much an alternative construal of Scanlon's statement about moral wrongness as an amendment to it. The sentence speaks of systems of rules "which no one could reasonably reject as a basis for informed, unforced general agreement" and, it might be thought, character-based treatments of wrongness require an amendment specifying instead that no one of such and such a kind could reasonably reject the rules as a basis for such agreement. But in fact, in perfectly literal though nonphilosophical talk, the most frequent understanding of the reasonableness of rejections and acceptances itself refers to the character expressed, without any commitment to further derivation from a formal account. This linguistic fact is philosophically important since formal contractualism might have more appeal than it deserves, on account of confusion between formal reasonableness and character-based reasonableness.

Someone who is unreasonable in accepting or rejecting proposed terms for assessing interactions is—on the most common construal—either too demanding or too intolerant of demands in others. Either he is less than minimally responsible in insisting that others acquiesce in his pursuit of advantage ("I'll play that radio AS LOUD AS I WANT") or he insists that others concede what they could assert without irresponsibility ("I don't care about your having to go to work, Mommy, YOU PROMISED"). The two excesses often come to the same thing, but not always—as when someone makes unreasonably severe demands on another not in excessive pursuit of her own advantage but in the interest of a third party ("You should pay her those five dollars with interest, even though she loaned you the taxi fare twenty years ago").

These distinctions between reasonable and unreasonable responses to proposed terms are, at least in the first instance, judgments of the character expressed in the choice. Unreasonable rejections express someone's being an unreasonable person, here, and the difference between an unreasonable and a reasonable person is primarily a matter of one-sidedness as opposed to balance. In old-fashioned language that emphasizes the priority of appropriate concerns over cognitive merit in this understanding of reasonableness, one might speak of the reasonable person as a person of good will. Alternatively, one might say that the standard for reasonableness, here, is the inclinations (i.e., the rational and informed inclinations) of a morally responsible person—provided it is understood that such a person would not insist on arrangements requiring more than minimal moral responsibility from others.

One learns what a reasonable person (i.e., a person of good will) is like through the variety of examples, warnings, punishments, praises and quite specific reasons that flow one's way as others teach one, or try to teach one, to be such a person. In late twentieth-century households in the United States, "You've got to cooperate," "Don't let him tell you what to do," "A promise is a promise," "Don't be stubborn," "Live and let live," and "You can't let him get away with that" are characteristic terms of instruction in this perplexing process.

Perhaps the understanding of reasonableness in interaction that one acquires, if all goes well, can be fully reconstructed on the basis of a formal principle. But perhaps not. If not, then the most common understanding of "reasonable rejection" produces a nonformal, character-based reading of Scanlon's account of moral wrongness. Whether this account is an impartial morality will depend on the nature of the constraints on relevant motivational systems. In the authoritative judgments of rule-systems as bases for unforced general agreement one imposes nonformal standards of morally legitimate interest on the motivational systems of potential cooperators. In other words, one excludes some rejections as irrelevant even though they are compatible with a goal of unforced general agreement with others equally desirous of such agreement. Perhaps the fundamental means for distinguishing relevant from irrelevant bases for rejection themselves permit favoritism toward intimates as a basis for such refusal. For example, rejection based on a desire specially to further the interests of one's friends might be counted as a relevant obstacle to general unforced agreement even though rejections reflecting the same amount of frustration and imposing no heavier burdens on others are not given such importance. If so, then the basic principles for distinguishing what is morally wrong from what isn't entail that favoritism toward friends is not always wrong. Contractualism is no longer impartial.

Though contractualism can rely on fundamental norms of character and still be worthy of the name, character-based contractualism is an unstable compound. The greater the reliance on motivational constraints other than the cooperative desire, the less the importance of the interest in cooperation in determining moral wrongness. At the furthest limit, moral wrongness is identified with disallowance by any system of rules that no morally responsible person could reject as a basis for informed, unforced general agreement. If the requirement of responsibility is not itself derived from a required cooperative desire, then the account of moral wrongness is extremely close to this: what is morally wrong is disallowed by any system of *self*-regulation that no morally responsible person could reject on the basis of rationality and full information. The crucial rejections in the latter account will be concerned with whether everyone capable of moral self-restraint should constrain his or her conduct in certain ways. However, this attention to people in general does not express an interest in cooperation, as such. It expresses a responsible person's awareness that she is not so special as to deserve freedom from the total basic system of constraints which others who are capable of self-regulation ought to impose on themselves. A commitment not to be so special is different from an interest in cooperation—though, of course, cooperation is an important subject of responsible choice. So once one crosses the line to the rule of responsible self-regulation (just the shift that I will eventually advocate), one's outlook is no longer worth calling "contractualist."

A third and final construal deserves a brief mention, since, through confusion, it can add unearned plausibility to the others. When moral wrongness is at issue, the rejection of proposed arrangements may be condemned as unreasonable just because it reflects an inability to tell right from wrong. Thus, someone convinced by arguments about social freedom in previous chapters of this book might characterize as unreasonable the rejection of a bill of rights in the choice of a constitution. Anyone who insists that such direct intrusion of the moral into judgments of reasonableness must be muddled should consider the fundamental role of the inability to tell right from wrong in the most common standard for insanity in Anglo-American criminal law. Deploying the third usage, one could convert Scanlon's proposal into a pronouncement that an act is morally wrong if it is disallowed by any system of rules whose rejection, by someone concerned with moral wrongness, would reflect a lack of insight into moral wrongness. Of course, no one would actually offer such an utterly unhelpful pronouncement as an account of moral wrongness. Only confident prior discernment of the moral wrongness of an act could support confidence that it falls under this pronouncement. Still, this tautologous connection between moral wrongness and "reasonable rejection" in one usage should warn us not to make too much of the ring of truth in Scanlon's formulation. The most securely true version is no account of moral wrongness at all.

NORMAL RESPONSIBILITY

Now that the options for contractualism have been distinguished, I will try to show that the contractualist account should be abandoned. First, I will argue that formal contractualism sometimes prohibits acts that are not wrong because of its impartial constraint on morally legitimate interests. Then, I will argue that character-based contractualism, despite its additional nonimpartial aspects, sets inaccurate limits on wrongness because it retains emphasis on cooperation that is artificial in a general account of moral wrongness.

In developing criteria of moral wrongness, formal contractualism must allow that any set of desires is a potential source of veto, provided that the desires are not intrinsically anti-cooperative. Its means of developing a definite morality in the face of this abundance is an impartial standard in social design: principles are only given moral force if they could serve as a basis for general, informed agreement if everyone had an equally intense desire for regulation by general, informed agreement. Because of its equal treatment of detached but demanding systems of desires, this impartial standard could impose morally excessive burdens on individuals whose concerns for particular people are robust.

Suppose that I am about to leave home to keep office hours when my son [supposing I had one] calls up from California. He is distraught (though not suicidal). His girlfriend has just left him and he urgently wants my friendly ear. "Do you really have to keep your office hour?" he pleads. It is the third week of the semester, and I have no particular reason to believe that any student of mine faces an imminent hard assignment, important judgment or crucial life-choice. The sort of student to whom I would hope to make excuses, if he asked me, next day, where I had been during office hours, would certainly understand.

But what about the sort of rigid and dour student who makes the late 'sixties glow all the brighter in my memories? My imagined dialogue with him does not go so well, since he might respond, "To me it is extremely important to be able to rely on the word of others, including such implicit but definite promises as posted office hours. Because of this interest in reliability, I would gladly share exacting principles forbidding promise-breaking even when otherwise important opportunities are foreclosed. No doubt, I wouldn't sacrifice everything for the keeping of a promise. But, if others were similarly willing, I would accept the disruption you avoided to a relation as close as yours is to your son. I would accept this cost so that general agreement would guarantee the reliability of promises no more important than yours to keep that office hour." The Grim Student's concern for reliability is that great, and his interests in personal attachments and surprising opportunities are relatively small.

Given his one-sided interests in life, the Grim Student has reason to reject, as a basis for general regulation, a system of rules permitting me the half-hour chat providing support in a crisis for someone I love while breaching my office hours during the least eventful week in the semester. My interests in life give me reason to reject such rigid rules in favor of others, more accepting of the unpredictable demands of intimacy. Formal contractualism responds to these ground-level desires by constructing rules whose acceptance by everyone would impose equal strains of commitment on each. In rejecting a system of rules of this kind, each of us is relevantly unreasonable, violating the universally ascribed cooperative goal.

This standard could perfectly well rule out my mild help to my son. Just suppose that the Grim Student is so rigid and remote that the strain on him in accepting general regulation by any system permitting my promise-breaking is greater than the strain on others less rigid and remote (including me) in accepting a more austere system. Reliance on equally intense cooperative desire is satisfied by adopting a system, prohibiting my mild, compassionate promise-breaking, that brings the Grim Student on board. But surely, these demographics of strain do not establish the moral wrongness of my listening to my son.

In response, a formal contractualist might attach moral significance to the fact that some interests are typical, some not, through a quasi-political understanding of the goal of unforced general agreement. The Grim Student is an eccentric. In this, he may well resemble other troubling people with diametrically opposed peculiarities, for example, the blithest spirit, who wants freedom to respond to every opportunity and really is willing to grant others this freedom. If they have morally legitimate interests, the eccentric are supposed to want general unforced agreement, just as much as the typical do, and (the argument goes) this desire may make it unreasonable for them not to favor the typical. They must acknowledge, after all, that pervasive strains of commitment threaten more extensive departures from general unforced agreement than strains on the part of a few eccentrics. So they will not reasonably reject arrangements that are accommodating to standard sets of desires.

This argument is tempting because a similar neglect of the highly atypical is compatible with justice in the provision of benefits by institutions. No system of institutions can be of precisely equal net benefit to all, regardless of differences in systems of desires. In political choices, it would be disastrous for all if each were committed even to approach as near as possible to that ideal of precise equality. For pursuit of this ideal would impose crushing burdens on information-gathering and coordination, or grant dangerous discretionary power to officials. Also, as Scanlon notes in "Preference and Urgency,"[9] a commitment to treat all individual systems of desires on an equal footing in providing benefits might create disastrous drainage of resources by encouraging the cultivation of inflexible, ineradicable and demanding desires. One might as well let the fantasy of being an arctic explorer become a deep-seated need, if that will make it an accepted source of demands for public provision. In sum, the side-effects of institutional sensitivity to atypical desires are often reasons why those with such desires should not insist on such sensitivity. They should accept a practice of basing political deliberations over benefits on some typical scale of preferences, emphasizing generally useful goods.

However, most questions of moral wrongness are not questions about the wrongness of a choice of institutions. In these matters, someone with atypical desires might not be swayed by considerations of typicality, and rightly so.

If I were marooned in a culture of extreme promise-worshipers with extreme interests in reliability like the Grim Student's, the pressure of the argument from typicality would be on me, and would force me to accept rules excluding listening to my son's troubles. No doubt, it would be impolitic, in such a culture, to risk being late for office hours, as it is impolitic in some subcultures to show up for work in blue jeans. Still, even living among the promise-worshipers, it would not be wrong of me to be humane and listen to my son, at the cost of being substantially late for an unimportant office hour.

Though this example is imaginary, it resembles the real background of Forster's statement about friendship, with which I first illustrated the many ques-

9 *Journal of Philosophy* 72 (1975), pp. 665–69.

tions about the burdens of morality. His declaration about betraying country for friend has an appropriately defiant air. Most people are more concerned than he was with the protection of their country's sovereignty and the styles of living most characteristic of their country. No doubt, misinformation, irrationality and monopolies of coercive power often play a role in sustaining their emphasis. Still, even discounting such influences, most people's patriotic attachments would probably be much more intense than Forster's, more intense absolutely and more intense as compared with their interest in sustaining connections of friendship. Whatever argument might be made against his willingness to choose friend over country, it would not be a good argument to remind him of what he doubtless knew, that the desires of most people would lead them to prefer rules for respecting the demands of country that are more patriotic than his. He might have agreed that there would be pervasive strains in people's commitment to his preferred set of rules, under which people are relatively liable to harms from betrayal of country on the part of those who attach Forsterian importance to their friends. He would have made no mistake about the nature of moral wrongness in refusing to be persuaded by such demographics of strain.

The Grim Student, a super-patriot and, conversely, someone who clings self-indulgently to intimate relations are all people who have not got their values right. In saying this, we do not mean that their lives are less worthwhile than others'. Perhaps this would be the effect of their distortions, all else being equal, but special achievements and enjoyments may more than balance the deficits. What we mean, generally and primarily, is that their motivational outlooks will lead to moral blindness, even if they are rational and well-informed. Because they lack appropriate concerns and emphases, what they would rationally reject does not have the same power to determine wrongness as the rational rejections of those whose concerns are within the moral norm. Evidently, the exclusion of certain motivational systems is substantive and fundamental, not derivable from a formal requirement of rational pursuit of unforced, informed general agreement. Systems within the norm, producing relevant rejections of proposed rules, involve special concern for the interests of one's friends. Since this permissiveness toward special attachment has entered the foundations of morality itself, this character-based morality is not impartial.

This rejection of formal contractualism could lead to a character-based construal of Scanlon's contractualist account of wrongness, rather as Rawls' contractualist account of justice, in its latest versions, relies on independent specification of the interests governing a moral person's social choices. However, the rejection of institutionally important arguments from typicality suggests that there is something wrong with the larger project of basing the whole nature of moral wrongness on the choice of a social contract.

What can one mean by the rejection of rules "as a basis for informed, unforced general agreement," and still be a contractualist worthy of the name? One essential feature has to do with the subjectmatter of the relevant choices. The acceptances and rejections establishing moral validity judge proposed systems of rules in light of what it would be like to live in a world in which people generally conform to such rules; as one consequence, concern will largely be directed to the possible effects on oneself of others' conformity. This concern with consequences of general conformity is the most obvious reason why Aristotle, for example, is not a contractualist. He agrees that right choice is determined by the deliberations of people with the motivational structures that every fully equipped human should try to have. But according to him, the primary concern in such choices is the person one is or becomes if one governs one's life in certain ways, not the effects of living in a world in which people generally conform to certain rules.

The contractualist emphasis on choices in light of the potential impact on oneself of general conformity is too all-embracing. There is no kind of general conformity that provides an accurate comprehensive basis for determining moral wrongness—so character-based contractualism shares too much of the pure version to set the right limits, just as Scheffler's hybrid theory shared too much of the consequentialist obsession with quantities of benefit.

Suppose, on the one hand, that each deliberator (appropriately corrected for morally illegitimate interests) is to consider what it might be like for him or her if all were actually to conform to a proposed system of rules. The assumption of full compliance would lead to inaccurate assessments of moral wrongness in our world of partial compliance. On the assumption of full compliance, no one would be reasonable to reject a proposal that no one possess weapons. Because of the same artificial removal of relevant anxieties, constraints on promise-breaking would be too loose, as well. If all could be expected to apply their principles scrupulously, it might be unreasonable to reject a principle that promises may be broken when one has well-grounded certainty that loss of the opportunity that arose would be substantially more serious than the loss created by the promise-breaking. After all, such well-grounded certainties seldom exist. Yet such a general permission seems excessive, and reference to its moderate cost under full compliance seems quite irrelevant. One would have plenty of cause for anxiety, importantly restricting the value of long-term planning in which one counts on others, if one had to count on compliance as it would actually be, given people's actual tendency to tailor epistemic appraisal in their own interests.

Suppose, on the other hand, that the relevant deliberations concern effects on oneself of conformity as one would expect it to be. This agenda for choice is too worldly to yield a sufficiently strict standard of wrongness. "Someone else will do it, if not me" becomes too powerful an excuse. If one knows that most villagers would yield to the temptation to rob and kill any shipwrecked sailors and that the whole village soon becomes aware of all shipwrecked sailors, one won't expect anyone to benefit from one's forbearance in these matters. Even a shipwrecked sailor will not benefit from a principle protecting his life if most would not abide by it in practice and the many are bound to cancel the attempted mercies of a few. Yet one may need a sailor's coat, and the one who kills him is apt to get it. Under circumstances in which the shipwrecked are bound to be killed, no one has a reasonable basis for rejecting the permission to plunder because of the impact on himself or herself given the actual prospects of compliance. Still, even under those circumstances, it is wrong to kill the sailor. Similarly, if the reward for catching a fugitive slave is bound to lead to her capture, the pointless sacrifice of the reward is still a dictate of morality.

As these examples show with special brutality, in nonideal circumstances the only gain from doing the right thing may be the responsible person's knowledge that she has not done wrong and the victim's awareness that at least some people ineffectually refused to treat him wrongly. But a standard that admits such gains as independent grounds for reasonable rejection would make wrongness too independent of cooperative considerations to be a contractualist account. Thus, contractualism is most plausible when the crucial acceptances and rejections are premised on an ideal of compliance. In addition to the difficulties in describing a satisfactory ideal, this idealizing tendency gives rise to the burden lifter's advice that what is morally wrong is not always wrong. For any idealization will sometimes force neglect of actual threats and rational anxieties with a bearing on wrongness. However, as with analogous suspicions inspired by consequentialism, the mistake in the burden lifter's response to contractualism would be the assumption that moral wrongness has been accurately described. I will now try to develop a more accurate description, and use it to criticize the burden lifter's advice.

Persons and Their Rules

If conduct is morally wrong, features of that conduct are reasons why it is morally wrong. If someone reaches the conclusion that an act is morally wrong, what makes her reasons valid? Consequentialism and formal contractualism are both answers to this question. For all their differences, they have much in common. In both cases, ultimate validation comes from a standpoint which everyone ought to adopt in judgments of morality, an impartial standpoint which does not in itself permit favoritism toward one's special attachments and projects. Any such permissiveness that is validated results from combining the impartial standard with psychological data provided by people's actual bases for preference. Also, in both cases, the authoritative judgments implement an impartial goal that ought to be prominent in the deliberations of lawmakers. Consequentialism singles out the promotion of well-being, formal consequentialism the goal of fairness. These conceptions of the authoritative goal in moral deliberation differ, yet each identifies a goal that is explicit in many lawmakers' deliberations but much rarer in moral constraints that people explicitly impose, in general. I will sum up these common aspects in the label "the legislative approach to morality."

Probably, the parallels with legislation reveal an important cause of the common assumptions. Legal figures of speech are unavoidable in talk of moral wrongness and moral responsibility. So it is natural to assume that one should pursue an impartial goal appropriate to lawmaking in choosing moral laws to govern one's own conduct.

In addition, the legislative approach is encouraged by the philosophical quest for generality that we have constantly encountered. Suppose that valid reasoning about moral wrongness rests entirely on a general rule for moving from a set of facts of the case at hand, none of them intrinsically moral, to a judgment of moral wrongness; if one is equipped with this standard for choice, no further capacity for moral discrimination is required for moral insight. Such a general principle will have to set limits, in light of the facts at hand, to the costs one may impose on others in pursuing one's own interests. Otherwise, it could not determine the demands of morality. But a description of such limits that does not require further moral discrimination always seems arbitrary unless it assigns self-concern an importance depending on its role in satisfying an impartial goal. And it is only the standard theories of the legislative goals that provide appropriately reductive accounts of sufficiently commanding impartial goals—or, in any case, claim that such accounts will be forthcoming when moral inquiry is complete. In this way, the image of rationality as based on general rules leads to the legislative perspective on moral wrongness.

The other theories that I have criticized can only avoid the legislative approach at the cost of lapsing into one or another kind of arbitrariness. Scheffler's hybrid theory is admittedly incomplete as it stands, since no general impact-ratio is described. But any such ratio would stand in need of further justification. And it is hard to see how a general ratio could be justified except by its role in achieving some impartial goal, of the legislative sort. As for character-based contractualism, it turned out to be an artificial grafting of contractualism onto a nonlegislative perspective.

The legislative approach has had a long history. Its failures up until now are reason to abandon it, seeking a basis for judgments of moral wrongness that is not impartial and does not provide an independently adequate general rule for determining moral wrongness. For apart from such philosophical prejudices as the conviction that general rules must ground rational judgments, there is no reason to suppose that morality is legislative. Morality addresses itself to people's interests and sets morally appropriate limits to their pursuit of their interests. Why suppose that appropriate permission for such pursuits is justified through applying a standard that itself includes no such permission at the start? Why suppose that there is any rule or set of rules whose application to nonmoral facts justifies all valid judgments of moral wrongness, yet whose application does not require any further moral discrimination?

It is time to move across the line that character-based contractualism uneasily straddles, making a radical break from the legislative approach. In this alternative, substantial permission to pursue the attachments and projects that give one one's full individuality is part of the ultimate standard one employs to validate choices. Such permission need not wait on an impartial assessment of data provided by people's actual, nonimpartial psychologies. Moreover, the concerns that guide authoritative deliberations are familiar aims in normal, nonlegislative practice. For these reasons, I will speak of the alternative approach as "person-centered."

But can there be a person-centered basis for choice that is a morality, generating judgments of moral wrongness? In his powerful discussions of the excesses of current moral theories, Williams has recommended something like the person-centered approach as a break from morality, or, in any case, modern moralities, specially attentive to moral obligation.[10] My concern will be to show that ordinary modern engagement with questions of moral wrongness is person-centered.

My proposal begins with the fact that an act is morally wrong just in case it is disallowed under the circumstances by any system of rules for the regulation of one's own conduct that no morally responsible person could refuse to impose on herself if she rationally responded to all relevant information but put the influence of coercion to one side. In short, one avoids moral wrongness by not doing what no morally responsible person would willingly do, rationally and with full information. Despite the banality of this claim, it is useful in criticizing the moral theories that we have encountered so far. To begin with, it conflicts with consequentialism. The consequentialist standard for acts is so demanding that morally responsible people, possessed of full information and uninfluenced by coercion, will fail to govern themselves by it, as even consequentialists admit. The agent-centered prerogative is excluded as well, once the role in moral responsibility of particular relationships and past choices is acknowledged. Since morally responsible people will not determine the terms of their self-regulation solely on the basis of consequences of general conformity, this standard is not contractualist, either. Finally, the concerns that guide a morally responsible person in choosing how to regulate her choices may involve some favoritism toward particular people and projects. So this approach to morality is not impartial.

So far, I have emphasized ways in which a person-centered morality can depart from legislative versions, avoiding the associated failures. But legislative moralities, formal contractualism in particular, also succeed in account-

[10] See *Ethics and the Limits of Philosophy*, chapter 10.

ing for certain truths about morality, whose role in the person-centered approach is not yet clear. In particular, three features of moral deliberation are a challenge. Morally responsible people seek moral judgments that are based on reasons; they do not pursue an ideal of spontaneous, unreasoned response to concrete situations. Second, morally responsible people only condemn actions as morally wrong if they think this conduct would be rejected from a perspective that everyone capable of morality ought to share. Finally, the particular arguments about potential gains and losses that emerge from legislative moralities are often relevant and broadly useful, whatever their ultimate inadequacies. If people were morally responsible in virtue of giving an authoritative role to an impartial perspective for assessing reasons for choice, these features of moral responsibility would be easy to explain. In any event, these features exist. A person-centered approach must also account for these needs for deliberation and these resources for deliberation.

If previous remarks about the worship of generality are right, a person-centered response to this challenge will differ in form from standard legislative accounts. Standard legislative moralities seek general rules connecting findings that are not individually intrinsically moral to conclusions about moral wrongness; no further moral discrimination would be needed to apply the rules. They are like the rules of empirical justification in positivist canons, which were supposed to connect purely observational findings with scientific hypotheses, and which were supposed to be applicable without the need for further scientific commitments. (It is a remarkable testimony to human hopes and philosophical ambitions that the pursuit of the moral canon is still so vigorous in ethics, despite its reduced appeal in the philosophy of science.) In contrast, the resources for deliberations about wrongness that emerge from a person-centered approach will, presumably, depend, for their application, on the capacity to make various further moral distinctions. Perhaps there will be fundamental reference to sensitivity, generosity or other moral properties. Perhaps there will be reference to thresholds of adequacy or considerations of balance that are specifically relevant to moral responsibility. The need for deliberation will be acknowledged, but it will not be filled using rules of the general yet reductive sort.

Further thought about moral responsibility leads to the following account of moral wrongness, in which needs and resources for deliberation find appropriate roles. An act is morally wrong just in case it would be excluded by the least demanding system of terms for self-reproach and reproach that is compatible with the virtues at which everyone capable of self-regulation should aim. By deriving this account from the concerns appropriate to a morally responsible person, but not from the authority of a detached and impartial point of view, one can reconcile the person-centered approach with the truths in the legislative approach to morality. I will base this explanation and defense on a series of banalities about the concerns that are characteristic of morally responsible people.

1. *A morally responsible person is not capricious.* A morally responsible person wants to regulate actions of hers that might impose costs on others in a stable way in the course of her adult life (i.e., her life from the time when she is capable of the self-regulation that I am describing). In other words, she wants the considerations in light of which she permits herself to do what may hurt others to be considerations to which she consistently attends.

Here, a number of qualifications must be understood. The considerations need not consist of descriptions of characteristics to be avoided which provide nontautologous principles that could be employed by someone with no capacity to balance rival considerations. If previous examples are right, talk of adequate, but not excessive concern for demands of love or of friendship may play an indispensable role.[11] Still, if she forbears on certain grounds in one case, she will want there to be some relevant difference in other cases in which she does not forbear—even if there is no nontautologous description of why the difference was enough. Perhaps she can say no more, for example, than that the loss to a stranger in one case was sufficiently small to permit attention to the competing interests of her friend, while in the other the loss to the stranger would have been too great. Still, it matters to her that there is that relevant difference, on the basis of which she can reconcile her responses. These things matter to her, not just because unpredictability has burdensome effects, but because she wants her actions to reflect the noncapricious person she is.

Another qualification is needed to distinguish noncapriciousness from stubbornness. Sometimes, a morally responsible person really will change the terms on which she regulates her conduct. However, when she does so, she will regret having employed different terms of assessment in the past, and will wish that her present standards had been her standards all along.

2. *A morally responsible person imposes constraints on herself.* The stable self-regulation constitutes willing forbearance, by which she would willingly refrain from choices even if no one else were able to impose costs on her for violating the rule. Of course, people can also avoid wrongdoing by acting as a morally responsible person would even though they are not the sort to do so except in response to the peril of imposed costs. But what makes the action morally wrong is its relation to self-regulating people's principles.

What of the person who regulates his conduct by certain rules because such regulation governs the approvals of someone else he respects? He is not guided, in the final analysis, by his concerns for others or his concern to be a

---

[11] John McDowell has emphasized this need for a sensitive balance in the most influential current project of basing morality on the virtuous person's ways of choosing. See, for example, "Virtue and Reason," *Monist* 62 (1979), pp. 331–50.

certain sort of person regardless of what anyone else might think. So one might say his regulation of his conduct is not genuinely self-imposed. On the other hand, he is guided by his own respect for another, which might be deep enough to sustain just the choices a morally responsible person would make.—Such people are ordinarily thought of as morally responsible, so long as they hold to rules that guide the conduct of morally responsible people who are not similarly dependent on others. And this breadth to the category will do no harm, so long as it is understood that the imitative are morally responsible because their self-regulation corresponds to that of people who work out the terms of their conduct in the more independent way. Respect links the former to the latter rather as respect links the scientific beliefs of the inexpert to the beliefs of scientists. In the scientific case, no one would have knowledge if someone didn't have independent access to truth. In the moral case, no one could tell the difference between right and wrong if no one could in the independent way. Since the proposed connection between moral wrongness and moral responsibility works just in case it fits the choices of the independents, I will confine attention to them.

3. *A morally responsible person reproaches others on the basis of terms for criticism that are also her basis for reproaching herself.* Whether or not someone is morally responsible depends on the nature and use of a system of self-imposed terms that serves this dual function. This entails, on the one hand, that a morally responsible person is not hypocritical, blaming another on the basis of terms for reproach that are not terms on the basis of which she stably regulates her own conduct. On the other hand, a morally responsible person is not a moral masochist; though she may hold herself to a higher standard than the terms she employs in reproaching others, she will keep this aspect of her life separate from the self-imposition of terms which she uses in reproach and self-reproach at once. Moral responsibility depends on the characteristics of this dual system.

Both the stability required in the first truism and the autonomy required in the second can characterize aspects of self-regulation that have no bearing on moral wrongness, because they lack this dual function. For example, when Mozart as a touring prodigy wrote to Papa, "I want to become great, like Handel and Hassler," he was announcing a self-defining goal by which he sought stable self-regulation, a goal which seems already to have expressed his independent concerns rather than the pressure of Leopold Mozart's approvals and disapprovals. Still, Wolfgang Amadeus would not have reproached others for a failure to advance toward musical greatness. Conduct violating this self-imposed standard would not be morally wrong, even on the part of the young Mozart, in his own view.

I have identified the crucial aspect of self-regulation in terms of function, but the function is not primarily social. The rules in question have the dual function of describing the transgressions for which one reproaches oneself (trying to do better thereafter) and the transgressions for which one reproaches anyone else who is capable of stable self-imposed self-regulation. Perhaps one should add (in a limited concession to social function) that the reproach in question is the kind of criticism that serves as a necessary, though not a sufficient, part of the approval of punishment on the part of a morally responsible person. [12]

4. *A morally responsible person seeks to avoid moral arrogance.* By "moral arrogance," I mean reproaching another for acts permitted by her terms for self-regulation when her employment of those terms does not reflect irrationality, ignorance of relevant evidence or concerns that should not govern the choice of such terms. Suppose a morally responsible person were to discover that the act he condemns in another was conscientiously chosen, and that the other's way of arriving at conscientious choices is not subject to any relevant criticism. Then he will withdraw the reproach.

In avoiding moral arrogance, one reduces one's terms for reproach to the least demanding that qualified people impose on themselves. Since a morally responsible person also avoids hypocrisy and moral masochism, these terms for reproach will also be her terms for self-reproach. So, just as in legislative moralities, morally responsible people all seek terms for judging everyone's acts that each morally qualified person is willing to impose on himself or herself. But the drive toward commonality need not be a drive toward impartiality. For the qualifications making one's system for reproach and self-reproach relevant to the search for a least demanding system may permit some favoritism toward one's special attachments and projects. As a result, the least demanding terms among relevant self-regulators, the terms that determine moral wrongness, may be different from the least demanding terms compatible with any of the impartial outlooks that might be taken to validate moral reasoning.

In sum, in matters of reproach and self-reproach, morally responsible people want to see eye-to-eye with one another. But what are the qualifications that put someone in this sphere of equality? More aptly, what are the defects that exclude someone (for the absence of relevant defects, not some standard of perfection, is the basis for exclusion)? A number of these defects have been specified already. If the terms of someone's self-reproach or reproach are due to capriciousness or hypocrisy, then one need not adjust one's system of self-reproach and reproach to fit his, in order to be morally responsible. And, of course, one need not see eye-to-eye with someone whose self-regulation is not self-imposed at all, but depends on fear, ignorance, unreason or imitation.

[12] Though the concerns characterizing a morally responsible person are not primarily social, the truth of the characterization might well be justified by appealing to an epistemology of a highly social kind. Such an argument will describe a truth-enhancing process giving rise to the person-centered morality in question. And this process is apt to involve distinctive social histories and interactions in the course of upbringing.

These various bases for a person's terms, which make it responsible to neglect them, are relatively abstract traits concerned with the relation between one's forbearances at different times, the relation between one's terms for self-reproach and terms for reproach, the relation between one's terms and others', or very general kinds of causes of holding to the terms. In addition, there have turned out to be concrete bases for responsible neglect of someone's terms, involving his failure to get his values right in his concerns (a failure that may be such in light of his history). The Grim Student cares too much about predictability as compared with concern for intimates. The super-patriot cares too little about those to whom he is not bound by ties of acquaintance, law or common custom.

The abstract norms for relevant self-regulation are entailed by the truisms about the general nature of moral responsibility that I have already presented. In addition, if one wonders whether someone's self-regulation is tainted by concrete traits of an inappropriate kind, one will hope for guidance. The following, final banality, imposing a kind of unity of the virtues, provides some help in these inquiries.

5. *One's system of reproach and self-reproach is compatible with moral responsibility just in case, in one's circumstances, imposing it on oneself is compatible with all the virtues that everyone capable of self-regulation ought to pursue.* There is no moral arrogance in reproaching someone for conduct he allows himself because his system violates this principle. On the other hand, if his self-imposition is compatible with all of the virtues at which everyone capable of self-regulation should aim—traits including, though not limited to, the formal traits corresponding to the previous four truisms—then it is excessive to condemn as wrong an act admitted by his terms for self-regulation.

This is not to say that moral responsibility entails all of the virtues. Stable conformity to the right rules is sufficient for literal moral responsibility, the sort that can be achieved by those who imitate appropriate others. Moreover, someone might recognize the need for compatibility with the relevant virtues, work out appropriate terms for assessing wrongness on those grounds, commit himself to these terms for self-regulation but lack some of those virtues. He would not adopt a system that a generous person could not adopt, but he is not a generous person. This is possible because a generous person would not reproach others just for the absence of generosity. Indeed, it would be downright ungenerous to want everyone capable of self-regulation, even grouchy, introverted people, to require generous conduct of themselves. Finally, as we shall see in more detail in the next chapter, there are traits whose presence ought to inspire admiration in everyone which are not traits at which everyone ought to aim, for example, utter benevolence at all costs as compared with mere generosity. Those admirable traits are virtues, but virtues that could certainly be absent from a morally responsible person.

The conduct of mine that the Grim Student condemned was due to terms of self-regulation compatible with all the virtues which everyone ought to pursue. I am sensitive to the needs of others yet noncapricious in adopting my relatively permissive system of self-reproach and reproach. So the Grim Student was morally arrogant. Indeed, he was something worse. His imposing his system on himself depended on inflexibility in dealing with others, a trait that everyone ought to seek to avoid. So there is no need to take his system into account in finding common ground with morally responsible people. On the other hand, the blithest spirit is either capricious or insensitive to the needs of others. So there is no moral arrogance in my condemning his acts in terms more demanding than his own.

Similarly, a system of reproach and self-reproach that only a super-patriot could have is not in the running as a system determining moral responsibility. For a super-patriot lacks compassion (which need not be identified with universal impartial sympathy. One need not recommend universal impartial sympathy in pointing out to a super-patriot that Iraqis are humans, too). The pharmacist whose response to calls does not depend on what sign he has posted is not reliable. But Phil is reliable and compassionate, while Frank is not.

It is not common in modern philosophy to base the judgment of deliberations on a diverse catalog of traits that ought to be expressed in deliberations. But outside of philosophical writings, criticisms of proposed terms for moral assessment are usually criticisms of the character expressed in a practice of reproach and self-reproach. That way of judging, one protests, would be callous, inflexible, insensitive or self-righteous—or, on the other hand, self-indulgent, sentimental or squeamish. There is no reason to suppose that all of these characterizations can be reduced to the abstract norms.

Though many of the traits at which everyone should aim require concern for strangers, they permit some partiality. One can be sensitive to the needs of others while paying special attention to oneself and those one loves. But there are limits to such special attention. Someone who won't call the police to help a profusely bleeding stranger when this means being ten minutes late for his daughter's birthday party is not sensitive to the needs of others. Quite generally, the traits that everyone ought to pursue lie between extremes, extremes of self-centeredness and impartiality for such traits as generosity, sensitivity and compassion, extremes of looseness and rigidity for such traits as flexibility in dealing with others.

Of course, the discernment of sensitivity, compassion, flexibility and other traits that everyone ought to pursue is itself morally contentious. There is, I think, no general rule adequate for discerning any of these traits on the basis of properties that are not, individually, intrinsically moral. Yet a catalog of such traits is essential to specifying what moral wrongness is. In general, my proposal about moral wrongness and moral responsibility does not lend itself to any reductive project of describing moral wrongness in terms that are not, individually, intrinsically moral.

Still, this abandonment of reductive hopes does not cast doubt on the obvious supervenience of moral properties on nonmoral facts. If one situation includes a morally wrong act and involves all factors with a bearing on that moral wrongness then any situation which is identical to it in nonmoral properties will include a morally wrong act as well. Such supervenience of the moral on the nonmoral requires no reduction. For it reflects the determination of wrongness by what any morally responsible person would disallow together with the fact that a morally responsible person seeks terms for self-restraint that dictate the same forbearances in the same circumstances as she wants all others to observe if they are capable of stable self-regulation. If identity of nonmoral properties insures that the circumstances, psychological capacities and actions or forbearances are the same, then the nature of moral responsibility insures that the moral characteristics will be the same.

What would require a reductive account is the further demand that situations which must share moral properties because of their similarity in nonmoral properties be situations involving nonmoral properties that are sufficient reasons for the ascription of the moral properties. A believer in moral truth need not make this demand unless he thinks that distributions of properties determining what moral truths there are must correspond to attributions of properties that justify the associated moral truth-claims. And this is an invalid demand, here as elsewhere. Spatiotemporal distributions of properties of chemical constitution, mass and momentum determine all meteorological truths, for example, that a hurricane occurred at a certain place and time. But there is no reductive account of hurricanehood in nonmeteorological terms, and, hence, there are no physicochemical ascriptions which are, by themselves, reasons sufficient to justify the truth claim about the hurricane. Similarly, there is no nonmoral vocabulary in which the terms for morally responsible self-regulation are adequately described.

No doubt, much more can be said about the nature of a morally responsible person and some more must be said for important purposes. Still, this account of moral responsibility is developed enough to establish appropriate needs and resources for deliberation without basing the deliberative aspect of moral responsibility on the ultimate authority of a detached and impartial standpoint for choice. By themselves, the first three truisms, involving the goal of stable self-imposed nonhypocritical self-regulation, establish deliberative needs and resources. Someone who pursues this goal will not be content always to decide whether to forbear just by consulting his immediate, spontaneous response to the question of what moral responsibility would permit. One's immediate, spontaneous response will be influenced by the concerns that are most salient on the given occasion. But one seeks a basis for decision in terms for stable, lifelong self-regulation. One wants to eliminate ignorance and intimidation as sources of choice. And one wants to avoid terms for self-regulation that require less than one's terms for reproaching others. These desires dictate some reflection, reflection which takes into account the variety of situations one might encounter. For example, an inclination of the moment to hold oneself to an absolute prohibition against promise-breaking is unlikely to withstand reflection on other situations that one may encounter in which the consequences of promise-keeping are dire. This is not a rule one would stably impose on oneself. Or suppose permissiveness beckons. Faced with the choice of breaking a promise to pursue an unexpected opportunity, one might be inclined to say that the promise-breaking is not wrong if the expected gain to oneself is greater than the expected loss. But if this is to be one's stable basis for self-regulation, it must also be one's stable basis for reproach. When one considers a case in which one's reliance on another turns out to be misplaced just because he sees some chance of net overall gain from promise-breaking, one sees that one would want to hold the other to a more demanding standard, in a system of standards that one also applies to oneself.

The other truisms add further needs and resources. The constraints on character force scrutiny of interests sustaining self-regulation in others and in oneself, while the desire to see eye-to-eye with others forces concern with needs and interests that one does not oneself expect to develop. For example, if one is a rich person wondering whether to give anything to the poor, one's future may be so protected that reflections on what might happen in one's own life would not, by themselves, force any requirement of minimal charity. But one must also consider whether adopting terms for self-reproach and reproach is compatible with compassion. Also, one's desire to see eye-to-eye with relevant others would lead to reflection on the moral personality that could sustain a poor person in terms for self-reproach permitting trivial theft in response to desperate needs. If the self-imposition of such terms is compatible with the traits that everyone ought to pursue, then, one will accept, such conduct is not morally wrong.

In these and other ways, moral responsibility requires the thought-experiments about potential roles and role-reversals characteristic of contractualism, without artificial emphasis on the effects of regulative social institutions. One's deliberations are forced far beyond one's spontaneous responses to immediate circumstances. Still, in her authoritative deliberations about moral wrongness, a morally responsible person employs standards which, intrinsically, permit favoritism toward special attachments and projects. At every level, she insists on normal virtues of sensitivity and compassion, not utterly impartial ones.

VINDICATED BURDENS

We have finally found an adequate basis for insisting that what is morally wrong is always wrong. In part, the new argument for the scope of morality is negative and defensive. Since morality obviously has great absorptive capacity to take partial interests into account, there is a burden of proof on someone who denies that what is morally wrong is always wrong. Before, it seemed that the burden could be sustained by the argument from impartiality. More precisely, the various descriptions of the moral point of view either imposed so much impartiality that they excluded what was not wrong or introduced some other overly rigid standard excluding considerations with a legitimate bearing on wrongness—for example, through the imposition of a general impact-ratio as the sole permission to fall short or artificial emphasis on a general constraint of social design. The account of moral wrongness in terms of moral responsibility is not liable to any charge of too-exclusive emphasis that could sustain the alleged limit on moral wrongness.

In the absence of the standard reason for denying that what is morally wrong is always wrong, we have a further reason for affirming this entailment. The denial would lead to a mystery that can now be avoided. Suppose that an act, though morally wrong, is not wrong all told. Still, moral wrongness always importantly bears on the wrongness of an act. It must be that some contrary consideration intervenes, having to do with wrongness of nonmoral kinds, so that moral wrongness here is not wrongness all told. Perhaps in this case, accurate comparison of the considerations does not lead to a judgment that it would be wrong not to do what is morally wrong. But it would be quite mysterious if such judgments were not appropriate elsewhere. For the different kinds of wrongness are not generally incommensurable. Obviously, considerations of moral wrongness can combine with considerations to the effect that the alternatives would be wrong in other ways in an overall judgment that an act is wrong. It would be wrong for me to bankrupt my family to avoid minor aesthetic wrongness in interior decoration. If comparing the different kinds of wrongness can yield a definite judgment that a morally wrong act is wrong, and if moral wrongness does not absorb other kinds of considerations, why shouldn't the other considerations sometimes make it wrong not to do what is morally wrong? But this possibility creates a deep mystery of its own. There would have to be some standpoint, process or attitude appropriate to comparing moral wrongness and other kinds of wrongness, which could lead to the outcome that the avoidance of a moral wrong is wrong. But when one looks for this perspective among actual bases for judgment, one cannot find it. The point is not that the judgment "wrong not to do what is morally wrong" is shocking, but that there seems to be no perspective broad and deep enough for comparing the moral and the nonmoral in reaching such a judgment.

Fortunately, there is a more positive justification for taking what is morally wrong always to be wrong. Though I have spoken of moral responsibility, the adjective is not doing much work. It is just a signal that the appropriate concerns potentially extend, to some degree, to everyone affected by one's choices, even those whose presence in the interaction would not have been one's choice and those with whom one has not joined in any psychologically meaningful interaction. Whatever one's faithfulness to professional, political or familial responsibilities may be, one isn't morally responsible if one is not concerned to see eye-to-eye with everyone in self-regulation and blame. A similar breadth is required by the fifth truism, about the other virtues, since someone utterly unconcerned with neediness in strangers lacks compassion. Once this breadth is understood, one can omit the adjective and simply speak of responsibility. A choice is morally wrong if it would be disallowed by the terms of self-regulation of every responsible person.—But a choice that could only be made on condition of irresponsibility (given the usual condition of rational processing of full information) is wrong. It would be absurd to accept this characterization and deny that one possessed a sufficient rationale for self-reproach.

In the previous chapter, worries about moral wrongness and wrongness began with the story of George and Jim. A final look at the same example may help to resolve them. If George knows what moral wrongness is, his belief that keeping Jim's secret would be morally wrong is a belief that such silence would be excluded by any terms for living one's life that a responsible person would want people to observe. Any less demanding terms would require capriciousness, an absence of concern to avoid reproaching others where one would not reproach oneself, an absence of concern to avoid moral self-indulgence and moral arrogance, some attitude incompatible with virtues everyone ought to pursue, or some other basis for dismissing a person's process of self-regulation as not responsible. George cannot comfort himself with the reflection that the special attachments of friendship are excluded from this description of appropriate choosing. Special, though not absolutely overriding attachments are included as an acceptable part of the outlook of a person whose self-regulation is not to be dismissed. If he concedes the moral wrongness of keeping silent (as, perhaps, he should not), George has no basis for denying that silence would be wrong. He has a compelling rationale for self-reproach, if he keeps the secret.

Still, George's choice to keep silent could be reasonable. A reasonable choice may impose unreasonable burdens on others.

Chapter Eleven

LIVING AS ONE SHOULD

An ASSESSMENT of the demands of morality is incomplete if it is limited to questions of wrongness. For a characteristic charge of those who criticize the demands of morality, or of modern versions of morality, is that there is too much emphasis on questions of obligation in the deliberations morality prescribes as decisive. This is one of Williams' central criticisms of "the morality system," and one of Stocker's reasons for supposing that modern styles of ethical thinking are psychologically distorting or incomplete.[1] An exclusive concern with questions of wrongness is apt to mirror the emphasis on obligation which they think is a central defect.

Certainly, there are other questions about which morality has something to say, above all, questions of what kind of person one should try to be and what one should and should not do. It is not wrong to be less than compassionate, generous and sensitive to others' needs, so long as one is a morally responsible person. And, as we have seen, one can be the latter but not the former. Still, one should try to be a compassionate, generous and caring person. This different force of "should" extends to assessments of acts, as well as assessments of one's personality. Once, when a friend called to give me directions to her father-in-law's funeral, I worried out loud, for longer than I should have, whether I could find time to come. I was not as sensitive as I should have been. Yet I was not so wild as to behave irresponsibly, I did not do wrong, and I did not violate an obligation.

In general, one may not be living as one should, even when one does not do wrong in falling short. Yet what one should and should not do is clearly a moral matter, at least in part. If the demands of morality are specially apt to be excessive where obligation is not at issue, these questions of how one should live seem likely to expose the excess.

I will conclude the discussion of the burdens of morality by considering the related questions of the decisiveness of morality and the completeness of morality in what it says about how one should live. The question of decisiveness is whether what one should choose morally speaking is always what one should choose. The question of completeness is a bit more complicated.

Is the converse of decisiveness correct, so that it is always the case that what one should choose is what one should choose morally speaking? The

---

[1] See, for example, Williams, *Ethics and the Limits of Philosophy*, pp. 180f., Stocker, "The Schizophrenia of Modern Ethical Theories," p. 465.

assessment of a choice as a choice "one should make" is ambiguous, in a way that can cause trouble, here. The assessment might be that the choice would serve the chooser's goals, satisfy her desires or be in her interests. Such choices need not be choices that she should make, morally speaking. For example, morality need not say that she should invest in a seven-year Treasury bill, when she should, on account of her interests. Still, we can raise a further question. Suppose we put to one side the questions of whether a choice would fit the chooser's goals, desires or interests. These questions are not the one we are, now, asking in asking what someone should choose (though facts about self-interest and the like might certainly be relevant to the right answer). Still, the question of what she should choose can have an objective answer, not just validated by the tastes or the decision of the person answering the question (which may also be a source of descriptions of "what she should choose"). The open question of completeness is whether there could be an objectively valid finding of what someone should do which is not a finding as to what would work for her own sake, and is not a finding as to what she should do morally speaking.

Once one has conceded that morality is not always decisive, it is hard to resist the further step of denying that morality is complete. Nondecisiveness entails that there are some cases in which what one should choose morally speaking is not what one should choose. Since morality always has an important bearing on these matters, other considerations must have intervened. Moreover, if no contrary considerations do intervene, what one should choose morally speaking provides the answer to the objective question of what one should choose that is not a question of one's interests. But why should the moral answer not be true in light of the nonmoral considerations, unless these are capable of sustaining objective answers to questions of the same kind?

It is natural to move in this way from nondecisiveness to incompleteness. And this has some further, momentous consequences. The claim that morality is not always decisive in questions of what one should choose, together with the claim that it is incomplete leads to the bold burden lifter's proposal that sometimes it is an objectively valid assessment, not concerned with self-interest and the like, that one should make a choice, when one should not make it morally speaking. For the nonmoral considerations that sometimes establish what one should do, ought sometimes to be powerful enough to establish what one should do in the face of moral considerations, if they are sometimes powerful enough to deprive those considerations of decisive force.

As in the analogous position on wrongdoing, the moral shock requires epistemic novelty. The combination of nondecisiveness and incompleteness implies the existence of a special perspective on choice, which might be called "the point of view of individual perfection," to borrow a phrase of Susan Wolf's. From this perspective, one balances moral and nonmoral considerations in order to discern objectively valid answers to questions of what sort of person one should try to be, which are not questions of what would be in one's interests.[2] After all, nonmoral considerations sometimes have a decisive bearing on the objective answers (incompleteness), and moral considerations are not always decisive (nondecisiveness). Yet moral considerations sometimes are decisive in case of conflict, so there is no general incommensurability here. So there must be a standpoint which is not the moral point of view from which the necessary comparisons can be made. Wolf notes that we appreciate a variety of traits that can interfere with doing good to others (a mordant wit, for example) or limit resources available to provide for urgent, legitimate needs (the skillful creation of *haute cuisine*, for example). Perhaps prospects of prowess along these lines must be balanced against morally attractive possibilities.

In investigating these issues of decisiveness, completeness and the point of view of individual perfection, I will emphasize questions of the kind of person one should try to be. Of course, the question of whether one should choose this or that particular action is more routinely on our minds. But the question of character has a certain logical priority. If one should do something, when not doing it would not be wrong, there must be some reason why. And the reason always is that the action would be characteristic of a kind of person one should try to be.

Moralistic Ideals

I will be arguing that morality is decisive and complete with respect to questions of how one should live, and that there is no point of view of individual perfection. This last denial should come as a relief. For when one reflects on the lives of perceptive people, it is hard to discern any process, attitude or outlook in which they accurately compare demands of morality with other considerations to reach a judgment of who they should be or what they should do which is not a matter of self-interest yet is objectively valid. As with the analogous attempt to impose limits on morality within a larger view of wrongness, no perspective seems wide and deep enough.

Still, many ways of thinking about morality would make morality nondecisive in these matters. Certainly, the legislative approach to morality would

---

[2] See Susan Wolf, "Moral Saints," *Journal of Philosophy* 79 (1982), pp. 436f. I am not sure whether Wolf herself would use the phrase to describe the standpoint I have just presented. That depends on whether she takes objectively valid answers to questions of what someone should try to be (which are not questions about self-interest) to be based on objectively valid answers to questions of what it is desirable for someone to be (which are not questions of self-interest). She explicitly identifies the point of view of individual perfection with the latter. But if it is not a means of access to the former, the whole subjectmatter of perfectionist deliberations starts to become mysterious.

make it excessive to insist that the sort of person one should try to be morally speaking is, in every respect, the sort of person one should try to be. This is clearest if the moral ideal to strive for is identified directly with decision-making from the favored impartial perspective. Advice to be such a person would be a dismaying counsel of priggishness. To adapt an example of Stocker's, such a person, no matter how closely his history was intertwined with yours, would only take pains to cheer you up because this is the most efficient way to create good consequences at the moment, or because he recognizes his duty to help those in need, or because no one could reasonably reject a system of rules requiring good cheer on such occasions.

The more plausible option for legislative morality is indirect. One is the sort of person one should be if, assessing who one is from the impartial standpoint of morality, and taking into account one's actual interests and one's potential for change, one would approve of the sort of person one is. But any such process of assessment is inaccurate, if it leads to judgments of the sort of person one should be.

All of the impartial standpoints that legislative moralities identify with the moral point of view are too rigid as bases for self-assessment. I have already described how the engineering standpoint of consequentialist self-assessment is too rigorous (and how the mere addition of a general permission to fall short is too insensitive to the variation of responsibilities, which certainly has a bearing on what one should try to be). Applied to the task of self-assessment, contractualism would be too political—the direction of distortion depending, as usual, on the nature of the assumed compliance. The traits that no one could reasonably refuse to impose on herself on the assumption of similar commitment on the part of all are not assertive and suspicious enough for the real world. But in some grim corners of the real world, the only reason not to take on a self-aggrandizing trait is that it leads one to act as one shouldn't—the sort of judgment that was to be fully explicated in the contractualist way.

Still, there is something right about these legislative approaches to character—something that makes it hard to accept the decisiveness of morality, even if ordinary moral judgments are not construed in a legislative way. The determination of what people should try to be, morally speaking, should bear some significant relation to the determination of what they must do to avoid wrongdoing. The "should" of morality may be softer than the "must" of morality. But if an understanding of what is required to do what one must to avoid doing wrong does not provide a basis for assessing how one should live, there seems to be no category of what one should do morally speaking. There will still be such tasks as being generous, being sensitive to others' needs, and being tolerant. There may be some standpoint of objective assessment according to which someone should engage in those tasks. But without some special connection to moral responsibility, it is hard to see why this standpoint should be any different from whatever standpoint might make it true that someone should try to be a funny guy, a good writer or a brilliant cook.

Adapting the two-tiered structure of the more plausible legislative approaches, one might think that the moral determination of the kind of person one should try to be seeks the motivational structure apt to give rise to the least wrongdoing. But this demands too little in some ways, too much in others.

The minimization of wrongdoing demands too little because there could, in principle, be someone who is extremely and successfully fastidious about not doing wrong yet who is not the sort of person he should try to be because (for example) he is not generous. In other cases, the proposal demands too much, because the engineering standpoint that seeks to minimize moral pollution is too rigid, like the engineering standpoint that seeks maximum production of goodness.

Consider Phil the pharmacist, again. Suppose that Phil, after fixing morally appropriate limits to his professional responsibilities, realizes, with appropriate shame and moral anxiety, that he has failed to live up to these responsibilities, on a number of occasions. He did not check his answering machine, he took off for the weekend, he told a timid sick person to wait until Monday morning—all on occasions when it was wrong to do so. Of course, he should try to do better. But Phil, like any sensible person, knows that mere resolutions to try to avoid past patterns of wrongdoing are often not enough. In this case, he can diagnose the source of the wrongdoing. He did not live up to his moral responsibilities because he so much enjoys being with his children and with his wife. The enjoyment distracts him from his obligations. Indeed, Phil concludes, the only way he is apt to do less wrong in his life is by becoming less attached to those dear to him, more of a detached workaholic.

If Phil refuses to detach in response to the mere fact that less total wrongdoing is apt to result, he does not fail to act as he should in self-assessment. It is not a valid principle that one should, in such moments, do whatever is needed to become a minimally polluting piece of moral equipment. But if he can decide not to change, without moral defect, then the minimization requirement does not describe the sort of person he should try to be. Of course, Phil's attachments, however lovable, do not make his negligent behavior less wrong. When he lets himself become so engrossed in his attachments that he does not check his answering machine, his failure to control his attention and interest is wrong. But this does not entail that he would be wrong not to alter the underlying attachment.

The same conclusion emerges from reflection on what the rule of minimal pollution would mean for those whose way of life is not yet settled. Someone with Phil's attachments will wrong nonintimates, as a result. But once these attachments are acquired, change in the direction of detachment will sometimes lead to the wronging of intimates or former intimates. Lucy and the kids are apt to be deprived of what they rightly expect on some occasions. If the minimization proposal is right, someone starting out in life and foreseeing these perils would have a strong reason to try to form no special attachments, avoiding tugs away from moral responsibility. But it would be ludicrously prim to suppose that this is the sort of person one should try to become, if possible.

MORAL IDEALS

In the person-centered account of wrongness that I developed before, a diverse catalog of intrinsically moral traits was fundamental in determining wrongness. It is these traits that provide the basis for the moral assessment of the sort of person one should try to be. When the nature of what one should do, morally speaking, is clarified in this way, morality turns out to be decisive and complete in such matters. Morality is decisive when it conflicts with self-interest or other considerations in determining what one should do, and morality takes up all the space left for objective judgments of what one should do, when the question is not about self-interest.

In accurate moral self-assessment, there are certain traits to which everyone should attend in determining what sort of person he or she should try to be. These include sensitivity to others, generosity, flexibility in dealing with others—in sum, the traits that must be compatible with the terms of reproach and self-reproach of a morally responsible person. So there is the right sort of connection between the moral "should" and the moral "must": understanding how moral wrongness is determined reveals the traits at which everyone should aim. Because of the latter connection it would be absurd to deny that such self-assessment is moral, or to condemn as arbitrary a categorical distinction between attention to these traits and attention to others.

Everyone should *consult* certain traits in self-assessment. But it would be excessive to propose that everyone should try to embody these traits. For personal limitations have to be taken into account. Even if an exceptionally irritable and shy person could, by straining every nerve, be a generous and sensitive person, it might be excessive to insist that he should try to be a generous and sensitive person. The concrete norms of character that keep recurring in every phase of moral judgment need to be supplemented with a proviso concerning authenticity. The proviso is that one may, though one need not, avoid strivings that impose excessive limits on one's capacity to identify with the attitudes one strives for.

To put the same proviso in other terms: it is permissible for one's self-assessment to be part of one's ongoing project of being a person. Part of this project is the effort to act in ways that express who one is, rather than responding to demands that one experiences as external. One does not want to engage in behavior that one does not own, psychologically speaking, even if one approves of that behavior. Also, though one wants to attend to other people (or, if sufficiently reclusive, at least to something beyond oneself) one doesn't want to be engulfed, losing one's sense of one's self as separate from one's world. To avoid both detachment from one's behavior and absorption by one's world, one seeks to sustain meaningful connections between the internal and the external, subjective feelings and objective demands. This process is exceptionally challenging. Yet someone with no concern for its goals would not be concerned to be a person. In this respect, the project is prior to that of being a moral person. One never acts as one should not in refusing to abandon this project of being a person, in the process of self-assessment.

Nonetheless, sometimes a person should put the project of authenticity on the back burner, as it were, doing some temporary violence to who she is to become a sort of person she should try to be. The proviso of authenticity only permits the rejection of excessive limitations on authenticity. It requires discrimination, discrimination which cannot be reduced to a formula, to determine these limits. But this does not mean that an extramoral yet objective viewpoint determines what one should do. For the needed discrimination is moral. Indeed, the awareness required to discern moral wrongness, the awareness that I previously described somewhat loosely as a grasp of the traits that everyone capable of self-regulation ought to pursue, is, more precisely, a grasp of the traits that every such person should try to have if the proviso of authenticity is satisfied.

This sketch of what a person should try to be, morally speaking, might seem horridly permissive in two respects. On the one hand, the permission to pursue authenticity might seem much too broad, since a proneness to harmful wrongdoing might be a central aspect of who someone is, which he could not change without ceasing to be a living center of experience and possessor of behavior.—But in fact, there is room for all the condemnation needed. When someone falls short of the traits that everyone should, at least, consult, he is not the sort of person he should be, morally speaking, even if the proviso obtains, so that there is no moral ground for saying that he should try to be . . . what he should be, morally speaking. (As far as I can see, this is the one way in which "should be" and "should try to be" can sometimes be pried apart, in moral matters.) And of course, the denial that someone should try to be different does not in the least mitigate the wrongness of wrongdoing to which he is prone because of who he is. Phil's family-based negligence was an aimiable instance of this fact. At most, the proviso of authenticity sometimes provides a reason to forgive wrongdoing. If a small wrong proceeds from a trait that someone could not extinguish without ceasing to be who he is, that is reason to forgive.

Though the proviso of authenticity is worrisome when it applies to people with extreme personalities, all of us need its protection to avoid a moral determination of what to strive for which would be much too demanding. When authenticity allows, each of us should try to be a generous person. But it is not the case that any of us should try to be the sort of person who is generous whenever generosity is called for. One should always regret having acted ungenerously, even to a distasteful person on a day of bad headaches and big tasks. But one need not regret being the kind of person who is not invariably as generous as he or she should be. The proviso of authenticity explains this limit to consistency and analogous limits for other virtues. To be that consistently generous, someone would have to be so guarded and unspontaneous that she would not even be a generous *person*.

The other appearance of permissiveness concerns the catalog of norms which everyone should consult. I have said that these norms are the ones with which responsible terms for reproach and self-reproach must be compatible. Though these norms are demanding, most, if not all, of them require to a lesser degree capacities which other traits, "maximal traits" as I will call them, demand to a heroic degree. For example, generosity is a trait that everyone should attend to, cultivating it if authenticity allows, but not utmost benevolence, the aim to do anything that promotes overall well-being.

For the following reason, it might seem that this moderation, while appropriate in an account of moral obligation, is inappropriate in an account of what one should try to be, morally speaking. Anyone would be a morally better person (the objection begins) if she had the maximal trait rather than the corresponding more moderate trait. And morally speaking, one should always strive to be a morally better person, if appropriate respect for authenticity allows. So, it might seem, my description of what one should try to be, morally speaking, must aim too low.

Something must be wrong with this argument if morality is decisive concerning what one should try to be. For striving to cultivate the maximal traits, even within the limits of authenticity, sets limits to projects and ambitions when it is not true that a person should respect those limits. If any teenager decides on a career less beneficent than one she could sustain without giving up on the project of being a person, one would have to condemn her for a failure to try to be the sort of person she should.

In fact, the argument for maximal moral demands is wrong in one premise or the other. The first premise was that someone is a morally better person for having a maximal trait, such as utmost benevolence, rather than the corresponding moderate trait in the catalog I have partly developed, for example, generosity. This is hardly obvious, once certain irrelevancies are noted and put to one side.

Granted, most of us, perhaps all of us would be morally better people if we were closer to ideals of utmost benevolence. But few, if any of us, can be said without qualification to be generous, compassionate, sensitive to others' needs and so on through the nonmaximal norms. Certainly, none of us displays these traits all the time. By moving closer to an idealized portrayal of Francis of Assisi, one avoids criticisms emerging from the moderate norms, as many middle-aged professors avoid apt medical criticism of their weight by moving closer to the physique of professional basketball players. This does not mean that one should be unsatisfied with satisfying less than maximal demands.

Also, it is often the case that someone would give rise to more morally good phenomena by acquiring certain maximal traits. But the production of more good effects does not, as such, make one a morally better person. At least in Eisenstein's portrayal, Ivan the Terrible was a sort of person it was desirable to have around to end the chaos of the boyars through ruthlessness and cunning. Because of overall consequences that were morally better, it was desirable that young Ivan made the choice to become a ruthless dominator, but in becoming terrible he did not become a morally better person.

To put irrelevancies to one side, compare two possibilities, reformed Scrooge and super-reformed Scrooge. Reformed Scrooge is the hero at the actual end of the story. He has resolved to be generous. But this does not entail a commitment to reduce his standard of living to a bootblack's if this is part of the way of life that will have the best effect on the world. Indeed, Scrooge is more interested in having a good time on his own account postconversion than he was pre-conversion. Super-reformed Scrooge embodies another ending, in which Scrooge does become utterly benevolent. To put to one side the question of which alternative gives rise to more morally good phenomena, suppose that the extra goodness resulting from the extra benevolence of super-reformed Scrooge is just enough to balance his extra self-imposed deprivations. Otherwise, his plans go awry, for reasons beyond his control.

Is super-reformed Scrooge a morally better person than reformed Scrooge? Many of us think not. We accept that reformed Scrooge is a morally better person than pre-reformed Scrooge, even if *his* generosity creates no more good consequences than his prior stinginess would have, for reasons beyond his control. But we take the verdict that super-reformed Scrooge is morally better yet to combine the worst of the world religions, the glorification of self-denial, with the worst of modern advertising, the principle that more is better. Of course, super-reformed Scrooge has embarked on a more heroic enterprise. But we take this project to be on a par with a commitment to being a brilliant actor or a great chef (i.e., to be such in addition to being generous, sensitive and the like). Denying that the embodiment of the maximal traits makes one a morally better person, we are willing to accept that, morally speaking, one should try to be as morally good a person as one can, within appropriate limits of authenticity.

Still, it is hard to resolve this question of moral superiority—above all, because of a difficulty in distinguishing the evaluation of persons from the evaluation of total phenomena. Someone's moral qualities may depend on her actual success in pursuing her projects. This is the contingency that Bernard

Williams has labeled "moral luck."[3] Perhaps, then, it is unfair to evaluate super-reformed Scrooge just by looking at a situation in which his extra effort to do good makes no proportionate contribution to goodness. Perhaps when he is successful he is a morally better person, even though the moral evaluation of persons is not the same as the moral evaluation of the total difference they make to the world.

It is extremely difficult to distinguish the moral value of the person in question from the moral value of the total difference he makes, when one compares successful reformed Scrooge with successful super-reformed Scrooge and accepts the possible impact of moral luck. It is so difficult that one cannot be sure that an utterly benevolent person, if he succeeds in his projects of utmost benevolence, is not a morally better person than a generous one who succeeds in his projects of generosity. Suppose he is. Then it will not be true that one should, morally speaking, always try to be a morally better person, within appropriate limits of authenticity. No doubt, Scrooge should have suffered his pangs, including moral pangs, when he squarely faced his failure to strive to be generous. But Scrooge, upon reform, need not have suffered any pangs, moral or otherwise, at his failure to move beyond generosity to utmost benevolence.

It is not the case, morally speaking, that one should strive for the maximum, but one should admire the maximum. Once it is granted that the maximal traits might make someone morally better than the moderate norms, the crucial distinction is between two different kinds of objectively valid ideals, ideals one should pursue and ideals one should admire.

Suppose that one should pursue a certain ideal, trying to be a certain kind of person. If this pursuit puts demands on a capacity, one should, then, admire those who have the capacity in abundance. But this does not mean that one should try to become like them, taking these objects of admiration to represent a goal to be pursued. Indeed, it could even be the case that one would not be as one should if one were just like them. Phil the pharmacist should pursue a reasonably strenuous ideal of self-discipline, tact and loyalty in dealing with those who depend on him. So he should admire the forty-seven samurai in the Japanese epic, who exercise such exquisite self-discipline in loyally plotting the murder of their late master's adversary and who show precise tact in the timing of their collective ritual suicide. However, he should not make this ideal for admiration an ideal for pursuit, even with requisite adaptation to modern circumstances. Outside the realm of anything like morality, the difference between the types of ideals is familiar enough. Given my interest in classic Italian cooking, I should admire Marcella Hazan. Given my lesser abilities and my other interests and responsibilities, I should not try to be like this much-admired maestro.

[3] See the title essay in his *Moral Luck*.

From a moral standpoint, super-reformed Scrooge and Francis of Assisi should be admired. For they display in abundance a capacity for concern for others required to be the sort of person one should. But it is not the case that one should, morally speaking, try to be a person of their sort. The denial that one should so strive does not require an intrusion of nonmoral considerations, reducing the force of moral ones, but only the distinction of the two kinds of ideals, within the moral realm.

THE ADEQUACY OF MORALITY

Doubt whether morality is decisive in questions as to how one should live might be based on concern that morality sometimes demands too much in the way of self-denial. Legislative moralities do demand too much, but they misdescribe the demands of morality. An accurate, person-centered account of morality does not demand too much. In self-assessment, morality requires attention to norms which are not maximal. The concerns that would permit one to strive for less, without aiming lower than one should, are respected in the proviso of authenticity.

What we have not yet considered is the possibility that morality is not so much excessive as one-sided, as a source of insight concerning what sort of person to be. Perhaps morality is incomplete, in the sense I previously described. This would, at least, cast doubt on the decisiveness of morality, as well. For the nonmoral bases for objective judgments not concerned with the person's interests could be quite important in cases in which moral considerations, though real enough, were relatively unimportant.—Note that this conflict with decisiveness depends on the specific kind of incompleteness I stipulated before, in which the objective judgment does not respond to a question about self-interest or the like. If no moral considerations intervene, then John's mere desire to get into medical school can make it the case that he should try to get a good grade in organic chemistry. But if, morally speaking, he should not cheat, when this is his only way of getting a good grade, the fit with his interests does not create the possibility that he should cheat, nonetheless. In any case, it does not if the account of what one should do, morally speaking, is as undemanding as the person-centered one.

The difficulty in locating a point of view of individual perfection suggests that there is no such incompleteness. And, in fact, the incompleteness of morality is, I think, an illusion. There is no nonmoral source of considerations needed to settle objective questions about what sort of person one should be which are not questions about one's interests.

Of course, I may legitimately impose on myself strivings that do not emerge from the process of moral self-assessment. But such self-regulation, though permitted, is not an instance of my striving to be a sort of person I should strive to be. If moral assessment permits the choice, then it is compatible with my living as I should, but not required for such living.

Moreover, one should, morally speaking, avoid lazy self-acceptance. One should develop some of one's capacities to some extent in the direction of excellence. In any case, it is arguable that some such norm of self-development exists. Here, the pursuit of goals that are not themselves moral plays a role in determining the sort of person one should be. But the role it plays is assigned by morality.

Any remaining, nonmoral considerations that might support an objective assessment of what a person should try to be will call for some positive objective evaluation of the person, as she might become. So, as Wolf has observed, the traits that can make a person wonderful without making her a morally better person are most likely to reveal this nonmoral support. Suppose that I have developed my potential to whatever moderate extent morality says I should. I still perceive in myself a potential for a trait that makes people wonderful. For example, I see that I could become quite witty. But I don't care to be that alert. I am not interested enough in being interesting. If a positive nonmoral evaluation of nonmoral traits has an objective bearing on questions of what sort of person I should strive to be, I should not be so self-accepting: I am objectively mistaken if I do not criticize myself on the grounds that I should try to be more like the scintillating people in Preston Sturges movies.—But this seems a confusion of the criticism of people with the criticism of works of art. At best, the fact that I would be mistaken in not admiring a trait is magnified into a claim that I should, as a matter of objective fact, strive to embody it if I can. This is the confusion between ideals one should admire and ideals one should pursue.

Admittedly, the nature and extent of the moral responsibility to develop one's potential are hard to determine. So the assessment of objective individual perfectionism is advanced by considering cases in which an enormous gain in someone's prowess depends on a somewhat immoral course of development, not enormously bad but bad enough that, clearly, one should not embark on it, morally speaking.

Gauguin's deserting his wife and children to be creative on Tahiti is good raw material for this inquiry. But it needs some modification. Perhaps a judgment that Gauguin should have chosen as he did is justified retrospectively and morally by the fact that his decision yielded enormous benefits to humankind. Prospectively, then, Gauguin took on a moral risk that his abandonment of family might turn out to be a decision he should not have made. This peril and Gauguin's consequent moral luck were, indeed, the point of Williams' introducing Gauguin into contemporary ethical discussion.

Enormous prowess without consequent enormous benefits beyond the prowess itself produces the real test of the completeness of morality. Suppose that Gauguin had decided to go to Tahiti and paint sublimely great murals, knowing that the Tahitian climate would soon turn them to mold. And suppose that he had succeeded. Surely, this Gauguin, tailored to our purposes, would not have made an objective mistake concerning the sort of person he should be, if he had decided to stay in France rather than desert his family. If he stayed, would someone *else* note an objective mistake, in remarking that he should have left his family and engaged in the wonderful, nonbeneficial acts of prowess?

Granted, it is not clear that our revised Gauguin would choose as he should *not*, in embracing the bohemian exotic. But that would depend on whether his desertion reflected a profound personal commitment. It depends on whether his choice falls within the proviso of authenticity. Suppose that he would put no pressure on his striving to lead a life authentically his own if he stayed in France, even though he is capable of Gauguin's prowess should he imitate Gauguin's flight. He could express who he is about as well by running an art gallery in Lyons. Then he should not desert his family—on account of considerations bearing on authenticity that are morally central, but have no such role to play in an ethic of prowess. (Being a figure of prowess would not be alien for him, either.)

Though morality is, in fact, decisive and complete, it is extremely tempting to suppose that nonmoral considerations play an additional, independent role in objective assessments of who one should try to be. Unless the truths that lead to this temptation are acknowledged, full-fledged acceptance of morality will seem smug and shallow.

The attractions of positing the viewpoint of individual perfection are due, in large part, to certain profound similarities in psychological function between the pursuit of nonmoral ideals and the pursuit of moral norms. As we saw in examining the life of reason of a responsible person, such a person can regulate herself by nonmoral ideals, apart from the dual system of regulation and self-regulation in which she seeks equality with all similarly responsible people. In fact, virtually everyone regulates conduct and attention by nonmoral strivings—say, trying to live up to a self-image as a good writer or a funny guy. In addition, virtually everyone pursues ideals which, though they may be dictated by morality, are taken as important regardless of their moral role, i.e., their role in responsibility, generosity, sensitivity and other norms. Though one's striving to be a good spouse and good parent may be dictated by one's striving to be responsible, sensitive and generous, people do not, in general, strive to be good spouses or good parents just as means of being responsible, sensitive and generous. This would be a sign of shallow attachment.

Striving to live up to extra-moral ideals and to ideals not pursued just because of their relation to morality is part of who one is. Without such long-term nonmoral commitments, one would lack a personality, and become a mere nexus of experiences and behavior. Admittedly, moral self-regulation is itself a part of this process of centering, among morally responsible people. But it is a universal experience that additional, nonmoral strivings are required to give one's life the shape of personality.

In sum, people have deep-rooted needs for noncapricious self-regulation by nonmoral ideals, just as, if morally responsible, they have a deep-rooted need for noncapricious self-regulation on the same terms for reproach and self-reproach that other morally responsible people employ. Moreover, both moral norms and nonmoral ideals are rationally pursued apart from the value attached to payoffs from such activity. In the case of one's nonmoral ideals, what is independently (though not exclusively) important is participation in the striving, for this participation, not the payoff from success, gives shape to one's life. If "What will I do today?" were an utterly open question every morning, unbound by any enduring striving, one would lose one's mind.

In these ways, the inner process of nonmoral striving resembles the inner process of trying to be the person one should. Indeed, it resembles the inner process of being a morally responsible person. When one falls short in either the nonmoral or the moral case, one feels pain and anxiety at oneself—so much so that the same word "shame" fits either sort of response, shame at one's stupidity, say, as well as shame at one's irresponsibility or insensitivity. No wonder, then, that the nonmoral strivings are often taken to resemble the moral strivings in aiming at the goal of living as one should. But the parallels concern psychological processes of self-reflection, not objective validity in the outcome. This helps to explain why certain nonmorally based judgments as to what a person should be seem plausible as expressions of that person's conclusion, but horrendous as assertions by someone else. Perhaps Anne Sexton concluded that she should remain in touch with madness and suicidal ideas in order to write poignant poems of madness. Perhaps, despite the risks in the decision, her way of reaching it was not defective. If there is an objective viewpoint of individual perfection, why is it, in contrast, so clearly wrong to suppose that a valid conclusion that Sexton should have remained in touch with madness and suicidal ideas could have been reached by someone else?

The psychological similarities to moral norms make it possible to suppose that one conforms to an objective answer to a question of what one should try to be, which is not a question about one's interests, in pursuing one's nonmoral ideals. In addition, the psychological role of nonmoral ideals creates a positive need for such confusion. It is essential to the role of nonmoral striving in personality that one does not normally interrogate one's nonmoral ideals, to assess their relation to one's self-interest. They provide the routine matrix for one's questionings and initiatives that makes these questionings and initiatives psychologically one's own. Thus, treating quite nonmoral norms, such as being a good writer and a funny guy, as if they were norms from which one should not depart is essential to one's deepest need to pursue them. To this extent, the assumption of a nonmoral standpoint of individual perfection is a necessary normal myth.

BACK TO THE PRESENT

There is a distinguished tradition, extending at least as far back as Nietzsche, in which modern moral anxieties are traced to the inadequacy of the modern moral outlook and ancient Greek accounts of virtue are recommended as hinting at the remedy, if not supplying it ready-made. The questions of truth, justice and conscience that I have considered in this book have provoked such warnings and recommendations, in recent years. For example, Bernard Williams has traced stultification and confusion to the inappropriate burdens of the modern basis for self-regulation that he calls "the morality system." This system, which he sometimes calls, simply, "morality" "is not," he writes, "an invention of philosophers. It is the outlook, or, incoherently, part of the outlook of almost all of us." Because of the bad fit of the modern moral outlook with our modern problems of living "very old philosophies may have more to offer than moderately new ones."[4] Alasdair MacIntyre has argued that the modern moral outlook is dominated by a liberal individualism that provides no coherent guidance for those responding to modern problems. Looking back to ancient ethics, in a famously eloquent conclusion, he says, "[I]f the tradition of the virtues was able to survive the horrors of the last dark ages, we are not entirely without grounds for hope."[5]

In these final chapters, I have tried to show that ordinary modern morality is sane enough to place no more than appropriate burdens on us—just as in the middle chapters, I tried to show that justice as social freedom commands the moral authority whose modern absence is MacIntyre's theme. Still, there is something to the familiar modern turn toward ancient Greek wisdom. Modern moral philosophies regulate choice by impartial, detached perspectives, and usually try to sum up their favored perspective in a general rule requiring no further moral discrimination. This legislative approach is very different from the ancient ethical emphasis on diverse concrete norms of how to live. No doubt that abstractness does partly reflect certain pervasive features of modern life. For example, now much more than in earlier times the most important practical deliberations seek to maximize economic quantities that are neutral in terms of concrete uses—maximizing profit, say, return on investment, savings, productivity or gross national product. Surely, this encourages the development of fundamental moral principles requiring maximization assessed from an impartial point of view.

In this and other ways, the abstraction and impersonality of most modern

---

[4] *Ethics and the Limits of Philosophy*, pp. 174, 198.

[5] *After Virtue* (Notre Dame: University of Notre Dame Press, 1981), p. 245.

moral philosophy is not a philosophers' invention. Yet it is a distortion of modern morality, or so I have tried to show. Our moral outlook is already Greek enough. It is governed by norms of character (not always ancient Greek ones—but that is no cause for anguish). The norms are, indispensably, learned from examples and piecemeal, concrete instruction. MacIntyre's despair to the contrary, our morality is sufficiently coherent and widely shared that it could sustain a community worthy of respect. In general, the study of moral conflict establishes the adequacy of modern morality. The great problems arise from ourselves and our societies, not our standards. Perhaps we should stop fussing about morality, and try to be good.

INDEX